Beckett's Dantes

To Ruby Cohn, Carla Locatelli,
and John Pilling,
my 'buoni maestri'

Beckett's Dantes
Intertextuality in the fiction and criticism

DANIELA CASELLI

Manchester University Press
Manchester and New York

distributed exclusively in the USA by Palgrave

Copyright © Daniela Caselli 2005

The right of Daniela Caselli to be identified as the author of this work has been asserted by her in accordance with the Copyright, Designs and Patents Act 1988.

Published by Manchester University Press
Oxford Road, Manchester M13 9NR, UK
and Room 400, 175 Fifth Avenue, New York, NY 10010, USA
www.manchesteruniversitypress.co.uk

Distributed in the United States exclusively by
Palgrave Macmillan, 175 Fifth Avenue,
New York, NY 10010, USA

Distributed in Canada exclusively by
UBC Press, University of British Columbia, 2029 West Mall,
Vancouver, BC, Canada V6T 1Z2

British Library Cataloguing-in-Publication Data is available

Library of Congress Cataloging-in-Publication Data is available

ISBN 978 0 7190 7157 7 paperback

First published by Manchester University Press in hardback 2005

This paperback edition first published 2009

Printed by Lightning Source

Contents

	Acknowledgements	*page* vii
	Introduction	1
1	**Dantes in Limbo**	10
	Detecting Dante in Joyce	10
	Recycling Dante in *Proust*	22
2	**Belacqua does not observe 'the rule of the road'**	35
	There is no real Belacqua in *Dream*	36
	Dante and Mr Beckett	45
	Sordello is in the shade	50
3	**Strata and mysteries: intratextuality in *More Pricks Than Kicks***	57
	Quick deaths	58
	Screechy flatfooted Tuscany peacocks	62
4	**Fatigue and disgust: *Murphy* and *Watt***	81
	Dante is kept out of sight: *Murphy* and the manuscripts	81
	Addenda and excorporations	88
5	**Who is the third beside you? Authority in *Mercier and Camier***	102
	Vague shadowy shapes	105
	No quotes at any price	112
6	***Déjà vu* beyond reach: from the *Novellas* to the *Three Novels***	120
	The calmative effects of one's classics	120
	Odds and ends	132
	Bits and scraps flickering on and off	138
7	**Staging the *Inferno* in *How It Is***	148
	A voice comes to one in the dark	149
	'E fango è il mondo': the *Inferno* performed	154
	Geometries of passion	162
	The witness and the scribe	169

8 'In the words of the poet': *The Lost Ones*   183
   Ravening eyes   184
   Closed places   188
   The sun and other stars would still be shining   194

Conclusion: farewell to the old lutist   201

Bibliography   206

Index   226

Acknowledgements

Many people have contributed to the making of this book. Carla Locatelli first kindled my enthusiasm for Beckett, and her inquisitive mind has never stopped being a source of inspiration. I am grateful to John Pilling for sharing with me some of his staggering knowledge of Beckett, and for his academic thoroughness, high standards, and witty criticism, which have taught me a lot over the years. Ruby Cohn's insight and rigorous scholarship have guided my work, and her friendship and generosity have made it all possible.

I would like to thank the expert staff at the Beckett International Foundation Archive at Reading University Library, and especially Mike Bott and Julian Garforth for their good humour and kindness, and the Library staff at Trinity College Dublin. My gratitude goes to Edward Beckett for granting permission to quote from unpublished material, to James and Elizabeth Knowlson for their help in reading manuscripts, to Zygmunt Baranski for his advice on matters relative to Dante, and to Anna Dolfi for her support over the years.

Instrumental to the writing of this book was the climate of friendship and real intellectual exchange created by Karín Lesnik-Oberstein, Jonathan Bignell, Stephen Thomson, Ciarán O'Kelly, Sue Walsh, and all the other members of the Cultural and Critical Theory Group at the University of Reading. I am grateful to Jonathan Bignell at the University of Reading and Erica Burman at Manchester Metropolitan University for their generosity and infectious intellectual enthusiasm and to John and Christine Bolland, John Sears, and Patricia Allmer for their advice and help when I most needed it. The School of English, Sociology, Politics and Contemporary History at the University of Salford provided me with a friendly, supportive, and stimulating working environment, which helped me complete this book and plan others.

My gratitude goes to my mother, Maria Luisa Pustetto, and to my father, Fulvio Caselli, for their unfailing support and encouragement to do what I liked most and to stick to it. My sister, Silvia Caselli, has shared joys and anxieties to do with this book and with much else besides, helping me by showing me how integrity, energy, and lightheartedness can work together.

I would also like to thank those friends whose input contributed to the making of this book in so many ways: Mara Zardini, Andrea Pappacena, Gabriele Troilo, Barbara De Rigo, Marisa Basile, Rezzonica Castelbarco, Alberto

Ottieri, Peter Buse, Núria Triana-Toribio, Cathy Gelbin, Riccardo Capoferro, Paul Bavister, Laura Hubner, Kaye Mitchell, and Laura Salisbury.

This book could not have been written without Karín Lesnik-Oberstein, an intellectual companion who constantly stretches my thinking and reminds me what scholarship is really about, and a great friend who has always been there for me.

To Emanuele Basile goes my love.

Introduction

There were 'no pictures on the wall, no obvious amenities, only a narrow bed, a desk and a table with several books, including a dictionary'. In the midst of this spare impersonal setting, a single object seemed to stand on its own. One book lay open on the table, close enough so that Gussow could see the notations in the margin. This book was, Beckett told him, his 'schoolboy copy of Dante's *Divine Comedy*'.[1]

Dante is a strange object in Beckett studies; it stands out and stands for Beckett's greatness and isolation. This single object breaks the disquieting impersonality of the setting; it evokes a nostalgia for times gone by, and it confirms the intellectual rigour of the author. Dante's presence is pervasive in Beckett studies. The student edition of the *Comedy* appears not only in Beckett's work as the 'beslubbered Salani edition'[2] but also – with remarkable frequency – in Beckett biographies, which refer to the Trinity College years during which Beckett's tutor Bianca Esposito guided him through the thicket of Dante's canticles,[3] to his rereading the *Inferno* 'between bouts of sand and sea' in Tangiers,[4] and to the last period of his life in the old people's home in the rue Rémy-Dumoncel, during which 'Beckett was rereading Dante in Italian'.[5] Most importantly, however, references to Dante and the *Comedy* are scattered throughout the Beckett *oeuvre*.

But what does Dante do in Beckett and for Beckett? This book hopes to answer these questions by arguing that Dante's presence in Beckett is part of a critique of value and authority. 'Quotation', 'source', and 'origin' are notions which are commonly read as positing the authority of a previous text, which supplies a later text with meanings while remaining autonomous and stable. This can be observed in most existing studies on Beckett and Dante which, while theorising the instability of Beckett's texts (often praised for lending themselves to many complex and conflicting interpretations), oversimplify and ultimately stabilise Dante as an authoritative predetermined meaning, reading him for instance, as 'symboliz[ing] the cultural heritage of Western civilization', or as 'a devout Christian' whose values and theology are subverted by Beckett.[6] Beckett's texts, however, while placing Dante as authority, source, allusion, and model to be parodied, also question the notions on which such concepts rely, namely the opposition between outside and inside, memory and invention, and source and end product. Most significantly, these different Dantes are part of a larger infernal (intratextual) strategy of reduplications, mirrorings, echoes, and *mises en abyme* which shape the Beckett corpus. It is my contention that Dante is assumed as an external source of literary and cultural authority in Beckett's work, and also participates in Beckett's texts' sceptical undermining of kinds of authority. I will therefore investigate this paradoxical movement rather than simply isolating discrete, identifiable fragments of Dante's texts in Beckett and then calling them 'quotations', 'sources', 'origin', a strategy which has not been able to do justice to the complex ways in which this literary relation works.

Many critics have isolated fragments of Dante's texts in Beckett's *oeuvre*.[7] These are then called quotations, sources, origin, and their function is explicated in terms of these labels. Other scholars have conducted thematic studies, often placing Beckett within a tradition or a context to which Dante is also argued to belong.[8] These comparative researches call Beckett texts 'purgatorial' and 'internal',[9] read such Beckettian infernos (or purgatories) as examples of the human condition,[10] or describe Beckett's anti-theological use of Dante as parodic and subversive.[11] And yet, neither can the complex Beckettian take on the problem of literary relations be expanded into some generalised comparison nor can it be condensed in the opposition between Dante's 'poetics of conversion' and Beckett's 'poetics of perversion'.[12] By contrast, I am interested in what it means to claim that an intertextual element comes from Dante, both in terms of the project of intertextuality and in terms of the explication of Beckett's texts in their own right. To look at what can be labelled as 'Dante' in Beckett leads us to reconsider the different kinds of intertextuality present in the Beckett *oeuvre*, and also how that same *oeuvre* can help us to reshape our ideas about literary intertextuality.[13]

In Beckett, the retrieval of the source (in this study finding references to specific passages from Dante) does not produce, as Michael Riffaterre would have it, 'a stable picture of the text'.[14] Instead, it raises questions regarding the very possibility of textual stability. For instance, as I will demonstrate in Chapter 2, Belacqua, the protagonist of *Dream of Fair to Middling Women* who shares his name with the slothful character in *Purgatorio* IV, is at once a character and his own critique; his artificiality and the process of his fabrication are constantly foregrounded and the many layers which make up this character (references not only to the *Comedy* but also to some of its fourteenth- and fifteenth-century commentaries) parallel at intertextual level the assertion that 'there is no real Belacqua' (121). Rather than explaining quirky Belacqua Shuah away, Dante's Belacqua adds to his literariness while taking away from his realism.

Central to this book is therefore the argument that the references to various aspects of Dante's works to be found throughout the Beckett *corpus* produce 'Mr Beckett' as the author 'with the bay about his brow', as *Dream* puts it (141). Beckett in this study is assumed to be not the origin of the texts but a figure of power emerging from them, which inevitably remains powerful even when professing his own powerlessness.[15] As Chapter 3 will argue, *More Pricks Than Kicks* is a good case study in this respect, as allusions to and parodies of Dante's lines echo specific passages in *Dream* and in many Beckett poems of the time, rather than referring directly to the *Comedy*. This complex web of internal references to Dante is one of the ways in which Beckett texts, from the early works up to *Company* and *Ill Seen Ill Said*, are interconnected and constitute themselves into the Beckett *oeuvre*. Rather than arguing that the Beckett *corpus* derives its coherence from its author, as previous readings of the Beckett/Dante relationship have done, *Beckett's Dantes* will demonstrate that 'Mr Beckett' as the authority behind the texts is produced by repetitions, echoes, and what Molloy calls '*déjà vu* ... infinitely beyond my reach' (103). Dante is one of the main actors in Beckett's theatre of authority.

Authority is thus a crucial issue when examining the relationships between these two canonical authors and indeed when thinking about any intertextual relationship.[16] It is not enough either to 'sense vague shadowy shapes' like Mercier and Camier do, or to exclaim, after 'Dante...Bruno.Vico.. Joyce': 'Basta!' Dante is 'here, and more substantially than would appear from this swift survey of the question'.[17] We need instead to ask what it means to claim that a linguistic element comes *from* Dante. I reformulate this question by exploring how some Beckett texts construct parts of themselves as repetitions of other texts, and by analysing how this strategy operates in many of Beckett's works of fiction and criticism, only tangentially referring to the dramatic works, for which it would be necessary to develop a theory of performance. My position is therefore very different from the Bloomian notion of misreading, often reproduced in Beckett criticism; in my interpretation the point becomes not that there is a text which is there to be repeated (or 'misread') but that the repeating text advertises its own repeating as such, thus enacting a retrieval and also labelling its function.[18] For instance, the second part of my first chapter focuses on how, in the essay *Proust*, Dante's function has changed from 'Dante...Bruno.Vico..Joyce'; in *Proust*, Dante no longer epitomises linguistic experimentalism but works instead as the quotable authority capable of strengthening the intellectual credentials of the writer. As will be further argued by my readings of other texts, there is in Beckett no stable Dante; there is, instead, a constant interrogation of how an antecedent text can be invested with a predetermined meaning and an exploration of how a text can be reproduced, understood, or subverted by another text. In order not to close down these questions, my study does not follow Bloom's tradition of replacing a Beckettian 'reading' of Dante with a 'misreading' of Dante, thus leaving firmly in place authorial intentionality (what Bloom calls 'wilful revisionism') and textual stability (against which a misreading can be measured). Having rejected the idea that there is only one Dante and only one Beckett whose relationship can be analysed, I work with a multiple and changeable notion of textuality which nevertheless configures itself in specific ways.[19] That is to say, to argue in favour of multiple Dantes does not mean to endorse the idea that any meaning can be attached to the sign 'Dante'. To move beyond the idea of authorial intentionality and of a stable prior text entails neither a claim that every meaning can be casually configured and attributed nor a claim that we can do away with the idea of authority. In Judith Butler's words, we could say that 'a loss of certainty is not the same as political nihilism'.[20] This approach entails an extremely close reading, which can demonstrate how these questions on intertextuality 'are enacted and staged through writing practices and not simply by mode of theoretical assertion'.[21] The notion of intertextuality that derives from the analysis of the interaction between Beckett's and Dante's texts is thus not easily liberating: rather than being a theory which 'reminds us that all texts are potentially plural, reversible, open to the reader's own presuppositions, lacking in clear and defined boundaries', intertextuality in Beckett never allows us to forget that there is always a price to pay for quotations, as Mercier and Camier put it.[22] To explore the ways in which Dante is produced and the political implications of these strategies (such as the construction of authority) does not mean to claim that anything (or nothing) can be called 'Dante' or that 'Dante' can occur in any form. *Beckett's Dantes* turns instead the question of fidelity, a central one in Beckett studies, into an exploration of authority: rather than asking how accurately or subversively Beckett (the author) reproduces Dante (the stable text), I will explore how Beckett's texts invent their own precursors, reversing the terms of the statement, similarly to what Borges does in his famous essay on Kafka.[23]

The issue can be developed further by looking at Dante as a function within Beckett's texts, asking why Dante is present in Beckett as source, quotation, or origin. Within the larger issue in Beckett of where meaning comes from, and if it indeed comes from anywhere, the insertion of Dante – in whatever way it occurs – simultaneously evokes and critiques this very strategy. Two questions follow: first, how does Beckett criticism deal with the notion of a Dantean intertext, and how might this be reformulated, taking into account the complex ways in which quotation, source, and origin operate in Beckett? And, secondly, how might Beckett's texts be read in the light of this different theoretical framework?

Approaches focused on quantifying 'how much Dante' can be found in Beckett, or on determining how accurate or illuminating Beckett's representations of Dante may be, are discouraged by Beckett's texts themselves, since such questions imply the assumption of literary value, hierarchy, authority, and canon. Instead, these notions are challenged by Beckett's prose works, which, by questioning the teleological and authorial implications of narrative, construct different Dantes. In turn, Dante's texts, and mainly the *Comedy*, produce Beckett the author: looking for the specific ways in which Dante appears in Beckett therefore means reconsidering both the Beckett and the Dante canons.

For instance, to locate *How It Is* and *The Lost Ones* in the *Inferno* or the *Purgatorio*, respectively, as Beckett scholarship has done in the past, does not account for how these texts tailor different Dantes to suit their respective poetics.[24] As I will argue in Chapter 7, *How It Is* mobilises *Inferno* VII to produce a notion of reality as the unreliable outcome of repetition. The canto in which Virgil translates the incomprehensible gurgling originating from the bubbles on the surface of the Styx into the 'hymn' sung by the invisible slothful damned illustrates how 'credence' for the reality of such a scene is won from the (rapidly diminishing) 'incontrovertibility' of Virgil's authority.[25] Conversely, the mud in *How It Is* is at once what permits the passing on of the murmuring and what hinders it, thus reproducing the situation of the slothful damned of the fifth circle, doomed to sing their almost unintelligible 'hymn' of damnation.

The Lost Ones, a text which oscillates between claiming to be the recording of a visual experience and the construction of a fiction based on 'notions', uses the last lines of the *Comedy* to interrogate, through Dante, the very process of construction of fictional spaces and of ways out. The issue of visibility, which will be analysed in relation to this text in Chapter 8, is central to both intertextuality and Beckett. We can observe its relevance in 'Dante...Bruno.Vico..Joyce', which struggles to establish which kind of intertexts can or cannot be seen in Joyce's work and ends up impatiently claiming, with regards to Vico and Bruno, that they are 'there, and more substantially than would appear from this swift survey of the question'. In this early work the argument in favour of an 'invisible' presence is based on a declared invisibility which becomes more 'substantial' than the essay has actually been able to show. This matter becomes very significant when considering the role of manuscripts in Beckett studies. In the so-called 'Whoroscope' notebook, a text often read as a precursor to *Murphy*, we find the following injunction: 'But keep whole Dantesque analogy out of sight'.[26] Dante's presence is stated and erased at the same time. The promise of such an invisible Dante in the 'Whoroscope' notebook has been read by critics into *Murphy* in ways that overlook the paradoxical nature of this promise, which prompts instead an examination of the status of invisible presences and visible absences in Beckett's ghostly *oeuvre*. Dante's visible absence is also significantly linked to Beckett's poetics of residua, fragmentariness, and marginality; the 'Addenda' section in *Watt*, which reproduces a fragment from the *Comedy* in which Virgil refuses to add 'fair words' to the scene of violence taking place before Dante's eyes in the fifth circle of Hell, will help us, as I will show in Chapter 4, to reassess from an intertextual point of view the roles of mimesis and authority in both Beckett and Dante.

Dante as invisible presence and visible absence is also related to the bilingual status of the Beckett *oeuvre*. Although this study focuses on the English texts of the bilingual Beckett corpus, the French texts are often referred to, since quotations and allusions migrate, are modified, or disappear from one version to the other. This is especially the case with *Mercier et Camier/Mercier and Camier*, the *Nouvelles et textes pour rien/Stories and Texts for Nothing*, *Comment c'est/How It Is* and *Le dépeupleur/The Lost Ones*. From Chapter 5 onwards, therefore, this study devotes more space to the French texts than in earlier chapters. My reading of *Mercier et Camier/Mercier and Camier* focuses on how Dante sometimes appears in the French and not in the English self-translated text and vice versa. In the texts from the *Novellas* to the *Texts for Nothing*, I look at how the few quotations and, occasionally, sustained allusions, challenge ideas of depth, origin, and ending. In this book English and French titles and quotations are given priority according to the critical focus of the argument rather than the chronology of composition.

Elaborating on the readings illustrated above, this book will do two things at once; on the one hand, it will find and explain the intertextual references to Dante to be found in Beckett's prose works. On the other hand, it will argue that a careful analysis of such references can lead to questioning given assumptions about intertextuality. Intertexts in Beckett do not work as the missing piece of the puzzle able to provide us with the complete picture. In an *oeuvre* which asks where meanings come from and how they come about, sources will not restore an allegedly desirable full meaning; what they can do, however, is to raise important questions about how meanings take shape in Beckett. Accounting for references to Dante will not solve the Beckett mystery, and this book makes no promises in this sense; it will, however, demonstrate through a close reading of texts by both Beckett and Dante that intertexts in Beckett productively question ideas of origin, stability, and repetition. Finally, it will contend that the outcome of these practices is 'Mr Beckett' himself, the author with 'the bay about his brow'.

Notes

1 Sighle Kennedy, 'Beckett's schoolboy copy of Dante: a handbook for liberty', *Dalhousie French Studies*, 19 (Fall Winter 1990), 11–19, 11. Kennedy quotes Mel Gussow, 'Interview with Samuel Beckett', *The New York Times* (31 December 1989), Arts and Leisure section.
2 Samuel Beckett, *Dream of Fair to Middling Women* (New York: Arcade, 1993), p. 51. Subsequent references are given in the text. The typescript of *Dream* reads 'the Fiorentia edition in the ignoble Salviani' (RUL MS 1227/7/16/8). For a more detailed discussion see Daniela Caselli, '"The Florentia edition in the ignoble Salani collection": a textual comparison', *Journal of Beckett Studies*, 9:2 (2001), 1–20.
3 James Knowlson, *Damned to Fame: The Life of Samuel Beckett* (London: Bloomsbury, 1996), pp. 51–54.
4 Samuel Beckett to Mary Hutchinson, 1 August 1975, the University of Texas, Austin; quoted in Knowlson, *Damned to Fame*, p. 618.
5 Kennedy, 'Beckett's schoolboy copy of Dante'; Gussow, 'Interview with Samuel Beckett'; Knowlson, *Damned to Fame*, p. 53; Anthony Cronin, *Samuel Beckett: The Last Modernist* (London: HarperCollins Publishers, 1996), p. 587.
6 Pietro De Logu, 'The unifying power of tradition: the presence of Dante in W. B. Yeats's and Samuel Beckett's works', in Wolfgang Zach (ed.), *Literature(s) in English: New Perspectives* (Frankfurt: Peter Lang, 1990), pp. 61–67, p. 66; Kelly Anspaugh, 'Faith, hope and – what was it?: Beckett reading Joyce reading Dante', *Journal of Beckett Studies*, 5:1 and 2 (1996), 19–38 and 'The partially purged: Samuel Beckett's "The Calmative" as Anti-*Comedy*', *Canadian Journal of Irish Studies*, 22:1 (1996), 30–41.
7 David Hayman, 'Quest for meaninglessness: the boundless poverty of *Molloy*', in W. O. S. Sutherland Jr (ed.), *Six Contemporary Novels* (Austin: University of Texas Press, 1962), pp. 90–112; John Fletcher, 'Beckett's verses: influences and parallels', *French Review*, 37:1 (October 1963), 320–331, 'Beckett's debt to Dante', *Nottingham French Studies*, 4 (May 1965), 41–52, and *Samuel Beckett's Art* (London: Chatto & Windus, 1971); Lawrence Harvey, *Samuel Beckett: Poet and Critic* (Princeton: Princeton University Press, 1970); Katherine Travers Gross, 'In other words: Samuel Beckett's art of poetry', Ph.D. thesis, Columbia University, 1972; Sighle Kennedy, 'Beckett's schoolboy copy'; Sebastian Neumeister, 'Das allegorische Erbe. Zur Wiederkehr Dantes bei Becketts (*Le dépeupleur*, 1970)', in Manuel Lichtwitz (ed.), *Materialen zu Samuel Becketts* Der Verwaiser (Frankfurt: Suhrkamp, 1990), pp. 107–28; Mary Bryden, 'Beckett and the three Dantean smiles', *Journal of Beckett Studies*, n.s. 4:2 (September 1995), 29–33, and 'No stars without stripes: Beckett and Dante', *The Romanic Review*, 87:4 (1996), 541–556; Knowlson, *Damned to Fame*; Francesca Del Moro, '"The Divine Florentine": Dante nell'opera di Samuel Beckett', dissertation (tesi di laurea), University of Pisa (Italy), 1996; John Pilling, 'From a (W)horoscope to *Murphy*', in John Pilling and Mary Bryden (eds), *The Ideal Core of the Onion: Reading Beckett Archives* (Reading: Beckett International Foundation, 1992), pp. 1–20, *Beckett Before Godot: The Formative Years (1929–1946)* (Cambridge: Cambridge University Press, 1997), *Beckett's* Dream Notebook (Reading: Beckett International Foundation, 1999), *Companion to Dream of Fair to Middling Women* (Tallahassee, FL: Journal of Beckett Studies Books, 2004); Jean-Pierre Ferrini, *Dante et Beckett* (Paris: Hermann, 2003); C. J. Ackerley and S. E. Gontarski, *The Grove Companion to Samuel Beckett* (New York: Grove Press, 2004).

8   A. J. Leventhal, 'The Beckett hero', in Martin Esslin (ed.), *Samuel Beckett: A Collection of Critical Essays* (Englewood Cliffs: Prentice Hall Inc., 1965), pp. 37–51; Terence McQueeny, 'Samuel Beckett as critic of Proust and Joyce', Ph.D. thesis, University of North Carolina, 1977; Per Nykrog, 'In the ruins of the past: reading Beckett intertextually', *Comparative Literature*, 36:4 (Fall 1984), 289–311; William Hutchings, '"Shat into grace" or, a tale of a turd: why it is how it is in Samuel Beckett's *How It Is*', *Papers on Language and Literature: A Journal for Scholars and Critics of Language and Literature*, 21:1 (Winter 1985), 64–87; Wallace Fowlie, 'Dante and Beckett', in Stuart Y. McDougal (ed.), *Dante Among the Moderns* (Chapel Hill: University of North Carolina Press, 1985), pp. 129–152; Paul Gleason, 'Dante, Joyce, Beckett and the use of memory in the process of literary creation', *Joyce Studies Annual*, 10 (Summer 1999), 104–142; Edward Colerick, 'The syntax of life: strategies of representation in Samuel Beckett's middle to late longer prose 1947–1983', Ph.D. thesis, University of Kent, 1997.

9   Phyllis Carey, 'Stephen Dedalus, Belacqua Shuah, and Dante's *Pietà*', in Phyllis Carey and Ed Jewinski (eds), *RE: Joyce 'n Beckett* (New York: Fordham University Press, 1992), pp. 104–116; Michael Robinson, 'From purgatory to inferno: Beckett and Dante revisited', *Journal of Beckett Studies*, 5 (Autumn 1979), 69–82; Renato Oliva, 'Appunti per una lettura dell'ultimo Beckett', in Samuel Beckett, *Senza e Lo spopolatore*, ed. Renato Oliva (Turin: Einaudi, 1972), p. 97; Kevin C. O'Neill, 'Two trilogies: notes on Beckett and Dante', *Romance Notes*, 32:3 (Spring 1992), 235–240 and 'The voyage from Dante to Beckett', Ph.D. thesis, University of California, 1985; Gabriele Frasca, *Cascando: Tre studi su Samuel Beckett* (Naples: Liguori, 1988).

10 Lois A. Cuddy, 'Beckett's "dead voices" in *Waiting for Godot*: new inhabitants of Dante's *Inferno*', *Modern Language Studies*, 12:2 (Spring 1982), 48–61; Eva Doran, 'Au seuil de Beckett: quelques notes sur "Dante...Bruno.Vico..Joyce"', *Stanford French Review*, 5:1 (Spring 1981), 121–127.

11 Kateryna Arthur, 'Murphy, Gerontion and Dante', *AUMLA, Australian University Language and Literature Association*, 55 (May 1981), 54–67, and 'T. S. Eliot, Samuel Beckett, and Dante', Ph.D. thesis, University of Sussex, 1982; Kelly Anspaugh, 'Faith, hope and – what was it?' and 'The partially purged'; Philip Terry, 'Waiting for God to go: *How It Is* and *Inferno* VII–VIII", *Samuel Beckett Today/Aujourd'hui: Beckett Versus Beckett*, 7 (1998), 349–360; Constantine Theoharis, '"Che la diritta via era smarrita: Dante's *Commedia* in Beckett's *Texts for Nothing*', *Journal of the Short Story in English*, 41 (2003), 25–39.

12 Terry adopts John Freccero's description of Dante's poetics. John Freccero, *Dante: The Poetics of Conversion* (Cambridge, MA: Harvard University Press, 1986).

13 Kristeva coins the term 'intertextuality' after Bakhtin. See Mikhail Bakhtin, 'Discourse in the novel', in Michael Holquist (ed.), *The Dialogic Imagination: Four essays by M. M. Bakhtin*, trans. Caryl Emerson and Michael Holquist (Austin: University of Texas Press 1981), pp. 259–422. Intertextuality initially means in Kristeva that every text is a 'mosaic of quotations'; it also indicates that it is a 'way in which a text reads history and places itself in it'. Intertextuality is later rejected in favour of what she calls 'transposition', that is a 'passage between one system of signs and another'. Julia Kristeva, 'Bachtin, le mot le dialogue et le roman', *Critique*, 239 (1967), 438–65, reprinted in *Desire in Language: A Semiotic Approach to Literature and Art*, trans. Thomas Gora, Alice Jardine, and Léon S. Roudiez (Oxford: Blackwell, 1980); 'Problèmes de la structuration du texte', *Théorie d'ensemble* (Paris: Éditions du Seuil, 1968); *Revolution of Poetic Language*

(New York: Columbia University Press, 1984). For a discussion of the historical and theoretical vicissitudes of the term see Graham Allen, *Intertextuality* (New York and London: Routledge, 2000). For an interesting intervention on intertextuality in Beckett see Enoch Brater, 'Intertextuality', in Lois Oppenheim (ed.), *Palgrave Advances in Samuel Beckett Studies* (Basingstoke: Palgrave, 2004).

14 Michael Riffaterre, 'Interpretation and undecidability', *New Literary History*, 12 (1981), 227–242, 227. Riffaterre's thesis is opposed by Gérard Genette, who maintains that in any hypertext (i.e. target text or primary text) 'there is an ambiguity which Riffaterre denies to the intertextual reading'; he advocates instead what he calls 'lecture palimpsestueuse'. Gérard Genette, *Palimpsestes: la littérature au second degré* (Paris: Seuil, 1982), p. 450.
15 Michel Foucault, 'What is an author?' (1969), in Paul Rabinow (ed.), *The Foucault Reader* (Harmondsworth: Penguin, 1984), pp. 101–120.
16 Cesare Segre, 'Intertestuale, interdiscorsivo: appunti per una fenomenologia delle fonti', in C. Di Girolamo and I. Paccagnella (eds), *La parola ritrovata: fonti e analisi letteraria* (Palermo: Sellerio, 1982), pp. 15–28.
17 Samuel Beckett, *Mercier and Camier* (London: Picador, 1988), p. 19 and 'Dante...Bruno. Vico..Joyce', in Ruby Cohn (ed.), *Disjecta: Miscellaneous Writings and a Dramatic Fragment* (New York: Grove Press, 1984), p. 29.
18 Harold Bloom, *The Anxiety of Influence* (New York: Oxford University Press, 1973).
19 Jacques Derrida, 'Qual quelle: Valéry's sources', trans. Alan Bass, *Margins of Philosophy* (Brighton: The Harvester Press 1982), pp. 273–306.
20 Judith Butler, *Bodies That Matter* (London and New York: Routledge, 1993), p. 30.
21 Daniel Katz, *Saying I No More: Subjectivity and Consciousness in the Prose of Samuel Beckett* (Evanston, IL: Northwestern University Press, 1999), p. 16.
22 Allen, *Intertextuality*, p. 209. Beckett, *Mercier and Camier*, p. 62.
23 Jorge Louis Borges, 'Kafka and his precursors' in Donald A. Yates and James E. Irby (eds), *Labyrinths: Selected Stories and Other Writings* (New York: New Directions, 1964), p. 201. The relevance of fidelity in Beckett studies has been discussed by Anthony Uhlmann, *Beckett and Poststructuralism* (Cambridge: Cambridge University Press, 1999), and Russell Smith, 'Someone (the other Beckett)', *Journal of Beckett Studies*, 10:1–2 (Fall 2000–Spring 2001), 1–16.
24 Carey, 'Stephen Dedalus, Belacqua Shuah, and Dante's *Pietà*'; Robinson, 'From purgatory to inferno: Beckett and Dante revisited'; O'Neill, 'Two trilogies: notes on Beckett and Dante'.
25 Such a problem is stated in *Company* as 'A device perhaps from the incontrovertibility of the one to win credence for the other'. Samuel Beckett, *Company* (London: Calder, 1980), p. 8.
26 Samuel Beckett, 'Whoroscope' notebook, RUL MS 3000.

1 Dantes in Limbo

Detecting Dante in Joyce

The early Beckett essay 'Dante...Bruno.Vico..Joyce', was written in 1929 at Joyce's suggestion about the debt of *Work in Progress* to Dante, Bruno, and Vico.[1] The essay opens by claiming that 'the danger is in the neatness of identifications'; such 'neatness' can reduce the comparison to 'a carefully folded ham-sandwich', an act of 'pigeon-holing' or of 'book-keeping' (19). Rather than limiting the analysis to the passages where 'explicit illustration' of one text within another can be found, the essay privileges what it calls 'reverberations' or 'reapplications'. The not-so-easily 'visible' literary contaminations are juxtaposed with 'the stiff interexclusiveness that is often the danger in neat construction' (22). Although presence and visibility are usually regarded as problems within the Beckett *oeuvre*, in this text they are asserted rather than probed, with the purpose of grounding Joyce's authority.

Bruno and Vico serve the argument of Joyce's linguistic experimentalism that will be the basis for the discussion of what *Rough for Radio II* will call, tongue-in-cheek, 'the divine Florentine'. Dante is introduced flippantly, in the third and last section of the essay:

> To justify our title, we must move North, '*Sovra'l bel fiume d'Arno alla gran villa*'.... Between '*colui per lo cui verso – il meonio cantor non è più solo*' and the 'still to-day insufficiently malestimated notesnatcher, Shem the Penman', there exists considerable circumstantial similarity. (30)

The two quotations are from the *Comedy* (*Inf.* XXIII, 95) and from Leopardi's *Sopra il monumento di Dante che si preparava in Firenze*, respectively.[2] The latter is a poem which describes Dante as the only poet capable of reaching Homer's perfection, while the quotation from the *Comedy* is a self-description of Dante replying to Catalano dei Malvolti and Loderingo degli Andalò in the sixth section of Malebolge. To the two hypocrites who ask him about his identity, Dante replies: 'I' fui nato e cresciuto / sovra 'l bel fiume d'Arno a la gran villa, / e son col corpo ch'i' ho sempre avuto' (I was born and grew up on the fair stream of Arno, at the great town, and I am in the body that I have always had) (*Inf.* XXIII, 94–95).[3] The quotation on Dante's origins 'justifies' the geographical movement from Vico and Bruno's Naples to Florence and is associated with the

Leopardi poem, which creates a *mise en abyme*. Just as in Leopardi the comparison between Homer and Dante guarantees Dante's poetic excellence, in Beckett Dante is proof of Joyce's artistic importance. The basis for such a relationship of authority between Dante and Joyce (their 'circumstantial similarity') is their common linguistic innovation, as 'they both saw how worn out and threadbare was the conventional language of cunning literary artificers, both rejected an approximation to a universal language' (30).

The essay fashions a modernist Dante; but, if a number of twentieth-century writers have seen Dante's modernism in the multilingualism of the *Comedy*, the ability to transform 'the poetical problem into a linguistic question', and the innumerable variations of register within the unity of tone, the argument developed by the essay rests mainly on the assumption that Dante's language is 'synthetic'.[4] While the *Comedy* is the text which sustains most twentieth-century theories supporting a modernist Dante, 'Dante...Bruno.Vico..Joyce' argues in favour of the similarity between Dante's and Joyce's linguistic experimentation mostly through quotations from *De vulgari eloquentia* and the *Convivio*.

Beckett's essay concentrates on the way in which the vernacular was theorised by Dante, and it contends that this new language broke the literary conventions of its time, thus causing the public's moral and aesthetic disapproval. The view that 'the *De vulgari eloquentia* postulated the need for an artificial, "synthetic" language – a refined and immutable version of the common language – was one of the predominant interpretations at the time of Beckett's essay, although several critics would dispute it'.[5] The ongoing debates about the theories illustrated in the Latin prose of *De vulgari eloquentia* and in the vernacular of the *Convivio* point to the fact that the two texts exhibit not only remarkable philosophical complexity but also a number of paradoxical and contradictory arguments. These paradoxes and contradictions are structured, according to Pier Vincenzo Mengaldo, as an attempt to give an inaugural 'formal' existence to a linguistic reality as 'in progress'.[6]

The rhetoric of the essay aims to demonstrate how the idea of Dante as the quintessentially classic author has developed over time, whereas his art was initially perceived as far too daring an experiment. Joyce's language, the text argues, is an artificial construction which can paradoxically 'desophisticate' language through the unity of form and content. Dante's language is correspondingly described as a similarly 'artificial' product, the result of a synthetic operation of skimming the best parts from a number of dialects (a theory which had been denounced as 'false' by Vico).[7] The reaction against the conventionality of a worn-out language – Latin in Dante's case, English in Joyce's – is for Beckett a common characteristic of the two authors, both free from narrow national or regional prejudices.

In order to bolster his argument, Beckett quotes excerpts from *De vulgari eloquentia* in which Dante expresses his contempt for anyone who thinks his own town the most delightful place, and who likes his own dialect better than any other:

> *Nam quicumque tam obscenae rationis est, ut locum suae nationis delitosissimum credat esse sub sole, huic etiam proe cunctis propriam volgare licetur, idest maternam locutionem. Nos autem, cui mundus est patria ... etc.'* When he comes to examine the dialects he finds Tuscan: *'turpissimum ... fere omnes Tusci in suo turpiloquio obtusi ... non restat in dubio quin aliud sit vulgare quod quaerimus quam quod attingit populus Tuscanorum.* (30)

The passage illustrates Dante's indignation with anyone who gives primacy to his own narrow reality. Yet, in *De vulgari* the passage in which Dante describes himself as someone 'for whom the world is fatherland as the sea is for fish' is followed by the declaration of his affection for Florence and the discussion differentiates between choosing the world as motherland and being forced to do so because one is exiled.[8] In order to connect Dante's openmindedness with his linguistic multidialectal operation, Beckett's quotation seems to refer only to the vernacular of Florence, but has in fact two different referents in *De vulgari*. The adjective 'turpissimus' is from chapter eleven of book one of *De vulgari* and refers to the vernacular of Rome, while the rest of the sentence comes from chapter thirteen. Although the omissions are indicated, they are misleading; once contextualised, Dante's assertion has very different implications. In chapter ten Dante describes every vernacular found in Italy, in order to exclude them all because none of them can be regarded as *vulgare illustre*. He starts from those furthest away from 'the panther whose smell is everywhere and which is nowhere visible' (I.xvi, 1); the first *vulgare* discussed in chapter eleven, the vernacular of Rome, does not even deserve that name, since it is a 'tristiloquium' (a noun used in I.xv, 7 for the vernaculars of Trento, Turin, and Alessandria too).[9] The vivid Dantean adjective 'turpissimus' is quoted (conjugated) in the Beckett text as if it referred to the Tuscan vernacular, whereas *De vulgari* is remarkably less harsh towards the dialect of Tuscany, which is nevertheless also judged as profoundly different from the *vulgare illustre*, as made clear by Dante's criticism of Guittone d'Arezzo's vernacular, regarded in chapter thirteen as merely municipal. The passage from which Beckett quotes reads:

> Sed quanquam fere omnes Tusci in suo turpiloquio sint obtusi, nonnullos vulgaris excellentiam cognovisse sentimus, scilicet Guidonen, Lapum et unum alium, Florentinos, et Cynum Pistoriensem, quem nunc indigne postponimus,

non indigne coacti. Itaque si tuscanas examinemus loquelas, et pensemus, qualiter viri prehonorati a propria diverterunt, non restat in dubio quin aliud sit vulgare quod querimus, quam quod actingit populus Tuscanorum. (I.xiii, 4–5)

But although almost all Tuscans have been deafened by their own wretched speech, I feel that some have understood excellence in the vernacular, to wit Guido, Lapo, and one other Florentine, and Cino of Pistoia, whom now, not unfittingly constrained, I unfittingly put last. And so if we examine the Tuscan vernacular and consider how men of the greatest fame have abandoned their own, there can be no doubt that the vernacular which I seek is other than that of which the people of Tuscany make use. (73)

The Tuscan vernacular cannot be the *vulgare illustre* precisely because the poets who come closest to the excellence of vernacular eloquence (among them Dante himself) have departed from it. In other words, *De vulgari eloquentia* tries to justify theoretically what in the text is presented as a contemporary poetic phenomenon, constituted by Dante's own previous poetic experiences – both the Stilnovistic and the moral – and by those of other poets, especially Cino of Pistoia and Guido Cavalcanti, the latter still regarded as a model vernacular poet, an attitude which will change in the *Comedy*. *De vulgari* wants to create the national project of the *vulgare illustre*; hence the paradoxical adoption of Latin, to give to the new *vulgare illustre* – a language defined in the first book as 'nobilior' than Latin – a rhetorical and poetical frame.

Thus, up to chapter fifteen of the first book of the *De vulgari*, *vulgare latium* indicates the sum of the different and dissonant dialects of the peninsula, none of which can be regarded as the *vulgare illustre*. However, from chapter fifteen to nineteen *vulgare latium* is designated as such by the 'doctores illustres qui lingua vulgari poetati sunt' (I.xix, 1). As Pier Vincenzo Mengaldo puts it: 'the theoretical construction of the illustrious vernacular lies between these two different meanings of the "vulgare latium"'.[10] While demonstrating in detail how none of the dialects spoken in any region of Italy corresponds to the illustrious vernacular, Dante also extensively describes a substantially unitary language, of the *doctores illustres*: that is to say the poets who write or have written in a non-municipal vernacular.[11] He insists on the differences among the municipal vernaculars just as much as he stresses the unity of this literary language. According to Mengaldo, this unity results not from the selection of the purest elements of all the different vernaculars but instead from the rational impetus towards the 'reductio ad unum', that is to say a metaphysical simplification.[12]

'Dante...Bruno.Vico..Joyce' highlights a theoretical tension in Dante's text. The poets mentioned in the passage quoted above are said to have moved away from the popular municipal vernaculars and at the same time to recognise the poetic excellence of the vernacular. They work in the text as actual examples and yet they are transformed into an abstract entity, summed into the divine number one, the 'simplicissima quantitas' by which the local vernaculars will be measured. Lucia Boldrini has maintained that such singular, perfect entity 'does not appear anywhere in particular but is reflected in all the particular vernaculars and reflects them in itself (I.xvi, 5). The *vulgare illustre* is qualified therefore as the *optimum* of vernaculars'; unlike Mengaldo, Boldrini interprets the opposition between *omnis* and *nullius* at the end of chapter sixteen as an indication that 'the task of the poet is to "(re)compose" [the illustrious vernacular], starting from the multiplicity of the local vernaculars and selecting from them what best reflects the perfection of the "one" – that is to say, extracting the noblest elements and reconstituting them in the *vulgare illustre*'.[13] Boldrini's Dante, the 'self-fashioned redeemer of the *felix culpa* of Babel' and absolute innovator, is in line with Beckett's – and even more with Joyce's – formulation of Dante's language as 'synthetic', distilled out of the 'purest elements from each dialect'.[14] While Boldrini interprets the idea of 'the *optimum* of vernaculars' as a process of synthesis and selection, one could argue, with Mengaldo, that the text does not indicate such modalities as the method followed to 'invent' the illustrious vernacular. Rather, the poetic examples in the *De vulgari* shape a *de facto* reality to which the Latin text gives a *de jure* consistency.

The notion of a Dantean 'synthetic language' creates further problems in relation to the neat contrast between this new language and Latin suggested by Beckett. Although Dante in *De vulgari* reacts against the 'conventionality' of Latin, he also adopts it, 'helped by his belief in the continuity between Latin and the vernacular, which enables him to incorporate any kind of tradition while he is getting ready for any kind of innovation'.[15] Dante's Latin in this text is very sophisticated and has numerous cultural echoes, most notably of the thriving Latin scholastic prose of those years (especially St Bonaventura and Egidio Colonna), but also of the philosophical prose of the radical Aristotelians.[16] It is precisely through the instrument of scholastic argument that Dante asserts the superiority of the vernacular over Latin, using the typical scholastic antinomy between 'natural' and 'artificial'. Latin is artificial because it is a 'gramatica', a 'lingua regulata' constructed by the 'inventores gramatice facultatis'; Dante's illustrious vernacular is, on the contrary, a 'natural' language.

Thus, Dante's dissatisfaction with the 'conventionality' of the language used by 'cunning literary artificers' is paradoxically demonstrated through examples from a text in Latin which discusses through a scholastic argument the relationships between the vernacular's naturalness and Latin's artificiality.

Latin is, in *De vulgari*, the human answer to the inevitable chaos of the languages after Babel; it is constructed through a 'gramatica' and therefore it is not subject to the erosion and the modifications of time and space.[17] Latin is the non-corruptible language, the model Dante has to use in order to give to his *vulgare* a literary existence. If the *vulgare*'s naturalness enables Dante to assert its superiority to Latin, it nevertheless carries with it the concepts of variability and mutability. These are the marks of the fall, which have to be amended precisely through the theoretical operation which Dante is conducting in *De vulgari eloquentia*, by the institution of a unitary and stable *vulgare illustre* (Boldrini's 'perfect entity' discussed above), capable of soothing the medieval anxiety of mutability.[18] *De vulgari eloquentia* is a productively paradoxical meditation, which does not provide an answer to the ultimate question of how the illustrious vernacular will remain a natural language once it has become 'lingua regulata'.

The corollary to the comparison between Joyce's and Dante's modernist experimentalism is that Dante 'did not write in Florentine any more than in Neapolitan'. As pointed out by many critics, the language of the *Comedy* is indeed illustrious Florentine, notwithstanding its many neologisms and borrowings from other dialects and languages, and surely it is more Florentine than Neapolitan.[19] The *De vulgari*'s theorisation however supports Beckett's refusal of the hypothetical objection that Dante's language was spoken in the streets whereas Joyce's language has never been spoken nor ever will be by any 'creature in heaven or earth'. In *De vulgari* the vernacular described as 'illustre, cardinale, aulicum et curiale', is indeed not a spoken language; Dante's language, he himself argues, will be the 'hinge' on which all other dialects will depend, it will be the unifying element of a still fragmented country.[20] The four adjectives point to the political and civic project implied in such a notion of language, which is also present in the *Convivio*, and has been read as 'an important force behind the *Wake*'s experimentation with narrative form'.[21]

As seen above, the claim that 'it is reasonable to admit that an international phenomenon might be capable of speaking [the language of *Work in Progress*], just as in 1300 none but an inter-regional phenomenon could have spoken the language of the Divine Comedy' leads us back to the quotation from *De vulgari* I.xiii, in which the 'viri prehonorati' or the 'doctores illustres' are indeed fashioned as 'phenomena' who have 'diverted' from their municipal vernacular. If their function is to create the possibility of a poetic activity in a non-municipal vernacular, and at the same time to operate as a consistent and unitary category, one might say that they point to the 'vulgar that could have been spoken by an ideal Italian who had assimilated what was best in all the dialects of his country, but which in fact was certainly not spoken nor ever had been' (30–31).

And yet, *De vulgari eloquentia* does not specify the modalities according to which such non-municipal vernaculars have 'diverted' from their local 'vulgar' languages. It remains unclear if the Joycean 'sifting' could be the method ideally or practically followed by these 'phenomena', who are 'inter-regional' not so much because they pick and mix from different local vernaculars but because they transcend their locality and are summed up into that 'simplicissima quantitas, quod est unum' (I.xvi, 6).

The figure of an experimental Dante who created a language that no one spoke, but 'that *could* have been spoken by an ideal Italian who had assimilated what was best in all the dialects of his country' (30) does not coincide with either the *vulgare illustre* theorised in *De vulgari* or the illustrious Florentine of the *Comedy*. However, this 'ideal Italian' brings to the fore both the political, anti-parochial, and unitary language of *De vulgari* and the innovative language in the *Comedy*. Most importantly, such a potential speaker prefigures Dante as Joyce the exile, the international phenomenon, and the innovator.[22]

The 'circumstantial similarity' between Dante and Joyce is both illuminating and partially fabricated. However, 'fabrication', 'sophistication', and 'synthetic language' do not necessarily carry negative connotations in this essay, as the quotations from the *Convivio* further demonstrate. They are described as 'two well made caps', which provocatively exhibits the artificiality of the parallel between Dante's and Joyce's texts. The first quotation, from chapter eleven of the first treatise, contains an image from Boethius used by Dante to characterise people who lack 'discrezione' (discretion) and therefore go 'contra nostro volgare' (against our vernacular).[23] The second quotation, from the end of the first book of the *Convivio*, reproduces Dante's claim that his vernacular will be like a 'new light' and a 'new sun'; Beckett compares it to Joyce's linguistic project. The subsequent 'translation' of 'in tenebre e in oscurità' (in darkness and obscurity) as 'bored to extinction' is an ironic modernisation. The prophetic dimension of Dante's claim is translated into a modernist ennui, which, however, will be the premise for a 'formal innovation'.

This agrees with a twentieth-century paradigm of a poetics able to break linguistic conventions. The classic modernist idea that any innovative work needs to frustrate conventional expectations, often encountered, for instance, in Ezra Pound's and Gertrude Stein's work, here applies to Dante. As Dante's audience was used to the 'suave elegance' of Latin – the text argues – so Joyce's readers are used to English, even though 'the language *commonly* spoken in Italy in Dante's time had not been Latin for several centuries'.[24] A shadow is immediately cast on this parallel by the assertion that 'Boccaccio never jeered at the "*piedi sozzi*" of the peacock that Signora Alighieri dreamed about'. The 'peacock Signora Alighieri dreamed about' is Dante himself, while the 'piedi sozzi' (filthy feet) represent the vernacular. This episode is narrated by Boccaccio in his *Trattatello in laude di Dante*.[25] According to Boccaccio's narrative, Dante's mother, while pregnant, dreamt that she was giving birth to a child who, feeding himself on laurel berries, became a shepherd and then transformed himself into a peacock. After having illustrated the allegorical meanings of the other events of the dream, Boccaccio explains that Dante's *Comedy* has the four most important characteristics of the peacock: 'penna angelica, e in quella ha cento occhi; ... sozzi piedi e tacita andatura; voce molto orribile ad udire; ... la sua carne è odorifera e incorruttibile' (angelic feather, and in it one hundred eyes; ... filthy feet and a silent way of walking; a voice horrible to hear; odorous and incorruptible flesh) (§221). The *Comedy* is like the flesh of the peacock because it tells the 'simple and immutable truth'; it is incorruptible, and the paradoxical smell of its incorruptibility is perceptible. The flesh of the peacock is covered with angelic feathers, as the *Comedy* is covered with 'the beauty of the history of the pilgrim, which resounds in the surface of the letter of the *Comedia*' (§224). The horrific voice of the peacock is Dante's voice, capable of 'morde[re] le colpe di molti viventi, e quelle de' preteriti gastiga[re]' (To bite the sins of many living people, and to castigate those of the dead) (§227). As the feet are the body parts that sustain the whole body, so language is the element on which any work of literature is based: 'e il parlare volgare, nel quale e sopra il quale ogni giuntura della *Comedia* si sostiene, a rispetto dell'alto e maestevole stilo letterale che usa ciascuno altro poeta è sozzo, come che egli sia più che gli altri belli agli odierni ingegni conforme' (and the vulgar language, in which and on which every juncture of the *Comedy* is based, is filthy if compared to the high and majestic literary style used by any other poet, even though more than others it is apt for contemporary minds) (§226).

The reference to Boccaccio's text highlights how the vernacular is still seen as 'piedi sozzi', low and dirty if compared with Latin, and yet, nevertheless, 'more than the others apt to modern minds'. Boccaccio's text, like *De vulgari eloquentia*, compares the vernacular with Latin and views the former as lower and less refined. The reference to the *Trattatello* makes of Boccaccio an *auctoritas*; unlike 'English eyes and ears', he did not 'jeer at the "*piedi sozzi*" of the peacock Signora Alighieri dreamed about' (31). Boccaccio, who calls his own vernacular and that of Dante 'our' Tuscan vernacular, is in Beckett an example of an illustrious author who could appreciate Dante's vernacular while still seeing it as 'piedi sozzi'. Boccaccio also serves another purpose: the opposition between the 'suave elegance' of '*ultima regna canam, fluido contermina mundo*' and the '"barbarous" directness' of '"*Nel mezzo del cammin di nostra vita*"' (31) is from the *Trattatello*. In Beckett such opposition serves the purpose of showing, once again, the innovative character of a Dante hardly preoccupied with irritating his Latin literary public. Boccaccio's point, however, is quite different, since he narrates that Dante had begun his work with the quoted Latin words, but had been forced to use the vernacular in order to be better understood by a society which despised Virgil and the classical authors (§192).[26] Boccaccio argues that it is precisely the wish to be understood that drives Dante to adopt the vernacular, thus implicitly admitting Latin's superiority but simultaneously defending Dante's novelty. Beckett's picture of the reception of Dante's work is further complicated by the following assertion:

> We know very little about the immediate reception accorded to Dante's mighty vindication of the 'vulgar', but we can form our own opinions when, two centuries later, we find Castiglione splitting more than a few hairs concerning the respective advantages of Latin and Italian, and Poliziano writing the dullest of dull Latin Elegies to justify his existence as the author of '*Orfeo*' and the '*Stanze*'. (32)

If 'Dante's mighty vindication of the "vulgar"' may be taken to refer exclusively to *De vulgari eloquentia*, historical studies indicate that the text was little known during the two centuries following its composition, both because it was left unfinished and because Dante had rejected it, never making it public.[27] But if Beckett refers to the general reception of Dante's works, and of the *Commedia* in particular, there is strong evidence of acclaim.[28] Furthermore, even assuming Beckett refers to *De vulgari*, the examples of Poliziano and Castiglione are surprising because they represent a well-documented reaction of the Renaissance against the vernacular and an attempt to go back to the Mannerist appreciation of Latin and of neo-Latin literature, as demonstrated by the rediscovery of *De vulgari eloquentia* at this time and its role in various contemporary skirmishes about language.[29] However, Poliziano and Castiglione – two examples of the Italian *Cinquecento*, historically the time in which the *Comedy* suffers its lowest degree of appreciation – are used as a rhetorical device to prove that Dante's unconventionality is comparable to Joyce's.

The text draws another parallel, this time between the reaction of the Church provoked by both Dante's and Joyce's art. The quotations from *Purgatorio* VI, 118 and XXXII, 149, together with a reference to the punishment of the three popes Niccolò III, Bonifacio VIII, and Clemente V (all appearing in *Inferno* XIX, 46–87) are examples of Dante's explicit attacks against the Church of his time. The 'storm of ecclesiastical abuse' raised by Dante and Joyce indicates that both authors break accepted conventions of the Catholic Church, whose rage against Dante is illustrated by the following assertion, paraphrased from a section of Boccaccio's *Trattatello*:

'*De Monarshia*' [*sic*] was burnt publicly under Pope Giovanni XXII at the istigation of Cardinal Beltrando and the bones of its author would have suffered the same fate but for the interference of an influential man of letters, Pino della Tosa. (32)[30]

In Beckett's essay, Dante is also mentioned in relation to his interpretation of the Bible in *De vulgari eloquentia*. Between parentheses, the texts claims:

(Dante makes a curious mistake speaking of the origin of language, when he rejects the authority of Genesis that Eve was the first to speak, when she addressed the Serpent. His incredulity is amusing: '*inconvenienter putatur tam egregium humani generis actum, vel prius quam a viro, fœmina profluisse*'. But before Eve was born, 'the animals were given names by Adam', the man who 'first said goo to a goose'. Moreover it is explicitly stated that the choice of names was left entirely to Adam, so [that] there is not the slightest Biblical authority for the conception of language as a direct gift of God...). (31)

The essay views Dante's position as a 'curious mistake', pointing out how in the Bible Adam's naming precedes Eve's address to the serpent. Although some scholars have, like Beckett, hypothesised a mistake on the part of Dante, others, such as Maria Corti and Roger Dragonetti, have drawn attention to the distinction in *De vulgari eloquentia* and in other contemporary texts between the act of naming and the act of speaking with an interlocutor.[31] Dragonetti's argument that 'primiloquium' indicates a dialogical act, rather than the act of naming, could account for Dante's 'curious mistake'. Moreover, according to Mengaldo, there was a medieval tradition – although not among 'professional' philosophers – which thought that Adam had spoken immediately after his creation in order to thank God.[32]

In any case, the essay highlights how in Dante femininity creates a clash between the ideas of *convenientia* and truth. Eve's 'overflowing' femininity is resisted in the *De vulgari* through scholastic argumentative strategies, based on the simultaneous use of reason and *auctoritates*, which are concepts opposed to Aristotelian notions of femininity. The two terms 'rationabilius' and 'rationabiliter', to be found in the passage partially quoted by Beckett, produce reason as the justification for a virile diversion from the Scriptures.

Beckett's statement asserting 'that there is not the slightest Biblical authority for the conception of language as a direct gift of God' also refers to a heatedly debated passage in *De vulgari*. Dante's text speaks of a 'forma locutionis concreata' (a definition deriving from the philosophy of the Modists) between Adam and God, in order to maintain his theory of the mutability of human language. The 'forma locutionis' is the 'formal cause and the generative and structuring principle of language', which is innate and independent from actual languages.[33] Maria Corti has maintained that, thanks to the notion of 'forma locutionis', *De vulgari* succeeds in harmonising the knowledge of the Bible and the exegetical tradition, with the idea of the mutability of language. *De vulgari* theorises that the original Adamitic language, the 'speculum' of God's perfection, was destroyed during the construction of the tower of Babel, when the 'forma locutionis' was also lost, and language was thrown into the chaos of arbitrary relations between *signa* and *res*.

The concept of 'forma locutionis' strengthens the idea of the naturalness of all languages while simultaneously working to overcome the theological obstacle represented by the idea that Hebrew was the Edenic and incorruptible language and the direct gift of God to Adam. The language of Adam is no longer a static and immutable language, although it remains, until Babel, a language in which 'forma locutionis' and world have the same relative position.[34] In Beckett's essay, the rejection of the divine origin of language is configured, in opposition to *De vulgari*'s theological mediations, as a way of assuming an exclusively human responsibility for the irretrievable arbitrariness of the linguistic sign.

The common 'preoccupation with the significance of numbers' is the next 'point of comparison' between the authors in question. This juxtaposition of examples, which asserts that for both Dante and Joyce numbers are relevant, calls Dante's use of the number three an 'obsession', without reference to its textual or cultural importance. The essay is quite vague in relation to Joyce's use of numbers too, claiming only that 'He is conscious that things with a common numerical characteristic tend towards a very significant relationship' (32).

The last paragraph of the essay establishes a comparison between Dante's and Joyce's Purgatories. The works of Joyce can be seen as purgatorial only if Dante's *Purgatorio* is purged of vice and virtue, punishment and reward, culmination, the Absolute, and unidirectional movement. In other words, only by openly abandoning the theological and teleological structure of Dante's voyage, the necessity of a linear progression and of an identity between ethical, religious, and literary enterprises, can Joyce's sphere hope to fit Dante's cone. As will be discussed later in this study, the space of 'real vegetation', Dante's Antepurgatory, will be adopted and refashioned in other Beckett texts. Joyce's and Dante's Purgatories are similar because both move; in Joyce, however, the movement has lost its redemptive guarantee, its fixed structure, its character of space-in-between. It has become a sphere, a vicious circle in which a step forward is a step back, thus collapsing in Bruno's theory of 'identified contraries'. Joyce's Purgatory metamorphoses into 'this earth', through a process that makes the Danteian structure a place in which 'eruptions' are 'simply a series of stimulants' necessary for the machine to proceed.[35]

Beckett's construction of Joyce's status through Dante, with its emphasis on Joyce's antitheological and antiteleological project, has often been adopted by critics as the authoritative starting point for any parallel between Dante and Beckett himself. For instance, Walter A. Strauss's article on Dante and Beckett concludes by claiming that 'Beckett, who has lost his belief in divine love – Dante's "l'amor che move il sole e l'altre stelle" and thereby comprises the divine and the human – is groping for whatever light and warmth may still be within the reach of human beings', while in Michael Robinson's work '*Molloy* and *Malone Dies* remain, in their combination of suffering and hope, closer to "this earth that is Purgatory"'.[36]

The juxtaposition of divine and human spheres based on 'Dante...Bruno. Vico..Joyce' is also present in Katheryna Arthur's study of Beckett, Eliot, and Dante, in which she states that 'Beckett uses Murphy to show how an individual liberated from old systems that fix universal hierarchies and enforce meaning, can invent meaning by setting up his own system. The new systems are however conceived in terms of the old. The Celia love/action chain mimics the Beatrice love/action chain and parodies elements of it.'[37] In a detailed reading of *How It Is* in relation to Dante, Philip Terry argues that Beckett operates a 'poetics of perversion' in contrast to Dante's 'poetics of conversion', maintaining that 'the radical goal of this text is severance from God', in line with its 'continual anti-theological activity'.[38] While the subversion of theology and teleology, parodic in various degrees, is an important aspect of this specific essay, I will argue in the course of this book that other works by Beckett establish a number of different relationships with Dante, often going against the ideas of authority, canon, and visibility which are adopted in this essay. While in 'Dante...Bruno.Vico..Joyce' the authority of the speaker results from a genealogy of *auctoritates* (often openly fabricated), the ways in which the parallel between Joyce and Dante is drawn cannot work as an authoritative model to explore the relationships between Beckett's and Dante's texts because it fails to interrogate how Beckett's different Dantes analyse and question the very idea of authority.

In 'Dante...Bruno.Vico..Joyce', Dante is fashioned as modernist not only by the attention devoted to the issue of language in his works but also by attributing to the 'divine Florentine' the impatience with contemporary literary models and the power to break through them. The quotations from *De vulgari eloquentia* create a Dante rather more cosmopolitan than the Latin text suggests, while those from the *Convivio* – and especially the translation of the end of the first treatise – draw attention to Dante as a fabrication. This modernist Dante is invested with the power of the *auctoritas*; it can guarantee Joyce's literary excellence, protect him from the accusation of unintelligible sophistication, and prefigure his status as a modernist classic.

Recycling Dante in *Proust*

Described as 'an explosive exercise in self-definition', *Proust* (1931) has been read as oscillating between being a critical study of the *Recherche* and a speculation on some aesthetic and narrative problems central to Beckett's writing.[39] The *Foreword* warns the reader about what will *not* be found in the book: 'no allusion ... to the legendary life and death of Marcel Proust, nor to the garrulous dowager of the Letters, nor to the poet, nor to the author of the Essays'. And 'the references are to the abominable edition of the *Nouvelle Revue Française*'. So much, as Beckett's *Enough* puts it, 'for the art and craft'.

The genre of the essay, although challenged by the bold and blunt syntax and by the derisive tone permeating many of the arguments, remains nevertheless the scaffolding of a text which often seems to be 'less interested in what is said than in the way in which it is said' (63). Beckett's early texts try to dismantle conventional notions of literature. Just as *Dream of Fair to Middling Women* challenges the realistic novel, so *Proust* questions the conventions of the critical essay. Intertextual practices such as allusion and quotation help achieve Beckett's goal. These allusions and quotations tend to be better integrated into the discussion than those present in 'Dante...Bruno.Vico.. Joyce'. This is true at least until the last section of the essay, in which we encounter

> a burst of comparative reference points ... Baudelaire, Dante, Spenser, Anatole France, Daudet and the Goncourts, Coppée, Cellini, Hugo, and Huysmans with a dash of Tennyson. Subsequently Dostoievski, Musset, Chateaubriand, Amiel and the Comtesse de Noailles are added; and in short order thereafter come Ernst Robert Curtius, Renan, Keats, Giorgione, D'Annunzio, Schopenhauer, Leibniz, Mantegna, Dostoievski, Spenser and Anatole France once again.[40]

This 'plethora of cultural baggage' allows Beckett to pose, through erudition, as what Estragon mockingly calls the 'crritic!' and to make his argument more dramatic and persuasive.[41] Nevertheless, allusions play at times a different role, as in the case of Leopardi's three quotations, which participate in the ontological and aesthetic preoccupations of the essay, framed by the philosophy of Schopenhauer.[42] *A se stesso* parallels a number of issues discussed in *Proust*, such as the relationship between time and desire, the impossibility of fulfilment, the tragic sense of life oscillating between suffering and boredom, habit as anaesthetised perception, and suffering as a moment of truth in the perception of reality.

If we now shift the attention to Dante's role in *Proust*, it becomes apparent that it works differently from the Dante of linguistic experimentation encountered in 'Dante...Bruno.Vico..Joyce'. In *Proust*, Dante's presence is geared to boost the authority of the critical 'I' rather than to justify Joyce's innovative techniques. The different Dantes constructed in the different Beckett texts indicate that 'Dante' is unstable in meaning. Francesco De Sanctis, who is a mediating authority in this text, was asking himself in 1870 'which is the real Dante?' For De Sanctis this was a question which presupposed the existence of a real Dante, of an ultimate answer.[43] Under the 'velame de li versi strani' (the veil of the strange verses) (*Inf.* IX, 63), De Sanctis wanted to find a concrete, ultimate truth. In my analysis, instead, I would like to argue that each Beckett text produces a different 'Dante', which has various functions in the text, thus creating different 'Becketts'. I will also explore how Dante is fashioned as an authority, in its turn shaping Beckett's authority. In other words, I would like to take into account the instability not only of Beckett's works but also of Dante's, trying to avoid attributing a predetermined meaning to them.

Most comparative studies devoted to Beckett and Dante assume a rigid definition of the meaning of 'Dante' or of the *Comedy*, and then proceed to analyse the difference between this and Beckett. For instance, Dante is seen as the 'culmination of the Christian tradition of the Middle Ages' and the *Comedy* is declared 'the greatest itinerary of the soul in Western literature'.[44] Thus, the conclusion is that the *Comedy* can be known, understood, and, usually, subverted by Beckett. As discussed above, the common discussion of Beckett's modernist rejection of the teleological and theological implications of the *Comedy* is a convincing argument in the case of 'Dante...Bruno.Vico..Joyce' (a text in which Dante's *Purgatorio* is a paradigm of theology and teleology), but that Dante cannot be generalised in an unqualified manner. Such predetermined meaning attributed to Dante is instead a sign of his authority as a long-established classic and of what is by now Beckett's established authority as a contemporary classic. In order to avoid reproducing Beckett's authority and to focus instead on how this authority is produced, it can be helpful to think of Dante as a discourse, rather than as a predetermined meaning. This enables us to look at how the construction of authorial texts takes place and helps to shape the canon instead of stubbornly asking the question of how accurately Dante has been understood by Beckett.

In *Proust*, the word 'inferno' is used to describe Marcel's inability to sleep in the unfamiliar room; later, in the fifth section of the essay, the narrator of the *Recherche* is described as being 'in the midst of this Tolomea' (12), as he suffers from Albertine's presumed betrayal (40). Tolomea, the third zone of the ninth circle, and the penultimate of the whole *Inferno*, is the zone of the betrayers of guests. If 'inferno' is a word which might not necessarily refer to Dante, 'Tolomea' works in a more specific way, pointing towards the *Comedy*.

The first direct quotation from a Dante text appears towards the end of the penultimate section of the essay, and it is from the second 'canzone' of Dante's *Convivio*, a text already quoted by Beckett in 'Dante...Bruno.Vico..Joyce'. The section describes Proust's involuntary memory; 'impertinently', *Le Temps retrouvé* is said to be an 'inappropriate description' of its content (as *Crime and Punishment* was, according to Joyce, a similarly inadequate title).[45] After the quip the section refers to the scene in the library. The quotation from Dante concludes an intricate passage on the role played by art in recreating the 'bounty of a subject' living an experience 'at once imaginative and empirical, at once an evocation and a direct perception, real without being merely actual'.

> For in the brightness of art alone can be deciphered the baffled ecstasy that he had known before the inscrutable superficies of a cloud, a triangle, a spire, a flower, a pebble, when the mystery, the essence, the Idea, imprisoned in matter, had solicited the bounty of a subject passing by within the shell of his impurity, and tendered, like Dante his song to the 'ingegni storti e loschi', at least an incorruptible beauty:
> 'Ponete mente *almen* com'io son bella' (57)

Edith Fournier has pointed out that 'ingegni storti e loschi' (crooked and shady wits) is a quotation from *Convivio* IV, xv.[46] Dante's 'song' is the second 'canzone' commented on in the second book of the *Convivio*, 'Voi ch'intendendo il terzo ciel movete', which ends as follows:

> Canzone, io credo che saranno radi
> color che tua ragione intendan bene,
> tanto la parli faticosa e forte.
> Onde, se per ventura elli addivene
> che tu dinanzi da persone vadi
> che non ti paian d'essa bene accorte,
> allor ti priego che ti riconforte,
> dicendo lor, diletta mia novella:
> 'Ponete mente almen com'io son bella!'

> Song, I think only few people will understand your meaning, since you speak it in such a difficult and strong manner. So, if you should come across people you think cannot understand, do not despair and tell them my beloved news: 'See at least how beautiful I am!'

The line quoted concludes this 'canzone' which speak[s] its 'ragione' in such a difficult and strong way; as Dante explains in his commentary, the song is 'strong' because what it says is new. Since it is difficult to understand, 'saranno radi / color che [t]ua ragione intendan bene' (will be rare those who will understand properly what you say). The 'ingegni storti e loschi' referred to by Beckett are the 'persone ... che non ti paian d'esser bene accorte' (people you think cannot understand); to them the song can say 'see at least how beautiful I am'.[47]

By saying that only the 'celestial intellects of love' are the addressees of this song, the authorial commentary proclaims its 'poetics of the new', at once seducing the implied reader and stimulating him/her to become one of the chosen addressees and to interpret the poem.[48] The last line incites the reader to recognise its formal beauty in its three aspects, grammatical, rhetorical, and musical; at the same time, however, it invites him/her not to stop at this stage, but to understand its 'bontade' (goodness), which for Dante is in the 'sentenza' (meaning), while 'bellezza' (beauty) is in the 'ornamento delle parole' (ornament of the words).

Dante's line is included in Beckett's text as an example of how art can have 'at least an incorruptible beauty' and is connected to Marcel's recognition of the 'necessity of art'; an art is here conceived in opposition to 'the grotesque fallacy of a realistic art'. The multiple subject of Beckett's sentence, 'the mystery, the essence, the Idea', tenders an incorruptible beauty, just as Dante offers his song to those who cannot understand.

The insertion of Dante in the passage brings to the fore the elitist choice of an art which can work at two levels, showing 'at least' its incorruptible beauty to those who cannot grasp its 'deeper' meaning. This passage, theorising artistic epiphany, has been read in conjunction to Schopenhauer's confutation of the Kantian 'doctrine of time', for which 'there can be no existence, essence, or reality *except in time*'. Schopenhauer instead elaborates a doctrine of the eternity of the present, which even though 'inaccessible to empirical consciousness' can however 'be seen as the supreme reality for the metaphysician'.[49]

Dante is also included in the paragraph which follows the quotation of 'Voi ch'intendendo'. Marcel's experience in the library made him realise that only art can reproduce the 'bounty of a subject' and therefore capture – in Beckettian terms – the 'negation of Time', or – in Proustian terms – the retrieval of time. Dante is an example of art as incorruptible beauty. When Marcel leaves the library he 'is confronted by the spectacle of Time made flesh'. If earlier on the two distant moments of time 'clashed', now

> the measure of their span ... is written on the face and frailty of the dying, curved, like Dante's proud, under the load of their years – 'unwieldy, slow, heavy and pale as lead'.

> 'e qual più pazienza avea negli atti
> piangendo parea dicer: – Più non posso.' (58)

The lines quoted are from *Purgatorio* X, 136–139:

> Vero è che più e meno eran contratti
> secondo ch'avien più e meno a dosso;
> e qual più pazïenza avea ne li atti,
> piangendo parea dicer: 'Più non posso'.

> They were truly more or less contracted according as they had more and less upon their backs; and he who showed the most suffering in his looks, seemed to say, weeping, 'I can no more'.

The reference to 'Dante's proud' renders the intertext more immediate than the previous one. Both quotations make clear that the borrowed phrases belong to Dante, thus reducing the impact resulting from their being in Italian and with no specified source. Both quotations indicate Dante as a literary authority; in the first case, his words show the potential of art, in the second case, his authoritative image describing the proud loaded by their sin like caryatids is compared to the Proustian description. The latter quotation conforms to a frequent habit in the *Comedy*, whose visual quality has often been one of Dante's intertextually most exploited traits; furthermore, the quotation reproduces the end of a canto, also a common practice in Dante intertextuality. In both cases then, Dante is included in Beckett's text as a distant classic, whose distance is enhanced by abrupt quotation.

Dante appears once more in the last section of Beckett's essay. He still plays the role of a literary authority; but here he is a negative *exemplum*:

> Dante, if he can ever be said to have failed, fails with his purely allegorical forms, Lucifer, the Griffin of the Purgatory and the Eagle of the Paradise, whose significance is purely conventional and extrinsic. Here allegory fails as it must always fail in the hands of a poet. Spenser's allegory collapses after a few cantos. Dante, because he was an artist and not a minor prophet, could not prevent his allegory from becoming heated and electrified into anagogy. (60)

The passage closely recalls Francesco De Sanctis's *Storia della letteratura italiana*, from which the quotation 'chi non ha la forza di uccidere la realtà non ha la forza di crearla' (who does not have the power to kill reality does not have the power to create it) is taken.[50] According to McQueeny, De Sanctis's anti-allegorical position with regard to Dante provides Beckett with an instrument to extend Schopenhauer's critique of allegory in the pictorial and plastic arts to poetics as well.

The De Sanctis passage from which the examples of Lucifer, the Griffin, and the Eagle come is the following:

> L'allegoria dunque allarga il mondo dantesco, e insieme lo uccide, gli toglie la vita propria e personale, ne fa il segno o la cifra di un concetto a sé estrinseco. Hai due realtà distinte, l'una fuori dell'altra, l'una figura e adombramento dell'altra, perciò amendue incompiute e astratte. La figura, dovendo significare non sé stessa, ma un altro, non ha niente d'organico e diviene un accozzamento meccanico mostruoso, il cui significato è fuori di sé, com'è il grifone del Purgatorio, l'aquila del Paradiso, e il Lucifero, e Dante con le sette P incise sulla fronte.

> Allegory, while it enlarges Dante's world, at the same time kills it, robs it of its own and personal life, and turns it into the sign and cipher of a concept outside itself. Thus there are two distinct realities, one outside the other, both of them incomplete and abstract. Dante's figures, having to symbolize not themselves, but something outside themselves, are unorganic, are a mechanical and monstrous mixture whose meaning is outside itself – as, for instance, the Griffin in Purgatory, the eagle in Paradise, Lucifer, and Dante with the seven Ps engraved on his forehead.[51]

Dante is included in the discussion on the 'intellectual symbolism of Baudelaire' as another example of how the 'concept' creates in art 'a unity *post rem*'; it is contrasted with a very Schopenhauerian 'Idea' associated with the 'concrete'. Dante is here an example of how even the unchallenged literary authority fails when using the conceptual instrument of allegory. The Dante we encounter here is a long way from the one emerging from 'Dante...Bruno.Vico..Joyce' and closer to the Dante, author of the *Comedy*, described by De Sanctis.

With De Sanctis, the *Comedy* is approached in a dualistic way, which will lead to the division into 'poetry' and 'non-poetry' theorised by Benedetto Croce. De Sanctis condemns allegory for its 'abstraction' and argues that this concept of poetry is the negation of poetry itself. Post-romantically convinced that the medieval period was 'not an artistic world; it was the contrary of art', De Sanctis reads Dante as the only artist able to surpass his age and therefore to achieve 'real poetry'. Dante, however, is for De Sanctis still sometimes tied to the allegorical and scholastic conventions of his time, which he partially overcomes by detaching the 'literal' from the 'allegorical' sense; giving independence to the former, he is able to limit the anti-artistic effects of the latter. De Sanctis conceives the artist as a free spirit able to create, outside allegory, free characters: tellingly, Dante is often compared to Goethe's *Faust*.

The sentence quoted by Beckett – 'who does not have the power to kill reality does not have the power to create it' – illustrates the De Sanctian notion of the true artist as capable of going beyond his own intentions. To disrupt reality in order to reconstitute a reality of a higher order, as Dante did, is the task of the true genius, who is both a poet and an artist, unlike Cavalcanti, who is an artist but not yet a poet. In the same passage from where the quotation 'chi non ha la forza ...' is taken, however, De Sanctis claims that if the poet is an artist, then he will be able to explode reality and create a reality of a higher sort, that of art. The division between artist and poet is thus in De Sanctis not ontological but pragmatic.

Beckett seems no longer to believe in the notion of artistic freedom, since he states in the opening of *Proust* that 'the writer ... is not altogether at liberty to detach effect from cause' (1). However, he accepts De Sanctis's dichotomy and uses it as a critique both of realism and of the symbolism *à la* Baudelaire, that is, against those literary practices which do not try to reproduce the artistic epiphany of the momentary abolition of passing time.

Dante is again referred to in relation to anagogy: 'Dante, because he was an artist and not a minor prophet, could not prevent his allegory from becoming heated and electrified into anagogy' (60). This passage has been described by McQueeny as 'puzzling', and certainly the insertion of anagogy as a way of 'heating and electrifying' allegory is not easy to come to terms with. Dante defines anagogy in the second book of the *Convivio*, in the commentary to the song 'Voi ch'intendendo', according to the medieval fourfold interpretation of the Scripture developed from John Cassian in the fourth century. In the late twelfth-century *Summa Theologica* by Alexander of Hale, we find Bede's exemplification of this methodology; Jerusalem can be interpreted as a city (literal sense), as the Church (allegorical sense), as the soul of any faithful Christian (moral sense), and as the life of all heavenly beings (anagogical sense).[52] The anagogical sense is the sense that etymologically leads up to the first principle, that is to say God. Dante follows the tradition and defines the anagogical sense as follows:

> Lo quarto senso si chiama anagogico, cioè sovrasenso; e questo è quando spiritualmente si espone una scrittura, la quale ancora [sia vera] eziandio nel senso litterale, per le cose significate significa de le superne cose de l'etterna gloria: sì come vedere si può in quello canto del profeta che dice che, ne l'uscita del popolo d'Israel d'Egitto, Giudea è fatta santa e libera. Che avvegna essere vero secondo la lettera sia manifesto, non meno è vero quello che spiritualmente s'intende, cioè che ne l'uscita de l'anima dal peccato, essa sia fatta santa e libera in sua potestate.

> The fourth sense is called anagogical, that is, transcending the senses: this is brought out when a work is expounded with regard to its spiritual meaning;

even though the work is true in a literal sense, what is said there speaks also of things beyond our knowledge relating to eternal glory. One can say this, for instance, in that song of the prophet which says that, when the people of Israel escaped from Egypt, Judah was made holy and free. For although what is said here is clearly true in a literal sense, the spiritual meaning of this word is no less true, namely, that when the soul escapes from sin it is made holy and free in its distinctive power.[53]

In the *Convivio* Dante 'does not actually deny the possibility of a fourfold interpretation of poetry', although he asserts that he wants to follow 'the manner of the poets' rather than that of the theologians, thus not going 'as far as explicitly equating his poems with the Biblical text'.[54] And yet, even if the *Convivio* focuses on the literal and the allegorical senses and only hints at the other two, the distinction between poets and theologians becomes blurred.[55]

Moral and anagogical senses, therefore, could be read as contributing to the *Convivio*'s, and later to the *Comedy*'s assertions of authority. And yet, Dante is in *Proust*, via De Sanctis, an example of the negative consequences of allegory in relation to poetry. If in the *Convivio* the juxtaposition of poets and theologians is part of a discussion of the meaning of *auctor*, in *Proust* the concept of the artist as opposed to that of the minor prophet seems to privilege, in De Sanctian terms, creativity over structural rigidity. However, the claim that Dante is an artist and not a minor prophet could mean that he is in fact a major prophet, capable of imparting an anagogical sense to his writing, vivifying what is called 'flat writing' (allegory). On the other hand, the opposition between artist and minor prophet, could also mean that, being an artist, Dante is not a minor prophet; in which case, Dante becomes a De Sanctian subject that goes beyond his time and intentions, incapable of preventing 'his allegory from becoming heated and electrified into anagogy'. If we follow this reading, anagogy has less to do with its scriptural tradition than with its function of asserting Dante's genius.

'Less interested in what is said than in the way in which it is said', *Proust* follows De Sanctis's critical line up to a certain point. For De Sanctis allegorical, anagogical, and moral senses are all doctrinal obstacles; in his reading, Dante wanted to follow the fourfold interpretative method of his time, and wanted to create abstract allegorical figures, but could not prevent his art from becoming much more than what he had in mind. The allegorical sense then, just like the anagogical one, is a medieval fossil, dead for the modern reader of the *Comedy*. The *Comedy* is, for De Sanctis, 'the Middle Ages realized as art, author notwithstanding and contemporaries notwithstanding' and, I would add, allegory notwithstanding. In Beckett's *Proust* anagogy is opposed to allegory ('that glorious double-entry, with every credit in the said account a debt in the meant, and inversely') in order to reproduce De Sanctis's justification of Dante's literary genius.[56] This electrifying verbal pyrotechnics can be read as part of the more general iconoclastic drive pervading Beckett's early writings.

The three Dantean insertions play different roles in *Proust*, a text which oscillates between using quotations and allusions to challenge the 'sacred rule and compass' of academic disquisitions and adopting them to reach the more conventional goal of drawing persuasive comparisons. In both cases, the intertextual references found in the text exhibit the erudition of the writing subject. The quotation 'chi non ha la forza ... ', obscurely left in Italian and with no trace of its origin, is part of the centrifugal drive of a text which often uses intertextuality to distance itself from the canons of academic discussion. The silently mediated reference to the role played by allegory in Dante belongs instead to the centripetal tendency of *Proust*, which here juxtaposes a literary authority in order to confute the validity of allegory as a mode and to enhance Proust's critique of Baudelaire. While the two Dante quotations juxtapose Dante and Proust (using in one case a famous 'canzone' and in the other an image from the *Purgatorio*), Dante as the genius proving the inadequacy of allegory mirrors the post-Romantic picture produced by De Sanctis's *Storia della letteratura italiana*.

If in 'Dante...Bruno.Vico..Joyce' Dante was interpreted from the point of view of his multilingualism and constructed through strategies of persuasion, in *Proust* Dante becomes a literary monument, whose genius remains undisputed; he is the *auctoritas*, citable and re-usable. In *Dream of Fair to Middling Women* Dante will instead become 'a great game', 'a brilliant pastiche'.[57]

Notes

1 Samuel Beckett, 'Dante...Bruno.Vico..Joyce', in Ruby Cohn (ed.), *Disjecta: Miscellaneous Writings and a Dramatic Fragment* (New York: Grove Press, 1984), p. 19; subsequent references are given in the text. Ruby Cohn explains that the essay 'appeared in 1929 in both book (*Our Exagmination Round his Factification for Incamination of Work in Progress*: Paris, Shakespeare and Company) and periodical (*transition* 16–17)', p. 169.

2 'D'aria e d'ingegno e di parlar diverso / per lo toscano suol cercando gia / l'ospite desioso / dove giaccia colui per lo cui verso / il meonio cantor non è più solo' (Differing from us in air mind and tongue / Strangers thro' Tuscan territory fared / Eager to find the grave / Of such a singer that no more among / The bards Maeonides stands forth alone). Carlo Muscetta and Giuseppe Savoca (eds), *Sovra il monumento di Dante che si preparava in Firenze, Canti, Poesie varie, Traduzioni poetiche e Versi puerili, Parnaso Italiano*, vol. IX (Turin: Einaudi, 1968), p. 10, lines 18–22; translated as 'On the monument of Dante to be erected in Florence', in Geoffrey L. Bickersteth (ed.), *Poems of Leopardi* (New York: Russell and Russell, 1973) p. 145.

3 When not otherwise stated, the edition of the *Comedy* adopted in this study is *La Commedia secondo l'antica vulgata*, ed. Giorgio Petrocchi (Milan: Mondadori, 1966–67). The translation used is *The Divine Comedy*, translated with a commentary by Charles S. Singleton (Princeton: Princeton University Press, Bollingen Series LXXX, 3 vols, 1973), vol. 1, p. 241.

4 Gianfranco Contini, 'Dante oggi', *Un'idea di Dante* (Turin: Einaudi, 1970) p. 63. See also Anna Dolfi, 'Dante e i poeti del Novecento', *Studi Danteschi*, 58 (1986), 307–342; Adelia Noferi, 'Dante: la parola dell'altro e l'altro della parola', *Il gioco delle tracce* (Florence: La Nuova Italia, 1979), pp. 1–41; T. S. Eliot, 'Dante' (1929), in Frank Kermode (ed.), *Selected Prose of T. S. Eliot* (London: Faber and Faber, 1975), pp. 205–230; Zygmunt Baranski 'The power of influence: aspects of Dante's presence in twentieth-century Italian culture', *Strumenti Critici*, n.s. 1:3 (September 1986), 343–376. When not otherwise stated, translations from critical writings are mine.

5 Lucia Boldrini, *Joyce, Dante and the Poetics of Literary Relations: Language and Meaning in Finnegans Wake* (Cambridge: Cambridge University Press, 2001), p. 19.

6 Pier Vincenzo Mengaldo, *Linguistica e retorica di Dante* (Pisa: Nistri-Lischi, 1978), p. 80.

7 Boldrini, *Joyce, Dante, and the Poetics*, p. 20.

8 The whole passage reads: 'Nam quicunque tam obscene rationis est ut locum sue nationis delitiosissimum credat esse sub sole, hic etiam pre cunctis proprium vulgare licetur, idest maternam locutionem, et per consequens credit ipsum fuisse illud quod fuit Ade. Nos autem, cui mundus est patria velut piscibus equor, quanquam Sarnum biberimus antes dentes et Florentiam adeo diligamus ut, quia dileximus, exilium patiamur iniuste, rationi magis quam sensui spatulas nostri iudicii podiamus' (For whoever reasons so disgustingly that he considers his birthplace to be the most lovely place under the sun, he also values his own language, that is, his mother tongue, above all others, and consequently he thinks that it was the very one which was Adam's. I, however, for whom the world is fatherland as the sea is for fish, although I drank from the Arno before I had teeth and so love Florence that for my love I suffer unjust exile, I prop up the shoulders of my judgement more by reason than by the senses) (I.vi, 3). *De vulgari eloquentia*, in Pier Vincenzo Mengaldo (ed.), *Opere minori* (Milan and Naples: Ricciardi, 1979), vol. V, ii. *Dante in Hell, The De Vulgari Eloquentia, Introduction, Text, Translation, Commentary* by Warman Welliver (Ravenna: Longo, 1981), p. 53. Subsequent references are given in the text. Beckett's text presents a few minor discrepancies.

9 Beckett's notebook on Ariosto also discusses the establishment of Italian as a common language and quotes a passage from *De vulgari eloquentia* in which the vernacular is referred to as the 'panther' to be hunted. TCD MS 10962, fol. 60.

10 Mengaldo, *Linguistica e retorica*, p. 78.

11 Dante, *De vulgari*, I.xix, 1.

12 Mengaldo backs his theory with the historical materialist hypothesis that manuscripts from different traditions (especially the Sicilian) may have been read by Dante in the 'Tuscanised' language of the copyists. Mengaldo, *Linguistica e retorica*, p. 80.

13 Boldrini, *Joyce, Dante, and the Poetics*, p. 102.

14 Boldrini, *Joyce, Dante, and the Poetics*, pp. 74–75.

15 Contini, 'Dante oggi', p. 63.

16 Mengaldo, *Linguistica e retorica*, p. 70; Maria Corti, *Dante a un nuovo crocevia* (Florence: Sansoni, 1981), pp. 33–76.

17 Dante believes that the three languages *oïl*, *oc*, and *sì* derive from a unique source, which, nevertheless, is not Latin, but one of the many languages formed after Babel. Latin is an artificial human construction which tried to rescue the mutability of the natural languages by fixing them in a set of 'regulae'. Dante, *De vulgari eloquentia*, I.X; Mengaldo, *Linguistica e retorica*, p. 65; 'gramatica' in Umberto Bosco and Giorgio Petrocchi (eds), *Enciclopedia dantesca* (Rome: Istituto dell'enciclopedia italiana, 1970–78), pp. 259–64; Boldrini, *Joyce, Dante and the Poetics*, chapters two and three.
18 Mengaldo, *Linguistica e retorica*, p. 31.
19 Boldrini, *Joyce, Dante and the Poetics*, pp. 19 and 113.
20 In the 'Letter to Cangrande', we read: 'ad modo loquendi, remissus est modus et humilis, quia locutio vulgaris in qua et muliercule comunicant' (As regards the style of language, the style is unstudied and lowly, as being in the vulgar tongue, in which even womenfolk hold their talk); this, however, is not the *vulgare illustre* discussed in the *De vulgari*. *Epistolae*, XIII, 31–32. *Dantis Alagherii Epistolae. The Letters of Dante*, trans. Paget Toynbee (Oxford: The Clarendon Press, 1920), p. 201.
21 Boldrini, *Joyce, Dante, and the Poetics*, p. 99.
22 Beckett's Dante is thus very different from Eliot's 'universal' poet: 'Dante, nonetheless an Italian and a patriot, is first a European'. T. S. Eliot, 'Dante', p. 207.
23 Dante, *Convivio*, in Cesare Vasoli and Domenico De Robertis (eds), *Opere minori* (Milan and Naples: Ricciardi, 1988), vol. I, ii; I.XI.
24 Boldrini, *Joyce, Dante, and the Poetics*, p. 19; the author's emphasis.
25 Giovanni Boccaccio, *Trattatello in laude di Dante*, in Pier Giorgio Ricci (ed.), *Tutte le opere di Giovanni Boccaccio*, Vittore Branca (ed.), vol. III (Milan: Mondadori, 1974), pp. 423–538, §§16–18. Subsequent references are given in the text. See also Terence McQueeny, 'Samuel Beckett as critic of Proust and Joyce', Ph.D. thesis, University of North Carolina, 1977, p. 49; Francesca Del Moro, '"The Divine Florentine": Dante nell'opera di Samuel Beckett', dissertation, University of Pisa, 1996, pp. 20–21; Lucia Boldrini, *Joyce, Dante, and the Poetics*, p. 21.
26 The legend is reported for the first time in Frate Ilario's letter to Dante's friend Uguccione, as Terence McQueeny clarifies. McQueeny, 'Samuel Beckett as critic', p. 49. Benvenuto de Rambaldis de Imola reports the same legend, polemically attacking those claiming that Dante was forced to interrupt his Latin poem because his Latin style was not sufficiently good for such an ambitious theme. See Bevenuti de Rambaldis de Imola *Comentum super Dantis Aldigherij Comœdiam*, J. P. Lacaita (ed.), 5 vols (Florence: 1887), I, pp. 78–79. See also Roberto Mercuri, 'Percorsi letterari e tipologie culturali nell'esegesi dantesca di Benvenuto da Imola', in Pantaleo Palmieri and Carlo Paolazzi (eds), *Benvenuto da Imola lettore degli antichi e dei moderni* (Ravenna: Longo, 1991), pp. 55–78, p. 61. The letter to frate Ilario and Boccaccio's narrative about Dante's mother's dream are also reported in J. A. Symonds, *An Introduction to the Study of Dante* (London: Adam and Charles Black, 1893), pp. 70–72 and p. 36, respectively. This critical volume is mentioned as a source in one of Beckett's early 'Dante notebooks', TCD MS 10962.
27 Mengaldo, *Linguistica e retorica*, pp. 22–4.
28 Michele Barbi, *Dante: vita, opere, fortuna* (Florence: Sansoni, 1933).
29 Mengaldo, *Linguistica e retorica*, p. 95.
30 See Boccaccio, *Trattatello*, §196–197. See also Pier Giorgio Ricci, *L'ultimo rifugio di Dante* (Ravenna: Longo, [1891] 1965), pp. 159–161.

31 Roger Dragonetti, *Aux frontières du langage poétique* (Gent: Romanica Gardensia, 1961), pp. 13–14. Corti, *Dante a un nuovo crocevia*, p. 50.
32 Pier Vincenzo Mengaldo, 'Adamo', in *Enciclopedia dantesca*, p. 48.
33 Corti, *Dante a un nuovo crocevia*, p. 47.
34 On the evolution of Dante's concept of the origin of language see Bruno Nardi, 'Il linguaggio', *Dante e la cultura medievale: nuovi saggi di filosofia dantesca* (Bari: Laterza, 1942), pp. 148–175. On Dante's adoption of the term 'forma locutionis' and its implications see Corti, *Dante a un nuovo crocevia*, pp. 46–52.
35 Pascale Casanova has argued that the theme of Purgatory in Beckett's works can be read in a political light, since, as Jacques Le Goff has pointed out, in the twelfth century Purgatory started to be located in Ireland. See Pascale Casanova, *Beckett l'abstracteur: anatomie d'une révolution littéraire* (Paris: Éditions du Seuil, 1997). Jacques Le Goff, *La naissance du Purgatoire* (Paris: Gallimard, 1981), pp. 256–273; translated into English by Arthur Godhammer as *The Birth of Purgatory* (London: Scolar Press, 1984). For a reference to St Patrick's Purgatory see James Joyce, *Ulysses*, eds Hans Walter Gabler, Wolfhard Steppe, and Claus Melchior, with a new preface by Richard Ellmann (Harmondsworth: Penguin, 1986), p. 272. See also Stephen Greenblatt, *Hamlet in Purgatory* (Princeton: Princeton University Press, 2001).
36 Walter A. Strauss, 'Dante's Belacqua and Beckett's tramps', *Comparative Literature*, 11 (Summer 1959), 250–261, 261; Michael Robinson, 'From purgatory to inferno: Beckett and Dante revisited', *Journal of Beckett Studies*, 5 (Autumn 1979), 69–82, 72.
37 Kateryna Arthur, 'Murphy, Gerontion and Dante', *AUMLA, Australian University Language and Literature Association*, 55 (May 1981), 54–67, 63–64.
38 Philip Terry, 'Waiting for God to go: *How It Is* and *Inferno* VII–VIII', *Samuel Beckett Today/Aujourd'hui: Beckett Versus Beckett*, 7 (1998), 349–360.
39 John Pilling, *Beckett Before Godot* (Cambridge: Cambridge University Press, 1997), p. 37. Samuel Beckett, *Proust* (New York: Grove Press, 1957). Subsequent references are given in the text.
40 Pilling, *Beckett Before Godot*, pp. 46–47.
41 Pilling, *Beckett Before Godot*, p. 47.
42 McQueeny, 'Beckett as critic', pp. 76–81; Daniela Caselli, 'Beckett's intertextual modalities of appropriation: the case of Leopardi', *Journal of Beckett Studies*, 6:1 (Autumn 1996), 1–24.
43 Francesco De Sanctis, *Storia della letteratura italiana* (Turin: Einaudi-Gallimard, 1996), p. 162.
44 Pietro De Logu, 'The unifying power of tradition: the presence of Dante in W. B. Yeats's and Samuel Beckett's works', in Wolfgang Zach (ed.), *Literature(s) in English: New Perspectives* (Frankfurt: Peter Lang, 1990), pp. 61–67, p. 61; Eric P. Levy, *Beckett and the Voice of Species: A Study of the Prose Fiction* (Totowa: Barnes & Noble Books, 1980), p. 41.
45 Beckett attributed to Joyce the quip about *Crime and Punishment* in an interview with Ellmann in 1954. McQueeny, 'Beckett as critic', p. 82.
46 Samuel Beckett, *Proust*, translation and preface by Edith Fournier (Paris: Les Éditions de Minuit, 1990), p. 117, note 110.
47 The 'canzone' also appears in TCD MS 10963a.
48 For a discussion of Dante's 'poetics of the new' see Teodolinda Barolini, *The Undivine Comedy: Detheologizing Dante* (Princeton: Princeton University Press, 1992).
49 McQueeny, 'Beckett as critic', p. 133.

50 De Sanctis, *Storia della letteratura*, p. 160.
51 De Sanctis, *Storia della letteratura*, p. 147. McQueeny's translation. McQueeny, 'Beckett as critic', p. 124.
52 A. J. Minnis and A. B. Scott, with the assistance of David Wallace, *Medieval Literary Theory and Criticism* (Oxford: Clarendon Press, 1988), p. 218.
53 *Convivio*, II.i,1, pp. 115–117; *The Banquet*, transl. Christopher Ryan (Saratoga: Anma Libri, 1989), p. 43. A reference to 'anagogy (Greek g if you don't mind)' is present in 'Draff'. Samuel Beckett, *More Pricks Than Kicks* (New York: Grove Weidenfeld, 1972), pp. 175–911, p. 188.
54 Boldrini, *Joyce, Dante and the Poetics*, pp. 30–31 and 29, respectively.
55 Boldrini, *Joyce, Dante and the Poetics*, pp. 31–35. Boldrini discusses how the variously attributed *Epistle to Can Grande* uses the fourfold method in relation to the *Comedy*.
56 De Sanctis, *Storia della letteratura*, p. 164; Beckett, 'An Imaginative Work!', in *Disjecta*, pp. 89–90, p. 90.
57 Mario Luzi, 'Dante, scienza e innocenza', *Vicissitudini e forma* (Milan: Rizzoli, 1974), p. 79; quoted in Dolfi, 'Dante e i poeti del Novecento', p. 330.

2 Belacqua does not observe 'the rule of the road'

O frate, andare in sù che porta? (*Purg.* IV, 127)
Oh sometimes as now I almost think: nothing is less like me than me
(*Dream*, p. 77)

In *Dream of Fair to Middling Women* intertextuality is both a dismantling practice and a verbal game. By establishing a constellation of texts of reference while reacting against that same literary legacy, *Dream* constructs a canon in order to question it.

The allusions to Dante in this text are very frequent: the *Comedy* is occasionally quoted by Belacqua, who repeats the phrase 'qui vive la pietà ...' from *Inferno* XX, 28 as a form of 'incantation', and by the narrator, who turns into a joke the lines from *Inferno* III, 95 and V, 23, 'Vuolsi così colà, dove si puote / ciò che si vuole, e più non dimandare' (Thus it is willed there where that can be done which is willed; and ask no more).[1] Dante also figures as both an author and a literary product. He is the poet buried in Ravenna, subject of the parodic conversation between the countess Parabimbi, the Man of Law, and the Paleographer, who 'translated his epitaph into heroic couplets' (221).[2] Dante is also 'a beautiful book', an actual volume, which Belacqua gives as 'a mark of esteem!' to the Syra-Cusa, who leaves it behind and is thus kicked out of the story (51).[3]

Dante's invocation to Apollo in *Paradiso* III, 8–9 is parodied, and so is one of the many references to ineffability: '*Da questo passo vinti ci concediamo ...*', which is, as John Pilling has pointed out, a misquotation from *Paradiso* XXX, 22 (112).[4] A number of Dantean female characters are mentioned, from the obvious Beatrice, who is hallucinated as 'lurk[ing] in every brothel' (41) to the Semiramis-like Syra-Cusa and the ethereal Constance and Piccarda, to the more obscure 'Miss Florence', who 'turned and turned again, on back, sides and belly', like Florence does in *Purgatorio* VI, 149–151, in which Dante compares his city to 'quella inferma / che non può trovar posa in su le piume, / ma con dar volta suo dolore scherma' (the sick woman who cannot find repose upon the down, but with her tossing seeks to ease her pain) (72).[5]

In these examples Dante is outside the text; allusions are often advertised and the text plays the 'who said this?' and 'have you spotted the style?' game (72). However, *Dream*'s intertextuality simultaneously maintains and challenges the structure of the *ipse dixit*, questioning the issues of power and authority implied in the use of quotations, allusions, plagiarism, criticism, and parody. By focusing on how the text shapes its more than 'trine' Belacqua, and looking at the figure of Sordello, I will argue that *Dream* at once evokes and critiques ideas of fictionality and authority through Dante.

There is no real Belacqua in *Dream*

Belacqua is one of the most evident intertextual features of *Dream* and one that has often been discussed in criticism. At once a character of *Purgatorio* IV and the protagonist of *Dream*, Belacqua will later be the main character of *More Pricks Than Kicks* and will also appear in *Murphy* and *Molloy*. As Peter Boxall has argued in relation to 'Dante and the Lobster', Belacqua inhabits two different geographies, that of *Purgatorio* IV and that of the Beckettian texts, questioning the boundaries of these two fictional spaces.[6] Thanks to his name, Belacqua, the 'overfed child pedalling, faster and faster, ... down a frieze of hawthorn after Findlater's van' (1), partially occupies the space of the slothful soul of the Dantean Antepurgatory.

In chapter 'TWO' of *Dream* Belacqua arrives in Germany suffering from 'a bout of hepatic colic'; after Bel and the Smeraldina-Rima enter a taxi, the narrator, addressing the 'gentle reader', introduces Belacqua. Elements from Dante's *Purgatorio* IV are listed and Belacqua's posture – 'with his head in his thighs as a general rule' – is mentioned; the comparison between Bel and Belacqua is called a 'merely ... intestinal incohesion' (66), a phrase not too subtly alluding to Bel's illness. The passage reads:

> BELACQUA
> we had to call him and no indolent virgin is his sister (indolent virgin!) and he does not much care whether he plays the tinkle-tinkle of a fourhander or not but he won't facing the keyboard observe the rule of the road (a megalomaniac you see with his head in his thighs as a general rule) so we ask you to humour now what naturally looks merely like so much intestinal incohesion, remember he belongs to the costermonger times of a pale and ardent generation, pray that he will let a few good sighs out of him ere it be too late and speedy promotion from the Godbirds. (66)

There are many specific references here to canto IV, which describes Belacqua as follows:

> E un di lor, che mi sembiava lasso,
> sedeva e abbracciava le ginocchia,

> tenendo 'l viso giù tra esse basso.
> 'O dolce segnor mio', diss'io, 'adocchia
> colui che mostra sé più negligente
> che se pigrizia fosse sua serocchia'. (*Purg.* IV, 106–111)

and one of them, who seemed to me weary, was sitting and clasping his knees, holding his face low down between them. 'O my sweet lord', said I, 'set your eye on that one who shows himself lazier than if sloth were his sister.'

Dream's Belacqua does *not* have indolence as his sister, and does *not* care about playing or making lutes, but shares with Dante's character the characteristic of not observing 'the rule of the road'; Bel is the result of the negative comparison with Belacqua of canto IV; both challenge the theo/teleological progression of narrative from their crouched posture, since Bel refuses to proceed and Belacqua questions Dante's progress along the terraces of the *Purgatorio*.[7]

The references to the few sighs, their lateness, and the promotion from the 'Godbirds' are specific allusions to canto IV, where Belacqua, after having asked 'O frate, andare in sù che porta?' (O brother, what's the use of going up?) explains that he has to wait in that position for the same number of years as his life, since he repented (that is, let the good sighs out of him) only at the end of his life:

> Ed elli: 'O frate, andare in sù che porta?
> ché non mi lascerebbe ire a' martiri
> l'angel di Dio che siede in su la porta.
> Prima convien che tanto il ciel m'aggiri
> di fuor da essa, quanto fece in vita,
> perch'io 'ndugiai al fine i buon sospiri,
> se orazïone in prima non m'aiuta
> che surga su di cuor che in grazia viva;
> l'altra che val, che 'n ciel non è udita?' (*Purg.* IV, 127–135)

'O brother, what's the use of going up? For God's angel who sits at the gate would not let me pass to the torments. First must the heavens revolve around me outside it, so long as they did during my life, because I delayed good sighs until the end – unless prayer first aid me which rises from a heart that lives in grace. What avails the other, which is not heard in heaven?'[8]

The Dantean context partially affects too the description of the Smeraldina-Rima, who is said not to have 'the conductive properties of the appropriate kind'

(66). The sentence, charged with the sexual overtones affecting female characters in *Dream*, can be related to the 'conductive' properties of the prayers said by persons in the grace of God, and thus accelerating Belacqua's ascent to the *Purgatorio*. Of course, the foremost amongst those in the grace of God is Beatrice.

In this passage, Bel is compared and contrasted to what is fashioned as his *alter ego*. This overt metanarrative technique uses intertextuality to proclaim the fictionality of the protagonist. Belacqua's artificiality is duplicated by a further intertextual dimension. The excerpt discussed above belongs to a section published in 1932 in *transition* under the title 'Sedendo et Quiesciendo' [*sic*].[9] The phrase 'sedendo et quiescendo' appears later in Beckett's novel and does not belong to the *Comedy*, but can be found, together with the information that Belacqua was a lute-maker, in two early commentaries, the *Comentum* of Benvenuto de Rambaldis de Imola (c. 1375) and that of the Anonimo Fiorentino (c. 1400).[10] The 'tinkle-tinkle of a fourhander' goes back to Benvenuto's 'aliquando etiam pulsabat', a phrase quoted verbatim in *Dream*:

> Whether *squatting in the heart of his store, sculpting with great care and chiselling the heads and necks of lutes and zithers, or sustaining in the doorway the girds of eminent poets, or coming out into the street for a bit of song and dance (aliquando etiam pulsabat)*, he [Belacqua] was cheating and denying his native *indolence*, denying himself to the ground-swell of his *indolence*, holding himself clear, refusing to be sucked down and abolished ... Sometimes he speaks of himself thus drowned and darkened as 'restored to his heart'; and at other times as 'sedendo et quiescendo' with the stress on the et and no extension of the thought into the spirit made wise. Squatting in the heart of the store he was not quiet. Cellineggiava finickety scrolls and bosses, exposed to the fleers of uneasy poets. *If to be seated is to be wise, then no man is wiser than thee*. That class of cheap stinger. (121–122; emphasis mine)

Benvenuto and the Anonimo belong to the early exegetical tradition of the *Comedy*; their comments on Belacqua used in *Dream* were reproduced in the entry 'Belacqua' in Toynbee's *Dictionary of Proper Names and Notable Matters in the Works of Dante*, the standard reference book for an English-speaking student of Dante in Beckett's time.[11] After a paraphrase of *Pugatorio* IV, Toynbee writes:

> Benvenuto says of him that besides being a maker of musical instruments, B. was something of a musician also, and adds that D., who was a lover of music, was intimate with him and on that account:
> – 'Iste fuit de Florentia, qui faciebat citharas et alia instrumenta musica, unde cum magna cura sculpebat and incidebat, colla et capita citararum, et aliquando etiam pulsabat. Ideo Dantes familiariter noverat eum, quia delectatus

est in sono'. (He was from Florence and built guitars and other musical instruments he then carved and engraved with much care the heads and the necks of these guitars, and sometimes he played some of them. For this reason Dante knew him well, since he was delighted by music)

The Anonimo Fiorentino says of him: –

Questo Belacqua fu uno cittadino di Firenze, artefice, et facea cotai colli di liuti et di chitarre, et era il più pigro uomo che fosse mai; et si dice di lui ch'egli venia la mattina a bottega, et ponevasi a sedere, et mai non si levava se non quando egli voleva ire a desinare et a dormire. Ora l'Auttore fu molto suo dimestico: molto il riprendea di questa sua nigligenzia; onde un dì, riprendendolo, Belacqua rispose colle parole d'Aristotile: Sedendo et quiescendo anima efficitur sapiens; di che l'Auttore gli rispose: Per certo, se per sedere si diventa savio, niuno fu mai più savio di te. (74) (This Belacqua was a citizen from Florence, an artisan who made such remarkable guitar's necks, and was the laziest man who ever existed; and it is said of him that he used to come to the shop in the morning and sit down, and he would never rise but when he wanted to go to eat and sleep. Now, the Author was very intimate with him: he used to reproach him much for his negligence; so that one day, while he was reproaching him, Belacqua replied with Aristotle's words: *Sedendo et quiescendo anima efficitur sapiens*; to which the Author replied: certainly, if to be seated is to be wise, then no man is wiser than thee.)[12]

Toynbee underlines Benvenuto's importance within Dante's exegetical tradition, and often refers to his interpretations of the *Comedy*. Benvenuto is among the first commentators to exalt Dante's literary excellence and consolidate his fame as a modern *auctor*, not only associating his name with that of the ancient *auctoritates* as Boccaccio was doing but also considering 'both Dante and the *Commedia* as peerless'.[13] The *Comentum* is a text that has been read as bridging the late medieval critical and theoretical framework with the pre-humanistic literary phase. Roberto Mercuri has argued in favour of the transitional position of Benvenuto, whose medieval Latin differs enormously from Petrarch's refined use, but who has nevertheless absorbed, and even modified, many aspects of the new cultural models proposed by Boccaccio and Petrarch.[14]

In his reception of Dante Benvenuto treats Boccaccio as an *auctoritas* and a source of reliable informative material, but nevertheless elaborates independent and sometimes even polemical interpretations. As Zygmunt Baranski has pointed out, the mixture between the *accessus* of type C and the Aristotelian *accessus* based on the *causae* in Benvenuto's prologue creates an innovative critical apparatus to account for what is diagnosed as Dante's groundbreaking originality and to solve the paradox that the title *Comedy* created for all the early commentators.[15] Benvenuto 'reveals not just a strong sense of the commentary tradition, but also of the novelty of its own exegetical structures'; his 'new sense of value and importance of the commentary and of the commentator ... is in keeping with contemporary views on the independent status of learning'.[16]

Thus, when Benvenuto discusses Belacqua, he shows traits of exegetical *amplificatio* mixed with his taste for the anecdote and the short story (*novella*); the text is the basis from which 'he can cut out an autonomous space for himself ... and experiment with a personal narrative freedom which often goes beyond the Dantean text'.[17] The passage from Benvenuto has become the main source for the biographical identification of Belacqua as a Florentine lute-maker and contemporary of Dante, a view shared by Toynbee as well. The description of Belacqua, however, does not have to be taken as a neo-positivistic biographical investigation into the historical source of a fictional character. The proliferation of details in this excerpt need not be read as oriented toward the retrieval of a factual truth, but can instead be understood in terms of how the commentator elaborates on his text and supports the authority of the *auctor*. Biographical investigations have retrieved only a few legal documents referring to a Duccio di Bonavia named Belacqua.[18] The nickname is all he shares with the Dantean character, and the value of this research remains very limited indeed. It is of greater interest, instead, to observe both the dynamics of the passage from the *Comentum* and the authoritative value it has gained in subsequent commentaries and critical works.

Benvenuto's Belacqua, as he appears in the short excerpt included in Toynbee, is characterised by colourful details such as might be found in the genre of the *novella*. Benvenuto's writing, which presents fictional traits, can be appreciated in the whole passage devoted to the lazy soul of *Purgatorio* IV:

> Hic est sciendum quod ista fuit vox cuiusdam pigri, qui vocatus est Bilacqua. *Iste fuit de Florentia, qui faciebat citharas et alia instrumenta musica, unde cum magna cura sculpebat and incidebat, colla et capita citararum, et aliquando etiam pulsabat. Ideo Dantes familiariter noverat eum, quia delectatus est in sono*; unde sicut superius in secundo capitulo posuit unum amicum Cantorem, ita nunc ponit alium sonitorem; et quia noverat istum tam pigrum ad omnia, non tamen pravum, sed satis purum, ideo cum bona conscientia fingit ipsum salvum ... Nunc poeta noster describit in speciali unum amicum, ciuis pigritia suo tempore omnes antecessit inter sibi notos; ... unde cum Dantes aliquando increparet eum de pigritia sua, iste erat solitus respondere quod anima sedendo et quiescendo fit sapiens.

> Here it must be known that that voice belonged to that lazy person named Belacqua. *He was from Florence and built guitars and other musical instruments he*

> *then carved and engraved with much care the heads and the necks of these guitars, and sometimes he played some of them. For this reason Dante knew him well, since he was delighted by music*; as Dante had put a friend who was a singer in canto two, here he has a musician; and since he was known by everybody as a very lazy person, although not depraved but rather pure, for this reason Dante has him saved. Now our poet describes in a special manner a friend whose laziness was greater than that of anyone he knew at the time; ... so that when Dante reproached him for his laziness, he used to reply that his soul would become wiser by sitting and resting. (Com. III, 133; emphasis mine)

Belacqua's 'purity' is, in the commentary, the premise of his collocation in the *Purgatorio*. This shows a specific legacy from medieval thought, concerned not with factual truth but with the production of texts capable in their turn of producing *auctoritates*. Alistair Minnis has argued in relation to medieval authorship that 'the thinking ... seems to be circular: the work of an *auctor* was a book worth reading; a book worth reading had to be a work of an *auctor*'.[19] A similar logic is at work in Benvenuto; since the Belacqua of the text waits to 'be purged', the Belacqua of the commentary has to be 'satis purum'. Moreover, Belacqua is said to be both an artisan and a player through a justification which is a commonplace of Dante exegesis; as Dante put Casella, a singer, in canto II, so he put a 'sonitorem' in canto IV. But in canto IV there is no hint of Belacqua's profession, and the 'neat' parallelism seems devised in order to have the 'identification'. Dante's love of music is part of the nobility of soul that necessarily characterises any *auctor*. The dialogue between Dante and Belacqua is an enhanced reproduction of the situation of the canto.

The Anonimo, whose 'vernacular text is too close to the Latin one to hypothesise anything but a material translation [from Benvenuto]', will adopt this dramatisation: this is not infrequent in the anecdotal fourteenth- and fifteenth-century commentaries.[20] Dante and Belacqua are made to speak the words of 'the Philosopher', that is Aristotle, who was for both Dante's and for Benvenuto's time the supreme and unchallenged authority of every age. The *auctoritas*, implicit in Benvenuto, is made explicit by the Anonimo Fiorentino excerpt reproduced by Toynbee.

Aristotle's words 'sedendo et quiescendo' in praise of the contemplative life – the life closest to God – are twisted in Benvenuto's commentary and mocked in the Anonimo's text, which lets Dante have the last word and reply to Belacqua 'Per certo, se per sedere si diventa savio, niuno fu mai più savio di te' (certainly, if to be seated is to be wise, then no man is wiser than thee), the quotation translated in *Dream*. In the Anonimo's early fifteenth-century commentary, the contemplative life can be an excuse for laziness, and Dante, now a character in this humorous dialogue, can make fun of it while becoming himself a humorous figure.

The commentaries referred to in the section 'Sedendo et Quiesciendo' [sic] play an important role later, in Beckett's chapter 'UND', where we find a long discussion of narratological problems concerning both structure and characterisation. *Dream*'s intertextuality underlines the conventional and historical nature of post-Romantic narrative strategies. The division between reality and fictionality is constantly threatened in this text, and the notion of character is vehemently questioned and tentatively dismantled. In *Proust*, the author of the *Recherche* is praised because 'His explanations [of characters] are experimental and not demonstrative. He explains them in order that they may appear as they are – inexplicable. He explains them away.'[21] In *Dream*, 'the Smeraldina-Rima is not demonstrable. She has to be taken or left' (13) and the narrator asks himself about Nemo: 'But what can you do with a person like Nemo, who will not for any consideration be condensed into a liŭ, who is not a note at all but the most regrettable simultaneity of notes' (11). The text cries, in Belacqua's words: 'please ... do not apply any system at me' (190) while exposing the multiplicity of systems at work in a novel. Plot and characters are uncovered as artificial precisely through the adoption of the self-declared artificial system of the (supposedly Chinese) 'scale of liūs'.[22] However, this system of relations is declared to be constantly failing, and the movement of the characters is said to be

> based on a principle of repulsion, their property not to combine but, like heavenly bodies, to scatter and stampede, astral straws on a time-strom, grit in the mistral. They are no good from the builder's point of view, firstly because they will not suffer their systems to be absorbed in the cluster of a greater system, and then, and chiefly, because they themselves tend to disappear as systems. (119)

The passage quoted is followed by the names of Balzac and 'the divine Jane' as examples of 'chloroformed worlds'; Balzac is 'absolute master of his material' and 'he can write the end of his book before he has finished the first paragraph' (119–120). Beckett's attack against the teleological law of the realistic novel becomes a metanarrative tirade, which also questions the notion of character: 'Why anything? Why bother about it? It covers good paper. A great deal of the above marginalia covers Belacqua, or, better: Belacqua is in part covered by the above marginalia' (120). The character of Belacqua is at first said to be submerged by the 'above marginalia', the secondary quality of which interferes with Belacqua's central position. However, the rectified sentence turns things upside down, implying that such marginal digressions 'cover' the topic or, better, the character in question. Through an eminently Shandean move, the idea of narrative progression is at first claimed to be stalled by digressions; in this way digressions themselves come to the fore and lose their secondary status; the marginalia spill on to the whole page, and the commentary becomes the text.

The passage goes on to describe the 'trine' nature of Belacqua, taking care to insert metanarrative comments such as 'the dots are nice, don't you think?' We are faced with the already familiar 'third being' of Belacqua, his 'Limbese' state, when he is 'bogged in indolence', and 'the cities and forests and beings were also without identity, they were *shadows*, they exerted neither pull or goad. His third being was without axis or contour, its centre everywhere and periphery nowhere, an unsurveyed marsh of *sloth*' (121; emphasis mine). References to Limbo, to indolence, and to sloth and shadows, prepare the ground for the next, more overtly intertextual paragraph.

> He is sorry it does not happen more often, that he does not go under more often. He finds it more pleasant to be altogether swathed in the black arras of his *sloth* than condemned to deploy same and inscribe it with frivolous *spirals*, *ascending* like the little *angels* and *descending*, never coming to head or tail, never abutting. Whether *squatting in the heart of his store, sculpting with great care and chiselling the heads and necks of lutes and zithers, or sustaining in the doorway the girds of eminent poets, or coming out into the street for a bit of song and dance (aliquando etiam pulsabat)*, he was cheating and denying his native *indolence*, denying himself to the ground-swell of his *indolence*, holding himself clear, refusing to be sucked down and abolished. But when, as rarely happened, he was drawn down to the blessedly sunless depths, down and down to the slush of *angels*, clear of the pettifogging ebb and flow, then he knew, but retrospectively, after the furious divers had hauled him out like a crab to fry in the sun, because at the time he was not concerned with such niceties of perception, that if he were free he would take up his dwelling in that place. Nothing less exorbitant than that! If he were free he would take up his dwelling in that curious place, he would settle down there, you see, he would retire and settle down there, like La Fontaine's catawampus. (121–122; emphasis mine)

The introduction of words such as 'sloth' and 'shadows' announces an intertextual passage which criticises the notion of character even more radically than does the 'Sedendo et Quiesciendo [sic]' section. The denial of Belacqua's reality – 'There is no authority for supposing that this third Belacqua is the real Belacqua ... There is no real Belacqua, it is to be hoped not indeed, there is no such person' (121) – is followed by a textual coalescence between the several Belacquas analysed above, that is to say Beckett's, Dante's, Benvenuto's, and the Anonimo's. This proliferation of sources mirrors and intertextually enhances the instability asserted in the statement 'there is no real Belacqua ... there is no such person'. The third person singular pronoun 'he' is a fragile device unable to mask the composite character of the protagonist, whose 'personality' multiplies as in a mirror game.

Bel contrasts with Benvenuto's and the Anonimo's Belacqua, more than Dante's. Beckett's Belacqua wants to become engulfed, to be Limbese, to become even stiller than Dante's Belacqua. The aspiration to the 'real vegetation' of the Antepurgatory is contrasted with the 'betrayal' of his indolent nature on the part of Benvenuto's and the Anonimo's Belacquas, who 'frivolously' chisel and play guitars. The composite Belacqua of the text is accused of 'cheating' when he works or plays; Dante's Belacqua's 'native indolence' is erased by Benvenuto's and the Anonimo's 'sonitor'. The commentaries of Benvenuto and the Anonimo are merged in the translation which, using 'zithers', privileges the phonic and etymological levels closest to the Latin and the Italian, while Benvenuto's late Latin (*aliquando etiam pulsabat*) is also partially maintained. The precision of the sculpting is described both in Benvenuto and the Anonimo, while the details of Belacqua seated in his 'store' (bottega) belong to the Anonimo; the reference to the 'squatting' posture seem further to blur the boundaries between the Belacquas from the Anonimo and Dante.

The 'he', referring to a multiplicity of subjects, once again slips into Dante's text through the metaphor of the divers and the crab, recalling Dante and Virgil trying to haul Belacqua out of his stone.[23] A further destabilisation occurs when we read that 'he would take up his dwelling in that place'. Which place? Belacqua's Antepurgatory, Dante's canto IV, Bel's 'third gulf' which however is a 'Limbo' (the first circle of Hell), Benvenuto's ideal Florence, or the Anonimo's 'bottega'? As the exclamation 'Nothing less exorbitant than that!' acknowledges, this intertextual Belacqua exerts notable pressure on the idea of a smooth course, of a track that can be followed. With 'its centre everywhere and periphery nowhere', the third Belacqua cannot be any more real than others Belacquas, scribbled in and scribbled over by the above marginalia, as 'there is no such person' and there is no 'authority for supposing' that this could be the case.

The proliferation of subjects and of references to different texts continues in what follows in *Dream*:

> Sometimes he speaks of himself thus drowned and darkened as 'restored to his heart'; and at other times as 'sedendo et quiescendo' with the stress on the et and no extension of the thought into the spirit made wise. Squatting in the heart of the store he was not quiet. Cellineggiava finickety scrolls and bosses, exposed to the fleers of uneasy poets. *If to be seated is to be wise, then no man is wiser than thee*. That class of cheap stinger. (122)

After a brief metanarrative intermission, the pronoun 'he' reappears, showing again how Belacqua is made up of odds and ends. Aristotle's words quoted by Benvenuto and the Anonimo refer to Bel's 'third being', but the stress is now on the copula, which questions the centrality of 'the spirit made wise'. Immobility and its ironically derived wisdom are contrasted with the activities going on in the Benvenuto's and the Anonimo's stores, where Belacqua not only 'squats', but also is 'not quiet', spending his time 'cellineggiando'. 'Cellineggiare' is a Beckettian coinage, which refers to the aptly named Benvenuto Cellini, who had been already used in an early notebook to characterise Ariosto as a 'mere Benvenuto Cellini of words' and now suggestively echoes Benvenuto's 'cum magna cura sculpebat et incidebat'.[24] The slothful – and yet paradoxically active – character has to endure Dante's 'cheap stinger'. In the earlier passage Belacqua was forced to 'sustain in the doorway [of an imaginary shop?] the girds of eminent poets'; now he is 'exposed to the fleers of uneasy poets'. The Anonimo Fiorentino's quotation from Aristotle follows, translated word for word and italicised. Dante, now a character answering back to a spirit 'made wise', is the 'eminent [but] uneasy poet'.

The fictionality inherent in the exegetical writings merges in *Dream* with the non-originality of creative writing. The 'he' works as a conventional device; the name of the character can grant neither unity nor originality, but is exposed in its multiple textuality. Belacqua, described by the Anonimo as 'artefice', foregrounds the artificiality of the commentaries, which do not simply describe the slothful character of the *Comedy* but 'inscribe' his sloth with Cellinesque 'frivolous spirals' (121). Such artificiality is unopposed by original simplicity: 'there is no authority for supposing that this third Belacqua is the real Belacqua'. The text comments on its own recycling of textual personae as a necessarily (and authoritatively) non-original form of writing, as indicated by the lack of 'freedom' that characterises Belacqua.

Belacqua has no origin, is not 'real'. However far back one goes, texts keep producing other texts and displacing their originality. Belacqua is a multiple and unlocatable subject who would like to dwell in a place that keeps changing: he migrates from one fictional space to the other. *Dream* works with the differences between the literary text and its commentaries and questions them; Dante's Belacqua blends into Benvenuto's and the Anonimo's, and all participate in a non-hierarchical fashion to shape the unstable protagonist of *Dream*.

Dante and Mr Beckett

Artificial compositions and chiselled creations are constantly played against one another and multiplied through the intertextual games. However, such strategies leave the narrator still in control both of his metanarrative assertions and of the description of the events. Although claiming to resist 'chloroformed' narrative criteria, the narrating voice never quite manages to get off his pedestal of omniscience; rather, he even knows that 'we do not quite know where we are in this story' (9). The passages analysed threaten to disintegrate the character as a single subjectivity, but they do this through an unchallenged narrator, who soon resumes his task, and tells us about Belacqua's disappointment in trying 'to induce at pleasure a state so desirable and necessary to himself [his "third being" or "dark gulf"]' (123), restoring some certainty about who this Belacqua is.

Later on in the text, the Alba thinks that Belacqua is always 'coiled up in the shadow', and she mentally accuses him of 'the sin against the Belacqua third person'. 'Personality! That old bugbear bastard of hell!' (194), cries an exasperated Alba, stressing once again the unreliability of the 'third person' and the absence of a stable substratum for personality. And yet, if the 'he' is unable to hold the self together, Belacqua's personality is still being discussed, *as if* Belacqua could have one; in *Watt*'s words, 'the only way one can speak of nothing is to speak of it as though it were something'.[25] And so Belacqua acquires, 'willy-nilly', 'that old bugbear bastard of hell'; in order to describe his self as split, he has to be given a self of some sort, and he has to occupy the place of the character previously challenged by the intertextual proliferation of referents. *Dream* oscillates between dismantling the notion of character through its textual and intertextual multiplication and adopting realistic strategies that describe their very limitations. In the last paragraph of the chapter 'UND' (the third chapter, after a first chapter of two brief paragraphs and a second one of more than a hundred pages), Belacqua shapes specific narrative questions only partially similar to those analysed previously. The quotation 'L'andar su che porta?' (what's the use of going up?), from Dante's *Purgatorio* IV, which closes the chapter, indicates how *Dream*'s Dante implies a reconsideration of the notions of source, authority, value, and theo/teleological progress.[26] The narrator stresses his power and the fictional quality of the narration:

> Thus dusk shall ere long gather about him – unless to be sure we take it into our head to scuttle at dead of night the brave ship where now he lies a-dreaming ... and Belacqua along with his palpitations and adhesions and effusions and agenesia and wombtomb and æsthetic of inaudibilities. L'andar su che porta? ...
> Oh but the bay, Mr Beckett, didn't you know, about your brow. (141)

In *Purgatorio* IV Belacqua answers to Dante's question about the reasons for his lazy posture as follows:

> O frate andare in sù che porta?
> ché non mi lascerebbe ire a' martìri
> l'angel di Dio che siede in su la porta. (*Purg.* IV, 127–129)

O brother, what's the use of going up? For God's angel who sits at the gate would not let me pass to the torments.

In the *Comedy*, the apostrophe 'O frate' makes the question explicitly dialogical, while its omission in *Dream* marks its rhetorical quality, and questions the whole fictional enterprise. In its turn, the question is followed by a voice addressing a 'Mr Beckett', which ironically re-transforms the quotation from a rhetorical into a dialogical and metanarrative question.

The quotation from Dante addresses the conventionally teleological scaffolding, which 'turns life into destiny'; *Dream* can be read as a critique of this teleological 'rule'.[27] This critique, however, is stated from a safely metanarrative level. As John Pilling puts it, the question, strategically 'placed at the end of "Und" … is an oblique reminder that *Dream*, too, will refuse to rise up, and will stay much where it was, even if the style and location change dramatically'.[28]

Fernando Salsano has argued that Belacqua's indolence is the result not of his own negligence or laziness but rather of the punishment he has to suffer, that is, a justification of his status in the text, and of the framework of the *Purgatorio*.[29] And yet, Belacqua's immobility, in contrast with the pilgrim's ascent, and his 'short words', in contrast with Dante's intellectual curiosity, also interrupt the vertical movement of this canto, in which almost every sentence refers either to the pilgrims' or to the sun's ascent. Belacqua's benevolent tone casts a disquieting shadow over the tension towards ascension; from his first address to the pilgrim, Belacqua is the immobile reminder of stasis which breaks Dante's and Virgil's narratives of ascent: 'Forse / che di sedere in pria avrai distretta!' (Perhaps you will need to sit before you get to the top!)

Dream, which quotes only a portion of Belacqua's question ('l'andar su che porta?'), constructs Belacqua as the critical, humorous, and anti-heroic voice which challenges the inherent teleological structure of narration. Through Beckett's text, we can read Belacqua at one and the same time as a soul who expiates a divine punishment, as a narratological necessity, and as an element which criticises the progress not only of Dante the pilgrim but also that of Dante the author of the *Comedy*, and, by implication, of literature in general.

Another remarkable feature of canto IV refashioned in *Dream* is the uncertainty of the source from where the voice speaks. As Dante the pilgrim first hears a voice and only later can identify Belacqua as the speaker, crouched in the shadow of a big stone, so the reader does not at first know where 'L'andar su che porta?' comes from. Although Dante's Belacqua speaks those specific words when he has already been recognised, in *Dream* we have a textual reproduction of the structure of canto IV, where 'a voice comes to one [in the dark]'.[30]

However, while it is still possible for Dante to climb a little in order to reach Belacqua and talk with him, the reader of *Dream* is confronted with two different sources; one is Dante's Belacqua, the other is 'Mr Beckett'. Beckett's Bel is not given the power of asking this question, although his sharing Belacqua's name creates an overlap. To 'L'andar su che porta?' a voice replies 'Oh but the bay, Mr Beckett, didn't you know, about your brow', identifying in this way the speaker of the Dantean misquotation as 'Mr Beckett'. The narrative voice therefore splits, creating different spaces: that of the rhetorical question in Italian, coming from an initially unspecified space, later attributed to Mr Beckett, and a second space, from where the voice addressing Mr Beckett mockingly speaks. It is therefore impossible to gain certainty as to the source of the voice, since the origin is already multiple: does the voice belong to Dante's Belacqua, Beckett's Bel, Beckett's 'Mr Beckett', or the split narrative voice?

Mr Beckett, once named, becomes part of the fictional world of the novel; it is, however, also the name of the author who guarantees that we are reading a text. Addressing Mr Beckett, the split narrative voice questions the notion of author as unitary biological identity, and reveals it as part of the intricate power structures that control the investment in literature. The recirculation of the Dantean discourse wreaths the laurel about 'Mr Beckett''s brow: Dante speaks, and Beckett becomes an author. The appropriation of Dante's voice means that 'Mr Beckett' can usurp the place of Dante, the literary authority par excellence, the *auctor*, thereby gaining recognition as an author.

The ironic remark that places 'Mr Beckett' in the position of Dante suggests that the ultimate negation of the progressive movement of the literary work is impossible. The very existence of the question 'what's the use of going up?' implies a critique from the inside. As Dante's slothful Belacqua continues to wait until the prayers of intercessors will permit his ascent, the narrative voice reminds 'Mr Beckett' that he cannot pretend that the text that bears his name is a pointless enterprise, since the act of writing and appropriating discourses entails the notion of the book as a product. It also constructs him as the author, as the instance granting literariness, homogeneity, and consistency to his products, as the literary authority institutionalised by 'the bay about [his] brow'. The subject 'Mr Beckett' is the author caught up in the web of powers which he tries to negate at the textual level. The voice ironically remarking on Mr Beckett's naivety, however, is an authorial voice in control from a safe external position, which reproduces a structure where there is still an unnamed guarantee of meaning, although coming from an unidentified place. 'The places in [discourse] where there is room for possible subjects' slip one on to the other, showing the conventional attribution of roles of the genre; however, the last metanarrative remark is still an assertion of authorial control.[31]

Dream is an attempt to discuss the reversibility of literary value; it is an early formulation that even the artistic practices which 'try to escape the contingency of economic exchange ... will always be liable to the criticism that their very challenge to the structures of artistic value, and value in general, will always themselves constitute forms of value in ways that allow them to be promptly restored to the fields of exchange and transaction which they had attempted to transcend'.[32] 'L'andar su' always brings something; even when 'we do not quite know where we are' (9); the act of appropriation of different texts and discourses which resists the literary tradition through parodic practices ends up having a value attached to it. Writing cannot be a completely disinterested practice, because it inescapably entails the birth and the institutionalisation of the figure of the author. 'Oh, Mr Beckett, but the bay about your brow' is an early metanarrative parodic assertion of the inanity of preferring negation to affirmation.[33] The 'work', although 'abandoned', is in the end retrieved and published and, implicitly, read.

Furthermore, Mr Beckett, speaking from Dante's place, speaks through the mouth of the *auctor*, a term which indicates not only the writer but also the authority.[34] This term, which before the twelfth century referred only to the ancient and revered Latin authorities, was used to describe Dante, a modern writer in the vernacular. Dante fashions himself as the author of the text able to reach the highest possible goal, that of speaking the truth, that of speaking God's words, and does this by 'neutraliz[ing] the betrayal of self-consciousness implicit in all narrative authenticating devices by making his authenticating devices outrageously inauthentic'.[35] To speak with Dante's voice is an 'outrageously inauthentic device', which in *Dream* is used to authenticate the narrative, that is to exist as an author. The narrative does not claim to be true, even if realism or, better, the relation between language and reality, is still Beckett's focus; however, the narrative can try to question itself from within, while ironising on this infinite negotiations of value, which is the basis for the existence of the literary work and of the author.[36]

As Beckett's texts construct a Dante, so Dante's texts, and mainly the *Comedy*, construct a Beckett. Dante, on the one hand, can be helpful to rethink issues such as authorship and authority in Beckett; Beckett, on the other, is useful for rereading the *Comedy*'s structure and its ideas of truthfulness. Analysing the ways in which Dante appears in Beckett means reconsidering both the Beckettian and the Dantean canons.

Sordello is in the shade

If Belacqua has 'its centre everywhere' in *Dream*, another Dantean character questions the relations between centre and periphery and text and margins. He is Sordello, a central character in the English poetic tradition thanks to Browning and, later, to Pound, and a soul of Antepurgatory for whom 'loco certo non ... é posto' (No fixed place is set) (*Purg.* VII, 39) and who goes with Dante and Virgil to the door of the *Purgatorio*; present in canto VI, VII, and VIII, he is also mentioned in canto IX.[37]

The Smeraldina-Rima, sadly brooding in chapter 'TWO' over Bel's imminent departure from the Schule Dunkelbrau, is described through Italian words quoted from *Purgatorio* VI and its translations:

> *Posta sola soletta, like the leonine spirit of the troubadour of great renown, tutta a se romita* (sic). So she had been, sad and still, without limbs or paps in a great stillness of body ... So he would always have her be, *rapt, like the spirit of the troubadour, casting no shade, herself shade.* Instead of which of course it was only a question of seconds before she would surge up at him, blithe and buxom and young and lusty, a lascivious petulant virgin, a generous mare neighing after a great horse, caterwauling after a great stallion, and amorously lay open the double-jug dugs. She could not hold it. Nobody can hold it. Nobody can leave here and hold it. *Only the spirit of the troubadour, rapt in a niche of rock, huddled and withdrawn forever if no prayers go up for him, raccolta a se, like a lion.* (23–24; emphasis mine)

Virgil, after having persuaded a doubtful Dante of the effectiveness of Christian prayers from the living in grace to speed the purgatorial souls' ascent, shows him to be a lonely soul:

> Ma vedi là un'anima che, posta
> sola soletta, inverso noi riguarda:
> quella ne 'nsegnerà la via più tosta'.
> Venimmo a lei: o anima lombarda,
> come ti stavi altera e disdegnosa
> e nel mover de li occhi onesta e tarda!
> Ella non ci dicëa alcuna cosa,
> ma lasciavane gir, solo sguardando
> a guisa di leon quando si posa.
> Pur Virgilio si trasse a lei, pregando
> che ne mostrasse la miglior salita;
> e quella non rispuose al suo dimando,
> ma di nostro paese e de la vita

> ci 'nchiese; e 'l dolce duca incominciava
> 'Mantüa ...', e l'ombra, tutta in sé romita,
> surse ver' lui del loco ove pria stava,
> dicendo: 'O Mantoano, io son Sordello
> de la tua terra!'; e l'un l'altro abbracciava. (*Purg.* VI, 58–75)

But see yonder a soul seated all alone, who is looking towards us; he will point out to us the quickest way.' We came to him: O Lombard soul, how lofty and disdainful was your bearing. And the movement of your eyes how grave and slow! He said nothing to us, but let us go on, watching only after the fashion of a couching lion; but Virgil drew on towards him, asking him to show us the best ascent; and he did not reply to his question, but inquired of our country and condition. And the gentle leader began, 'Mantua – ; and the shade, all in himself recluse, rose towards him from his place there, saying, 'O Mantuan, I am Sordello of your city!' – and they embraced each other.[38]

Sordello, 'the leonine spirit of the troubadour of great renown', is described in De Sanctis's *Storia della letteratura italiana* as that who 'esce dalla sua calma di leone' (comes out of his leonine calm).[39] The Smeraldina-Rima is rapt, so 'tutta in sé romita' that she loses her femininely uncontainable corporeality and becomes a shade, just like Sordello, 'rapt and withdrawn'.[40] Some elements of Beckett's rereading of the Belacqua episode recur here; the loneliness, the detachment, the corporeality reduced to shadow, the prayer upon which the length of the stay depends, the plasticity of the pose. The shadow of the troubadour can be 'without the ... poor anger that rises when stillness is broken, our anger, the poor anger of the world that life cannot be still, the live things cannot be active quietly' (24); after all, he inhabits the 'real vegetation' of the Antepurgatory. While in the case of Belacqua the texts were blended into each other, destabilising the notion of character, here the allusion works as a simile, juxtaposing and not merging the two texts.[41]

The rapt and lonely character serves Belacqua to spiritualise a Smerry disturbingly perceived as far too 'bodily'. On the structural level, the Dantean passage alluded to casts a new light on the often mentioned 'purgatorial quality' of many Beckettian texts. This intertext, and the recurrence of the Anteinfernal term 'Limbo', then altered into 'Limbese', to indicate Belacqua's tentative seclusion from the world, underlines the relevance of the textual problem of tracing boundaries, of beginning and ending, which will characterise many Beckett texts dealing with liminal spaces and thresholds.[42]

After the opening 'But' to be found in the Chaucer quotation, *Dream* multiplies its beginnings, with a two-paragraph chapter 'ONE' which provides a parodically elliptic background from Belacqua's childhood and youth. The long 'TWO', which opens with an almost immobilised Belacqua, is a new beginning. In John Pilling's words, '*Dream* commits the narrative "sin" of beginning twice, without really beginning at all.' 'UND', a digressive and metanarrative chapter, which is placed between 'TWO' and 'THREE', can be paired with 'AND', the final chapter, characteristically sealed by the word 'END'.[43] The final sentence, however, describes a voice demanding that Belacqua 'move on', creating an almost circular connection with the 'unpleasant ultimatum' of the wharfinger 'requiring him to go' (7) at the beginning of the 'story'. Belacqua's 'happiness' to 'move on' is far from the 'I can't go on, I'll go on' of *The Unnamable*, but, nevertheless, it states an uneasiness with traditional notions of beginning and end which can be traced back to the literary legacy of texts such as *Tristram Shandy* or *Tom Jones*.

Sordello, together with Belacqua, belongs to the specific liminal space of Antepurgatory. De Sanctis, upon whom the use of Dante in *Proust* depended, says of the Antepurgatory:

> This ante-purgatory is almost a transition between the *Inferno* and the *Purgatorio*; sin is and is not here; it is still in the habit but no longer in the soul … The soul does not belong to the flesh any more, but once it had as its master, and it remembers it. Flesh is no longer a reality, as in the *Inferno*, but a memory.[44]

Barolini argues that 'the solitary and unplaceable figure of Sordello (scholars have debated whether he should be grouped with those who died violently or with the princes of the valley) is emblematic of the ambiguities raised by this liminal space'.[45] The liminal space of Antepurgatory can thus be compared to that of Limbo as examples of the strategy in the *Comedy* of 'multiple beginnings, so that each beginning undermines the absolute status of the new beginning'. This 'textual fabric that implicitly counters the artifice of beginning' produces the realism of the text. Textuality works to render invisible its fictionality, to present itself as true; to begin again and again blurs the conventional division between text and non-text and presents each difference as a new beginning. Belacqua and Sordello are both inhabitants of in-between spaces, which Barolini connects to the *Comedy*'s 'poetics of the new' and its strategies to represent the unrepresentable process of transition, the passing of time. The term 'Antepurgatory' is a label created by scholars to set boundaries between two spaces divided by the door appearing in canto IX but not presenting substantial difference in terms of the treatment or of the salvation of the souls. Antepurgatory, as well as Limbo (which, however, is the first circle of Hell), are narratological devices which 'institute difference where otherwise there would be an undifferentiated expanse'. In this way every beginning can be a new beginning while the accumulation of different beginnings erodes the clear-cut narrative necessity of excising narration from the flow of time.[46]

It is precisely this 'middling' space which *Dream* strives to reproduce and reshape, claiming that 'the experience of my reader shall be between the phrases, in the silence, communicated by the intervals, not the terms, of the statement' (138). *Dream* begins twice, thus claiming the artificiality of realistic convention, attempting to escape a long 'chloroformed' tradition, and resisting the lie of a possible transposition of 'reality' into text. Moreover, the multiple beginnings also create an undifferentiated narrative flux in which new events can be described while resisting the principle of progression. In *Dream*, which has been described as an 'intricate, demystifying parody of the world in discourse and of realism and truth in literature', the preoccupation with the limit between text and non-text is central, and the reference to Sordello shapes and yet questions the notion of a 'middling' space.[47]

Belacqua and Sordello share another function; both Belacqua's friendly 'forse che di sedere in pria avrai distretta' (Perhaps before then you'll need to sit) and Sordello's stern 'Vedi? sola questa riga / non varcheresti dopo 'l sol partito' (Look, even this line you would not cross after the sun is set) (*Purg.* VII, 53–54) act as reminders of the limits of the poet and question the pilgrim's ascent.[48] *Dream* is a purgatorial enterprise in that it strives to deny any progression while remaining a literary work, and being therefore obliged to proceed, following Galileo Galilei's modified motto: 'fair to meedling. The poem moves, eppure' (203). Even the 'Limbese' Belacqua is, after all, 'only too happy' to 'move on' (241).

Notes

1. Beckett, *Dream of Fair to Middling Women* (New York: Arcade, 1993), pp. 148, 37. Subsequent references are given in the text. The line is also quoted in TCD MS 10963, fol. 16, TCD MS 10963a, fol. 3, and TCD MS 10966, fol. 3.
2. Dante's tomb in Ravenna is often referred to in English literature, from Richard Duppa (1770–1831) to Byron, from Shelley to Thomas Medwin (1788–1869). See Paget Toynbee, *Dante in English Literature from Chaucer to Cary (c.1380–1844)* (London: Methuen, 1909).
3. The character is named after St Lucy's birthplace, thus the association with Lucia Joyce. In the '*Dream*' notebook Beckett records that Lucia, one of the 'tre donne benedette' from *Paradiso*, comes from Syracuse. James Knowlson, *Damned to Fame: The Life of Samuel Beckett* (London: Bloomsbury, 1996), p. 151. Toynbee also records her origins. Paget Toynbee, *Dictionary of Proper Names and Notable Matters in the Works of Dante* (Oxford: The Clarendon Press, 1898), p. 343. Details about the blind martyr of Syracuse who allegorically stands for the illuminating grace can also be found in the 'Dante' notebooks,

TCD 10963a, fol. 1 and 10963, fol. 6; the latter corresponds to note 97 of the Enrico Bianchi 1922 edition of the *Comedy* for Salani used by Beckett. See Daniela Caselli, '"The Florentia edition in the ignoble Salani collection": a textual comparison', *Journal of Beckett Studies*, 9:2 (2001), 1–20.

4 In the '*Dream*' notebook, this line is transcribed with a few other lines from *Paradiso* XXX, 22–24 and 31–33. The '*Dream*' notebook also reproduces *Inf.* XXX, 128; *Par.* III, 10–18; *Par.* XXIX, 12; and *Par.* XXXI, 83–84. See John Pilling, '*Beckett's* Dream *Notebook*' (Reading: Beckett International Foundation, 1999) and my '"The Florentia edition"'.

5 The passage is reproduced in one of the MacGreevy letters as: 'Ché non può trovar posa in su le piume / Ma con dar volta suo dolore scherma (*Purg.* IV 150–51)'. TCD MS 10402, undated. James Knowlson has dated it 20 June 1930. Semiramis appears in *Inferno* V, 58–60, on the list of the 'luxurious' damned (a pun on the italian 'lussuriosi', i.e. lustful damned) in the 'Whoroscope' notebook (erroneously grouping them in *Inferno* IV instead of V), and TCD MS 10963. Costanza and Piccarda, 'eternal pearl of Costance and Piccarda' (130, 175) are among the inhabitants of the first Heaven of the Moon (*Par.* III); they surface in 'Le Concentrisme' (*Disjecta*, p. 37) and in a passage transcribed and translated in the '*Dream*' notebook. For a more detailed discussion of such passages see Caselli, '"The Florentia Edition"'.

6 Peter Boxall, 'Negative geography: fictional space in Beckett's prose', Ph.D. thesis, University of Sussex, 1996.

7 Kathrin Schödel, apparently unaware of my previous work on this topic, has also later discussed Belacqua in relation to narrative progression in *Dream*. Kathrin Schödel, 'Intertextuelle Dialog: Dantes "Belaqua" in Samuel Becketts Roman *Dream of Fair to Middling Women*', *Deutsches Dante Jahrbuch*, 77 (2002), 149–173.

8 'L'andar', 'andar' and 'andare' are variants; so are 'uccel di Dio' and 'angel di Dio'. Petrocchi prefers 'andare' and 'angel', while it seems that the edition quoted in *Dream* uses 'l'andar' and 'uccel'. See my '"The Florentia edition"'. In *Purg.* II, 38 and VIII, 104 angels are called 'birds of God'.

9 Samuel Beckett, 'Sedendo et Quiesciendo' [*sic*], *transition*, 21 (March 1932), 13–20. Variants not relevant to my purposes can be observed between the two versions.

10 For the dating of the commentaries see Zygmunt G. Baranski, 'A note on the Trecento: Boccaccio, Benvenuto and the dream of Dante's pregnant mother', in *Miscellanea di Studi Danteschi in memoria di Silvio Pasquazi* (Naples: Federico & Ardia, 1993), pp. 69–82, p. 71. See also Franco Quartieri (ed.), *Benvenuto da Imola: Un moderno antico commentatore di Dante* (Ravenna: Longo, 2001).

11 Toynbee, *Dictionary of Proper Names*, p. 74 (the 1968 reprint of Toynbee's volume revised by Charles S. Singleton is appreciably different). I would like to thank Zygmunt Baranski for pointing out to me that the excerpts from Benvenuto and the Anonimo were reproduced in Toynbee. See also Daniela Caselli, '"Looking it up in my big Dante": a note on "Sedendo and Quiescendo"', *Journal of Beckett Studies*, 6:2 (Spring 1997), 85–93, and '"L'andar su che porta?": Dante nel primo Beckett', *The Italianist*, 18 (1998), 130–154. The relevance of Toynbee and of the commentaries is later reiterated by Jean-Pierre Ferrini, who however does not acknowledge my previous work on this topic. Jean-Pierre Ferrini, *Dante et Beckett* (Paris: Hermann, 2003), pp. 24–25.

12 The excerpts from Benvenuto and from the Anonimo are also reproduced in the '*Dream*' notebook, together with a passage from the *Postille Cassinesi*; see Caselli, '"The Florentia edition"'.

13 Baranski, 'A note on the Trecento', p. 74; see also, by the same author, 'Benvenuto da Imola e la tradizione dantesca della "Comedía": appunti per una descrizione del *Comentum*', in Pantaleo Palmieri and Carlo Paolazzi (eds), *Benvenuto da Imola: lettore degli antichi e dei moderni* (Ravenna: Longo, 1991), pp. 215–230.
14 Roberto Mercuri, 'Percorsi letterari e tipologie culturali nell'esegesi dantesca di Benvenuto da Imola', in Palmieri and Paolazzi (eds), *Benvenuto da Imola*, pp. 55–78, p. 78.
15 Baranski, 'A note on the Trecento', p. 228; about the Type C *accessus*, see P. W. Hunt, *The History of Grammar in the Middle Ages* (Amsterdam: G. L. Bursill-Hall, 1980), pp. 117–144; A. J. Minnis, *Medieval Theory of Authorship: Scholastic Literary Attitudes in the Later Middle Ages* (London: Scolar Press, 1984), pp. 18–27. For a discussion on the notion of 'comedía' see Teodolinda Barolini, *Dante's Poets: Textuality and Truth in the Comedy* (Princeton: Princeton University Press, 1984), p. 277.
16 Baranski, 'A note on the Trecento', p. 81.
17 Alfredo Cottignoli, 'Realismo "creaturale" e "comparatio domestica" nel commento dantesco di Benvenuto', in Palmieri and Paolazzi (eds), *Benvenuto da Imola*, pp. 215–230, p. 208.
18 Santorre De Benedetti, 'Comunicazione su Belacqua', *Bullettino della Società Dantesca Italiana*, 13 (1906), 222–233.
19 Minnis, *Medieval Theory of Authorship*, p. 12.
20 De Benedetti, 'Comunicazione', 223.
21 Samuel Beckett, *Proust* (New York: Grove Press, 1957), p. 67.
22 For a discussion on the 'scale of liūs', see John Pilling, *Beckett Before Godot* (Cambridge, Cambridge University Press, 1997).
23 Elizabeth Barry draws attention to the parallels between Belacqua's and Molloy's foetal position and Wordsworth's 'Resolution and Independence'. Elizabeth Barry, '"Take into the air my quiet breath": Beckett and English Romanticism', *Journal of Beckett Studies*, 10:1–2 (Fall 2000–Spring 2001), 207–221.
24 TCD MS 10962, fol. 44.
25 Samuel Beckett, *Watt* (New York: Grove Weidenfeld, 1959), p. 77.
26 For a discussion of the textual variants between the line quoted in *Dream* and alternative versions, such as Petrocchi's 'O frate andare in sù che porta?' see Caselli, '"The Florentia edition"'.
27 'Fait de la vie un destin, du souvenir un acte utile, et de la durée un temps dirigé et significatif', Roland Barthes, *Le degré zéro de l'écriture* (Paris: Gonthier, 1965), p. 37; quoted in Carla Locatelli, *La disdetta della parola: l'ermeneutica del silenzio nella prosa inglese di Samuel Beckett* (Bologna: Patron, 1984), p. 9.
28 Pilling, *Beckett Before Godot*, p. 66.
29 Fernando Salsano, 'Belacqua', in Umberto Bosco and Giorgio Petrocchi (eds), *Enciclopedia Dantesca* (Rome: Istituto dell'Enciclopedia Italiana, 1970–78), pp. 556–558.
30 Samuel Beckett, *Company* (London: Calder, 1980), p. 7.
31 Michel Foucault, 'What is an author?' (1969), in Paul Rabinow (ed.), *The Foucault Reader* (Harmondsworth: Penguin, 1984), pp. 101–120, p. 120.
32 Steven Connor, 'Negativity and the question of value: Beckett's *Worstward Ho*', *Paragraph*, 15:2 (1992), 121–135, 122.
33 In *Murphy* 'yes and no' are defined as the 'eternal tautology'. Samuel Beckett, *Murphy* (London: Picador, 1973), p. 27. Charles Juliet writes that Beckett once claimed: 'La négation n'est pas possible. Pas plus que l'affirmation. Il est absurde de dire que c'est

absurde. C'est encore porter un jugement de valeur. On ne peut pas protester, et on ne peut pas opiner.' Charles Juliet, *Rencontre avec Samuel Beckett* (Paris: Éditions Fata Morgana, 1986), p. 49.

34 On Dante as *auctor* see A. J. Minnis, *Medieval Theory of Authorship*, and A. J. Minnis and A. B. Scott (eds), with the assistance of David Wallace, *Medieval Literary Theory and Criticism* (Oxford: The Clarendon Press, 1988). See also Baranski, 'A note on the Trecento', pp. 69–82.

35 Teodolinda Barolini, *The Undivine Comedy: Detheologizing Dante* (Princeton: Princeton University Press, 1992), p. 15.

36 For an argument about narration which addresses similar issues in a different context see Karín Lesnik-Oberstein, '*Oliver Twist*: the narrator's tale', *Textual Practice*, 15:1 (2001), 87–100.

37 Robert Browning, *Sordello*, in *The Poetical Works of Robert Browning*, eds Ian Jack and Margaret Smith, vol. 2 (Oxford: Clarendon, 1984). Ezra Pound's Canto II famously teases Browning: 'Hang it all, Robert Browning, / there can be but the one "Sordello". / But Sordello, and my Sordello? / Lo Sordels si fo di Mantovana.' Ezra Pound, *Selected Poems 1908–1969* (London: Faber and Faber, 1975), p. 115. See also Mary Bryden, 'No stars without stripes: Beckett and Dante', *The Romanic Review*, 87:4 (1996), 541–556.

38 The third of the three 'Dante postcards' reads: 'In *Purg* all pray save: scomunicati (3), violenti (4), accidiosi (18)'. RUL MS 4123. See also Mary Bryden, 'Beckett and the three Dantean smiles', *Journal of Beckett Studies*, n.s. 4:2 (September 1995), 29–33, 29.

39 Francesco De Sanctis, *Storia della letteratura italiana* (Turin: Einaudi-Gallimard, 1996), p. 219. T. S. Eliot also quotes from this canto in 'Dante' (1929), in Frank Kermode (ed.), *Selected Prose of T. S. Eliot* (London: Faber and Faber, 1975), pp. 205–230, p. 219.

40 *Purgatorio* XIV, 67–72. 'In se' and 'a sé' are variants.

41 Gian Biagio Conte, *Memoria dei poeti e sistema letterario: Catullo, Virgilio, Ovidio, Lucano* (Turin: Einaudi, 1974 and 1985).

42 Occasionally, a few place names from the *Comedy* are employed in *Dream*. Giudecca, the lowest level of the *Inferno*, is used to indicate the centre of Smeraldina's palm (67). The Stygian speculum appears in 'TWO' in connection with Narcissus, and Malebolge is equated to section 'THREE'.

43 Pilling, *Beckett Before Godot*, pp. 58–9, 60, and 66.

44 Francesco De Sanctis, *Storia*, p. 200.

45 Barolini, *The Undivine Comedy*, p. 34.

46 Barolini, *The Undivine Comedy*, pp. 22 and 33.

47 Locatelli, *Unwording the World*, p. 58.

48 Barolini, *The Undivine Comedy*, p. 114.

3 Strata and mysteries: intratextuality in *More Pricks Than Kicks*

Dream of Fair to Middling Women argues that the realistic notion of character is conventional and 'chloroformed', questioning it through a Belacqua whose multiple intertertextual dimensions mirror his declared 'unreality'. Thus, Belacqua is at once a character and its own critique and dissolution. In *More Pricks Than Kicks*, Belacqua is, once again, the protagonist.[1] In this text, he is not only an explicitly intertextual figure but also an intratextual one, in so far as he inherits many features of the *Dream* Belacqua.

More Pricks Than Kicks is a Beckett work which not only re-elaborates texts by other authors but also reinscribes and reformulates Beckett's own previous works. In this sense, it is a significant case study for understanding how intratextuality – that is to say the relationship between different texts by the same author – operates in Beckett. The most explicit cases of intratextuality are the two stories 'A Wet Night' and 'The Smeraldina's Billet-Doux', almost verbatim transcriptions of two episodes in *Dream*. *More Pricks Than Kicks* also explicitly and ironically refers to *Dream* as a work in progress, or, better, as an actual book by Walter Draffin at the '*limae labor* stage for the past ten or fifteen years' (143), while in *Dream* the book the reader is reading is also the book Belacqua himself is writing (138). Furthermore, there are several allusions to *Dream*, replete with common phrases: in 'Fingal' Belacqua is a 'fat overfed boy' (29) as in the opening of *Dream*, in which the 'overfed boy' is 'pedalling' (1); Belacqua is in both texts 'bogged in indolence' (36 and 121); the same Florentine fire brigade station appears in 'A Wet Night' (49), in *Dream* (202) and in 'Ding-Dong' (40); and the Smeraldina is described as 'Lucrezia del Fede' both in 'Draff' (176) and in *Dream* (15). As the Frica does in 'A Wet Night', in *More Pricks* one feels that 'all this had happened ... before, by hearsay or *in a dream*' (80): intratextuality keeps 'faintly alive a book effectively dead'.[2]

More Pricks Than Kicks also incorporates material from some of the poems, and the last, unpublished, story of the collection is entitled 'Echo's Bones', like the homonymous poem included in the collection *Echo's Bones and Other Precipitates*, also published in 1935. Another title, 'What a Misfortune' – the translation of half a quotation from Voltaire's *Candide* – had already been used by Beckett in 1929 for a satirical article for the *T.C.D.: A College Miscellany*.[3]

In *Dream*, Mr Beckett receives an ironic 'bay about his brow' speaking Dante's words; the *auctor* serves to provide Mr Beckett with the status of author and simultaneously to ridicule it. By repeating portions of other Beckett texts, *More Pricks Than Kicks* inaugurates a constant feature of the Beckett *oeuvre*, which H. Porter Abbott has described as follows: 'by repeating names, images and motifs from one work to another – sufficiently developed to be recognizable, insufficiently developed to connect – Beckett was constantly reinveinting his entire *œuvre*.'[4] Although I question notions of intentionality, the analysis by Porter Abbott is helpful to my argument, as it is my contention that intratextuality is a major contributor to the constitution of the Beckett canon. If 'the greatest influence on the texts of Samuel Beckett are the texts of Samuel Beckett', Samuel Beckett the author is himself the product of this constant process of incorporation.[5]

More Pricks Than Kicks can be read as deferring its own origin while contributing to an idea of consistency in the *oeuvre*: it is a text whose origin is always somewhere else, in unlocatable spaces which nevertheless belong to other Beckett works. The repetition of Dante in its many forms (quotations and characters from the *Comedy*, the recurring name of Dante, references to the *Convivio* or the *De vulgari eloquentia*) is one of the main ways in which the Beckett *oeuvre* constructs itself. Dante is part of a double movement – toward texts by other authors and toward texts by Beckett himself. Such movement interrogates how ideas of consistency and similarity between texts by the same author operate.

The name of Belacqua is an evident sign of intratextual continuity, and it is also the most relevant unifying device in a volume in which the episodic and open nature of each story is counterbalanced by a series of internal allusions.[6] Among the most visible allusive strategies, we find cross-references to events that will happen later on or that have already happened (as in the openings of 'Ding-Dong' and 'What a Misfortune', respectively) and ironic footnotes that point towards previous stories (in 'Walking Out' the reader is referred to 'Fingal', while in 'What a Misfortune' s/he is referred to 'Walking Out').

The blanks which separate the stories – always suspended in *medias res* – work as a graphic device showing the inability to cover completely (to 'petrify', to 'itemise') Belacqua's life.[7] 'The intervals of the statement' indicate that this idea of realism can survive only in a fragmentary and open story. Yet, the web of internal allusions creates a structure for the sequence of episodes.

Quick deaths

> It was morning and Belacqua was stuck in the first of the canti in the moon. He was so bogged that he could move neither backward nor forward. Blissful Beatrice was there, Dante also, and she explained the spots on the moon to him. (9)

The opening of 'Dante and the Lobster' is centred on the instability of the notion of Belacqua's identity. Here Belacqua moves – although he is 'stuck' – from the Dante to the Beckett text. In *Dream* Belacqua meanders through Dante's, the Anonimo's, and Benvenuto's fictional spaces; similarly, in the opening of 'Dante and the Lobster' a subtle use of the pronouns merges Belacqua Shuah – the reader of *Paradiso* II – with Dante's Belacqua of *Purgatorio* IV, and with Dante the protagonist of the *Comedy*. Further, 'the location of Belacqua on the morning of the story is blurred across the boundary between his existence as a character in Beckett's story, and as a sinner in Dante's poem, to suggest that Beckett's Belacqua is occupying Dante's geography, and that he has travelled from Dante's Purgatory to this "Paradise that is not terrestrial"'.[8] The intertextual Belacqua of *Dream* is in *More Pricks Than Kicks* a reader of the *Comedy* itself. His experience as a reader of the *Comedy* – a text in which author, narrator, and protagonist coincide – is told as a paradoxical crossing of the conventional limits between reader and character, and between the outside and the inside of the text: Belacqua is 'stuck in the first of the canti in the moon', 'bogged' as a student struggling with Beatrice's explanation of the spots on the moon, but 'bogged indeed' as the damned of *Inferno* VII.[9] To know that 'blissful Beatrice was there, Dante also', does not help to locate that *there*, but rather merges the dimension of the reader with that of the characters of the *Comedy*.[10] Belacqua is not supposed to travel through the canticles, being 'stuck' in *Purgatorio* IV; he ought to move 'neither backward not forward'. On the contrary, here he is in *Paradiso* II, and 'impatient to get on to Piccarda', that is to say to *Paradiso* III. The pronoun 'he' is the most important strategy through which the different spaces are merged: '[Beatrice] had it from God, therefore he could rely on its being accurate in every particular' (9). If Dante could indeed rely on the accuracy of Beatrice's explanation, Belacqua Shuah is only bogged and bored by her 'proof', although not by her 'refutation', which is 'plain sailing'.[11] This expression is an allusion to the beginning of *Paradiso* II, in which Dante warns his readers against the dangers of what will be a difficult navigation:

> O voi che siete in piccioletta barca,
> desiderosi d'ascoltar, seguiti
> dietro al mio legno che cantando varca,
> tornate a riveder li vostri liti:
> non vi mettete in pelago, ché forse,
> perdendo me, rimarreste smarriti. (*Par.* II, 1–6)

O you that are in your little bark, eager to hear, following behind my ship that singing makes her way, turn back to see again your shores. Do not commit yourselves to the open sea, for perchance, if you lost me, you would remain astray.[12]

Further, the pronoun 'he' has a function analogous to the one analysed above in the sentence that closes the first paragraph:

> Still he pored over the enigma, he would not concede himself conquered, he would understand at least the meanings of the words, the order in which they were spoken and the nature of the satisfaction that they conferred on the misinformed poet, so that when they were ended he was refreshed and could raise his heavy head, intending to return thanks and make formal retraction of his old opinion. (9)

The pronoun refers both to Belacqua, who shows all the determination of a Dante – or a Beckett – scholar, and to Dante, who narrates how, after Beatrice's explanation, he did raise his head: 'e io, per confessar corretto e certo / me stesso, tanto quanto si convenne / leva' il capo a proferer più erto' (and, to confess me correct and assured, I raised my head more erect to speak) (*Par.* III, 4–6). The 'toiling' reader (Belacqua) is both a character in the text he is reading and a character reading that text. Belacqua's oxymoronic immobile ubiquity produces an implied reader who struggles to understand where to place the protagonist, thereby mirroring the protagonist's paradoxically 'bogged' backward and forward movement.

After this long paragraph illustrating that this 'art has nothing to do with clarity, does not dabble in the clear and does not make clear' but that, rather, it has to do with playing with the limits between texts, midday strikes, as in *Purgatorio* IV, and we are catapulted into Belacqua Shuah's Dublin, a place where Dante is a mere book that can be 'slammed shut' (10).[13]

An important ring in the intertextual chain is the reference to Piccarda, whom Belacqua is 'impatient to meet'; she was already present in *Dream* (130) in a passage alluding to Cain, who also appears here 'with his truss of thorns' (12). Cain is mentioned in *Paradiso* II as a legend used to explain the presence of the spots on the moon; he is also referred to in *Inferno* XX, 126, where he is used as a periphrasis indicating the moon.[14] Reference to the 'branded moon' can also be found in Beckett's poem 'Alba' (1929), where Dante is explicitly mentioned:

> before morning you shall be here
> and Dante and the Logos and all strata and mysteries
> and the branded moon
> beyond the white plane of music
> that you shall establish here before morning[15]

The passage in 'Dante and the Lobster' referring to Cain abruptly interrupts the hyperbolic description of Belacqua charring the two slices of bread for his lunch. In this paragraph Cain is said to be 'dispossessed, cursed from the earth, fugitive and vagabond. The moon was that countenance fallen and branded, seared with the first stigma of God's *pity*, that an outcast might not die *quickly* (12; emphasis mine)'. The paragraph introduces the *leitmotiv* of the story, which is built upon Dante's 'superb pun' from *Inferno* XX, 28: 'Qui vive la pietà quand'è ben morta', quoted by Belacqua later on in the text, during the Italian lesson. Belacqua ponders on how it would be possible to translate Dante's 'great phrase' but he is discouraged by the Ottolenghi's remark on the inanity of the project. He will nevertheless still be thinking about the double meaning of 'pietà' later on in the story: 'why not piety and pity both?' (21). Dante's 'superb pun' was present in *Dream* as one of Belacqua's favourite lines to mumble in moments of crisis (148). Dante's line also has a second intratextual dimension, since it appears translated in the poem 'Text', as 'pity is quick with death'.[16] The 'superb pun' central to 'Dante and the Lobster' stimulates Belacqua's skill as a translator; that it has already been published adds a further ironic dimension to the pun.

The anecdote about Cain introduces two of the story's linguistic elements – 'pity' and 'quick' – which, in connection with 'death', dominate the complex web of allusions and references culminating in Dante's line and concluding the story:

> Well, thought Belacqua, it's a quick death, God help us all.
> It is not. (22)

Dante therefore plays a crucial role in the orchestration of the story. Cain does not die quickly, and he is an example of the absence of God's pity, like McCabe, 'star[ing] up at [Belacqua]', and the lobster – 'Christ! ... is alive'. The assassin and the lobster are examples of the absence of human and godly 'piety and pity both': while Belacqua asks himself 'why not mercy and Godliness together?' 'poor McCabe, ... would get it in the neck at dawn' (21).

References to death are scattered throughout the story, which establishes a web of correspondences between McCabe's death, Belacqua's lunch, and the lobster dinner bought for his aunt. The profusion of hyperboles gives a ritualistic character to the act of toasting two slices of bread. McCabe, staring from the newspaper spread on the table, observes the loaf being 'evened off on [his] face'; the stump of the loaf then goes 'back into prison', and the slices of 'spongy and warm' bread, so soft as to be described as 'alive', will soon be deprived of their 'plush feel' and 'fat look'. Later on, the Gorgonzola cheese is described as 'alive' only when it has a 'good stench'; Belacqua 'slip[s] the cadaverous tablet of cheese between the hard cold black boards of the toast'; 'each mouthful' 'die[s]' in the mouth; the alive spongy bread is charred, the spicy mixture scorches the palate (14).[17] This constellation of words creates the contrapuntal structure of the story, synthesised by Dante's 'great phrase', and closed by the effective and abrupt comment of the narrator.

As in the case of *Dream*, Dante also plays minor roles in this story. Dante stands for the book by Dante, which Belacqua can 'slam shut', and which the signorina Ottolenghi promises to look up when confronted by Belacqua with 'the moon enigma'. Signorina Ottolenghi, Belacqua's 'Professoressa', is set by him 'on a pedestal in his mind, apart from other women', gaining a status comparable to that of 'blissful Beatrice' (possibly a pun on Dante Gabriel Rossetti's *Beata Beatrix*) or to the Alba of the poem, who can 'establish ... the white plane of music'.[18] The presence of the 'three large obligations' in Belacqua's day recall the tripartite division of the *Comedy* and the central importance of the number three in Dante, which had been recorded by Beckett in 'Dante...Bruno.Vico..Joyce'.[19] I have discussed how the idea of progression is linked in *Dream* not only with the notion of teleology, but also, via purgatorial 'culmination', to that of theology. The divine tripartite structure, apparently reduced to that something 'that one ha[s] to do next' (10), can be seen as recuperating a (resisted) theo/teleological dimension, if that something that one has to do next is the necessary condition for the story to exist, for the 'poem' to 'move'. The number three will reappear later on in *More Pricks*: in 'Ding-Dong' and in 'A Wet Night' 'the Bovril sign' refers, via Joyce, to Dante and the three colours of the theological virtues, transformed now into 'Doubt, Despair, and Scrounging';[20] Nick Malacoda, in 'Draff' as in the poem 'Malacoda', 'measures, coffins, and covers'; 'Echo's Bones' is divided into 'three scenes' (2).

Screechy flatfooted Tuscany peacocks

The presence of Dante in the stories of *More Pricks Than Kicks* is not consistent; it is largely present in 'Dante and the Lobster', 'Ding-Dong', and 'Draff', but less so in the other stories. In 'Fingal' there are no direct allusions to Dante, although Anthony Farrow has argued in favour of what I regard as a rather tenuous link between the inhabitants of the first heaven of the moon in 'Dante and the Lobster' and the lunatics of 'Fingal'.[21] 'One of the gangs' of lunatics, 'walking round and round the playground' (30) and Belacqua, who will 'follow the road round' (31), anticipate however the circular motion of 'Ding-Dong'. The well-known contrast established in 'Dante...Bruno.Vico..Joyce' between Dante's *Purgatory*, which is 'conical and consequently implies culmination' and Joyce's, which 'is spherical and excludes culmination' (33), is mirrored in *More Pricks Than Kicks* by the circular, aimless movements of Belacqua around Dublin and environs. Belacqua's goal is partially that already encountered in *Dream*, that is to say to 'be back in the caul, on my back in the dark for ever' (29), but in *More Pricks Than Kicks* Belacqua does not try any more to 'troglodise himself', opting instead for a constant movement 'from place to place ... But as for sites, one was as good as another, because they all disappeared as soon as he came to rest in them' (36).[22] In *Dream* Belacqua wants to write a book in which 'the experience of [his] reader shall be between the phrases, in the silence, communicated by the intervals, not the terms, of the statement' (138); in 'Ding-Dong' this 'old story' reappears: 'torment in the terms and in the intervals a measure of ease' (36).

In 'Ding-Dong' a number of elements coincide with those present in *Dream*. Belacqua is described as 'by nature sinfully indolent, bogged in indolence' (36), repeating a phrase used in *Dream* (121); the expression can also be found in the '*Dream*' notebook, in which it is preceded by the Italian equivalent 'impaludito in pigrizia'.[23] The Italian version does not belong directly to the *Comedy*, which uses ''mpaluda' only once, in *Inferno* XX, the same canto containing Dante's 'superb pun'. The word is used by Virgil during his description of the origin of Mantua, which is located on the bog where Manto's bones lay.[24] Although the Dantean coinage means 'to make a marsh' in the context of the canto, and 'impaludare' ('to be bogged') has been used by a few commentators, 'impaludare in pigrizia' seems to be a Beckettian coinage, allusive to *Inferno* XX and VII.[25]

Also the 'Beethoven pause' (37), the 'moving pause' (38) which Belacqua is said to inhabit, is linked to the same passage of *Dream* mentioned above, where Belacqua thinks of 'Beethofen' in connection to the silence of the intervals. This is another example of a Beckettian expression migrating from one text to another, as the much quoted letter to Axel Kaun (1937) indicates.[26]

'Ding-Dong' also adopts one of the narrative strategies observed in *Dream*.[27] If the narrative voice is omniscient in the first two stories, here the narrator acts as a witness, as somebody whom the reader can trust since Belacqua was a 'sometime friend' of his. Thus, the first seven paragraphs 'are offered as a commentary on a story which will soon get told, but which has not yet been told'.[28] The narrator claims, as a guarantee for what is being said:

> I know all this because he [Belacqua] told me. We were Pylades and Orestes for a period, flattened down to something very genteel; but the relation abode and was highly confidential while it lasted. I have witnessed every stage of the exercise. I have been there when he set out, springing up and hastening away without as much as by your leave, impelled by some force that he did not care to gainsay. I have had glimpses of him enjoying his little trajectory. I have been there again when he returned, transfigured and transformed. (37)

The passage works ironically; meant on one level as a persuasive piece of rhetoric to reassure the reader about the veracity of what s/he is reading, the hyperbolic definition of their friendship as that between Pylades and Orestes is undermined both by the opening remark 'my sometimes friend Belacqua' and by the following addition 'I gave him up in the end because he was not *serious*'. Moreover, the narrator asserts that he knows 'all this' because he has been told and he also claims to know it because he was there. The coexistence of both claims decreases the credibility of the narrating voice. A further ironic dimension which makes the narrator even more unreliable lies in the fact that Belacqua's 'exercises', which the narrator witnesses, seem indeed to 'imply culmination'. But if Belacqua is here said to come back 'transfigured and transformed', the whole structure of the story denies this progression; Belacqua only moves 'from place to place' and 'one [is] as good as another'; he can only go 'round and round, like the spheres, but mutely', like the 'Bovril sign', like an endless 'da capo'. As Lawrence Harvey has maintained, the frequent presence of circularity indicates stasis.[29]

The position of the narrator oscillates. While at first he claims to come from the same fictional space as Belacqua, exposing his own fictionality, he then slips into the omniscient position, becoming invisible and all-controlling. The story alternates sections told from an omniscient point of view with sections in which the narrator becomes visible again, makes 'enquires', is engaged in a dialogue with Belacqua (41–42), and stresses how his story is only a partial reportage (43) of what Belacqua laboured to make clear (37). To state that Belacqua 'seemed to derive considerable satisfaction from his failure' to make things clear to him is a further admission of unreliability.

Intertextuality and intratextuality mirror the narrative complexity of 'Ding-Dong' since they, too, question the authenticity of the story: references to Dante stress the artificiality of the account while still resorting to the authority of the 'divine Florentine' as a justification either to proceed or to refuse to do so. In 'Ding-Dong' there are both explicit references and structural analogies with the Dantean text. Belacqua 'squat[s], emerging ... from the underground convenience in the maw of College Street', because 'for the moment there were no grounds for his favouring one direction rather than another' (38–39). The squatting position refers to Dante's Belacqua via *Dream*, in which there are a number of variations on the image of squatting. His immobility recalls the Belacqua of 'Dante and the Lobster', 'stuck in the first of the Canti in the moon', who could move 'neither backward nor forward'; this same expression is used to define the position of 'Buridan's ass' to which Belacqua's indecisiveness is compared: 'Yet he found he could not [move on], any more than Buridan's ass, move to right or left, backward or forward' (39). Unable to decide from which heap of hay he should eat, the legendary ass starves to death. Anthony Farrow has identified the Buridan ass as a reference to *Paradiso* IV, which however does not mention it, but only evokes it (*Par.* IV, 1–9).

Dante is present also in the subsequent passage, extensively analysed by Kelly Anspaugh. The 'Bovril sign' rotates around *Purgatorio* XXIX in which the three theological virtues – 'Faith, Hope, and – what was it? – Love' (39) – are personified as dancing women and associated with the three colours white, green, and red.[30] It is also mirrored in the following story – 'A Wet Night' – an excerpt from *Dream* in which the Bovril sign reappears, while being also doubled in the poem 'Home Olga'.[31] As Anspaugh has argued, the passage alludes not only to the 'three graces of the Dublin musical world' of Joyce's 'The Dead', but also to the 'three principal women' of his story, who can be seen as corresponding not only to 'the three Graces of classical myth' but also to the 'classical Furies', mentioned twice in 'Ding-Dong'. Furthermore, the three colours reverberate in the three principal women of *More Pricks Than Kicks*, the Smeraldina, the Alba, and Ruby Tough, who will revisit the Beckett canon in the guise of Flo, Vi, and Ru in *Come and Go*.[32] While red is the colour of the cloud in which Beatrice and the God of Love appear in the *Vita Nuova*, the three colours are also the three colours worn by Beatrice during her first appearance to Dante in *Purgatorio*:[33]

> così dentro una nuvola di fiori
> che da le mani angeliche saliva
> e ricadeva in giù dentro e di fori,
> sovra *candido* vel cinta d'uliva
> donna m'apparve, sotto *verde* manto
> vestita di color di *fiamma viva*. (*Pur.* XXX, 28–33; emphasis mine)

> so within a cloud of flowers, which rose from the angelic hands and fell down again within and without, olive-crowned over a *white* veil a lady appeared to me, clad, under a *green* mantle, with hue of *living flame*.

This additional Dantean echo anticipates the appearance of the 'hatless woman advancing slowly' towards Belacqua (43); she tells him that 'heaven goes round ... and round and round and round and round and round' (45), a motion prefigured in its turn by the Bovril sign which 'went nowhere, only round and round, like the spheres, but mutely' (39), and reproduced in its endless circularity through the repetition of 'round'. The parallel between the woman advancing in the pub and Beatrice is sustained by 'her face, ah her face', which 'was what Belacqua had rather refer to as her countenance, it was so full of light. This she lifted up upon him and no error. Brimful of light and serene, serenissime' (44). Furthermore, 'her speech was that of a woman of the people, but of a gentlewoman of the people ... The one deplorable feature of her get up ... was the footwear' (44). This sentence has intratextual and intertextual overtones. In 'Dante...Bruno.Vico..Joyce', Beckett had alluded to 'the peacock Signora Alighieri dreamed about', referring to Boccaccio's *Trattatello in laude di Dante*, in which Dante's mother's allegorical dream is described.[34] I have analysed Boccaccio's parallel between Dante's *Commedia* and the four most important characteristics of the peacock. It is worth remembering that, according to Boccaccio, as the feet sustain the whole body, so language sustains any work of literature:

> e il parlare volgare, nel quale e sopra il quale ogni giuntura della *Comedia* si sostiene, a rispetto dell'alto e maestevole stilo letterale che usa ciascuno altro poeta è sozzo, come che egli sia più che gli altri belli agli odierni ingegni conforme. (§226)

> and the vulgar language, in which and on which every juncture of the *Comedy* is based, is filthy if compared to the high and majestic literary style used by any other poet, even though more than the others it is apt for contemporary minds.

The text plays with Boccaccio's *Trattatello* and with its repetitions both in 'Dante...Bruno.Vico..Joyce' and in a poem already mentioned, 'Text', which presents a number of allusions to Dante:

> Not so but perhaps
> at the sight and the sound of
> a screechy flatfooted Tuscany peacock's
> Strauss fandango and recitative
> not forgetting he stinks eternal.

This roundelay revolves around Dante as much as it does around previous Beckett elaborations of Dante. Beatrice speaks in vernacular, so her speech is indeed that of 'a woman of the people, but of a gentlewoman of the people', hinting back at the discussion about the illustrious vernacular in the *De vulgari eloquentia*. Like the feet of the 'screechy flatfooted Tuscany peacock', her feet are a deplorable feature in so far as they do not have the (previously deplored) 'suave elegance' of Latin (31); the woman approaching Belacqua says 'rowan an' rowan an' rowan', 'dropping the *d*'s and getting more of a spin into the slogan' (45). If the description of the woman's aspect has been read as an example of Belacqua 'recoil[ing] from her "feminist" footwear',[35] it can also be seen as reconsidering the discussion about Dante's linguistic innovation inaugurated in 'Dante...Bruno.Vico..Joyce'.

The features of this 'gentlewoman of the people' are transfigured and stylised in 'Ding-Dong', reduced to a very Dantean 'null'; they are 'only luminous, impassive and secure, petrified in radiance, or words to that effect, for the reader is requested to take notice that this sweet style is Belacqua's' (45). 'Petrified' has been read as allusion to Dante's 'rime petrose', while the radiance may well refer to the many episodes in which Beatrice is associated with the radiance of eternal light.[36] The text waltzes with both Dante's *vulgare illustre* and with his 'dolce stil novo', mocked as the 'sweet noo style' in 'Home Olga' and as 'sweet, facile, and plain' style in the unpublished short story 'Echo's Bones' (12). The passage in 'Ding-Dong' when Dante's style is evoked is declared to be simultaneously the most inauthentic and the most authentic: the narrator claims to produce a Dantean style ('only luminous, impassive and secure, petrified in radiance') and yet disavows it by saying that the words uttered were probably different, since they belonged to Belacqua. The authenticity of the text which pretends to reproduce Belacqua's 'sweet style' (itself a mockery of Dante's style) is questioned by the presence of a Dantean style, thus intertextually duplicating the contradictory positions occupied by the narrator.

The final 'desublimation' of Dante is represented by the reversed structural analogy.[37] After having emerged from the underground convenience, Belacqua, following his alleged 'strong weakness for oxymoron', 'moves on' from his 'moving pause' and crosses the river. But if Dante's trajectory can be roughly described as emerging from the underground of Hell, spiralling uphill to meet Beatrice (a 'female dog of a pixy with her tiresome Ptolemy', who at last goes away with Belacqua's sixpence) and finally crossing the Lethe to be 'puro e disposto a salir le stelle' (pure and ready to rise to the stars') (*Purg.* XXXIII, 145), Belacqua goes 'beyond the river' to reach Railway Street, a part of town famous for prostitution: 'Beatrice lurks in every brothel.'[38]

The structural significance of Dante continues in 'A Wet Night', one of the two stories of *More Pricks Than Kicks* which directly derives from *Dream*. As briefly mentioned above, this story begins in a way very similar to the previous one. Belacqua once again 'emerges' from the 'hot bowels of McLoughlin's' (47) and is confronted with the three colours of the Bovril sign. He is stuck in an eternal *da capo*, in which the three theological virtues are reduced to 'Doubt, Despair, and Scrounging'.

Dante is recalled twice in 'A Wet Night': once is during the conversation between the Parabimbi and the Man of Law at the Frica's party, in which he is the author of the *Divine Comedy* who died in Ravenna, which I have briefly discussed in relation to *Dream*. Another is the (mis)quotation of *Inferno* V, 122, a canto which is a commonplace in the history of the reception of the *Comedy*.[39] After the Alba has entered the Frica's party sporting her 'scarlet gown', reminiscent of Beatrice's gown of the colour of the living flame, 'The Gael, the native speaker, a space-writer and the violist d'amore got together as though by magic' (68). After a while Larry asks:

> 'You don't happen to know' he said finally 'does she?'
> 'They all do' said the violist d'amore.
> 'Like hell they do' groaned the Gael, *ricordandosi del tempo felice*. (69)

The explicit reference to *Inferno* V leads the reader to connect the Gael's sexually allusive answer to Francesca da Rimini's illicit love story on which she still looks back with regret and anguish:

> E quella a me: 'Nessun maggior dolore
> che ricordarsi del tempo felice
> ne la miseria; e ciò sa 'l tuo dottore. (*Inf.* V, 121–123)

> And she to me: 'There is no greater sorrow than to recall, in wretchedness, the happy time; and this your teacher knows.[40]

Anthony Farrow has remarked that Dante is here 'trivialised and reduced'; such a reading, which needs to posit Dante's greatness as a *datum*, highlights how this specific Dante diverges from that of 'Dante and the Lobster' or from that of 'Ding-Dong'.[41] If in those stories Dante, like the illustrious vernacular, is the hinge (*cardine*) around which the whole story revolved, linguistically and thematically, here *Inferno* V is a visibly (italicised) and foreign (Italian) intrusion. Such 'groan' indicates that the 'like' in the phrase 'like hell they do' creates a relationship between *Inferno* V and 'A Wet Night', but, rather than bridging the two texts, it increases their distance like Hell.

The following story, 'Love and Lethe', does not present Dantean intertexts, although the title recalls the Lethe crossed by Dante in *Purgatorio* XXXI and the river crossed by Belacqua in 'Ding-Dong'. In 'Walking Out' a few terms conjure up a shadow of Dante; so Belacqua's 'Kerry Blue bitch sat on the emerald floor'. The colour emerald echoes not only the Smeraldina-Rima and the emerald dressed 'Faith' reduced to a 'fungus of hopeless green' in the Bovril sign but also the valley of the princes where Sordello leads Dante and Virgil.[42] Another echo of the *Purgatorio* is 'the way they screwed uphill' (109), that is, Lucy and 'her partner in the life's journey' (108).[43]

The intratextual links are stronger in 'What a Misfortune', in which the opening is thematically related to the previous story, as indicated by the note referring to 'Walking Out'. The second paragraph refers to 'Dante and the Lobster':

> He could produce no tears on his own account ..., his small stock of *pity* being devoted entirely to the *living*, by which is not meant this or that particular unfortunate, but the nameless multitude of the current *quick*, life, we dare almost say, in the abstract. This impersonal *pity* was *damned* in many quarters as an intolerable supererogation and in some few as a positive sin against God and Society. (114; emphasis mine)

The play with 'pity' and 'quick' is not only an intratextual allusion but also an intertextual one; 'Dante and the Lobster' serves as a medium to refer back to *Inferno* XX:

> Se Dio ti lasci, lettor, prender frutto
> di tua lezione, or pensa per te stesso
> com'io potea tener lo viso asciutto,
> quando la nostra immagine di presso
> vidi sì torta, che 'l pianto de li occhi
> le natiche bagnava per lo fesso.
> Certo io piangea, poggiato a un de' rocchi,
> del duro scoglio, sì che la mia scorta
> mi disse: 'Ancor se' tu de li altri sciocchi?
> Qui vive la pietà quand'è ben morta;
> chi è più scellerato che colui
> che al giudicio divin passion comporta? (*Inf.* XX, 19–30)

> Reader, so God grant you to take profit of your reading, think now for yourself how I could keep my cheeks dry when near at hand I saw our image so contorted that the tears from the eyes bathed the buttocks at the cleft. Truly I wept, leaning on one of the rocks of the hard crag, so that my guide said to me: 'Are you even yet among the other fools? Here pity lives when it is altogether dead. Who is more impious than he who sorrows at God's judgement?

The 'many quarters' in which the sin is damned as a supererogation can be explained as referring to the 'reader', or better to a multitude of them, invoked by Dante to understand how it was not possible for him to restrain his tears; 'some few' can be interpreted as referring to Virgil. The 'many quarters' 'damn' as 'supererogation' the 'impersonal pity' demonstrated by Dante the pilgrim by crying, while Virgil, belonging to 'some few', 'damns' it as a 'sin against God and Society'. Virgil accuses Dante of being like the other fools ('sin against Society') and of contesting God's judgement ('sin against God'). The verb 'to damn' recalls Hell; Virgil can 'damn' pity in Hell as a sin, and therefore induces Dante to 'move on' from his present false conceptions and harmonise with God's judgement. The reader has the power to 'damn' Dante's attitude, of not following his textual invocation. In other words, this excerpt from *Comedy* constructs its implied reader through an apostrophe which leads him to make the same mistake Dante the pilgrim is making, so that Virgil's harsh rebuke works not only against Dante but also against the implied reader. If Dante the character wishes to share his pity, Dante the 'difficult poet' chastises such an attitude. And yet, Belacqua's 'impersonal pity' is not towards the dead but towards the 'undead', the nameless multitude not of the damned souls but of the 'current quick'. Furthermore, Belacqua's impersonal pity is perceived by the 'public' as 'callousness in respect of this or that wretched individual' but is said to have very great 'private advantages' (115). Dante's misdirected pity is 'damned' and killed off by Virgil, while Belacqua's apparently misdirected pity is damned in many quarters, but it is not counterbalanced by a more appropriate form of pity: as 'Text' puts it, 'pity is quick with death'.[44]

The references to Dante in 'What a Misfortune' are both to the *Comedy* and to other texts by Beckett; the previous example indicates the way in which Dante provides a structural link between this story and 'Dante and the Lobster'. This link is further enhanced by Thelma's surname 'bboggs', which connects her to the Belacqua of 'Dante and the Lobster', 'bogged and bored' and that of 'Ding-Dong', 'bogged in indolence'. Further references to Dante point to both *Dream* and the poem 'Text', as when the narrator incidentally describes the elder daughter of the bboggs family, Una, as somebody for whom 'an ape had already been set aside in hell' (118). The sentence alludes to *Inferno* XXXIII, in which Frate Alberigo dei Manfredi, confined to the ice of Cocytus, in the third zone of the ninth circle of Malebolge, explains to a sceptical Dante how both he and Branca Doria seem to be still living while in fact their souls are already in Hell:

> 'Io credo', diss'io lui, 'che tu m'inganni;
> ché Branca Doria non morì unquanche,
> e mangia e bee e dorme e veste panni'.
> 'Nel fosso sù', diss'el, 'de' Malebranche,
> là dove bolle la tenace pece,
> non era ancora giunto Michele Zanche,
> che questi lasciò il diavolo in sua vece
> nel corpo suo (*Inf.* XXXIII, 140–147)

'I believe you are deceiving me,' I said to him, 'for Branca d'Oria is not dead yet and eats and drinks and sleeps and puts on clothes.' 'In the ditch of Malebranche above,' he said, 'where the sticky pitch is boiling, Michel Zanche had not yet arrived when this one left a devil in his stead in his own body'

Barolini accounts for this Dantean strategy as follows:

> Alberigo ... persuade[s] the pilgrim to believe him ... by appealing to 'reality', namely the fiction to which he belongs. His reply is one of the most remarkable intratextual moments of the *Commedia*, as the text buttresses the text, the fiction supports the fiction ... By working relentlessly to situate us within his *speculum*, he seeks to reorient us: if we see things from inside, from within the *Commedia*'s possible world, then perhaps we will not notice that the laws that govern this ultimately textual universe are in fact less God's laws than his own.[45]

Una is placed in the narrative in the category of those damned who betrayed their family members, through a veiled reference to a typical Dantean textual strategy. The *Comedy* emphasises the idea that the person's real life is where his/her soul is, namely in Hell; however, as Barolini points out, it is through a double fictional move that this separation between an idea of fiction and one of reality is produced by a text which therefore constructs itself as real. 'What a Misfortune' plays with the idea of the double privileging of the textual existence of Una as a character, as it is her 'ape' which had already been set aside in Hell. If Una, whose name indicates the 'simplicissima quantitas' of the one (*unum*), lives in a double dimension which questions her originality, Mrs bboggs is described as 'almost as non-partisan as Pope Celestine the fifth. Dante would probably have disliked her on this account' (126). The reference is to the well-known passage of *Inferno* III, 60, where Dante claims:

> Poscia ch'io v'ebbi alcun riconosciuto
> vidi e conobbi l'ombra di colui
> che fece per viltade il gran rifiuto. (*Inf.* III, 58–60)

After I had recognized some among them, I saw and knew the shade of
him who from cowardice made the great refusal.

Generations of commentators have identified this unnamed shadow with Pope Celestine V, who abdicated in favour of Boniface VIII. However, Dante duplicates the paradox of Antehell, not naming the souls that abide there, and therefore denying them the fame that his own poem would have granted them. Indeed, he forces those shadows to live 'senza infamia e senza lodo' (without infamy and without praise), leaving the commentators to decide about their identity. The Beckett text dispels such textual ambiguity referring directly to Celestine V; however, a less direct reference to the same infernal canto can be found in the poem 'Text', already mentioned above:

> We are proud of our pain
> our life was not blind.
> Worms breed in their red tears
> as they slouch unnamed
> scorned by the black ferry
> despairing of death
> who shall not scour in swift joy
> the bright hill's girdle
> nor tremble with the dark pride of torture
> and the bitter dignity of an ingenious damnation.

The narrator's remark on Dante's hypothetical judgement on Mrs bboggs links to *Inferno* III as produced in 'Text'.[46] In 'Text', Canto III is at once parodied – now the damned are 'proud' of their pain and claim that their life was not blind – and fashioned as an acknowledgement of the 'ingenious' nature of Dante's system of damnation, to which this particular ingenious denial of greater torments belongs.[47] A comparison with Dante's lines can aptly show the precision of the Beckett allusions:

> Ed elli a me: 'Questo misero modo
> tegnon l'anime triste di coloro
> che vissero sanza 'nfamia e sanza lodo.
> ...
> Caccianli i cieli per non esser men belli,
> né lo profondo inferno li riceve,
> ch'alcuna gloria i rei avrebber d'elli'.
> ...
> Questi non hanno speranza di morte,
> e la lor cieca vita è tanto bassa,
> che 'nvidïosi son d'ogne altra sorte.
> Fama di loro il mondo esser non lassa;
> misericordia e giustizia li sdegna:
> non ragioniam di lor, ma guarda e passa'.
> ...
> Questi sciagurati, che mai non fur vivi,
> erano ignudi e stimolati molto
> da mosconi e da vespe ch'eran ivi.
> Elle rigavan lor di sangue il volto,
> che, mischiato di lagrime, a' lor piedi
> da fastidiosi vermi era ricolto.
> (*Inf.* III, 34–36; 40–42; 46–51; 64–69)

And he to me, 'Such is the miserable condition of the sorry souls of those who lived without infamy and without praise ... The heavens drive them out, so as not to be less beautiful; and deep Hell does not receive them, lest the wicked have some glory over them.' ... These have no hope of death, and their blind life is so abject that they are envious of every other lot. The world does not suffer that report of them shall live. Mercy and justice disdain them, Let us not speak of them, but look, and pass on ... These wretches, who never were alive, were naked and were much stung by gadflies and wasps there, which were streaking their faces with blood that mingled with their tears and was gathered by loathsome worms at their feet.

Dante reappears in 'What a Misfortune' in an intratextual and intertextual reference: *Dream*'s 'Turned he hath the audacious soul, turned and turned again, on back, sides and belly, like little Miss Florence on the tick while Virgil and Sordello – yet all this was very sore' (72) mirrors 'the forces in his [Belacqua's] mind would not resolve, he had tossed and turned like the Florence of Sordello, and found all postures painful' (136).

The precious vocabulary of *Dream* has become more accessible in *More Pricks Than Kicks*, in which the personification of Florence is abandoned. Both passages, however, work as juxtapositions of texts constructed as 'external', as 'margaritas' which stand out. The passage on the Florence of Sordello creates a relationship between these two texts which is amplified by the way in which 'What a Misfortune' mentions *Dream* as Walter Draffin's work in progress. Draffin is an 'Italianate Irishman' whose '*Dream of Fair to Middling Women* [has been] held up in the *limae labor stage* for the past ten or fifteen years' (143). The construction of the author through the reification of the book which had already been pursued in *Dream* here reaches a parodic dimension, amplified by the self-advertising 'if ... it ever reaches the public, and Walter says it is bound to, we ought all be sure to get it and have a look at it anyway' (144).

Dante connects 'What a Misfortune' with 'Dante and the Lobster', *Dream*, and 'Text'; in 'Draff' Dante is again a mediated presence, since it intratextually refers to the contemporary poem 'Malacoda', in which the same imagery borrowed from Malebolge is adopted. Lawrence Harvey has described in detail the correspondences between the poem and *Inferno* XXI, the canto in which Dante and Virgil meet the ten devils of Malebranche. The poem presents a tripartite structure; it begins with 'thrice he came' and it is subdivided according to the three actions performed by Malacoda, 'to measure', 'to coffin', and 'to cover'. 'Malacoda' and 'Scarmilion' are named; Malacoda is also described as 'this malebranca knee-deep in the lilies'; line 105 of canto XXI, 'posa posa Scarmiglione', is translated in Beckett as 'stay Scarmilion stay stay', and the bawdy Dantean 'ed elli avea del cul fatto trombetta' (and he had made a trumpet of his arse) becomes the less noisy Beckettian 'Malacoda for all the expert awe that felts his perineum mutes his signal / sighing up through the heavy air' and 'allow me hold your sulphur'.[48]

Malacoda reappears in 'Draff' as a 'fat drab demon', Nick Malacoda, who, ironically, cannot muffle 'his uproarious endeavour not to intrude on the gravel' while approaching the house to measure Belacqua's body. As in the poem 'Malacoda', Nick Malacoda (who, like 'blissful Beatrice', sports a tautological name) 'measures, coffins, and covers' (187) Belacqua's body. Endowed with the agility characteristic of the infernal demons, he can be observed 'springing up the stairs with a tape in his black claws' (178) while the Smeraldina does not manage to prevent him from doing his job. The hearse of 'Malacoda & Co.' is 'black as Ulysses's cruiser' (184), and his 'assistant ungulata', the 'Scarmilion' of the poem, here becomes his driver 'Scarmiglione', whom Hairy exhorts to 'temper full speed' in a reminiscence of Malacoda's 'stay Scarmilion stay stay'. 'All aboard all souls / half-mast aye aye / nay' of 'Malacoda' remains unaltered in 'Draff'; only the punctuation is changed. The line possibly alludes to Charon, the boatman of *Inferno* III who transports the soul across the Acheron into Hell.

There are a few more Dantean echoes in the story; Belacqua is said to have 'often looked forward to meeting the girls, Lucy especially, hallowed and transfigured beyond the veil' (181). Although generic, the allusion could be to Beatrice who shows her 'countenance' without the veil at the end of *Purgatorio* XXXI.

Dante is alluded to once more in 'Draff', in a note which supposedly should clarify which part of Smeraldina died with Belacqua but which ironically multiplies the complex relationships between surface and depth and presence and absence established by the text:

> She had definitely ceased to exist in that particular part which Belacqua had been at such pains to isolate, the public part so cruelly made private for his convenience, her last clandestine aspect* reduced to a radiograph and exploited to ginger his secret occasions.
>
> * What a competent poet once called the *bella menzogna*. (187; the 1974 Picador edition reads 'least clandestine')

The footnote is part of those 'marginalia' which enjoy such an unstable position in Beckett's texts. The Smeraldina's 'clandestine aspect' situated in the body of the text should be brought to the surface, revealed, by the note at the foot of the page. The marginal note should be able to explicate the central point, the obscurity of which works as a promise of clarity. Yet, such clandestine aspect is the competent poet's – or 'the only poet' who gives the title to the uncollected poem 'From the Only Poet to a Shining Whore' – 'bella menzogna' (beautiful lie) as discussed in *Convivio*, II, I, i.[49]

Belacqua, the 'defunct', could be 'incorporated in the daily ellipses of Capper Quin without him having to face the risk of exposure.' The absence indicated by the term 'defunct' is played against the materiality of the body which, however, is contrasted with the lack indicated by these regular (daily) ellipses. Furthermore, this paradoxical operation that juxtaposes presence and absence is paralleled by the relationship between surface and depth in so far as Capper Quin does not have to *face* the risk of *exposure*. So if Belacqua's spiritual/corporeal absence is not complete ('[he] was not wholly dead, but merely mutilated'), Smeraldina 'has suffered the inverse change'. She 'has ceased to exist' in her 'public part so cruelly made private for his [Belacqua's] convenience, her last clandestine aspect reduced to a radiograph and exploited to ginger his secret occasions'. With Belacqua's death the Smeraldina dies in that public part which has been made private; if the privatisation of the public seems to work 'cruelly' in favour of the man in the first part of the sentence, the relationship is turned upside down in the second part. Her last clandestine aspect, the privatisation of which now seems cherished rather than deplored, has been transformed into a 'radiograph', something which transforms the invisible into the visible and yet – in so far as it *exposes* – can titillate Belacqua's *secret* occasions. This 'last clandestine aspect' is therefore called, in borrowed words, 'bella menzogna'. In the *Convivio* Dante comments on the fourfold meanings of his *canzoni*, among which is 'Voi ch'intendendo' quoted by Beckett in *Proust*, and characterises the allegorical sense as 'veritade ascosa sotto bella menzogna' (truth hidden under a beautiful lie). The 'beautiful lie' is the ornate style, and allegory is a special kind of truth, which is not simply visible but is hidden under a beautiful lie. According to Dante's definition, the 'literal sense' is therefore not simply a surface but part of a series of layers. What is visible and beautiful can be a lie, while allegory, to be discovered under such a stratum, is the truth. The idea of 'bella menzogna' is related in Dante to the opposition between poetry and theology and is part of what I have briefly discussed in Chapter 1 as the justification of using the scriptural fourfold method to analyse his own secular poetry. In the context of 'Draff', however, this formulation operates within a system that questions the relationship between surface and depth and centre and margin. Just as the Smeraldina's clandestine aspect is a radiograph, it is also a 'bella menzogna', a lie which promises a truth, a surface which promises a depth and yet cannot operate 'simply' as surface, a literalness which also points to something else. The marginality of this ironically illuminating footnote questions the relationship between marginality and centrality, surface and depth, body and spirit.

Dante's presence and absence in *More Pricks Than Kicks* is linked to the notion of death and absence, from the lobster dinner to Una bboggs and the oxymoronic static circularity of the Bovril sign. The preoccupation with death and absence is mirrored at structural level by 'Echo's Bones', a story which is absent from the published volume and which, like several other texts by both Beckett and Dante, 'turns the question of place into the question of writing'.[50] 'Echo's Bones' was meant to be the last story of the volume, if the publisher – after having asked Beckett for one more story to add to the collection – had not turned it down.[51] 'Draff' is based on the absence of dead Belacqua; 'Echo's Bones' pushes the matter further, narrating Belacqua's afterlife: he is 'back at his old games' although he has departed 'from among the quick' (1).[52] Belacqua does not share the posture with Dante's Belacqua or with the *Dream* Belacqua any more, he sits instead 'bent double on a fence' (1), although, when he 'wrap[s] his tights', he can still feel that 'that is [his] position' (12). Many phrases and references to *Dream* are scattered throughout the text, which, being a story of Belacqua's afterlife, is in itself an allusion to the conceptual basis of the *Comedy*, while also contributing to the paradoxically 'bogged' backwards-and-forwards oscillation between incorporation and excorporation discussed in relation to 'Draff'.[53] The narrating voice opens the story commenting: 'The dead die hard' and paradoxically tries to confer truth value to the statement through the self-reflexive comment: 'This is a true saying', which, however, he immediately modifies: 'At least it can be truly said of Belacqua' (1). The artifice is here exposed of trying to be credible when narrating about the unknown, which in Dante is explored through an infinite gamut of narrative devices. The 'true saying' and the adjective 'truly' are deprived of their truth value by the provocative artificiality of the story, which seems to repeat in an 'endless da capo' the structure of *More Pricks Than Kicks*. The text foregrounds itself as, in Belacqua's words, 'a piece of rhetoric', a definition reinforced by the narrator's claim 'he is right'. Although the shadow of a plot is still present in the story, the obscurely allusive nature of its language and its structure are brought to the fore. The structure parodically involves 'three scenes' described as 'the first, the central and the last', an assertion which epitomises the evasive and parodic character of the story. The appearance of Zaborovna echoes the appearance of Beatrice in Dante, and Zaborovna's comment on her use of 'we' suggests such a correspondence: 'and we, why little we is just an impersonal usage, the Tuscan reflexive without more' (2). The comparison between Belacqua's thought which 'burst[s] from his brain as a phosphate from the kidney' recalls once again the emended Dantean bawdiness of 'Malacoda' and 'Draff'; there are no other linguistic references to Dante. However, the 'visions', the appearances of monsters, the allegorical and stylised description of the two parodic processions, allude to Dantean *loci* in the *Comedy*.[54]

Dante's narration of the afterlife world is based on the creation of a 'ver c'ha faccia di menzogna' (a truth that has the face of a lie); by situating art (the beautiful lie) within a prophetic framework (witnessing afterlife) Dante constructs the *Comedy*'s realism.[55] Beckett's narration of Belacqua's afterlife moves in the opposite direction: the rhetorical quality of the text is constantly exposed, the impossibility of guaranteeing any truth is repeated over and over again, and the intertextual overdetermination works as a signal pointing outside the text but failing to establish a larger system in which to retrieve a full meaning. In 'Echo's Bones' the act of narrating an afterlife is not different from that of narrating a life.

In *More Pricks Than Kicks* Dante has a number of functions, establishing a linguistic and spatial framework for 'Dante and the Lobster' and 'Ding-Dong', working as a foreign intrusion in 'A Wet Night' and 'What a Misfortune', questioning progression and presence in 'Draff' and 'Echo's Bones', and most significantly, acting overall as one of the main links among the short stories. In *More Pricks Than Kicks* Dante echoes passages in *Dream* and in many Beckett poems of the time, rather than referring only to the *Comedy*. *More Pricks Than Kicks* is an early example of what occurs to the whole Beckett canon: inter- and intratextual references to Dante interconnect Beckett texts and constitute them into the Beckett *oeuvre*.

Notes

1. Samuel Beckett, *More Pricks Than Kicks* (New York: Grove Weidenfeld, 1972). Subsequent references to this edition are given in the text. For a dating of the short stories see John Pilling, *Beckett Before Godot* (Cambridge: Cambridge University Press, 1997), pp. 93–113.
2. Pilling, *Beckett Before Godot*, p. 106.
3. Raymond Federman and John Fletcher, *Samuel Beckett: His Works and His Critics* (Berkeley: University of California Press, 1970), p. 5.
4. H. Porter Abbott, *Beckett Writing Beckett: The Author in the Autograph* (Ithaca: Cornell University Press, 1996), p. 20.
5. Andrew Renton, '"He all but said ..."': evasion and referral in the later prose and drama of Samuel Beckett', Ph.D. thesis, University of Reading, 1989, p. 3.
6. Anthony Farrow, *Early Beckett: Art and Allusion in* More Pricks Than Kicks *and* Murphy (Troy, NJ: The Whitston Publishing Company, 1991).
7. Pilling, *Beckett Before Godot*, pp. 101–102.
8. Peter Boxall, 'Negative geography: fictional space in Beckett's prose', Ph.D. thesis, University of Sussex, 1996, p. 40.
9. Peter Boxall argues that the expression recalls the damned 'fitti nel limo' of *Inf.* VII, 121; Boxall, 'Negative geography', p. 40. For a discussion of the presence of such words in the '*Dream*' notebook see Daniela Caselli, '"The Florentia edition in the ignoble Salani collection": a textual comparison', *Journal of Beckett Studies*, 9:2 (2001), 1–20, and John Pilling, *Beckett's 'Dream' Notebook* (Reading: Beckett International Foundation, 1999), p. 45.
10. Lawrence Harvey records the etymological redundancy of the adjective: Beatrice means 'blissful'. Lawrence Harvey, *Samuel Beckett: Poet and Critic* (Princeton: Princeton University Press, 1970), p. 106, note 50. The same redundancy is present in the Pre-Raphaelites' reinvention of Beatrice, and especially in Dante Gabriel Rossetti's *Beata Beatrix*.
11. Vittorio Sermonti argues that Beatrice's 'proof' is not an orthodox Scholastic explanation and briefly sketches the multi-faceted Scholastic cosmological theories in his *Il Paradiso di Dante* (Milan: Rizzoli, 1993), p. 36.
12. A similar metaphor occurs in *Purgatorio* I, 1–3.
13. Samuel Beckett, 'Intercessions by Denis Devlin', in Ruby Cohn (ed.), *Disjecta: Miscellaneous Writings and a Dramatic Fragment* (New York: Grove Press, 1984), pp. 91–94, p. 94.
14. In *Paradiso* II, 49–51, Dante mentions the popular belief about the nature of the spots on the moon in his question to Beatrice regarding the true nature of the spots: 'Ma

ditemi: che son li segni bui / di questo corpo, che là giuso in terra / fan di Cain favoleggiare altrui?' (But tell me, what are the dusky marks of this body which there below on earth cause folk to tell the tale of Cain?).

15 Lawrence Harvey establishes a connection between the 'before morning' of the poem and the time of the beginning of Dante's ascent to the mount Purgatory. Harvey, *Samuel Beckett*, p. 102. For a discussion of this poem see also Katherine Travers Gross, 'In other words: Samuel Beckett's art of poetry', Ph.D. thesis, Columbia University, 1970, pp. 184–205.

16 Samuel Beckett, 'Text', *The European Caravan: An Anthology of the New Spirit in European Literature* (New York: Brewer, Warren, and Putnam, 1931), pp. 478–480; reprinted in *The New Review*, 1:4 (Winter 1931–32), 338–339. Lawrence Harvey extensively discusses the references to Dante in 'Text'; Harvey, *Samuel Beckett*, pp. 287–296. Francesca Del Moro draws attention to the allusions to Tiresias via *Inferno* XX, 40–45 and Ovid's *Metamorphoses* and to the 'sad maimed shades' of *Inferno* XXIX, 6. Francesca Del Moro, '"The Divine Florentine": Dante nell'opera di Samuel Beckett', dissertation, University of Pisa (Italy), 1996, pp. 44–45.

17 In the 'Hades' section of Joyce's *Ulysses*, Leopold Bloom calls cheese 'corpse of milk'. James Joyce, *Ulysses* (Harmondsworth: Penguin, 1986), p. 116. The cadaverous gorgonzola cheese is connected to a similar moral preoccupation in Beckett's poem 'Casket of Pralinen for the Daughter of a Dissipated Mandarin': 'so all's well with the gorgonzola cheese of human kindness'. Beckett, *The European Caravan*, pp. 477–478.

18 Disparaging references to Italian nineteenth-century literature are made in the story when the Italian lesson is approaching. Belacqua is disgusted by Manzoni's poem devoted to Napoleon, *Il cinque maggio*, and the text incorporates a proverb which can be found verbatim in the *'Dream'* notebook and which can be roughly translated as 'Napoleone, that second-rate person, makes love to little Jackie'. Silvio Pellico gets his share of insults, together with Carducci, who in the *This Quarter* version of the story is described as an 'intolerable old bitch'. *This Quarter* (December 1932), 222–236, 230. In an early student essay which compares Carducci's poetry to D'Annunzio's 'sick' literature Beckett writes of Carducci: 'Ispira la sua freschezza!' (His freshness is inspiring!), TCD MS 10965a, fol. 3. This is not consistent with what is said in other student notes on Carducci, who is quoted saying 'Sono tentato di far due altre poesie su Assisi e San Francesco' (I am tempted to make other two poems on Assisi and Saint Francis). To this Beckett adds: 'No-one but a verse manufacturer could express himself like that. Imagine Leopardi being "tempted" to write poetry! Or Shelley writing for Italy: "I'd rather like to write a poem about the Lombard plain but I can't think of a rhyme for 'Euganean'". Carducci, with all his enormous & complicated metres, was not a poet. His work is stamped with a desperate subconscious effort.' TCD MS 10965, fol. 30.

19 Pilling, *Beckett Before Godot*, p. 104.

20 Kelly Anspaugh, '"Faith, hope, and – what was it?": Beckett reading Joyce reading Dante', *Journal of Beckett Studies*, 5:1–2 (Autumn 1995 and Spring 1996), 19–38.

21 Farrow, *Early Beckett*, p. 95.

22 See also 'Sanies I' where 'Portrane' occurs; Harvey, *Samuel Beckett*, p. 139.

23 John Pilling, *Beckett's 'Dream' Notebook*, p. 45 and Daniela Caselli, '"The Florentia edition"'.

24 A reference to Manto can be found in 'Text': 'Manto me dear / an iced sherbet and me blood's a solid.'

25 Among these was Pompeo Venturi, who, in 1732 commenting on *Purg.* IV, 108, writes '*tra esse le ginocchia. Mirabil pittura di tutte le proprietà della persona, degli atti, delle parole di un pigro, che ha gli spiriti vitali impaludati nella pinguedine*' (*between them his knees*. Wonderful picture of all the personal characteristics, acts, and words of a lazy person, who has his vital spirits bogged in fatness/indolence); Luigi Portirelli will, in 1804, quote Venturi. See *La Divina Commedia di Dante Alighieri col commento di Pompeo Venturi* (Florence: Ciardetti, 1821 reprint) and *La Divina Commedia di Dante Alighieri illustrata di note da Luigi Portirelli* (Milan: Tipografia dei classici italiani, 1804–5). For a further discussion see Caselli, '"The Florentia edition"'.
26 'Is there any reason why that terrible materiality of the word surface should not be capable of being dissolved, like for example the sound surface, torn by enormous [black] pauses, of Beethoven's seventh Symphony, so that through whole pages we can perceive nothing but a path of sounds suspended in giddy heights, linking unfathomable abysses of silence?' Samuel Beckett, 'Letter to Axel Kaun', in Cohn (ed.), *Disjecta*, p. 53.
27 Farrow, *Early Beckett*, p. 103.
28 Pilling, *Beckett Before Godot*, p. 103.
29 Harvey, *Samuel Beckett*, p. 48, note 21.
30 The third virtue is here called love, although in Dante it is 'carità', from the Latin *caritas*, and semantically quite close to the piety discussed at length in 'Dante and the Lobster'.
31 Anspaugh, '"Faith, hope, and – what was it?"', 23.
32 Farrow, *Early Beckett*, p. 204, and Anspaugh, '"Faith, hope, and – what was it?"', 23–24 and 27–28.
33 Paul Gleason links the third chapter of the *Vita Nuova* to Joyce's *A Portrait of the Artist as a Young Man* in his article 'Dante, Joyce, Beckett and the use of memory in the process of literary creation', *Joyce Studies Annual*, 10 (Summer 1999), 104–142, 119.
34 Giovanni Boccaccio, *Trattatello in laude di Dante*, in Pier Giorgio Ricci (ed.), *Tutte le opere di Giovanni Boccaccio*, Vittore Branca (ed.), vol. III (Milan: Mondadori, 1974), pp. 423–538.
35 Mary Bryden, *Women in Samuel Beckett's Prose and Drama* (Basingstoke: Macmillan, 1993), p. 37. See also her *Beckett and the Idea of God* (New York: St Martin's Press, 1998), pp. 149–157.
36 Harvey, *Samuel Beckett*, p. 322. See, for instance, *Purg.* XXXI, 139.
37 Anspaugh, '"Faith, hope, and – what was it?"', 24.
38 Ptolemy is the Greek astronomer, mathematician, and geographer (100–178); however, the term might also refer to Tolomea, the last circle of Hell mentioned in *Proust*, p. 40. Beckett, *Dream*, p. 102; but see also 'Sanies II', in which 'Dante and blissful Beatrice are there / prior to the Vita Nuova'.
39 Lucia Boldrini demonstrates that this canto, together with *Inf.* XXXI, is one of the most translated into English, while also being Joyce's favourite. Lucia Boldrini, *Joyce, Dante, and the Poetics of Literary Relations: Language and Meaning in* Finnegans Wake (Cambridge: Cambridge University Press, 2001), pp. 142 and 206, note 7. *Inferno* V, 40–48, in which 'the souls of the lustful are compared to wheeling flocks of sterlings and to cranes chanting their lay', is present in the poem 'Hell Crane to Sterling'. Federman and Fletcher, *Samuel Beckett*, p. 10. A quotation from Dante's *De Monarchia*, II, i provides the title for the poem 'Yoke of Liberty', *The European Caravan*, p. 480; see Harvey, *Samuel Beckett*, p. 312, note 136. Dante is referred to also in 'Enueg I', where the line 'its secret things' has been identified by Harvey as coming from Dante's 'le secrete cose', *Inferno* III, 21.
40 Francesca Del Moro points out that the phrase 'memories of past felicities' appears in *All Strange Away* (London: Calder, 1979), p. 56. Del Moro, '"The Divine Florentine"', p. 174.

41 Farrow, *Early Beckett*, p. 110.
42 'Oro e argento fine, cocco e biacca, / indaco, legno lucido e sereno, / fresco smeraldo in l'ora che si fiacca' (Gold and fine silver, cochineal and white lead, Indian wood bright and clear, fresh emerald at the moment it is split) (*Purg.* VII, 73–75).
43 In 'Walking Out' the 'motive of voyeurism and punishment is clearly indebted to the Phoenix Park incident in *Finnegans Wake*, and if the *Wake* coins "Waterloo" as a term of reference for the girls' pee in the park, we should remember that Belacqua ... can also be "etymologized" in perfect Wakeian fashion into "pretty water"'. Daniel Katz, *Saying I No More: Subjectivity and Consciousness in the Prose of Samuel Beckett* (Evanston, IL: Northwestern University Press, 1999), p. 35.
44 'Text' also refers to *Inf.* XX in the lines 'no blade has smoothed the forrowed cheeks / that my tears corrode'. In *All That Fall*, Mr Rooney says: 'Like Dante's damned, with their faces arsy-versy. Our tears will water our bottoms', *Collected Shorter Plays of Samuel Beckett* (London: Faber & Faber, 1984), p. 31. The image recurs also in *Watt*, pp. 164–169, and in *Mercier and Camier*, p. 11. In *Mercier and Camier* it is also said: 'The tears flowed, overflowed, all down the furrowed cheeks and vanished in the beard' (32). In *The Unnamable* we read: 'tears stream down my cheeks from my unblinking eyes', and 'For I feel my tears coursing over my chest, my sides, all down my back.' *The Beckett Trilogy: Molloy, Malone Dies, The Unnamable* (London: Picador, 1979), pp. 269 and 279, respectively.
45 Teodolinda Barolini, *The Undivine Comedy: Detheologizing Dante* (Princeton: Princeton University Press, 1992), pp. 95 and 98.
46 Samuel Beckett, *Eleuthéria* (Paris: Les Éditions de Minuit, 1995), p. 159. Francesca Del Moro, '"The Divine Florentine"', p. 86.
47 In *The Unnamable* there is also reference to an 'incomprehensible damnation', *The Beckett Trilogy*, p. 282. A brief note on Celestino V and a transcription of *Inferno* III appear in TCD MS 10966, fol. 3.
48 Harvey, *Samuel Beckett*, pp. 108–112.
49 The lines 'verità ascosa sotto bella mensogna' (sic) and 'il vero sotto il velame della parola oscuro' appear in TCD MS 10963a, fol. 2.
50 Bruno Clément, *L'Oeuvre sans qualités: rhétorique de Samuel Beckett*, préface de Michel Deguy (Paris: Éditions du Seuil, 1994), p. 366.
51 Beckett's letter to MacGreevy of 6 December 1933 reads: 'the last story, into which I had put all I know and plenty that I was better still aware of'. Quoted in Pilling, *Beckett Before Godot*, p. 98.
52 All the page references are to the typescript held at Dartmouth College Library.
53 The phrase 'sedendo et quiescendo' is included in the narrative, followed by the provoking remark 'Who said it?' (10); 'no smoking in the torture chamber' (1) is to be found in *Dream* (71); 'restored to the jungle' (1) recalls *Dream*'s 'restored to his heart' (122); 'Womb-tomb' (2) is also in *Dream* (123 and 175). The text presents, however, many more cross-references to the other stories of *More Pricks Than Kicks*.
54 The vision of the Alba; Lord Gall; Belacqua is transported on his back, like Dante and Virgil on Geryon's back; the griffin of Purgatory, which opens the procession in *Purgatorio* XXIX–XXXIII had been chastised by Beckett in *Proust*, which follows verbatim De Sanctis's condemnation of purely allegorical figures (60).
55 Barolini, *The Undivine Comedy*, p. 13.

4 Fatigue and disgust: *Murphy* and *Watt*

> Actually, [the Corrected Draft] turns out to be beautifully accurate when you once make the plunge and compel yourself to open your eyes in the limpid depths under its confused surface. (Vladimir Nabokov, *Pale Fire*, 1962)

In *Dream of Fair to Middling Women* and *More Pricks Than Kicks*, Dante is not only ever-present in the figure of Belacqua but is also a means to question notions of fictionality, teleological progression, and textual boundaries. In *Murphy* and *Watt*, Belacqua is no longer a character and Dante becomes an absence; an analysis of the ways in which Dante can *be* an absence in these texts will illustrate how the intertextual relationships between Beckett and Dante affect notions of authority, source, and influence.

Dante is kept out of sight: *Murphy* and the manuscripts

Dante as an absence in *Murphy* implies the adoption of the Foucauldian notion of author-function.[1] Comparing different texts by Beckett to find – or not to find – certain recurrent elements in them – namely, Dante – means to think of how the notion of authorial signature, which lies behind the idea of *oeuvre*, enables us to think of both a Dante and a 'non-Dante' in Beckett. Dante, one of the *auctoritates* of *Dream* and *More Pricks*, is visible in *Murphy* in the name of Belacqua, mentioned twice, and in a few other occurrences. Transforming an intertextual reference into an intratextual one, the name of Belacqua (now no longer a character) acts as the device which, inscribing the *auctoritas* of Dante, consolidates the continuity among Beckettian texts. The name of Belacqua confers visibility upon Dante's absence.

Critical tradition has made Dante's absence visible in *Murphy* not only through the name of Belacqua but also through sections of the 'Whoroscope' notebook, a manuscript which is by now effectively part of the Beckett canon, since the power of the author-function has expanded what is perceived as *oeuvre*; once the name 'Beckett' has become authoritative enough, anything attributed to Beckett becomes a text worth investigating.[2] Manuscripts and notebooks not only enlarge the Beckett canon but also help us to reconsider the function of unpublished writings within an *oeuvre* in which 'residua' play a major role.[3]

I will analyse portions of the 'Whoroscope' notebook to explore how Dante's absence is constructed in Beckett and the implications of regarding this absence as an invisible presence. There are many points of contact between the heavily fragmented notebook and *Murphy*. Structurally, the notebook presents thirty-four sections which stop to give way to a sequence of materials of a different kind; within the thirty-four sections, a discontinuity can be observed between section fifteen and sixteen.[4] The first fifteen sections of the notebook are ideas for a future text, addressed to an implied reader who is simultaneously constructed as a writer. Even though some of the preoccupations discussed in *Murphy* are present in these sections, it is difficult to establish a direct relationship. While the first fifteen sections narrate about a narration, section sixteen is a direct narration similar to the opening of *Murphy*. Although there is no internal consistency – for example sections seventeen and eighteen are notes that record material to be inserted – section sixteen marks a turning point from which a number of remarkable intratextual correspondences with *Murphy* become visible, as few examples from the text illustrate:

6
Journey through the 'careers' like D. & V. along the Purgatorial cornices, except that V. goes back, H goes out. Purgatorial atmosphere sustained throughout, by stress on Anaximander, individual existence as atonement.

7
H. mentor and squire, principle of knowledge and dissolution. Suggest it [ha]s life of its own by its inexplicable dis- and re appearances, changing bent, etc.

8
Choose 'careers' carefully, on some such principle as that of V.'s distribution of sins and punishments. But keep whole Dantesque analogy out of sight. [three lines completely erased].

10
Each 'cornice' is occupied by the physical failure which is the metaphysical achievement, in so far as it narrows the physical field (petites perceptions) & constitutes an increase in the apperceived.
Vocation the essence of *Purgatory*, de-function its negation.

14
Difficulty of dealing with 'careers', of which I know nothing, more apparent than real, since they are to be stated <u>via</u> X, whose impotence and bewilderment before the 'réel naïf' are precisely what releases the comic (and Cain from the darkness!).

16
Exordium I: X, naked, bound with silk scarves to a chair, ... hears endless chime of cuckoo ... and QUI PRO QUO, sees all the colours of the rainbow on floor beyond curtain. Telephone rings. He must answer, because if he does not the landlady will come etc. ...

The first sections of the 'Whoroscope' notebook (all crossed over in blue pencil) invoke and evoke Dantean structures that will not be 'explicitly illustrated' in the text yet to be written: the 'Dantesque analogy' will be 'kept out of sight'.

The comparison in the 'Whoroscope' notebook between X. and H. and Dante and Virgil generalises the motive of the couple to the point of converting it into a mechanism which would allow a narrative to be constructed. The comparison between the 'journey through the "careers"' of X. and H. and that of "D. and V." along the Purgatorial "cornices"' (6), transforms Purgatorial ascent into a journey through stages, which mediates some general and fundamental problems of literary architecture.[5] In the first fifteen sections of the notebook, the *Purgatorio* is one of the structural devices helping to give form to a project. Dante and Virgil are two poles, which exemplify a certain distribution of forces within the narrative; their spiral progression along terraces parallels in this text the journey in which 'individual existence' is 'atonement'. The *Purgatorio* shapes an idea of literary 'architectonics', just as it does in 'Dante...Bruno.Vico..Joyce', where a Purgatory which is 'conical, and therefore implies culmination' is not the mould for the casting of Joyce's world but the negative model against which Joyce's 'circular Purgatory' operates. In both 'Dante...Bruno.Vico..Joyce' and the notebook, the *Purgatorio* is a structural and taxonomic principle (as further confirmed by the presence of a scheme of 'Purgatorial Distribution' on the verso of folio 2).[6]

'Keep whole Dantesque analogy out of sight', in section eight, can be read as an indication of the way in which the first fifteen sections work, namely as a promise. The cancellation of Dante gives presence to its invisibility, and projects it outside the text. The cancellation is not cancelled, and promises an invisible presence: these notes evoke an absent (future) text structured around Dante's invisible authority. Stating the invisibility of the Purgatorial structure of the planned text creates a presence while deferring it, both in another place and in another time.

Direct quotations from Dante reappear further on in the notebook, after the sections intratextually related to *Murphy*. These floating fragments exist in the same textual space as the references to the *Purgatorio* of the first sections. Their sharing a common volume, however, does not imply a common critical status.[7] It is not certain if the notebook's entries follow a chronological progression and therefore if the Infernal residua are to be dated after *Murphy*.[8] In any case, the promise of an invisible Dante has led Beckett scholars to privilege the Purgatorial Dante of the first fifteen sections over the more fragmented Infernal one.

By adopting an intra- and intertextual perspective in analysing the relationship between the 'Whoroscope' notebook and *Murphy*, I do not presuppose a hierarchy between the two texts. *Murphy* is regarded neither as the finished product capable of giving meaning to a fragmentary source nor as a surface of which the manuscript is a deeper layer. As part of my exploration of how 'ideas of Dante' (to modify Contini's expression) are constructed in Beckett and in turn construct different 'Becketts', I am interested in how *Murphy* constructs the notebook and in how the notebook constructs *Murphy*. The two texts implicate each other in different ways, which, as Almouth Grésillon and Jean-Louis Lebrave have argued, cannot be stabilised in the traditional 'source *versus* text' opposition.[9]

I wish to acknowledge the incessant negotiation of meaning implied in the intra-intertextual perspective, which would be lost if the manuscript were interpreted exclusively as a source. Consequently, I do not read *Murphy* as the revelation of the 'Whoroscope' notebook prophecy; I read them as two texts that, in different ways, keep promising a presence while stating an absence. I am interested in how one text reproduces the dynamics of the other and not in reading one as the fulfilment of the other's promise. Rather than framing them into a teleological structure, I will map out how *Murphy* and the notebook differently structure Dante as a promise, deferring its presence while inscribing its authority.

My specific concern here is with the power exerted by the idea of a canonical author on a series of texts. I have mentioned above how the concept of author is the basis for including various unpublished materials in a canon. On the one hand, these materials are often regarded as less important than the published text, less authoritative, less under the control of the author. On the other hand, however, manuscripts and typescripts are taken to be proofs of the genesis of that same work, even more original than the original, more meaningful and revealing, capable of explaining the intentions of the author. These are contradictory views, which claim the complete subordination of the unpublished material to the published, and simultaneously project a higher value on it, since it is seen as the source, the origin of the book, the writing in act rather than already dead on the page.

These problems can be often encountered in the criticism devoted to modernist texts, and Richard Ellmann's 'Preface' to James Joyce's *Ulysses* can be helpful to illustrate in detail the issues at stake in my arguments.[10] Exploring the implications of the unpublished material also means examining the notion of obscurity itself. In describing the edition he is prefacing, Ellmann writes that 'what Gabler aims at is an ideal text, such as Joyce would have constructed in ideal conditions. The new edition relies heavily upon the evidence of existing manuscripts; where these have been lost, it attempts to deduce from other versions what the lost documents would have contained.' Ellmann justifies this by Joyce's practice of writing: 'Joyce ... did not always notice details of this kind [punctuation and spelling]', furthermore, 'it appears also that he rarely had an earlier version beside him when he was correcting a later one. Relying on memory, he sometimes sanctioned the inadvertent dropping of phrases; at other times, not recalling the earlier version exactly but sensing something was missing, he devised a circumlocutory substitute.'[11] When the editor's aim seems to be that of improving upon Joyce's own decisions on the basis of an ideal Joyce (without his 'defective eyesight and frequent haste') we are also told that, thanks to Gabler's 'touching up' and 'high polish', *Ulysses*'s 'small perfections have been recovered'. If on the one hand 'typist and typesetters' are accused of having a tendency to 'conventionalise Joyce's mannered punctuation and spelling', on the other, Gabler's 'substantive changes ... are obvious improvements'. Sentences which in the previous edition 'make ... no sense', are now crystal clear, since 'the new edition has recovered some lost words' and 'shows' what 'Joyce intended', even deciding when he intended it. What emerges from these few quotations is, first, that Joyce is used as the source of authority, from which it follows that a 'good edition' is an edition capable of accurately retrieving his intentions. Second, however, not only are Joyce's intentions unknowable, but also his working methods are highly questionable, so much so that the task of the good edition is to improve them to the point of creating an ideal text. The manuscript and earlier typescripts are regarded at once as the proof of Joyce's purest intentions, capable of making us retrieve his 'small perfections' and as the site of Joyce's sloppiness, in urgent need of emendation. The unpublished material is at once the fragmentary, unfinished stage of what will be the perfect, although difficult, work of art, and the original source of the author's ideal intentions from which the pure, clear text can be reconstructed.[12]

Jerome McGann has argued that Gabler's approach represents a variation 'from the usual "genetic" edition', but that it is not not so much a '"continuous manuscript text"' (as Gabler has called it) but a "continuous production text", where the effort is to display the work's evolution from its earliest to its latest productive phases in the author's lifetime'.[13] McGann distinguishes among various editorial practices not in order to claim that one system always displays advantages over the others but to contend that any editorial option 'impinges on the interpretation of the work': the opposition between editors who '"establish" the texts' and critics who 'then go on to "interpret"' crumbles.[14]

The specific set of problems displayed by Ellmann's comments on Gabler's editorial choices is relevant to Beckett, since often his manuscripts have been contradictorily read at the same time as the genuine expression of the author's intentions and as stages leading to the finished product. Nowhere is this clearer than in the studies devoted to Beckett's bilingualism, an aspect of the Beckett *oeuvre* which questions the notion of reliable texts, providing a good example of the importance in Beckett of a poetics of 'residua', 'disjecta membra', and 'odds and ends'. It is precisely within the criticism devoted to Beckett's bilingual output that we find early examples of scholars dealing with the problems raised by manuscripts. For instance, in his study of Beckett's self-translating practice and of the status of his bilingual works, Brian T. Fitch explored the paradoxical relationships between texts and manuscripts, and texts in the two languages. He argues that these relationships have often been overlooked and systematised by the critical tradition, transforming chronological priority into ontological pre-eminence.[15]

The study of Beckett manuscripts, however, has reproduced the contradiction of critical assumptions seen in the case of Ellmann's preface, and in the oversimplification criticised by Fitch's study. With specific reference to the 'Whoroscope' notebook, J. D. O'Hara for instance asserts that 'A glance into the "Whoroscope" notebook in which Beckett began to construct *Murphy* indicates rather startlingly that the finished novel is a smooth film of oil over troubled waters'. O'Hara – questionably – regards the first sections of the manuscript as the source of *Murphy*; consequently, he allocates to them the explicative power implicit in the very notion of source.[16] For this reason the manuscript is described as 'rather startlingly' obscure; the search for the explanation which the 'source' should provide is unfulfilled by the 'troubled' characteristics of what is taken to be the deeper layer of the novel. By comparison, the 'surface' of the novel is metaphorised into a 'smooth film of oil', through a use of depth and surface specular to the one parodied in the Nabokov epigraph to this chapter. If reassuring power is foisted on the notebook, the disquieting character of these troubled waters is maintained and functionalised; Beckett's self-addressed directive 'But keep whole Dantesque analogy out of sight' is described as 'a warning that he may have expanded to cover his later uses of depth psychology'.[17] If *Murphy*'s obscurity cannot be explained by a manuscript that is even more obscure, that same obscurity has to be read as seductive, because it can promise not only the invisible Dante but, by analogy, even the invisible 'uses of depth psychology'. This reading of the unpublished material struggles to stabilise the manuscript as the place where the full sense of Beckett's texts can be recuperated. But the same denial of fullness is mirrored, rather than solved, in the unpublished material, which disappoints the wish for the end of interpretation.

Since Dante's absence is projected outside the manuscript, we should think of Dante as a circulating absence in Beckett's *oeuvre*; this critical operation can shift the focus from the problem of location to that of *auctoritas*. To consider Dante as a circulating *auctoritas* in Beckett's *oeuvre* means to analyse how its invisible authority is at once constructed and displaced by the promise of the manuscript. Dante's absence becomes a guarantee of literariness and participates in the construction of the *auctor* Beckett.

The first fifteen sections of the 'Whoroscope' notebook use Dante as a mediating presence, evoking the authority of a literary monument and deferring its invisible presence; similarly, *Murphy* inscribes Dante as an authoritative absence using the figure of Belacqua and the astrological references. Like everything in *Murphy*, what is there stands for an aspect of literature to be dismantled; if there is 'no real Dante' the only way to speak of Dante is 'as though' it were there: 'for the only way one can speak of nothing is to speak of it as if it were something, just as the only way one can speak of God is to speak of him as though he were a man, which to be sure he was, in a sense'.[18] It is possible to speak of Dante in relation to *Murphy* because the text points to an authority while deferring the promise of its presence.[19]

In *Murphy* Belacqua is not a character but a structured presence in Murphy's mind: Belacqua is a state to which Murphy aspires. Belacqua in *Murphy* does not wait for salvation like in *Purgatorio* IV, but waits for Antepurgatory, although he still follows the Dantean rule, which prescribes a detention for a number of years equal to those spent on earth. But this happens only if the waiting is not mercifully shortened by the prayers of the living in the grace of God. Murphy therefore wishes for longevity and paradoxically prays to God *not* to have anyone praying for his salvation:

> Murphy would willingly have have waived his expectation of Antepurgatory for five minutes in his chair, renounced the lee of Belacqua's rock and his embryonal repose, looking down at dawn across the reeds to the trembling of the austral sea and the sun obliquing to the north as it rose ... Then he would have a long time lying there dreaming, watching the dayspring run through its zodiac, before the toil up hill to Paradise ... God grant no godly chandler would shorten his time with a good prayer. (47–48)

C. J. Ackerley has pointed out in detail the correspondences between *Purgatorio* I and IV and this passage; the reference to 'looking down at dawn across the reeds to the trembling of the austral sea' is to *Purgatorio* I, while the 'sun obliquing to the north as it rose' is to canto IV, in which Virgil tells Dante that his surprise in seeing the sun rising from the west can be explained by the fact that they are at the antipodes of Zion. And it is precisely the 'vision of Zion's antipodes' that Murphy vows to 'erase ... for ever from his repertory if only he were immediately wafted to his rocking-chair and allowed to rock for five minutes' (48).[20]

Murphy vows to give up the Belacqua fantasy, to 'renounce the lee of Belacqua's rock and his embryonal repose' (47–48) in order to be allowed to rock in his chair, to be 'improved of all knowledge' in order to reach 'the Belacqua bliss' (65) and other 'scarcely less precise' fantasies. This wished-for state is the second zone of Murphy's mind, as described in Chapter 6. It has been suggested that the tripartite division of the zones is a reversal of Dante's *Inferno*, *Purgatorio*, and *Paradiso*, in which the *Paradiso* is, however, characterised by complete darkness, while it is in the light that 'the kicks that the physical Murphy received, the mental Murphy gave' (65).[21] If so, this would intratextually reproduce the tripartite description of Belacqua in *Dream*. The second zone, where 'the Belacqua bliss' is referred to, is the one containing 'the forms without parallel'; nevertheless, at least one of these forms, which are 'more or less precise', is given a name that creates more than one parallel. The name of Belacqua refers back to the passage previously analysed, revives the protagonist of *Dream* and *More Pricks*, and contributes to setting up a tripartite structure. More than anything else, however, Belacqua acts as a reminder of Dante's presence, thereby investing the tripartite division with a lost meaning, by which I mean an authoritative, transcendental, harmonious division, which still survives as a structure that helps the narrative to go on while exposing itself as an empty shell. It is 'pleasant to lie on the shelf beside Belacqua, watching the dawn break crooked'; but we are reminded that this is only part of the 'painful duty' of relating a 'bulletin' (66).

There are a number of other elements that can be related not so much to Dante as a body of work but to Dante as previously constructed in Beckett's work. These intratextual references inscribe Dante's absence as the invisible presence of an authorial signature, and transform it into a consolidating element between different texts. The promise of a Dante that cannot explain or sustain the structure of the novel, and which, nevertheless, is evoked as an invisible presence, is to be found both in the first fifteen sections of the 'Whoroscope' notebook and in *Murphy*. Dante, even in the form of 'non Dante', is one of the unifying elements that constitute the Beckett *oeuvre* as such, by at once conferring and deferring additional value.

Addenda and excorporations

The inscription of Dante's authority can be observed also in *Watt*, a text which questions its own status as text in a number of different ways, among which the most prominent are repetition and mirroring. We encounter a quotation from *Inferno* VII, 60 in the 'Addenda', and a number of Dantean allusions in the text. In order to discuss the role played by Dante in this novel, it is important to explore how the 'Addenda' problematise notions of textual stability, memory, visibility, and repetition.

The term 'Addenda' advertises itself as 'what has to be added'. This title is accompanied by a note claiming: 'the following precious and illuminating material should be carefully studied. Only fatigue and disgust prevented its incorporation' (246). At once within and without the novel, the 'Addenda' as paratextual notion destabilise the boundaries of the text. However, 'no beginning, end, or continuity can be assigned' to *Watt* and therefore 'only a non-linear reading' is able 'to account for [its] perplexing narrative structure', and its 'horizontal and vertical repetitions and discontinuities'.[22] A non-linear reading will help explore the specific problems raised by the 'Addenda' to and in *Watt*.[23] Genette's notion of paratextuality is also useful. He views paratextuality as the relationship between what is usually called the text and what he calls the paratextual apparatus, such as title, subtitle, preface, notes, illustrations, etc.[24] For Genette, the notion of paratextuality is important because it focuses attention on the problems related to drawing the boundaries between text and non-text.

By presenting itself as additional material, an addendum does two things at once: it creates the notion of texts as text through its marginal position, and it creates a lack in the text, by proposing itself as supplement.[25] Acknowledging this dialectical process means to avoid reading the addenda at once as hierarchically inferior because marginal (material discarded by the author) and as the source of those same authorial intentions. In other words, not to acknowledge the problems raised by paratextuality results in paradoxically investing any addendum with the power of integrating a text already conceptualised as whole. This means that any paratextual material draws attention to the mutual relationship between margin and centre in the construction of a reality whose plenitude is created by the cancellation of their reciprocal implication.

The 'Addenda' to/in *Watt*, however, confront us with further problems. If 'this material stands outside the work and yet obviously forms part of it', it stands within and without a work which is constructed as a challenge to these same notions.[26] In other words, the 'Addenda' in *Watt* reproduce the dynamics of repetition, fragmentariness, seriality, displacement of origin, and impossibility of closure which characterise *Watt* as a text overtly struggling with the process of making sense. 'Addenda' cannot be incorporated because the corpus into which they should be absorbed does not construct itself as fullness but as the very process of its construction. Furthermore, its lack of incorporation (explained as the 'fatigue and disgust' caused by the notion of 'full meaning') is also a deferral of the promise of full meaning; this deferral mirrors the endless oscillation of openness and closure and excess and deficiency of the rest of the text. Trying to 'incorporate the appended material' would not so much mean, as in the case of other hypothetical addenda, to practise, as Connor claims, an 'incision [which] might us make us think that the novel itself is just an arbitrary incision within a series which is endlessly open'.[27] Rather, the seriality is already constructed by every single one of the other four parts of the text. The 'Addenda' section cannot be added, because it acts as a mirror, further reproducing the chronological instability of the text by its refusal to function as origin.[28]

In this sense too, the note appended to the 'Addenda' cannot be ironically dismissed and the 'Addenda' read as *not* 'precious and illuminating' but merely as a pile of discarded, meaningless material. This reading would rely on the assumption that in another, ideal world there could be addenda able to restore plenitude, only these Beckett ones cannot do it. Rather, it is crucial to acknowledge how the 'Addenda' challenge the notion of secondariness.

The reading I propose consists instead in seeing the 'Addenda' in *Watt* as part of the potentially infinite reduplication of themes and narrative structures which construct the novel.[29] The 'Addenda' section can be 'seriously' read as 'illuminating' because it echoes what the rest of the text does: it refuses to be incorporated into an idea of fullness; it reflects on how the ideas of fullness and lack are reciprocally implicated; and it questions this relationship. After all, this is a text which asks: 'and it is not strange most strange that one says of a thing that is full, when it is not full at all, but not of a thing that is empty, if it is not empty?' (95). In this sense, the 'Addenda' section, like the entire volume of *Watt*, is a repetition which 'enact[s] the arbitrariness and emptiness of language', 'attempt[ing] to efface the signifier, the materiality of the sign' and which, at the same time, 'can ... be read as an attempt to close the gap between word and thing, even though it is repetition [itself] which insistently opens up that gap'.[30] However, the 'Addenda' section does not merely repeat an 'original', but further questions the very notion of originality: in *Watt* the centre lies outside the circumference, and time does not progress in a linear fashion.

The 'Addenda' section is therefore a *mise en abyme* of the same structures that constitute the rest of the text; it self-revealingly deconstructs itself as a secondary language, defying a linear reading. It might be helpful to observe how a linear reading, which attempts to regard the 'Addenda' as secondary, is forced to posit the rest of the text as fullness while paradoxically acknowledging its being 'full of holes'. C. J. Ackerley, reading the 'Addenda' in *Watt*, asks: 'with a text so deliberately violated, how can an approach to the purpose via discarded drafts restore integrity?'[31] If the 'Addenda' is read as a series of 'discarded draft', secondary to the rest of the book, the text just described as 'full of holes – gaps, hiatuses, lacunae, deliberate errors and contradictions' has paradoxically to be described as a 'violated' fullness which the drafts can restore to integrity. In order to do this, Ackerley is gradually forced to separate the 'Addenda' from *Watt* altogether, as showed by his next paragraph, which begins: 'The Addenda, *in relation to the text* called *Watt*, thus constitutes an enigma of the deepest kind'.[32]

To read the 'Addenda' as a secondary text which, from its marginal position, challenges the finitude of the text but at the same time proposes itself as the possible source of meaning (and threatens it with the possibility of non-meaning) is not sufficient to account for its function. The 'Addenda', I argue, can instead be read as a portion of the text in the same hierarchical position as the rest, participating in the construction of infinite *mises en abyme*, which make of this an abandoned, rather than a finished book.

What I have identified as critical problems in reading the 'Addenda' in *Watt* and my proposed alternative reading can help interpreting the quotation from the *Comedy* (also about 'adding'), which appears in the 'Addenda': 'parole non ci appulcro' (I add no fair words to say).[33] The line belongs to a passage in *Inferno* VII in which Virgil explains to Dante the dynamics of the two groups of the avaricious and the prodigals, doomed to clash and hit each other violently:

> Mal dare e mal tener lo mondo pulcro
> ha tolto loro, e posti a questa zuffa:
> qual ella sia, parole non ci appulcro.
> Or puoi, figliuol, veder la corta buffa
> de' ben che son commessi a la fortuna,
> per che l'umana gente si rabbuffa;
> ché tutto l'oro ch'è sotto la luna
> e che già fu, di quest'anime stanche
> non potrebbe farne posare una. (*Inf.* VII, 58–66)

Ill-giving and ill-keeping have robbed them of the fair world and set them to this scuffle – what that is, I add no fair words to say. Now can you see, my son, the brief mockery of the goods that are committed to Fortune, for which humankind contend with one another; because all the gold that is beneath the moon, or ever was, would not give rest to a single one of these weary souls.

Embedded in the 'Addenda', the Dantean fragment works as a further *mise en abyme*; from the narrative point of view, the refusal to add embellishments reproduces the play with notions of originality, source, and fullness; from the structural point of view, it further mirrors the displacement of linearity. The Dantean Latinate neologism (from Latin *pulchrum*) rhymes with 'pulcro' ('beautiful', archaic 'wonderful') to indicate heaven; Virgil's refusal to add ornate words to describe the situation to Dante the character can be read as a refusal to adopt the ornate style – the 'bella menzogna' (beautiful lie) – to depict an infernal situation. Since 'pulcro' here means 'Heaven', we can infer that a style that recalls paradise is not suitable to picture Hell. Also, as seen in relation to *More Pricks Than Kicks*, the *Convivio*'s 'veritade ascosa sotto bella menzogna' (truth hidden under a beautiful lie) metamorphosises in the *Comedy* into the 'ver ch'ha faccia di menzogna' (truth which has the face of a lie). The elevation of poetry through the fourfold method of interpretation in the *Convivio* becomes one of the main strategies through which the *Comedy* constructs its truth by exposing it as what 'has the face of a lie'. If, following Teodolinda Barolini's argument, one develops 'a way of reading that attempts to break out of the hermeneutic guidelines that Dante has structured into his poems', it becomes possible to 'detheologise' Dante and to look at how the *Comedy*'s rhetoric works.[34] From this perspective, the claim 'parole non ci appulcro' can be read as a device to create the realism of the scene: Virgil claims that he does not need to describe the actual situation to Dante the character since he is there and can see what is going on. In other words, Virgil's refusal to add fair words creates visibility *as* reality. Furthermore, Dante the poet has already described the specific retribution of these damned spirits before Dante the pilgrim asks Virgil about the nature of their sin. Dante the poet makes Virgil claim that he does not want to add ornate words to portray a situation at once already described in detail by himself – and only reinforced by some of Virgil's words – and witnessed by Dante the character. By creating a supplement, Virgil's refusal rhetorically produces the mimesis in the canto and the authority of Dante the poet.

This refusal to add words to reality creates Dante the poet as the authority upon which this reality depends and Dante the character as the authority capable of witnessing it as reality. Dante's authority can paradoxically guarantee through his words a 'true' picture of what 'really' happened, while Virgil's words can only 'unnecessarily' reproduce it. If Virgil's words are declared unnecessary, Dante the poet's words and Dante the character's role of witness become indispensable to construct visibility as evidence. Tellingly, the figurative use of 'veder' immediately follows: Virgil, by encouraging the pilgrim to 'look' is in fact encouraging him to 'understand' the caducity of material good. In this sense, Virgil's invitation to look creates something which for the pilgrim is, although visible, still not completely clear. While Dante the poet constructs the 'reality' and Dante the traveller witnesses its 'truth', Dante the spiritual pilgrim still has some things that he cannot see properly. At this point of their journey, Virgil is superior as a guide (although doubts about his 'ornate words' have already been cast). The Dantean passage sets up through language the division between what is true and what is rhetorical (in the sense of 'non true') in order to construct visibility as self-evident presence, and authority as source and guarantee of reality.

Virgil's refusal to add fair words is appropriated by the 'Addenda' section of *Watt*, a portion of the text that refuses to be 'incorporated'. The Dantean fragment acts as a *mise en abyme* of the role of the 'Addenda' because they both refuse to add. In the *Comedy* Virgil's words construct Dante the poet's words as reality; Virgil's refusal to add words is a refusal to embellish what is in this way posited as fullness, visibility, presence. The refusal to add authenticates the narrative and creates it as reality. The 'Addenda''s refusal to 'add fair words' is a refusal to participate in the silent construction of an authenticity questioned by the rest of text; it is a refusal of hierarchy. In this sense Dante's words are, by their being placed among the 'Addenda', a *mise en abyme* of the whole movement of *Watt*. The novel enacts the endless process of producing meaning through the categories of lack and fullness, within and without, openness and closure; at the same time, it overtly shows how they are mutually implicated and therefore questions the pre-existence of a stable reality. The Dantean fragment is a residuum not because is a left-over, secondary to the text but because the whole text is produced as residuum; it is a supplement of a text which constructs itself as supplement, in the sense of both addition and substitution, as argued by Derrida.[35] The 'Addenda' section to/in *Watt*, by working as a *mise en abyme* of the whole text, is both thus creating and questioning the authority of the preceding portions of the text.

Existing scholarship has refused to interpret the 'Addenda' as reproducing the dynamics of the rest of the novel; instead the 'Addenda' have been read ironically. Rubin Rabinovitz, for instance, views the irony in the fact that, although close to the end of the book, the passage is nevertheless followed by two fragments in the English and only one in the French version, in which the order of the entries is occasionally different and some of them are missing. C. J. Ackerley sees the irony of the fragment in 'that Virgil, by describing the corruption of avaricious cardinals, is unable to remain silent'; however, this is a misreading of Virgil's 'I add no fair words to describe it'. Virgil's words are referred to the 'scuffle', that is to the description of the punishment, not to the moral lesson on the vices of avarice and squandering (and not corruption). Virgil is not 'describing the corruption of avaricious cardinals', but confirming Dante's doubt that the tonsured damned are in fact members of the clergy (not only cardinals, but also popes and clerics), a category among which avarice is said to be predominant.

Furthermore, Virgil is not 'unable to remain silent' but claims that he does not want to embellish with words the description of their punishment, which has been depicted first by Dante the poet.[36]

These ironic interpretations read the presence of the fragment from the *Comedy* as creating a parallel between the text's and Virgil's inability to remain silent; however, they fail to reach their goal to 'incorporate' the fragments in the 'novel' in order to reconstitute 'integrity' because they cannot take into account how the 'Addenda' mirror the rest of the text.[37] The movement between addition and residue provokes 'fatigue and disgust', which are, however, not opposed to the fullness of the body of the text, but reproduce instead, to borrow from 'Draff', its 'delightfully excrementitious' quality, its endlessly pleasurable excorporation.

Reading the 'Addenda' as participating in the process of *mise en abyme* of the rest of the text can account for other fragments. For example, the fragment 'never being properly born', that referring to the 'foetal soul', and that to a 'soulscape' are all reproductions of the theme of the 'disunion of things from their origins' analysed by Moorjani in connection with her discussion of thematic reduplications.[38] Furthermore, as pointed out by Rabinovitz, the passage 'limits to part's equality with whole', although reminiscent of Euclid's axiom, is a suggestion that 'the part can sometimes, but not always, be equated with the whole'.[39] In other words, this item asserts the principle of the 'simple *mise en abyme*', defined by Lucien Dällenbach as 'a fragment which resembles the work that contains it'.[40]

The 'Addenda' mirror the overt process of construction of meaning of the rest of the text, and the appropriation of the Dantean fragment is a further reflection. This 'infinite reduplication' is a movement that invests the Beckett canon in general, beside *Watt*, as the presence of the same line from *Inferno* (followed by the translation used above) in the 'Whoroscope' notebook indicates.[41] Rather than reading this presence in the manuscript as proving that the 'Addenda' is material 'actually' coming from other Beckettian manuscripts, I would contend that the movement of *mise en abyme* proliferates outside the published text, further displacing the notion of source, and constructing the Beckett canon as 'murmurs' and 'residua'.[42]

There are other Dantean elements in *Watt* that are generated, once again, by repetition: these are the allusions to the *Comedy*. If in the 'Addenda' we have the only Dantean quotation, in the rest of the volume we find a small number of allusions, most of which have been traced by Beckett scholars.[43]

Among them, I would like to discuss in more detail what *All That Fall* calls the 'arsy-versy' damned of *Inferno* XX, which Katherine Travers Gross reads in *Watt*. Travers Gross writes:

FATIGUE AND DISGUST

> Much of his canon ... on which ... Beckett's reputation finally rests, might in all justice be described as a reworking of Dante's *Inferno* and *Purgatorio*. Such, for example, is the method of not only his 'Dante and the Lobster' and this 1931 poem called 'Text' itself but, in other slightly different ways, of his poems entitled 'Enueg', 'Malacoda', and 'Serena III' in the *Echo's Bones and Other Precipitates* group, and in many other of his works besides. Dante's description in *Inferno* XX of the twisted body of the blind Tiresias which Beckett makes mocking use of for the first time in this 1931 poem of his ['Text'], in particular, recurs, either alone or in conjunction with Dante's description of those made food for worms by wasps in *Inferno* III and Freudian-colored images of conception and childbirth, in very many of his subsequent works including the 1953 *Watt* (58, 162, 165), the 1954 *Waiting for Godot* (48), the 1957 *All That Fall* (74–5), and the 1961 *Happy Days* (24–5), where it takes a different form upon each reappearance. (91)

Although I cannot agree with the assertion that much of Beckett canon is a 'reworking of Dante's *Inferno* and *Purgatorio*', it is interesting to note how these images from the *Inferno* have different functions. Gross does not specify the passages from *Watt* that she apparently connects with *Inferno* XX and III, but the page references allow us to hypothesise what she means. The first one is that which describes the 'I' and Erskine as similar since they both have 'a little fat bottom sticking out in front and a little fat belly sticking out behind' (58). In the next passage Watt is said to approach 'awkwardly buttoning his trousers, which he was wearing back to front' (162). The third passage – 'These were sounds that at first, though we walked breast to breast, made little or no sense to me' (165) – Travers Gross also refers, later in her work, to a different canto of the *Inferno*, namely canto XXXII.

Observing a re-elaboration of *Inferno* XXXII, 34–48 in the poem 'Serena III', Travers Gross asserts that 'Dante's image of the intertwined damned occurs in various forms in many of his subsequent works including *Watt* (164–169) and *How It Is* (275)':

> These were sounds that at first, though we walked face to face, were devoid of significance for me. (164)
>
> These were sounds that at first, though we walked breast to breast, made little or no sense to me. (165)
>
> These were sounds that at first, though we walked belly to belly, were so much wind to me. (166)
>
> These were sounds that at first, though we walked pubis to pubis, seemed so much balls to me. (167)
>
> These were sounds that at first, though we walked glued together, were so much Irish to me. (169)[44]

Gross relates the second passage to both *Inferno* XXXII and XX, therefore hypothesising that the two treacherous brothers immersed in the ice of the 'Caina', who are addressed by Dante as 'voi che sì strignete i petti' (you who thus press your breasts together) (*Inf.* XXXII, 43) merge in the Beckettian text with the 'arsy-versy' soothsayers of *Inferno* XX.

Ruby Cohn has read the passage as alluding to canto XX; if being 'face to face', 'belly to belly', 'glued together' implies an image similar to that of canto XXXII, it is only in canto XX that the damned are forced to walk backwards by having their faces turned towards their loins.[45] Therefore, it is canto XX which provides us with a figure of inversion. Virgil, describing the identities of the damned to Dante the pilgrim (after having rebuked him with the 'great phrase' 'qui vive la pietà quand'è ben morta'), explains how the one after Tiresias is 'Aronta [è] quel ch'al ventre li s'atterga' (He that backs up to the other's belly is Aruns) (*Inf.* XX, 46). The image of inversion is condensed in this line which paradoxically joins 'attergare' (to follow close to one's back) with 'ventre' (stomach, belly). Furthermore, in canto XX, Dante and his guide talk while they are walking, just as Watt and Sam do in the space between their gardens.[46] In canto XXXII the damned souls are unable to move and the two brothers (who will appear again in *How It Is* and *Ill Seen Ill Said*) are 'breast to breast' and cannot speak; they can only, by trying, produce a noise similar to those of storks' beaks ('mettendo i denti in nota di cicogna'), a noise we might describe as 'devoid of significance', or in the words of 'dread nay': 'in hellice eyes / stream till / frozen to / jaws rails / gnaw gnash / teeth with stork / clack chatter'.[47] In *Watt*, however, there is another allusion to canto XX; Sam reports his encounter with Watt as follows:

> Continuing my inspection, like one deprived of his senses, I observed, with a distinctness that left no room for doubt, in the adjoining garden whom do you think but Watt, advancing backwards towards me. His progress was slow and devious, on account no doubt of his having no eyes in the back of his head ... Then he turned, with the intention very likely of going back the way he had come, and I saw his face, and the rest of his front. (159)

The remark 'on account no doubt of his having no eyes in the back of his head' is at once an example of the typical destabilising redundancy of *Watt* and an intertextual *mise en abyme* of the figure of inversion. It is in *Inferno* XX that we find a specific reference to the connection between vision and advancing backwards:

> Come 'l viso mi scese in lor più basso,
> mirabilmente apparve esser travolto
> ciascun tra 'l mento e 'l principio del casso,
> ché da le reni era tornato 'l volto,

> *e in dietro venir li convenia,*
> *perché 'l veder dinanzi era lor tolto.*
> (*Inf.* XX, 10–15; emphasis mine)

As my sight went lower on them, each seemed to be strangely distorted between the chin and the beginning of the chest, for the face was turned toward the loins, *and they had to come backwards, since seeing forward was denied them.*

The apparently redundant specification of Watt having no eyes in the back of his head acts as a *mise en abyme* of the figure of inversion. Dante's soothsayers have their face twisted towards their back, and are therefore forced to walk backwards in order to see. Watt does not 'simply' invert the normal way of walking by advancing backwards; he also inverts a figure of inversion. If we extend this reading to the excerpts from *Watt* quoted above, we can see how the proliferation of Watt's linguistic inversion is accompanied by the *mise en abyme* of the figure of inversion. The image of walking 'breast to breast' is an 'imperfect inversion' of the image of the twisted soothsayers walking breast to back facing in the same direction. The allusions to Dante do not work as 'neat parallels': indeed 'from this will perhaps be suspected ... that the inversion was imperfect; that ellipse was frequent' (164). This reading would also confirm the movement of infinite mirroring and reduplication of the whole text. The vertigo of permutations is intertextually and intratextually produced.

In the case of both the quotation of Dante in the 'Addenda' and these allusions, I question a simply ironic reading of both the paratextual and the intertextual material. My analysis of the mechanisms of duplication and reiteration at work in *Watt* has tried to interpret the Dantean elements as part of the movement of repetition through which *Watt* radically questions the production of meaning and texts.

Both in *Murphy* and in *Watt*, Dante challenges the idea that a source is an origin able to integrate the text by providing a fuller intertextual meaning. In *Murphy*, Dante's authority plays a crucial role in shaping Beckett's authority, blurring given notions of textual boundaries. In *Watt*, Dante questions notions of source and origin; it is a supplement not only because it challenges the opposition of fullness and lack but also because it questions originality by being an intertextual *mise en abyme*.

Notes

1. Michel Foucault, 'What is an author?' (1969), in Paul Rabinow (ed.), *The Foucault Reader* (Harmondsworth: Penguin, 1984), pp. 101–120.

2 RUL MS 3000. See John Pilling, 'From a (W)horoscope to *Murphy*', in John Pilling and Mary Bryden (eds), *The Ideal Core of the Onion: Reading Beckett Archives* (Reading: Beckett International Foundation, 1992), pp. 1–20; *Beckett Before Godot* (Cambridge: Cambridge University Press, 1997); *Beckett's Dream Notebook* (Reading: Beckett International Foundation, 1999); *Companion to* Dream of Fair to Middling Women (Tallahaseee, FL: Journal of Beckett Studies Books, 2004); see also J. D. O'Hara, *Samuel Beckett's Hidden Drives: Structural Uses of Depth Psychology* (Gainesville: University Press of Florida, 1997).

3 The case of *Dream of Fair to Middling Woman*, which was published after Beckett's death, is one example of a residuum which suddenly became part of the canon.

4 For a detailed description of the fragmentary nature of the manuscript see Pilling, 'From a (W)horoscope to *Murphy*' and *Beckett Before Godot*, pp. 125–128. For a dating of the manuscript see Fredrik N. Smith, 'Dating the "Whoroscope" Notebook', *Journal of Beckett Studies*, n.s, 3:1 (1993), 65–70, and Geert Lernout, 'James Joyce and Fritz Mauthner and Samuel Beckett', in Friedhelm Rathjen (ed.), *In Principle, Beckett Is Joyce* (Edinburgh: Split Pea Press, 1994), p. 26.

5 John Pilling argues that the concern with 'architectonics' in *Murphy* is among the distinctive features which separate this phase of Beckett's writing from the previous one. Pilling, *Beckett Before Godot*, p. 130.

6 This table corresponds to the Enrico Bianchi edition of the *Divina Commedia* for the publisher Salani (1921 edition and most subsequent ones), as I have argued in '"The Florentia edition"'. For a discussion of the relations between the 'Whoroscope' notebook and the TCD notebooks, in which both 'D. & V.' and 'cornices' appear, see Daniela Caselli, 'The promise of Dante in the Beckett manuscripts', *Samuel Beckett Today/Aujourd'hui*, forthcoming.

7 Lernout dates the Mauthner fragments in the manuscript as post-*Murphy*; the quotations from *Inferno* appear after the Mauthner's transcriptions. See Pilling, *Beckett Before Godot*, p. 252, note 45.

8 Fredrik N. Smith argues that Beckett was not consistent in his use of the notebook and he did not keep it in any chronological fashion. Smith, 'Dating the "Whoroscope" Notebook', p. 65.

9 Almouth Grésillon, *Élements de critique génétique: lire le manuscrits modernes* (Paris: PUF, 1994); *Literarische Handschriften: Einführung in die 'critique génétique'* (Bern: Peter Lang, 1999); Almouth Grésillon and Jean-Louis Labrave, *Écrire aux XVIIe et XVIIIe siècles: genèses de textes littéraires et philosophiques* (Paris: CNRS Éditions, 2000).

10 James Joyce, *Ulysses*, eds Hans Walter Gabler, Wolfhard Steppe, and Claus Melchior (Harmondsworth: Penguin, 1986), pp. ix–xiv.

11 Nevertheless, Ellmann will later argue in favour of the concluded nature of the book by writing: 'But Joyce had put a fullstop to them.' Ellmann, 'Preface', p. xii.

12 Ellmann, 'Preface', pp. x–xi.

13 Jerome J. McGann, 'Literary pragmatics and the editorial horizon', in Philip Cohen (ed.), *Devils and Angels: Textual Editing and Literary Theory* (Charlottesville: University of Virginia Press, 1991), pp. 1–21, p. 10.

14 McGann, 'Literary pragmatics', p. 7.

15 Brian T. Fitch, *Beckett and Babel: An Investigation into the Status of the Bilingual Work* (Toronto: University of Toronto Press, 1988).

16 O'Hara, *Samuel Beckett's Hidden Drives*, pp. 43–44. O'Hara concentrates his analysis on the first fifteen sections of the manuscript and connects them directly to *Murphy*.

Curiously, after having described the 'Purgatorial distribution chart', he writes: 'the notebook's further entries offer us little help in moving from these first ideas to the finished work'. This is valid only in so far as the entries from 16 to 34 offer no allusions for O'Hara's concerns; in fact, these sections are those in which points of contact with *Murphy*'s opening can be observed.
17 O'Hara, *Samuel Beckett's Hidden Drives*, p. 44.
18 Samuel Beckett, *Watt* (New York: Grove Weidenfeld, 1959), p. 77.
19 Carla Locatelli reads *Murphy* as a 'critical' novel and views Beckett 'literary space' as constructed by the connections between texts. Carla Locatelli, *La disdetta della parola: l'ermeneutica del silenzio nella prosa inglese di Samuel Beckett* (Bologna: Patron, 1984), pp. 12–13.
20 C. J. Ackerley, 'Demented particulars: the annotated *Murphy*', *Journal of Beckett Studies*, 7:1 and 2 (Autumn 1997 and Spring 1998), 1–234, 76–77.
21 O'Hara describes the quoted passage as 'a childish version of Dante's Inferno'. O'Hara, *Samuel Beckett's Hidden Drives*, p. 53.
22 Angela B. Moorjani, *Abysmal Games in the Novels of Samuel Beckett* (Chapel Hill: North Carolina Studies in the Romance Languages and Literatures, 1982), pp. 36 and 26, respectively.
23 A number of scholars have written on the Addenda in *Watt*. See J. M. Coetzee, 'The English fiction of Samuel Beckett: an essay in stylistic analysis', Ph.D. thesis, University of Texas at Austin, 1969; Rubin Rabinovitz, *The Development of Samuel Beckett Fiction* (Urbana: University of Illinois Press, 1984), pp. 15–175; C. J. Ackerley, 'Fatigue and disgust: the Addenda to *Watt*', *Samuel Beckett Today/Aujourd'hui*, 2 (1993), 175–188.
24 Gérard Genette, *Palimpsestes: la littérature au second dégrée* (Paris: Éditions du Seuil, 1982), pp. 9–10.
25 Jacques Derrida, *Of Grammatology* (Baltimore: Johns Hopkins University Press, 1976) and *Writing and Difference* (London: Routledge, 1978).
26 Steven Connor, *Samuel Beckett: Repetition, Theory and Text* (Oxford: Blackwell, 1988), p. 31.
27 Connor, *Samuel Beckett*, p. 31.
28 *Watt* radically destabilises the notion of origin in different ways, among which it is worth recalling the complex series of narrators, as Angela Moorjani argues. Moorjani, *Abysmal Games*, pp. 27–28.
29 The 'infinite reduplication' is one of the three categories into which Lucien Dällenbach divides the *mise en abyme*, the other two being the 'simple reduplication' and the 'paradoxical reduplication'. Lucien Dällenbach, *Le récit spéculaire: essai sur la mise en abyme* (Paris: Éditions du Seuil, 1977), p. 51.
30 Connor, *Samuel Beckett*, p. 32.
31 Ackerley, 'Fatigue and disgust', 175.
32 Ackerley, 'Fatigue and disgust', 175; emphasis mine.
33 In this case, the translation is mine, since Singleton translates the expression as 'I spend no fair words to say', converting addition into expenditure.
34 Barolini, *The Undivine Comedy: Detheologizing Dante* (Princeton: Princeton University Press, 1992), p. 17.
35 Derrida, *Of Grammatology*.
36 In *Watt*, Mr Spiro, whose nickname is 'D-U-M. Anagram of mud', in describing his role in the publication of the 'popular catholic monthly, *Crux*' claims 'We keep our tonsure

above water' (27). This brings us back not just to the tonsured heads of the clergy in canto VII but also to the fraudulents of the eighth *bolgia* immersed in excrement (*Inf.* XVIII, 115). Dante spots a soul whose head is so filthy that it is impossible to decide if he is a layman or a clergyman: 'E mentre ch'io là giù con l'occhio cerco / vidi un col capo sì di merda lordo, / che non parea s'era laico o cherco' (And while I was searching down there with my eyes, I beheld one whose head was so befouled with ordure that it did not appear whether he was layman or cleric) (*Inf.* XVIII, 115–117).

37 Ackerley, 'Fatigue and disgust', 185–186.
38 Moorjani, *Abysmal Games*, pp. 86–87.
39 Rabinovitz, *The Development*, pp. 161–162.
40 Moorjani, *Abysmal Games*, p. 21.
41 RUL MS 3000. The pages are not numbered and the entry is towards the end of the notebook. See Pilling, 'From a (W)horoscope to *Murphy*', p. 8.
42 I would argue, in line with my discussion of *Murphy*, that *Watt* also defies any identification between the lost, misread, misrepresented, tattered notebook in which some of the inverted words of Watt are said to have been recorded by one of a series of unreliable narrators, and the manuscripts which are catalogued as the 'early drafts' of *Watt* (although their relationship is interesting and worth investigating).
43 Richard Begam connects 'all the old windings, the stairs with never a landing that you screw yourself up ... the wild country roads where your dead walk beside you' (40) to *Purgatorio* XXVI, 145–146. However, since the *Purgatorio* is structured as a series of stairs that the pilgrims climb it is difficult to justify the choice of a specific passage from the *Purgatorio* as a source. Begam also relates *Inferno* I, 113–123 to the passage in which Erskine is said to 'go by your side, to be your guide, and then for the rest you will travel alone, or with only shades to keep you company' (63). Richard Begam, *Samuel Beckett and the End of Modernity* (Stanford: Stanford University Press, 1996). The word 'guide' carries with it a Dante intertext, but Ruby Cohn has persuasively related this passage to *Everyman*. Ruby Cohn, *Samual Beckett: The Comic Gamut* (New Brunswick: Rutgers University Press, 1962), p. 76. Shades accompanying characters appear in *Mercier et Camier/Mercier and Camier*, as I will argue in the next chapter. Watt's appearance as 'lit less and less by the receding lights, until it was scarcely to be distinguished from the dim wall behind' (16) and Mr Hackett's uncertainty about Watt's status can recall Virgil's appearance to Dante as 'chi per lungo silenzio parea fioco' (one who seemed faint through long silence) (*Inf.* I, 63) and Dante's insecurity about his being 'od ombra od omo certo' (shade or living man) (*Inf.* I, 66). However, Virgil becomes gradually clearer rather than dimmer. 'Hoarse from long silence' (*Inf.* I, 63) occurs both in Italian and in English in the 'Whoroscope' notebook, and it is reproduced in *The calmant/The Calmative* and in *How It Is/Comment c'est*, as I demonstrate in the next chapters. See also Caselli, '"The Florentia edition"'. The dynamic between appearing and disappearing also has a Dantean intertext in the image of the mist dissipated by the sun: 'If Erskine had been a snorer ... then the mystery, it seemed to Watt, would have been dissipated, as the mist, by the sun' (122). In *Purgatorio* XVII, 1–12 Dante uses the image of the mist dissolving into the rays of the sun to depict its walking out of the thick smoke which envelops the wrathful souls. Significantly, in *Watt* the possibility of the mist dissolving is posited only to be denied: 'But there, Erskine was not a snorer' (122). Another possible allusion to Dante related to this theme of fading is the one to 'the trembling of the sea' (245). In the first of the 'Three Dantean Postcards', we read: 'Purgatorio I, 117, "Dawn: *il tremolar*

della marina".' RUL MS 4123. Dante begins his journey in the *Purgatorio* at dawn, and perceives the trembling of the sea, which towards the end of *Watt* 'could not but be admired' (245). In the Belacqua passage of *Murphy* we also have 'the trembling of the austral sea' (48).

44 Katherine Travers Gross, 'In other words: Samuel Beckett's art of poetry', Ph.D. thesis, Columbia University, 1972, pp. 274–275: 'or on Butt bridge blush for shame / the mixed declension of those mammae' is related to 'livide, insin là dove appar vergogna / eran l'ombre dolenti ne la ghiaccia' (*Inf.* XXXII, 34–35) and '"Ditemi, voi che sì strignete i petti", diss'io, "chi siete?"' (so, livid up to where the hue of shame appears, were the doleful shades within the ice ... 'Tell me, you who thus press your breasts together ... who are you?') (43–4). See also *Text 6* in *Texts for Nothing*.

45 Cohn, *The Comic Gamut*, p. 71.

46 Canto XX ends with 'Sì mi parlava, e andavamo introcque' (Thus he spoke to me, and we went on the while) and canto XXI begins: 'Così di ponte in ponte, altro parlando / che la mia comedìa cantar non cura, / venimmo' (Thus from bridge to bridge we came along, talking of things of which my Comedy is not concerned to sing).

47 Samuel Beckett, 'dread nay', in *Collected Poems 1930–1978* (London: Calder, 1984), p. 33.

5 Who is the third beside you? Authority in *Mercier and Camier*

> Who is the third who walks always beside you?
> When I count, there are only you and I together
> But when I look ahead up the white road
> There is always another one walking beside you
> Gliding wrapt in a brown mantle, hooded
> I do not know whether a man or a woman
> – But who is that on the other side of you?
> T. S. Eliot, *The Waste Land*, 1922

Beckett scholarship has long noted that in *Mercier and Camier* 'the real issue concerns the relationship between the author and his two dupes' and that the 'true "pseudocouple" is not Mercier and Camier but the author linked with his two creations.'[1] I propose to expand on this point by P. J. Murphy, in order to observe how the issues of authority, visibility, and invisibility can be helpful to assess the role played by Dante in *Mercier and Camier* in relation to both *Mercier et Camier* and other texts by Beckett.

Written in French in 1946, *Mercier et Camier* was published only in 1970, while the self-translated *Mercier and Camier* appeared in print in 1974. In the opening of both versions, the narrator takes up the first person pronoun and declares complete control over the story: 'The journey of Mercier and Camier is one I can tell, if I will, for I was with them all the time', 'Le voyage de Mercier et Camier, je peux le raconter si je veux, car j'étais avec eux tout le temps'.[2] The position of witness assumed by the narrator is not adopted as a realistic device; rather, the text questions the very possibility of such a position. The 'if I will' not only creates the narrator as the instance in control but also underlines the redundant quality of the story, its dependence on the narrator.[3] The 'I', therefore, cannot only be regarded as a witness, but is the instance upon which the existence of the very story depends.

The witness is a convention that usually enables the narrator to disappear, and the narrative to present itself as mimesis, showing what 'really' happened. However, the extreme visibility of the narrating 'I' and his assertion of control over the narrative ('if I will') immediately shift attention to narration as diegesis. The visibility of the narrator and its double status of witness and of controlling force privilege the act of narrating over the narration itself.

Moreover, although the journey of Mercier and Camier is at first described as 'fairly easy going', soon we read: 'Mercier and Camier did not remove from home, they had that great good fortune' (7). After denying the existence of what had been declared to be the subject of the story, namely the journey as progression, the narration of the journey continues while the reliability of the narrator is destroyed.

From the opening of *Mercier and Camier* we witness a double movement: on the one hand the narrator claims to be a witness, therefore to be in the position to report something that has happened. Reality seems to be something external, which the narrator will reproduce in the story. At the same time, however, by overtly stating that the story will be 'an object for his manipulation' and by emptying the story of its subject, the narrator also devises a story, which will be completely dependent on him.[4]

Throughout the text we observe a number of changes in the position of the narrator, which go beyond the simple movement from the past tense describing what happened and the present tense referring to the time of the narrating act. The narrator occasionally becomes omniscient, and in chapter three the place of the 'I' is appropriated by a character while the narrator temporarily disappears. Furthermore, some descriptions are told in the present tense; every two chapters we encounter a 'Summary of the two preceding chapters', and the narrative presents a number of metanarrative comments.

This self-declared 'fairly easy going' text plays with the visibility and invisibility of the sources of control of the narrative (narrator as witness, omniscient narrator, and implied author), questions the very possibility of 'reporting', and metanarratively comments upon its own status as fiction. The text exposes its artificial character and its dependence on a deviser who is creating a fictional mechanism: in *Mercier and Camier* the two characters approaching the door of the shelter in the public garden is 'the signal for the sky to darken again and the rain to redouble in fury' (11).[5] As in *Murphy* the sun shone, 'having no alternative', stressing the necessary dependence of the text on the controlling author, here the narrative exposes its machinery, disturbing the possibility of a 'neutral' reportage.[6] When the narrator tells us that 'an altercation ensued, too foolish to be recorded, so foolish was it' (30), he tells us what he is leaving out of the story, thus giving existence to the 'foolish altercation' precisely by claiming to exclude it from the narrative. The structure of the sentence, moreover, underlines its redundancy and the ultimate inanity of the story as a whole. This questioning of the very idea of plot foregrounds the telling of the story, which is not so much the act of recounting witnessed events, but rather of controlling and organising them. Furthermore, if we look at the French version, the 'foolish altercation' over the 'massepain à la crème' is in fact recorded; the narrator's comment in the English text is a commentary on the French text (46). With Steven Connor, it can be argued that 'the comment which the English narrator makes is directed at the French narrative, and the translation makes sure that it can have no meaning except by reference to this other, absent version of the text'.[7] In the light of this discussion, it becomes clear how the existence of the two texts creates another problem in relation to authorial control, as indicated by a number of metanarrative statements. An example of this is the statement which follows the table illustrating the times of arrival and departure of Mercier and Camier at the place which they had appointed for their 'launching out, into the unknown' (8). The table is followed by the assertion: 'What stink of artifice' (9). In my reading of *Dream of Fair to Middling Women*, I have analysed the passage stating that 'Mr Beckett' was acquiring 'the bay about [his] brow', as an example of undecidable insecurity about the source of the narrative. In that instance, the voice ironising on Mr Beckett's naivety was seen to be in control from a safe external position, reproducing a structure where there is still an unnamed guarantee of meaning, although coming from an unidentified place.

In the case of *Mercier and Camier*, we have a similar situation when the metanarrative assertion 'what stink of artifice' has the function of indicating how the narrator (contradictorily both a witness and a deviser) is inextricably caught within the story he claims to be controlling. With Mark Currie, we can argue that, if we interpret metafiction, or, in this case, metanarration, as 'that something which is defined by its self-consciousness', then it follows that it 'must surely be conscious of its own definitive characteristic. It is not enough that metafiction knows that it is fiction; it must also know that it is metafiction if its self-knowledge is adequate, and so on in an infinite logical regress.'[8] If, within the narrative, we are told that what has just been narrated is 'artificial', two things happen at once. On the one hand, the assertion carries with it authoritative potential, affecting what has been written from its textual higher ground; on the other hand, however, the text provides no guarantee that this comment is any less artificial than the rest. If the metanarrative statement is attributed to the narrator himself, this makes a Cretan liar out of him; if the narrator tells us that his narrative is artificial – untruthful – then we have to assume that the statement that tells us so is itself part of this artificiality, and yet we only have the narrator's word for it. It remains undecidable because the comment upon the rest of the narrative is part of what is claimed to be artificial. If the narrative is labelled as artificial within the narrative, then it all has to be a 'lie' – 'all balls' as *How It Is* puts it – including the metanarrative statement we are reading. If there is no guarantee of truth, even what seems to distinguish between truth and lie cannot be taken as truth.

Furthermore, in 'what stink of artifice', the notion of artificiality itself is interesting in so far as it implies the possibility of non-artificiality, of a truthful report of events. We have seen, however, how the contradiction at the beginning of the text casts a shadow over this very possibility; the realistic narration is a sham, or at best a convention among others; the positions of narrator, characters, and goal of the story (the quest) are advertised as inescapably artificial, like any other story. The metanarrative assertion, however, also presents itself as an authoritative claim, as if it could escape the very game of which it is part and could guarantee the reality or unreality of what is written. Although there is no ground to decide what is artificial, since the claim belongs to the same fictional world that it denounces, the rhetoric creates the illusion that, by judging what the narrator has just said, it stands on a higher ground. The metanarrative statement occupies an ambiguous position, as it is implicated in the narrative it criticises and it also stands above it in order to judge it. By questioning the division between artifice and reality, such metanarrative statements disturb the verisimilitude on which *Mercier and Camier* is ostensibly based.

Vague shadowy shapes

The link between verisimilitude and narrative artifice is important in order to understand how *Mercier and Camier* plays with the visibility and invisibility of the different instances of control in the narrative. The narrator can sometimes disappear, as in the case of the monologue of Mr Madden, and he can shift from the position of witness to that of deviser or omniscient narrator. This hide-and-seek game is also a theme in the text, created by the appearance and disappearance of strange figures which follow or meet the characters, and by the invisible presences sensed by the characters.

The opening sentence of the novel, in which the narrator claims that he 'was with them all the time', sets up that third party which allows the couple to exist as such; as the epigraph to this chapter puts it, there is always 'another one walking beside you / Gliding wrapt in a brown mantle, hooded'.[9] Mercier and Camier are constantly under the 'strange impression' that they 'are not alone' but that there is something 'like the presence of a third party ... enveloping us', and, as Mercier puts it, he is 'anything but psychic' (100). Among the various strange impressions who increasingly bother the protagonists, the unnamed 'gentleman wearing ... a simple frock-coat and top-hat' (25) has been taken by P. J. Murphy to be the 'author who is following the same road as them' and of whom they catch a glimpse.[10] Although Murphy does not explain his deduction, he records the allusiveness of these unrealistic figures, which can assume different meanings, notably that of being instances of control over the narration. In *Mercier et/and Camier* references to anything external – at both thematic and textual level (casual encounters and quotations) – are linked to authority and control. The characters who cross Mercier and Camier's path intratextually create the oscillation between the world of the narrator within the texts of *Mercier et/and Camier* and that of the author-function Samuel Beckett, the instance responsible for the characters appearing and reappearing in the texts which bear his name. For instance, the 'old man of weird and wretched aspect, carrying under his arm what looked like a board folded in two' (75–76) and the 'ragged shaggy old man plodding along beside a donkey' (77) are both images shared with *The End/La fin* (67; 112–113 and 58; 97). Moreover, Mercier's memory of having seen the old man somewhere before is followed by that of the old man himself, who 'busied himself for a space with trying to recall in what circumstances' he had seen Mercier before (76), thus shaping a textual memory which prevents the Beckett texts from being placed in a relation of linear temporal progression.[11] These occurrences shape a web of intra- and intertextual relations that, as seen in the case *More Pricks Than Kicks*, constitute the Beckett *oeuvre* as strangely familiar. Dante is part of this negotiation of authority and control through intra- and intertextual references, as the following passages illustrates:

> The sun comes out at last, said Camier, that we may admire it sink, below the horizon.
>
> That long moment of brightness, said Mercier, with its thousand colours, always stirs my heart.
>
> The day of toil is ended, said Camier, a kind of ink rises in the east and floods the sky.
>
> The bell rang, announcing closing time.
>
> I sense vague shadowy shapes, said Camier, they come and go with muffled cries.
>
> I too have the feeling, said Mercier, we have not gone unobserved since morning.
>
> Are we by any chance alone now? said Camier.
>
> I see no one, said Mercier. (19)

Le soleil sort enfin, dit Camier, afin qu'on admire sa chute, à l'horizon.

   Ce long instant de clarté, dit Mercier, aux mille couleurs, il me touche toujours.

   La journée de labeur est terminée, dit Camier. Une sorte d'encre surgit à l'orient et inonde le ciel.

   La cloche sonna, annonçant la fermeture.

> Je garde l'impression, dit Camier, de formes vagues et cotonneuses. Elles vont et viennent, en criant sourdement.
> En effet, dit Mercier, je crois que nous avons des témoins, depuis ce matin.
> Serions-nous seuls, à present? dit Camier.
> Je ne vois personne, dit Mercier. (28–29)

The sinking of the sun below the horizon and the 'toil' – a term appearing in connection with Dante in *Dream of Fair to Middling Women* – are elements that in the Beckettian vocabulary are intratextually related to Dante, as seen with regard to *Murphy*.[12] The references to the bell striking and the vague shadowy shapes can be read in connection respectively with the ending of *Purgatorio* IV via 'Dante and the Lobster' and with the *Purgatorio* in general, pervaded as it is by shades and shadows. While the souls being purged are termed as shadows or shades ('ombre'), Dante's shadow is the only proof that he is alive, that he has a body which casts a shadow, unlike the other inhabitants of the *Purgatorio*, as the first of the 'Three Dante postcards' records: 'Dante's shadow, Virgil transparent. Seeing only one on ground D thinks V gone.'[13]

The vague shadowy shapes who, like the narrator, observe, witness, and keep the couple some sort of company, circulate an intratextual Dante that fashions Samuel Beckett as the authority (at times invisible or hard to make out) in control of a narrative which in turn questions both authority and control. The appearances of Watt, claiming to be 'unrecognizable' (111), Murphy (whose body was never found), and Quin contribute further to shaping the intratextual, and ironic, figure of the author:

> I am Watt, said Watt. As you say, I'm unrecognizable. Watt? said Camier. The name means nothing to me. I am not widely known, said Watt, true, but I shall be, one day. Not universally perhaps, my notoriety is not likely ever to penetrate to the denizens of Dublin's fair city, or of Cuq-Toulza. (111)

As in *Dream*, authority goes hand in hand with cultural value and is ironically underplayed. In this case, the 'appearance' of the author fades in thanks to the proper name of a character, Watt, which gives the title to two other Beckett texts. The character Watt, but also the book *Watt*, claims his/its almost universal 'notoriety'. Only Cuq-Toulza and Dublin (in the English version), and Cuq-Toulza and London (in the French) are excluded.[14]

Like Watt, Dante contributes to the production of Mr Beckett as the author, and Eric P. Levy has analysed in detail the pervasive references to Dante in *Mercier and Camier*.[15] Levy's study is helpful in so far as it points out many references, such as the parallel between the public garden and the earthly paradise; the figure that Mercier glimpses in the morning mist 'suggestive of Camier's' and the appearance of Virgil to Dante in *Inferno* I; the choir of *Purgatorio* X; and the curse with the umbrella similar to that of Vanni Fucci in *Inferno* XXV. Others parallels drawn by Levy are justified more by the variety of the material treated in the *Comedy* than by an intertextual relationship: the *Comedy* is a text sufficiently vast to provide correspondences for all kinds of comparisons.[16] The question becomes what is the function of these parallels, rather than whether they can be hypothesised. Levy's informative study is representative of many comparative analyses of the Beckett/Dante relationship; his argument that *Mercier and Camier* is a journey 'in search of subjectivity' modelled 'upon the greatest itinerary of the soul in Western Literature: Dante's *Divine Comedy*', but one in which the characters 'have lost all notion of goal or end' (41) reproduces the model developed in 'Dante...Bruno.Vico..Joyce'. Stamped with the mark of Beckett's authority, that model is applied to read Dante's conical, teleological progress guaranteed by theology, but no longer in Beckett. But whilst this is certainly one aspect of Dante in Beckett, it is not sufficient to account for the different 'Dantes' produced by Beckett's texts, nor for the ways in which Dante produces 'Mr Beckett'.[17] Moreover, if used as an assumption, this argument is far too general; most twentieth-century rewritings of Dante imply the loss of the theo/teleological framework.

Different levels of authority within *Mercier et/and Camier* are produced by the presence of a third party, the names of other Beckett characters, and Dante as a shadowy shape able to create intratextual references to other Beckett texts. *Mercier et/and Camier* is a palimpsest in which different levels of authority coexist; Dante is one of them.[18]

'Palimpsest', 'a parchment whence writing has been erased' (literally, 'scraped again'), also means 'paper, parchment, or other writing material prepared for writing on and wiping out again, like a slate', 'a parchment or other writing-material written upon twice, the original writing having been erased or rubbed out to make place for the second', and 'a manuscript in which a later writing is written over an effaced earlier writing'.[19] While in the case of *Company* and of the 'Second Trilogy' the 'erosion' and the 'compression' are more marked, *Mercier et/and Camier* also plays with depth and surface, and visibility and invisibility, in order to criticise verisimilitude. What initially appears to be true or real is – as argued above – gradually shown to be dependent on different kinds of authority. Eroded by contradictions, destabilised by different positions of the narrator and consequent changes in his degree of control, and questioned by the metanarrative statements whose source remains unclear, the text fabricates a series of allusions to texts by other authors (especially the *Comedy*) and to texts by Beckett himself (*Watt*, *Murphy*). Moreover, the encounters of the characters with the 'long line of maleficent beings' (13) seem to call for an 'external' explanation, just as the man in frock-coat and top-hat ('that third who always walks beside you') calls for an external authority. This series of layers constitutes a palimpsest of *auctoritates* upon which the text depends. These numerous and shifting authorities contribute to the dismissal of the subject of the story (in the sense of plot) and draw attention to themselves as subjects of the story, as instances able to control the act of telling.

By adopting the notion of palimpsest, I wish to explore further how Dante becomes a figure of authority by contributing to ideas of depth and surface, and visibility and invisibility, which make *Mercier et/and Camier* a textual investigation into the possibility of narrating and the notion of control over the narrative.[20] In this way, I also wish to avoid what I have suggested as the main problems in Levy's analysis of the English text, namely a thematic comparison that invokes Dante's authority and attributes a predetermined meaning to the 'source-texts' analysed, claiming Dante as 'the greatest itinerary of the soul in Western literature'.[21] I maintain that Dante is one of the invisible authorities that control the narrative and I will consider the interesting shifts between Dante's visibility and invisibility from the French to the English version, an aspect previously ignored by Levy and others.[22]

Like Mercier and Camier's reported dialogue, which records the presence of an observer who is not only the invisible narrator/witness but also a figure of control, chapter VI, after the description of Mercier's embarrassing entry in the saloon, reads:

> An acute observer, had one been present, but none was, might well have been put in mind of a flock of sheep, or a herd of oxen, startled by some dark threat. Their bodies rigid, drawn with fixed glare to face the common foe, they are stiller for a moment than the ground on which they graze. (81)

In the French version, chapter VIII:

> Un observateur, s'il y en avait eu, mais il n'y en avait pas, aurait pensé peut-être à un troupeau de moutons, ou de bufles, mis en émoi par un danger obscur. Les corps figés, les visages tendus et irrités qu'aimante la menace, ils sont un instant plus immobiles que la nature qui les emprisonne. (136–137)

Levy comments, referring only to the English version:

> The narrator can only note the reaction; he cannot explain it. Yet, his extended comparison of the clientele to a flock of sheep 'startled by some dark threat' recalls Dante's description in Canto III [of *Purgatory*] of the troop of souls' frightened response to his shadow. (48)

In *Purgatorio* III, 79–93, we read:

> Come le pecorelle escon del chiuso
> a una, a due, a tre, e l'altre stanno

> timidette atterrando l'occhio e 'l muso;
> e ciò che fa la prima, e l'altre fanno,
> addossandosi a lei, s'ella s'arresta,
> semplici e quete, e lo 'mperché non sanno;
> sì vid'io muovere a venir la testa
> di quella mandra fortunata allotta,
> pudica in faccia e ne l'andare onesta.
> Come color dinanzi vider rotta
> la luce in terra dal mio destro canto,
> sì che l'ombra era da me a la grotta,
> restaro, e trasser sé in dietro alquanto,
> e tutti li altri che venieno appresso,
> non sappiendo 'l perché, fenno altrettanto.

As sheep come forth from the fold by one and two and three, and the rest stand timid, bending eyes and muzzle to the ground; and what the first does the others also do, huddling themselves to it if it stops, simple and quiet, and know not why; so saw I then the head of that happy flock move to come on, modest in countenance, in movement dignified. When those in front saw the light broken on the ground at my right side, so that my shadow was from me to the cliff, they halted and drew back somewhat; and all the others that came after did the same, not knowing why.

The parallel detected by Levy is clearer in the English than in the French, which lacks the allusion to grazing and bending muzzles towards the ground. The allusion testifies to Dante's presence and continues the parallel between Mercier and Camier's and Dante and Virgil's progression; however, this allusion is an example of how Dante is one of the items through which the text constructs itself as a series of layers of authority. The narrator, who at this point occupies the role of witness, is the observer of the scene, which he reports. The denial of the 'presence' of an acute observer can be read ironically; if no acute observer was present, then the invisible observer who is telling us what he, supposedly, has 'seen', must be everything but acute. The source of humour is also the source of instability; if the narrator describes himself as not acute, he is undermining his reliability. At the same time, however, the obtuse observer is precisely the one who hypothesises what an acute observer 'might well have been put in mind of' (81). As argued above, by denying the presence of an external authority, the narrator creates that presence in the text. Furthermore, the metaphor of the flock of sheep alludes to Dante, declaring him an 'acute observer'. Dante's authority is that of the artist capable of observing and reproducing what he has seen, unlike the obtuse narrator of this text. At the same time, however, the example of reliability in narration is constituted by a simile, that is, by juxtaposing text as 'reality' and text as 'narrative', thus producing verisimilitude while resorting to another narrative. Dante is at once present while his presence is denied, and absent while alluded to. Moreover, the allusion to Dante, just by being there, inscribes the authority of Beckett the author on to that of the narrator.

> They advanced into the sunset (you can't deny yourself everything), burning up the sky higher than the highest roofs.
> A pity Dumas the Elder cannot see us, said Watt.
> Or one of the Evangelists, said Camier. (112)

The absent authorities of a realist writer and of one of the Evangelists are evoked but decreed absent. Levy reads the passage as an allusion to *Purgatorio* XXV in which 'Dante, Virgil, and Statius ... walk toward the setting sun to enter the Seventh terrace' (50). If the time in canto XXV is two in the afternoon (hardly sunset) Levy's reading nevertheless indicates how this passage demands some sort of attribution. The names of Dumas the Elder and of one of the Evangelists add a different value to the narrative which constitutes itself as a *tableau vivant* precisely through the evoked presence of illustrious observers. The dialogue transforms Watt and Camier as characters in an alternative narrative; the narrative we are reading, the result of the witnessing practice of the narrator as observer, is then placed at the same level as those of Dumas the Elder or of one of the Evangelists. The presence of these 'big names' within a narration that exists by dismissing the subject of its story, is at once ironic and 'serious'. The text simultaneously puts some distance between the *auctoritates* quoted and underlines two of the main preoccupations of the text, namely the problem of realism in literature and that of a text able to guarantee its own truth. The text creates its own genealogy, advertising its literary nature.

Teodolinda Barolini points out how the *Comedy* displays a similar textual strategy, although without the ironic element: 'the pilgrim's concern that: "Io non Enëa, io non Paulo sono" ("I am not Aeneas, I am not Paul" *Inferno* II, 32), is a supreme example of the double bind in which Dante is placed as the guarantor of his own prophetic status: the very act by which the pilgrim demonstrates humility serves the poet as a vehicle for recording his visionary models and for telling us, essentially, that "Io sì Enea, io sì Paulo sono"'.[23] Dante the pilgrim claims not to be on the same level as Aeneas or St Paul, and Dante the poet places himself at the top layer of religious authorities who have previously described a journey in the afterlife. Beckett's text wishes for the presence (thus denied) of two literary and religious authorities and, by doing so, ironically places the narrative as a pitiful failure in comparison to those of more authoritative writers. At the same time, however, it also establishes this narrative as the product of a narrator that can at least be compared to the other illustrious observers.

No quotes at any price

The presence of partially visible authorities is a phenomenon that overflows the limits of the single text in English or in French, affecting both *Mercier et Camier* and *Mercier and Camier*. The 'summaries of the two preceding chapters', for instance, go back to Beckett's early critique of the division between 'form' and 'content', promising a relation of identity and failing to fulfil such a promise, and questioning the issue of authority and control upon which the entries of such lists depend. In the French version, this phenomenon (and its kinship with the larger problem of self-translation) is ironically illustrated in the 'résumé' of chapter VIII, in which we read a rather bawdier version of the Pylades and Orestes dyad found in 'Ding-Dong': 'Le cul et la chemise, avec graphiques (passage entièrement supprimé)' (163).

As the summaries can promise to reproduce what comes before them but can differ both from the text and from each other, *Mercier and Camier* can differ from *Mercier et Camier*, while promising a relation of identity. Brian T. Fitch has explored in detail the complex relationship of dependence, interdependence, and independence that Beckett's self-translated texts enjoy.[24] Steven Connor has analysed how *Mercier and Camier* 'discarnates' characters, omitting some twelve per cent of the material of the French version, and how it 'does not just tamely replicate the original but comments upon it and upon the act of translation'.[25]

Levy's analysis of the English version has shown how many allusions to Dante are embedded in the text. However, while some of these allusions are to be found both in the English and in the French versions, others appear only in one or the other. The most striking example is the following passage:

> Oui, dit Camier ... Tu n'ignores pas cependant ce que nous avons arrêté à ce sujet: pas de récits de rêve, sous aucun prétexte. Une convention analogue nous interdit les citations.
> Lo bello stilo che m'ha fatto onore, dit Mercier, est-ce une citation?
> Lo bello quoi? dit Camier.
> Lo bello stilo che m'ha fatto onore, dit Mercier.
> Comment veux-tu que je sache? dit Camier. Ça m'en a tout l'air. Pourquoi
> Ce sont des mots qui me bruissent dans la tête depuis hier, dit Mercier, et me brûlent les lèvres.

> Tu me dégoûtes, Mercier, dit Camier. Nous prenons certaines précautions afin d'être le mieux possible, le moins mal possible, et c'est exactement comme si on fonçait à l'aveuglette, tête baissée. Il se leva. Te sens-tu la force de bouger? Dit-il. (99–100)

The English version reads:

> Yes, said Camier ... And yet you know our covenant: no communication of dreams on any account. The same holds for quotes. No dreams or quotes at any price. He got up. Do you feel strong enough to move? he said. (61–62)

The quotation in the French comes from *Inferno* I, 87, when Dante recognises Virgil:

> 'Or se' tu quel Virgilio e quella fonte
> che spandi di parlar sì largo fiume?',
> rispuos'io lui con vergognosa fronte.
> 'O de li altri poeti onore e lume,
> vagliami 'l lungo studio e 'l grande amore
> che m'ha fatto cercar lo tuo volume.
> Tu se' lo mio maestro e 'l mio autore,
> tu se' solo colui da cu' io tolsi
> *lo bello stilo che m'ha fatto onore.* (*Inf.* I, 79–87; emphasis mine)

> 'Are you, then, that Virgil, that fount which pours forth so broad a stream of speech?' I answered him, my brow covered with shame. 'O glory and light of other poets, may the long study and the great love that have made me search your volume avail me! You are my master and my author. *You alone are he from whom I took the fair style that has done me honor.*

Mercier and Camier are reported as discussing the 'convention' and the 'covenant' which rules in their relationship and which forbids quotations and 'the communication of dreams'. But in the French text, while expressing this unmotivated convention, they wonder about the 'nature' of a quotation. Can the line in Mercier's head, which describes Dante recognising Virgil as his *auctoritas*, be defined as a quotation?[26] Can this internal buzzing, connected to the words burning Mercier's lips, be seen as something external? We are led back to 'Draff''s 'marginal metabolism' and its critique of 'incorporation' and to *Watt*'s supplementary 'Addenda', resulting from a 'disgust' identical to Camier's.

The interrogatives on the limit of what is internal and what external to the text, and around the marginality of excremental residua, which cannot be opposed to full bodily presence, hinge on the lines from the *Comedy*. Virgil's role as an *auctoritas* within Dante's text fashions Dante as an *auctoritas* in Beckett's text. The line refers to Dante's 'beautiful' or 'fair' style, which has 'honoured' him. In the case of *Watt*, the line 'parole non ci appulcro', which works as a silent construction of reality in the *Comedy*, casts doubt on the idea of reality. In *Inferno* VII, Virgil's words act as an embellishment on the words of the poet, guaranteed by the pilgrim as a witness. In *Inferno* I, Dante characterises his own 'beautiful style' as coming from Virgil, the 'source'. The style described as 'beautiful' is Dante's style before becoming the author of the *comedìa*, his 'sacrato poema' (sacred poem). Seen from the perspective of the finished text, Dante's attribution of authority to Virgil also works to distance his 'poema sacro' from Virgil's tragedy.[27] In *Paradiso* XXX, Dante 'makes it clear that the usual distinctions between *comedìa* and *tragedìa* are irrelevant' in the following lines:

> Da questo passo vinto mi concedo
> più che già mai da punto di suo tema
> soprato fosse comico o tragedo (*Par* XXX, 22–24)

> At this pass I concede myself defeated more than ever comic or tragic
> poet was defeated by a point in his theme[28]

This passage, the first line of which is (mis)quoted in *Dream*, also appears in the '*Dream*' notebook. The evocation of the distinctions between 'comico' and 'tragedo' underscores Dante's belief that while other poets (either writing in the comic or in the tragic genre) could not attempt such a description, he could go beyond genres: 'the paradox of the method ... corresponds to the paradox of the genre that surpasses and eliminates genre: the *comedìa* that is higher than the highest *tragedìa*'.[29] Further, the category of beautiful is associated with mortality, and opposed to the truth, of which the poet is the scribe, and therefore the ultimate guarantor. In this sense, the highest recognition of Virgil's authority and the clearest inscription of his *auctoritas* in the text is also the basis of Dante's own authority. Dante's admission that his beautiful style, which 'has done him honour', comes from Virgil, is also a manoeuvre which distances it from the 'true' style of the *Comedy*, which will allow the 'difficult poet' to go back to Florence and get the 'bay about his brow'.

Mercier et Camier contradicts the characters' asserted 'convention' of not using quotations by quoting Dante in the original. While forbidding the presence of authorities, the text not only inscribes the presence of Dante, but also that of Virgil and of 'Mr Beckett', with his 'bay about his brow'. By reproducing a passage where Dante seems to deny his own originality in favour of his *auctoritas* – but which in fact is the prelude to the birth of Dante the scribe of God, the true poet – the text constructs a very visible authority while denying it the status of quotation. The context creates the maximum visibility for a quotation, given in the Italian, and by the discussion on its status as quotation. At the same time, the characters deny the authority of the quotation: Camier's remark 'lo bello quoi?' works as an ironic denial of Dante's beautiful style, and Mercier's uncertainty regarding the source of 'des mots qui [me] bruissent dans la tête' works as a denial of 'originality' while also questioning the opposition between a 'within' and 'without' the text (made even more unstable by the lack of the Dante quotation in the English text). Dante's line is described as something that both buzzes in the head and burns the lips. If the first description is a denial of originality, it is also a further confirmation of that originality. The buzzing of the words in the head seems to indicate the pervasive and unavoidable character of these words; like the 'murmurs' that can be heard better in the dark, these buzzing words are part of the character's 'skullscape'. To utter them is painful: the lips get scalded. The memory of the 'source' has been lost, the *auctor* has become part of the words within the head; however, his words still 'stink' of quotation.

The English text has none of the Dante material in it, and reads: 'No dreams or quotes at any price' (62). This sentence works as a commentary on a passage which has been omitted, therefore alluding to how the relationship between the two texts is under the author's control. Camier's words comment on the absence of Dante while reinforcing the presence of the author, who at once institutes and disobeys a prohibition. The prohibition is phrased in terms of 'price', which can be read as a further allusion to the notion of the alleged 'added value' that the presence of an *auctoritas* gives to the text. Dante in the English text is, thus, present under erasure.

Furthermore, in the French the passage is followed by the repetition of the word 'comédie' twice, in 'les bras allaient et venaient devant la poitrine, de la comédie' and 'A ton âge, se dit-il. Et ainsi de suite. Comédie aussi' (100–101). These references are not present in the English text, in which 'comedié' is translated as 'an act'. However, the English text has a much stronger allusion to Dante in the following sentence, which reads 'I was about to go, said Mr Conaire, all hope abandoned' (62), while the French text has: 'J'allais partir, dit monsieur Conaire, en désespoir de cause' (101). The allusion to the almost stereotypical 'Abandon every hope, you who enter' (*Inf.* III, 9) can be read as a means to draw the attention to Dante's erasure.

The Dantean allusions scattered in *Mercier et/and Camier* illuminate a barely visible substrate, partially effaced by a second writing. However, the first layer, which seems to add value to the journey of the two characters, is, in turn, shown to be dependent upon a further authority, a further layer. The text creates its own potentially endless genealogy: Dante has 'taken away' his 'fair style' from Virgil, Beckett from Dante, and so on. Rather than lending itself to a Bloomian reading, this endless genealogy exposes however the 'price' of quoting, foregrounds the act of telling the story, and undermines the notion of originality. The text sabotages strong misreadings, painstakingly argues that it is impossible to simply report events, and regards as impossible the existence of an upper layer, of a beautiful lie that simply acts as surface. *Mercier et/and Camier* constantly fabricates ideas of depth, strata of authority constructed by other authorities, strange impressions of *déjà vu*, as the reappearance and disappearance of Sordello indicates:

> les raisons ne manquent jamais pour s'arrêter, et que l'autre arrive, celui qui était derrière, et voit cette sorte d'ombre de Sordel, mais sans y croire, enfin sans y croire assez pour pouvoir se jeter dans ses bras, ou lui flanquer un coup de pied à l'envoyer cul par dessus tête dans les fondrières. (184)

The English text reads:

> good reasons are never lacking for coming to a stop, and that the other catches up, the one left behind, and seeing this kind of shade does not believe his eyes, at least not enough to run to its arms, or to kick it arse over tip into the quags. (105)

Here, as in the case analysed above, the allusion is more explicit in the French, which, by naming Sordello, makes clear the reference to the embrace between him and Virgil. Unlike Virgil, who embraces his fellow shade Sordello (and unlike Dante, who clumsily attempts three times to embrace the shade of Casella in *Purgatorio* II), Mercier (or Camier) knows better. They do not believe that the shade is real: therefore they can neither hug it nor kick it, unlike Virgil, who in the firth circle thrusts the wrathful Filippo Argenti off the boat into which he is trying to climb, back into the Styx quagmire (*Inf.* VIII).

Another Dantean proper name, which appears in the French but not in the English, is that of Manto, already encountered in the Beckettian canon. The French version has it:

> Quel temps fait-il, à présent? dit Camier.
> Pour qui me prends-tu? dit Mercier. Pour Manto?
> Je suis tout entier à mes équilibres, dit Mercier. (110)

The English text reads:

> What's the weather like now, said Mercier, if I look up I'll fall down. (67)

The reference to the soothsayer Manto creates the joke about being 'tout entière a mes équilibres'. As already observed in relation to *Watt*, to the poem 'Text', and to *More Pricks Than Kicks*, the twisted bodies of those who have challenged God's power are described in such moving terms in *Inferno* XX as to provoke Dante's 'piety and pity both'. The reference to the damned souls' loss of 'équilibre' makes Mercier's joke possible. While in this case the English does not have any of those references, it presents the Beckettian formula 'arsy-versy' (11), referring to *Inferno* XX, which has an intratextual dimension via *Watt*, *Texts for Nothing* and *All That Fall*, whereas the French 'cul-à-cul' (14) lacks it.[30]

In *Mercier et/and Camier* Dante is part of a complex textual construction that interrogates the idea of text as either surface or depth. Through the muffled voices of difficult poets, the shadowy presence of acute observers, and the fleeting impressions of familiar characters these texts question the status of the words that have 'tout l'air' of being quotations and allusions. Dante fades in and out of *Mercier et/and Camier*, indicating how the authority on which Beckett's *oeuvre* rests is constituted by the residual and the marginal.

Notes

1. P. J. Murphy, 'Language and being in the prose works of Samuel Beckett', Ph.D. thesis, University of Reading, 1979, p. 57. This part of Murphy's discussion does not appear in his later *Reconstructing Beckett: Language for Being in Samuel Beckett's Fiction* (Toronto: University of Toronto Press, 1990). Wishing not to transform chronological priority into ontological pre-eminence, in my discussion I will at times quote the English and at times the French text first.
2. Samuel Beckett, *Mercier and Camier* (London: Picador, 1988), p. 7; *Mercier et Camier* (Paris: Les Éditions de Minuit, 1970), p. 7.
3. Murphy, 'Language and being', pp. 55–56.
4. Murphy, 'Language and being', p. 56.
5. This does not happen in the French text: 'Mais aussitôt le ciel s'assombrissait de nouveau et la pluie redoublait de violence' (14).
6. For a discussion of the opening of *Murphy* see Carla Locatelli, *La disdetta della parola: l'ermeneutica del silenzio nella prosa inglese di Samuel Beckett* (Bologna: Patron, 1984), p. 20.
7. Steven Connor, *Samuel Beckett: Repetition, Theory and Text* (Oxford: Blackwell, 1988), p. 96.
8. Mark Currie (ed.), *Metafiction* (London: Longman, 1995), p. 1. On the limits of the definition of metalangue see also Carla Locatelli, '"My life natural order more or less in the present more or less": textual immanence as the textual impossible in Beckett's works', in Lois Oppenheim and Marius Buning (eds), *Beckett On and On ...* (Madison, NJ, and London: Associated University Press, 1996), pp. 127–147, p. 135.
9. While in Eliot the hooded third party's gender is explicitly undecidable, in *Mercier and Camier* the narrator, and most of the figures encountered by the pseudo-couple, are male.
10. Murphy, 'Language and being', p. 56.
11. Eric P. Levy unpersuasively claims that this man 'remind[s] us of Cato at the base of the mountain of Purgatory'. Eric P. Levy, *Samuel Beckett and the Voice of Species: A Study of the Prose Fiction* (Totowa: Barnes and Noble, 1980), p. 48.
12. 'The moon had raised her lamp on high, Cain was *toiling* up his firmament.' Beckett, *Dream*, p. 130; *Murphy*, p. 48. *Malone Dies* reads: 'I sometimes see shining afar and how is it the moon where Cain toils bowed beneath his burden never sheds its light on my face?' Samuel Beckett, *The Beckett Trilogy* (London: Picador, 1979), p. 203.

13 RUL MS 4123. The comment precedes the transcription of *Purgatorio* III, 19–21, 26, 37. In TCD MS 10963 'shadowy figures' (fol. 7) describes the crowd in *Inferno* III.
14 'il y a peu de chances par exemple que ma notoriété pénètre jusq'aux habitants de Londres ou de Cuq-Toulza' (193); In *Molloy* we read: 'just imagine that, for they had never heard of Watt, just imagine that too.' Beckett, *The Beckett Trilogy*, p. 71.
15 Jean-Pierre Ferrini later recorded the Dante intertexts in *Mercier et Camier*, although he does not cite either Levy or my previous work on the subject. Jean-Pierre Ferrini, *Dante et Beckett* (Paris: Hermann, 2003), p. 7.
16 The examples are numerous. I record here as unpersuasive: the parallel between Mr Conaire's horror of childbirth and Dante's fear of entering the fire wall in *Purgatorio* XXVII; the image of the goat, which, although it does appear in the *Purgatorio*, does not seem to have any relevance in this context; the identification of the man carrying the folded board with Cato and of Watt with Forese Donati; the interpretation of the phrase 'the flowers are in the vase and the flock back in the fold' as coming from *Purgatorio* XXVII and IV respectively.
17 As seen in my readings of *Dream*, *Murphy*, and the 'Whoroscope' notebook, the 'defunctionalisation' of the structure of the *Purgatorio* plays a relevant role in Beckett.
18 The notion of palimpsest has been used by John Pilling in his review of *Company*, and developed by Carla Locatelli, who extends it to the whole 'Second Trilogy'. Angela Moorjani also uses this idea in relation to Beckett's novels, when she discusses the inscription of traces and the function of the 'archives of the mind' in Beckett's texts. John Pilling, 'Review article: *Company* by Samuel Beckett', *Journal of Beckett Studies*, 7 (Spring 1982), 127–131; Carla Locatelli, *Unwording the World: Samuel Beckett's Prose Works After the Nobel Prize* (Philadelphia: University of Pennsylvania, 1990), pp. 41, 18, and 226; Angela B. Moorjani, *Abysmal Games in the Novels of Samuel Beckett* (Chapel Hill: North Carolina Studies in the Romance Languages and Literatures, 1982), pp. 107 and 149. See also Rubin Rabinovitz, 'Molloy and the archetypal traveller', *Journal of Beckett Studies*, 5 (Autumn 1979), 25–44 (p. 31).
19 *OED*.
20 On the notion of palimpsest see Jacques Derrida, *Writing and Difference* (London: Routledge, 1978), p. 224.
21 Levy, *Samuel Beckett*, p. 41. The same problem is present in Ferrini's work.
22 While Levy focuses only on the English text, Ferrini analyses only the French text.
23 Teodolinda Barolini, *The Undivine Comedy: Detheologizing Dante* (Princeton: Princeton University Press, 1992), p. 57.
24 Brian T. Fitch, *Beckett and Babel: An Investigation Into the Status of the Bilingual Work* (Toronto: University of Toronto Press, 1988).
25 Connor, *Samuel Beckett*, pp. 90 and 95.
26 The first '*Watt*' notebook of 1941 reads: 'tu se' lo mio maestro / e il mio autore'. HRHRC, University of Texas, Austin, fol. 53.
27 I refer to Virgil's epic poem as 'tragedy' following the *Comedy*, which juxtaposes 'alta tragedìa' to 'bassa comedìa' (*Inf.* XX and XVI). For a discussion of how Dante connects 'alta tragedìa' with 'menzogna' ('lie') see Barolini, *Detheologizing Dante*, pp. 59, 76, 79, and note 17, p. 293.
28 Teodolinda Barolini, *Dante's Poets: Textuality and Truth in the* Comedy (Princeton, Princeton University Press, 1984), p. 272.
29 Barolini, *Dante's Poets*, pp. 272–273.

30 However, Levy argues in favour of Dante's presence, claiming that the following passage in the English text refers to *Inferno* XVII, 115, that is to say the episode of Dante and Virgil's descent to the eighth circle on the back of the monster Geryon. The texts read: 'Let our watchword be, said Mercier. / Ah, yes, said Camier, lente, lente, and circumspection, with deviation to right and left and sudden reversals of course. ... / What's the weather like now, said Mercier, if I look up I'll fall down' (67), 'Que notre devise soit donc lenteur et circonspection, avec des embardées à droite et à gauche et de brusques retours en arrière, selon les dards obscurs de l'intuition' (109). Levy's assertion that 'Camier's advice ... follows Dante's description of the flight to the point of actually quoting two words from the Italian text' (47), does not take into account the misspelling of 'lenta lenta' (*Inferno* XVII, 115) into 'lente, lente'. As John Pilling has pointed out to me, this misspelling makes the parallel much less convincing, especially in the light of the following passage from Marlowe's *Doctor Faustus*: *O lente, lente, currite noctis equi.* / The stars move still, times runs, the clock will strike. / The devil will come, and Faustus must be damned. / Oh, I'll leap up to my God: who pulls me down?' Christopher Marlowe, *The Complete Plays*, ed. J. B. Steane (Harmondsworth: Penguin, 1986), p. 336. Marlowe's text also accounts for the Mercier's remark: 'If I look up I'll fall down'. In this case, then, the reference to Manto in the French is no longer there in the English, and the allusion to Dante has vanished.

6 Déjà vu beyond reach: from the *Novellas* to the *Three Novels*

> Having nothing to say, no words but the words of others, I have to speak.
> (Beckett, *The Unnamable*, p. 288.)

In my reading of *Mercier et/and Camier* I observed how Dante migrates from one text to the other. Sometimes allusions to Dante are repeated in Beckett's self-translated version; alternatively, the quotations from Dante are erased and this erasure is commented upon; other times still, some allusions are replaced with different ones, always from the *Comedy*. These shifts intratextually contribute to the construction of the author Samuel Beckett and make each of the two versions part of a process of self-commentary.

Dante is a significant discourse also in the prose texts from the *Nouvelles/Novellas* (alternatively called *Stories*) to the *Textes pour rien/Texts for Nothing*.[1] In these texts, especially from *Le calmant/The Calmative* (the last written novella) onward, the levels of control and authority are less apparent than in *Mercier et/and Camier*, since the distinctions between narrator and characters are gradually collapsed by the interplay of invention and memory, which questions the conceptual possibility of opposing memory as repetition to invention as originality. In all the texts from the *Novellas* to the *Texts for Nothing* the narrative voice can exist neither as singular and original nor as perfectly repeatable, because 'every attempt to identify itself utterly in repetition leaves some infinitesimal residue of difference unaccounted for, a residue that points back to the originating self'.[2]

Dante is part of this oscillation between memory and invention. Dante is a fragment of the unavoidable intratextual memory, which cannot be reduced to simple and reassuringly self-identical repetition. Various intratextually connoted terms, different textual places from the *Comedy*, most of which are by now textual commonplaces in the Beckett canon, and a number of quotations, make Dante part of the flickering, unavoidable, non-coinciding memory of the voice who says 'I'.

The calmative effect of one's classics

In the *Nouvelles/Novellas*, we see some intriguing parallels with the situation analysed in the previous chapter. The *Novellas* create a web of internal references, which makes it impossible to attribute to each of them only one place within a linear progression. This creates interesting effects, as John Pilling has noted in the case of *The Calmative*, which 'is obviously to some degree conceived of as occurring after the boat incident in *The End*, during which "I swallowed my calmative" (67). It is also, in time terms (if time terms can actually be applied here), after *The End* in its opening acknowledgement that this voice comes from beyond the grave: "I don't know when I died".'[3] In the *Nouvelles* 'the very issue of what is "in time" is turned topsy-turvy by the order of composition', which, differing from the order in which the stories were published, does not help to reconstitute a smooth temporal sequence; rather, it further complicates it, making the author participate in the destabilising movement of the texts.[4] The *Nouvelles* are also part of a larger web of intratextual relations. For example, the protagonist of *La fin/The End* says:

> I had perfected my board. It now consisted of two boards hinged together, which enabled me, when my work was done, to fold it and carry it under my arm. I liked doing little odd jobs. (67)

> J'avais perfectionné ma planchette. Elle consistait maintenant en deux morceaux réunis par des charnières, ce qui me permettait, une fois mon travail fini, de la plier et de la porter sous le bras, j'aimais bien bricoler. (112–113)

Elsewhere in this study I have pointed out that the image of the board folded in two, together with that of the man with the donkey, occurs in *Mercier et/and Camier*. The reciprocal recognition of Mercier and the unnamed man carrying the board is a further example of how temporal linearity is smudged by the merging of the different textual spaces of the author and the narrator.

Also, in the case of *Premier amour* and *First Love* we have a similar phenomenon to that observed in relation to the unstable passage referring to *Inferno* I, 67 present in *Mercier et Camier*, but not in *Mercier and Camier*, which makes Dante's authority appear and disappear while confirming the controlling power of the author.[5] *Premier amour* reads:

> Donnez un vase de nuit, dis-je. J'ai beaucoup aimé, enfin assez aimé, pendant assez longtemps, les mots vase de nuit, ils me faisaient penser à Racine, ou à Baudelaire, je ne sais plus lequel, les deux peut-être, oui, je regrette, j'avais de la lecture, et par eux j'arrivais là où le verbe s'arrête, on dirait du Dante. Mais elle n'avait pas de vase de nuit. (44)

The English version reads:

> Give me a chamber-pot, I said. But she did not possess one. (41)

Unlike *Mercier and Camier*, *First Love* radically erases the *auctoritates* and does not comment on the cancellation. Since all Beckett's self-translated texts enjoy a paradoxically parallel existence, Dante's absence from the English text is nevertheless relevant to a discussion of the Beckett *oeuvre*.[6] The scatological context is associated with the names of Racine, Baudelaire, and Dante, three great literary authorities of the Western canon. The protagonist of *Premier amour* thus implies, in a way similar to that of Winnie in *Happy Days*, that 'one loses one's classics'.[7] Memory is related to the soothing, calming effect of repeating from a text; in the words of *The Unnamable*: 'if I could learn something by heart I'd be saved'.[8] The impossibility of absolute repetition, of perfect coincidence, is mocked through the humorous contrast between the triviality of the words 'vase de nuit' and the three literary champions. The specification that it is about the '*mots* vase de nuit', stresses that even the most trivial words can recall, being 'words', those of the greatest authors. The characteristic of 'being words' is the sufficient condition for the reminiscence to exist. Once the reminiscence is inscribed in the text, however, another quality is immediately shared between the present text and those evoked, namely their 'being literature'. The juxtaposition of the names of these authors as signs of their literary value and the less valuable words 'vase de nuit', and of the lofty worlds evoked by the big names and the trivial context of the story, creates a contrast. But what seems to be a mere dismissal of authorities by mockingly raising the scatological matter to the heights of great literature, highlights how ephemeral and variable is the 'value' of words, while also placing the text within the canon. The alleged lack of value of the text is foregrounded in order to reclaim its own status of literature while commenting on the processes of attributing value to literature.

The distance between the most trivial words and the greatest ones is at first annulled by the memory of a single 'source', which, however, is uncertain. The interchangeable quality of Racine and Baudelaire underlines that they are names standing for a corpus of words, and stresses the reassuring quality of their value. These names guarantee a source for words whose repetitiveness acquires a special meaning. The parallel with *Happy Days* is revealing, since in both cases a calming effect is attributed to quotation, to the act of repeating from a guaranteed source. However, 'one loses one's classics', memory fails not just because it can no longer capture its object but also because it gradually erodes it. Words are always repetitions of other words but they cannot be either completely repeated or anchored to the tranquillity of the source. The failing memory becomes a figure of the impossibility of both repetition and originality: 'ils me faisaient penser à Racine, ou à Baudelaire, je ne sais plus quelle, les deux peut-être' (44).

Dante is positioned slightly differently in this context. The 'I' claims to have arrived through Racine and Baudelaire to the threshold of silence represented by Dante. The name of Dante is not isolated, but accompanied by an allusion to the limits of representation, to the speechlessness characterising the *Paradiso*.

One of the most quoted examples of the ways in which the impossibility of representation and communication is exploited as a literary device in the *Comedy* is encountered in the '*Dream*' notebook. A short misquotation of the same passage appears in *Dream* too: 'Da questo passo vinti ci concediamo ...'.[9] *Paradiso* XXX, 22–24 is transcribed in the notebook as follows:

> Da questo passo vinto me [*sic*] concedo
> più che giammai da punto di suo tema
> soprato fosse Comico o Tragedo
> ....
> ma or si convien che il mio seguir desista
> più dietro a sua bellezza, poetando
> come all'ultimo suo ciascuno artista
> (30.22. ...)

> At this pass I concede myself defeated more than ever comic or tragic poet was defeated by a point in his theme ... but now my pursuit must desist from following her [Beatrice's] beauty further in my verses, as at his utmost reach must every artist.

Through the authorities of Racine and Baudelaire, the 'I' claims to have arrived at the threshold of silence and representation, and he refers to Dante as the example of ineffability in literature. Dante is what 'remains' of 'la lecture'; it is still an identifiable source. Although Dante's name forms a trio with the other two authorities, it does not merge with them and is not directly and humorously connected to the words 'vase de nuit'. It is through the other two writers that the 'I' claims to have arrived at speechlessness, thus making speechlessness resonate with the words of both Racine and Baudelaire and of Dante. Dante still works as a fragmentary authority on the limits between silence and word, as a soothing residue of memory to which the 'I' can resort.

In *Le calmant/The Calmative* another kind of Dantean 'speechlessness' is alluded to as a comforting memory, connected with the oscillation between silence and speech.[10] The only passage in *Le calmant/The Calmative* that explicitly refers to the *Comedy* reads:

> I resolved to speak to him. So I marshalled the words and opened my mouth, thinking I would hear them. But all I heard was a kind of rattle, unintelligible even to me who knew what was intended. But it was nothing, mere speechlessness due to long silence, as in the wood that darkens the mouth of hell, do you remember, I only just. (33)

> Je préparai donc ma phrase et ouvris la bouche, croyant que j'allais l'entendre, mais je n'entendis qu'une sorte de râle, inintelligible même pour moi qui

connaissais mes intentions. Mais ce n'était rien, rien que l'aphonie due au long silence, comme dans le bosquet où s'ouvrent les enfers, vous rappelez-vous, moi tout juste. (53)

This passage explicitly refers to *Inferno* I, 61–63, in which Dante encounters Virgil for the first time:

> Mentre ch'i' rovinava in basso loco,
> dinanzi a li occhi mi si fu offerto
> chi per lungo silenzio parea fioco.

> While I was ruining down to the depth there appeared before me one who seemed faint through long silence.'

The passage is also quoted in the 'Whoroscope' notebook:

hoarse from long silence: Virgil to Dante
(Chi per lungo silenzio parea fioco: Inf. I)

The translation adopted in the notebook interprets 'fioco' in its acoustic sense.[11] By rendering it 'hoarse', the ambivalent dimension of 'fioco' as both an acoustic and a visual adjective is lost, and the passage indicates Virgil's difficulties in speaking after a long silence. In the critical tradition of the *Comedy*, 'che per lungo silenzio parea fioco' is usually interpreted as an 'acoustic metaphor', as a translation of 'a phonic emotion into a visual one' to indicate a blurred image, surfacing from the surrounding darkness as if from a long absence.[12] The ghost-like appearance of Virgil is translated into the image of the threshold between speechlessness and voice. In *Le calmant/The Calmative* the allusion to the Dantean episode seems to work as the soothing promise of repetition. The *Comedy* is a memory, shared by the 'I' and the 'you', able to neutralise the threat of speechlessness and estrangement through the image of a dialogue marking the beginning of a story. The text foregrounds its own allusiveness through the narratee, a 'you' to whom the question of memory is posed. The remarks 'do you remember, I only just', 'vous rappelez-vous, moi tout juste' blur the limit between narrator and author and between narratee and reader. The reference to the *Comedy* as a memory shared by the 'I' and the 'you' has an effect similar to that described in relation to *Mercier et/and Camier*: it 'overstep[s] ... a boundary *that is precisely the narrating (or the performance) itself*: a shifting but sacred frontier between two worlds, the world in which one tells, the world of which one tells'.[13]

In the allusion the *Comedy* is an external, 'calmative' text, able to convince the 'you' that this silence is nothing to worry about. In the tradition of 'Dante and the Lobster', the geographical textual spaces are confused, and the outside of the text is suggested as being itself textual. However, this memory is 'only just' remembered, and therefore cannot be a perfect repetition; it has lost its power of reintegrating the estranged self. The allusion is consistent with the whole text, which is a 'story' that the 'I' tells to calm himself, to fight the estrangement felt 'listen[ing] to [him]self rot' (27). This estrangement reappears in the 'rattle', which makes the subject face his own unintelligibility. The crumbling of the 'marshalled words' seems to indicate the crumbling of the subject as the product of his intentions ('even to me who knew what was intended'). The allusion works as a temporary reassurance that this discrepancy indicated by speechlessness is 'nothing', nothing to worry about, '*mere* speechlessness', 'aphonie', similar to Virgil's 'speechlessness'/'aphonie'/ 'hoarseness', which is just the prelude of a long soothing story. However, uttering the words is not the beginning of a calming experience of integration for the subject: 'The words were hardly out of my mouth when for shame I covered my face' (34), 'Cette phrase à peine prononcée, de honte je me couvris le visage' (54). Even when the words do come out according to the intentions of the speaker, the speaker cannot recognise himself in them, and estrangement is experienced. This is indicated also by the different uses of 'mouth' in the English text, in which the speechlessness of the mouth of Hell is echoed in the ingestion of the sweet, in the shame caused by the words out of the 'I''s mouth, and in the pity he feels towards the 'little unfortunate at the mouth of life'.[14] The mouth of Hell cannot guarantee the reassuring experience of the repetition of a beginning; the words uttered from the mouth of the 'I' increase, rather than soothe, his estrangement.

In this passage we can see how Dante is evoked as calming memory, as repetition, predictability and progression, as common ground shared by narrator and narratee. However, the repetition cannot be the simple reproduction of the identical, the memory is fading, and the calming power of the mouth of Hell is contrasted with the estrangement of the mouth of life. The repetition of 'mouth' in a context in which the materiality of the voice is paired with a sense of estrangement can be linked to *Mercier et Camier*, in which the quotation from Dante is related to the 'buzzing' or 'rustling' in Mercier's head and to the 'burning' of his lips.[15] The murmuring inside the head illustrates the impossibility of identical repetition of the 'source', encountered in *The Calmative* as a fading memory. The burning of the lips is a metaphor for the estrangement of utterance, of the non-coincidence of the subject who cannot recognise/hear ('entendre') as his the words uttered by his mouth.

If in *The Calmative* the allusion to Dante promises to transform the 'rattle' into 'mere speechlessness', in *Text 2* speechlessness becomes at once a threat and a promise of death:

> To need to groan and not be able, Jesus, better ration yourself, watch out for the genuine deathpangs, some are deceptive, you think you're home, start howling and revive, health-giving howls, better be silent, it's the only method, if you want to end, not a word but smiles, end rent with stifled imprecations, burst with speechlessness, all is possible, what now. (83)

> Avoir à gémir, sans le pouvoir, aïe, mieux vaut se restreindre, guetter la bonne agonie, elle est trompeuse, on croit y être, on se met à hurler, on revit, bienfaisants hurlements, plutôt se taire, c'est le seul moyen, si l'on veut crever, pas piper, crever craquant d'imprécations rentrées, éclater muet, tout est possible, la suite. (140)

Although explicitly referred to only once, Dante in *Le calmant/The Calmative* has a number of different functions, some of which recall the play between visibility and invisibility observed in *Mercier et/and Camier*. The allusions to the *Comedy* turn the story that the 'I' tells himself into a *déjà vu*. However, as the 'I' in *Molloy* puts it, since the notion of *déjà vu* suggests the possibility of sameness, of identical repetition, 'even the simple *déjà vu* seemed infinitely beyond [my] reach' (103). Dante works as an *auctoritas* because its presence in the text characterises the text as 'literature', but it does not work as a 'source' because it does not reconstitute the sense; rather, it questions the notion of source as explanation and restoration of full meaning.[16] Furthermore, by being merely one of the possible texts alluded to, Dante is only one of the ways in which the text signals its necessary unoriginality: it is one of the ways in which language is conceived as secondary, thus indicating the impossibility of both absolute repetition and absolute originality. What Angela Moorjani says about the 1961/1964 texts can be applied to the works from *Le calmant* to the *Textes pour rien* as well: 'not only is fiction a past narrative, but the past is narrative fiction.'[17]

In *Le calmant/The Calmative* the journey of the 'I' can be linked to some of Dante's movements in the *Inferno* and *Purgatorio*. I have stressed the problems of a thematic parallelism such as that elaborated by Levy in his study of *Mercier and Camier*. I have also underlined that some of the allusions detected by Levy are helpful to understand the text as palimpsest. Dante in *Le calmant/The Calmative* is one of the means through which the story is characterised as secondary and unoriginal. The journey of the *Comedy* cannot function as a source, but is rather a literary space towards which the text intermittently gestures, while refusing to be assimilated.[18] The *Comedy* does not explain the movements of the 'I' of the story, and does not clarify what the story means. What it does, however, is help us understand *how* the story means, that is, how *Le calmant/The Calmative* questions the opposition of fiction and memory by oscillating between them.

The opening of *Le calmant/The Calmative* – 'I don't know when I died' (27), 'Je ne sais plus quand je suis mort' (41) – creates a situation that can be described, as the summary of chapter VIII of *Mercier and Camier* puts it, as 'the life of the afterlife'.[19] In his 'icy bed', (27), 'lit glacé' (41), the character speaks from the 'outrageously inauthentic' position of the characters of the *Comedy*.[20] Unlike *Mercier et/and Camier*, the first person narrator presents the narrative as just 'another story, to try and calm myself' (27), 'encore une histoire, pour essayer de me calmer' (42), that will be told 'in the past none the less, as though it were a myth, or an old fable' (28), 'Je mènerai néanmoins mon histoire au passé, comme s'il s'agissait d'un mythe ou d'une fable ancienne' (43–44). Dante is one of the means through which this story operates *as if* it were a myth or an old fable.

The narrative is, once again, the story of a journey in which most of the elements are strongly allusive and overdeterminedly literary.[21] The character finds himself among trees ('au milieu des arbres'), in a 'grove', 'bosquet', and it is the light that indicates to him the end of 'this little wood', 'ce petit bois'.[22] Although the fact that the story begins in a wood refers to Dante, the attention of the narratee is drawn to another literary work: 'oh, look the trees!' are the paradoxically 'perishing oaks immortalized by D'Aubigné' (28), 'les chênes périssant de d'Aubigné' (44). The pun between 'perishing' and 'immortalise' sums up art's failure to make the text into an eternal artefact, as made clear by the association between the 'gleam of this pale light', 'ce jour plus pâle' with 'God knows what fatuous eternity' (29), 'gage de je ne sais quelle sotte éternité' (44). The ditch which girdles the wood is crossed by the character 'unmindingly', 'distraitement', and later on, we encounter a 'comedian', 'un diseur'. The little wood or grove as starting point and the light as sign of eternity (granted, now fatuous) indicating the end of the wood can be related to *Inferno* I.[23] The ditch limiting the wood, crossed 'unmindingly' by the 'I', can be read as a negative intertext. In *Inferno* I two *terzine* are occupied by a comparison between Dante crossing the limit of the wood, the border between life and death, and a shipwreck survivor.[24]

Later on, we have other scattered details, which, unlike the previous examples, are not in a sequence. Dante works as one of the possible literary meanings of the elements of the story, which, exposing their overdetermination, creates the narrative as unstable and secondary, privileging the act of telling over the subject told.[25] The character's limp is stressed, reminiscent of Dante's limp in *Inferno* I, 30.[26] His painful legs and his feeling gradually 'lighter' point to the *Purgatorio*, in which the pilgrim gradually feels lighter as his efforts in climbing the mount decrease. Parallel to the constant need of directions of Dante and Virgil in their ascent to the Earthly Paradise is the recurrent question of the 'I': 'The Shepherds' Gate for the love of God' (37 and 39).[27] The bowed head is reminiscent of the opening of 'Dante and the Lobster', in which Belacqua Shuah was bowing and raising his head like Dante in *Paradiso* II and III, during and after Beatrice's explanation of the spots of the moon. Other structural correspondences, such as the 'the spiral staircase which I began to climb at top speed' (36) and the 'clockwise' movement followed by the 'I' round the 'projecting gallery' (36) parallel the 'Journey through the "careers" like D. & V. along the Purgatorial cornices', as the 'Whoroscope' notebook puts it.[28] Another word occurring in *The Calmative* and in the 'Whoroscope' notebook is 'impetus', which in the notebook is described as 'given by H. throughout', and in the story remains unexplained. The 'I' realises that he 'was going downhill' and consequently 'turn[s] about and set[s] off in the other direction. For I was afraid if I went downhill of returning to the sea where I had sworn never to return' (37).[29] This, like the clockwise spiralling ascent, is an allusion to *Purgatorio* I, 112–114:

> El cominciò: 'Figliuol, segui i miei passi:
> volgianci in dietro, ché di qua dichina
> questa pianura a' suoi termini bassi'.

> 'Son,' he began, 'follow my steps: let us turn back, for this plain slopes
> that way to its low limits'.

Furthermore, the recorded impression that the 'wide street' is 'vaguely familiar' (37), constructs the familiarity of this 'dream' and intensifies the allusiveness of the passage.[30]

Also reminiscent of the *Purgatorio* is the image of 'overhaul[ing] more than one pedestrian' (35), as Dante and Virgil do.[31] The reference to the 'I''s shadow is also interesting:

> My shadow, one of my shadows, flew before me, dwindled, slid under my feet, trailed behind me the way shadows will. This degree of opacity appeared to me conclusive. (39)

> Mon ombre, une des mes ombres, s'élançait devant moi, se raccourcissait, glissait sous mes pieds, prenait ma suite, à la manière des ombres. Que je fusse à ce degré opaque me semblait concluant. (63)

Although neither of the versions specifies what are the conclusions of this 'conclusive' phenomenon, the French version refers more clearly to the Purgatorial motif of the purging shadows, inferring that Dante is alive because he casts a shadow. There are many examples from the *Purgatorio* in which the shadow is a proof of Dante being alive, thus different from the purging shadows. In *Mercier et Camier* we also encounter a 'sorte d'ombre de Sordel, mais sans y croire, enfin sans y croire assez pour pouvoir se jeter dans ses bras' (184). In the *Unnamable* the 'I' says: 'I wondered if I cast a shadow' (268), and 'For sometimes I confuse myself with my shadow and sometimes don't' (312), and again 'my shadow at evening will not darken the ground' (317). *Purgatorio* III, 88–93 and *Purgatorio* V, 1–9 can be helpful examples to show the relevance of Dante's 'opacity' in the canticle:[32]

> Come color dinanzi vider rotta
> la luce in terra dal mio destro canto,
> sì che l'ombra era da me a la grotta,
> restaro, e trasser sé in dietro alquanto,
> e tutti li altri che venieno appresso,
> non sappiendo 'l perché, fenno altrettanto

When those in front of me saw the light broken on the ground at my right side, so that my shadow was from me to the cliff, they halted and drew back somewhat; and all the other that came after did the same, not knowing why.

> Io era già da quell'ombre partito,
> e seguitava l'orme del mio duca,
> quando di retro a me, drizzando 'l dito,
> una gridò: 'Ve' che non par che luca
> lo raggio da sinistra a quel di sotto,
> e come vivo par che si conduca!'
> Li occhi rivolsi al suon di questo motto,
> e vidile guardar per maraviglia
> pur me, pur me, e 'l lume ch'era rotto.

I had now parted from those shades and was following in the steps of my leader, when one behind me, pointing his finger, cried, 'See, the rays do not seem to shine on the left of him below, and he seems to bear himself like one who is alive!' I turned my eyes at the sound of these words, and saw them gazing in astonishment at me alone, and the light that was broken.

Furthermore, as I have already pointed out in relation to *Mercier et/and Camier*, in the first of the 'Three Dante postcards' lines 19–21, 26, and 37 of *Purgatorio* III are reproduced, preceded by the statement: 'Dante's shadow, Virgil transparent. Seeing only one on ground D thinks V gone.'[33]

All the above examples allude to the *Comedy* but do not explain the story; they reinforce the stated 'vague familiarity' of a *déjà vu*, of 'another story' still.[34] This is also obtained by merging together lines from the *Comedy*. The following image is a synthesis of two passages of the *Comedy*, *Inferno* II, 126–129, and *Purgatorio* I, 134–136. Beckett's texts read:

And the little bruised stems soon straighten up again, having need of air and light, and as for the broken their place is soon taken. (30–31)

Et les petites tiges froissées se relèvent vite, ayant besoin d'air et de lumière, et quant aux cassées elles sont vite remplacées. (48)

Dante's passages read:

> Quali fioretti dal notturno gelo
> chinati e chiusi, poi che 'l sol li 'mbianca,
> si drizzan tutti aperti in loro stelo,
> tal mi fec'io di mia virtude stanca, (*Inf.* II, 126–219)

As little flowers, bent down and closed by chill of night, straighten and all unfold upon their stems when the sun brightens them, such in my faint strength did I become

> oh maraviglia! ché qual elli scelse
> l'umile pianta, cotal si rinacque
> subitamente là onde l'avelse. (*Purg.* I, 134–136)

O marvel! that such as he plucked the humble plant, even such did it instantly spring up again, there whence he had uprooted it

Another passage, followed by a metanarrative comment, is a conflation of two images, one from the *Inferno* and one from the *Purgatorio*:

I saw on the horizon, where sky, sea, plain and mountain meet, a few low stars, not to be confused with the fires men light, at night, or that go alight alone. Enough. (37)

Je vis à l'horizon, là où rejoignent le ciel montagne, mer et plaine, quelques basses étoiles, à ne pas confondre avec les feux qu'allument les hommes, la nuit, ou qui s'allument tout seuls. Assez. (59)

> Io dico, seguitando, ch'assai prima
> che noi fossimo al piè de l'alta torre,
> li occhi nostri n'andar suso a la cima
> per due fiammette che i vedemmo porre,
> e un'altra da lungi render cenno,
> tanto ch'a pena il potea l'occhio tòrre. (*Inf.* VIII, 1–6)

I say, continuing, that long before we had come to the foot of the high tower, our eyes went upward to its summit because of two little flames we saw set there, while yet another returned the signal from so far off that the eye could hardly catch it.

> I' mi volsi a man destra, e puosi mente
> a l'altro polo, e vidi quattro stelle

> non viste mai fuor ch'a la prima gente.
> Goder pareva 'l ciel di lor fiammelle:
> oh settentrïonal vedovo sito,
> poi che privato se' di mirar quelle!
> Com'io da loro sguardo fui partito,
> un poco me volgendo a l'altro polo,
> là onde 'l Carro già era sparito (*Purg.* I, 22–30)

> I turned to the right and gave heed to the other pole, and saw four stars never seen before save by the first people. The heavens seemed to rejoice in their flames. O northern widowed clime, that are deprived of beholding them!
> When I had withdrawn my gaze from them, turning a little to the other pole, there whence the Wain had already disappeared

The stars of *Purgatorio* I, called in the canto 'fiammelle', are merged with the 'fiammette' (both words mean 'little flames') of *Inferno* VIII; the 'little flames' become 'fires'. The intertextual reading is corroborated by the metanarrative comment 'enough', which indicates the 'fatigue and disgust' of 'adding' another inevitable allusive layer to the story.

A similar phenomenon can be observed in the encounter of the 'young woman, perhaps of easy virtue' (38), shadow of the 'puttana sciolta', of *Purgatorio* XXXII, 149, encountered in 'Dante...Bruno.Vico..Joyce', and *Mercier et/and Camier*.[35] The reference to the 'young woman' is followed by the remark 'That is all I had to add' (39), 'Voilà tout ce que je voulais ajouter' (62), which turns the image into a superimposition or a foreign body. And yet, as in the previous example and in the case of *Watt*, the addition can no longer be contrasted with an original, more valuable writing. Rather, it confers visibility upon the inescapable unoriginality of any writing.

At the end of *Le calmant/The Calmative* there is a further reference to *Purgatorio* I, 22–24 and 28–30:

> I said, The sea is east, it's west I must go, to the left of north. But in vain I raised without hope my eyes to the sky to look for the Bears. For the light I steeped in put out the stars, assuming they were there, which I doubted, remembering the clouds. (45–46)

> Je dis, La mer est à l'est, c'est vers l'ouest qu'il faut aller, à gauche du nord. Mais ce fut en vain que je levai sans espoir les yeux au ciel, pour y chercher les chariots. Car la lumière où je macérais aveuglait les étoiles, à supposer qu'elles fussent là, ce don't je doutais, me rappelant les nuages. (75)

The 'I' raises his eyes to the sky to look for the Bears, but now he is without 'hope', a term charged with Dantean connotations from *Dream* on. The light too can be referred to the 'sweet hue of oriental sapphire' (*Purg.* I, 13) characterising the *Purgatorio* after the 'dead air' of the *Inferno*. Furthermore, the movement west and the position of the sea on the east are strongly suggestive of *Purgatorio* IV, 53. The reference builds hopelessness into the theme of the stars through an act of appropriation of Dante's authorial signature, as seen in relation to *Dream*. By concluding the story with a characteristically modified intertextual reference, the text constructs its own ending as a preceding ending, thereby at once deferring its own 'being over' and marking it as 'authoritative' and originally unoriginal.[36]

Odds and ends

Dante is also one of the many elements connecting the *Three Novels* to the *Novellas*. The function of Dante in *Molloy*, *Malone Dies*, and *The Unnamable* is more markedly intratextual than in the *Nouvelles*. Towards the beginning of *Molloy* we read:

> He [C] hadn't seen me. I was perched higher than the road's highest point and flattened what is more against a rock the same colour as myself, that is grey. That rock he probably saw. He gazed around as if to engrave the landmarks on his memory and must have seen the rock in the shadow of which I crouched like Belacqua, or Sordello, I forget. (12)

> Il ne m'avait pas vu. J'étais juché au-dessus du niveau le plus élevé de la route et plaqué par-dessus le marché contre un rocher de la même couleur que moi, je veux dire gris. Qu'il aperçut le rocher, c'est probable. Il regardait autour de lui, je l'ai déjà fait remarquer, comme pour graver dans sa mémoire les caractéristiques du chemin, et il dut voir le rocher à l'ombre duquel j'étais tapi, à la façon de Belacqua, ou de Sordello, je ne me rappelle plus. (13)

This Dante is an intratextual rather than an intertextual reference. The image of Belacqua is confused with that of Sordello, and the 'I' identifies himself with the two figures. The very Beckettian 'Belacqua posture' and the confusion between Belacqua and Sordello are appropriated by the 'I', who hides from his creation/*alter ego*, absorbed in trying to memorise the landmarks. Angela Moorjani writes that 'in a reduplication of the Hackett-Watt encounter at the beginning of *Watt*, this opening episode stages Molloy watching two parts of himself meet and part'.[37]

The image of 'coming and going' had already been mediated by a Dante memory in *Watt* and in *Le calmant/The Calmative*. Here Sordello mediates the description of the 'elevated observer', and the context of the passage presents various Dantean elements, such as the sea in the east and characters climbing 'slower and slower, up the winding stones' (11).[38] Furthermore, the detail of being flattened against a rock of the same colour as the 'I', namely grey, can be read against *Purgatorio* XIII, 46–48:

> Allora più che prima li occhi apersi;
> guarda'mi innanzi, e vidi ombre con manti
> al color de la pietra non diversi.
>
> then more than before I opened my eyes: I looked in front of me and saw shades with cloaks no different in color from the stone[39]

Moorjani helps us to understand how pervasive is the allusiveness to Dante. She writes:

> The corresponding episode [to the one mentioned above of A and B] in Part II occurs during the last third of Moran's self-narration. During the three days he is waiting for his son to return with a bicycle ..., Moran, at dusk, comes face to face with his versions of B (the old man with the club) and A (the dim man). On the first day, Moran, after contemplating his wavering reflection in a stream, meets an old man whose face he desires as his own. On the second day, he sees first an unidentifiable face in the flowing depths of an inner glass and later a man by the campfire whose face, described in terms reminiscent of Moran's likeness in a mirror, resembles Moran's own. (42)

As observed above, the 'dim man' can inter- and intratextually be associated with 'one who seemed faint through long silence'. The image of the face emerging from the flowing depths of an inner glass can also be found in *Paradiso* III, 10–18, in *Dream of Fair to Middling Women*, in the '*Dream*' notebook, and in the essay *Le Concentrisme*, in which it appears as 'un caillou à peine visible contre une front exsangue'.[40] I reproduce below the passages from *Molloy*, from *Dream of Fair to Middling Women*, and from the '*Dream*' notebook quoting the *Comedy*:

> And then I saw a little globe swaying up slowly from the depths, through the quiet water, smooth at first, and scarcely paler than its escorting ripples, then little by little a face, with holes for the eyes and mouth and other wounds, and nothing to show if it was a man's face or a woman's face, a young face or an old face, or if its calm too was not an effect of the water trembling between it and the light. (137)

> Et je voyais alors une petite boule montant lentement des profondeurs, à travers des eaux calmes, unie d'abord, à peine plus claire que les remous qui l'escortent, puis peu à peu visage d'homme ou de femme, jeune ou vieux, ni si son calme aussi n'est pas un effet de l'eau qui le sépare du jour. (230)

> So that as from transparent and polished glass or, if you prefer, from tranquil shining waters, the details of his face return so feeble that a pearl on a white

brow comes not less promptly to his pupils, so now he sees her vigilant face and in him is reversed the error that lit love between the man (if you can call such a spineless creature a man) and the pool. For she had closed her eyes.

'Spirit of the moon' he said.
She begged his pardon. (175)

> Quali per vetri trasparenti e tersi,
> ovver per acque nitide e tranquille,
> non si profonde che i fondi sien persi,
> tornan dei nostri visi le postille
> debili sì, che perla in bianca fronte
> non vien men tosto alle nostre pupille:
> tali vid'io più facce a parlar pronte:
> per ch'io dentro all'erro [sic] contrario corsi
> a quel ch'accese amor tra l'uomo e il fonte
> (the Spirits of the Moon)

The translation which follows the passage in the '*Dream*' notebook reads:

> As from transparent polished glass or from
> tranquil shining shallows the details of my
> face return so in faint that a pearl on a white
> brow comes no slower to my pupils, so
> I saw the eager faces and in me who re-
> versed the error that lit a fire of love between
> the man & the pool.

The calm and smooth water, and the surfacing of the faces allude to a passage of *Paradise* in which the Ovidian myth of Narcissus is reversed, as in a mirror, to describe the 'Spirits of the Moon.'[41] A similar image surfaces in *Text 6*, in which the Ovidian myth creates a further *déjà vu*:

> The eyes, yes, if these memories are mine, I must have believed in them an instant, believed it was me I saw there dimly in the depths of their glades. (103)

> les yeux, oui, si ces souvenirs sont miens, j'ai dû y croire, un moment, croire m'y voir, obscurément, au fond de leurs perspectives. (171)

The Dantean allusion is part of the process of mirroring and duplication at work not only in single texts such as *Watt* but also intratextually, as can be observed from the excerpts reproduced above.

The name of Sordello and the crouching Belacqua posture recur towards the end of *Malone meurt/Malone Dies*, where Murphy, Watt, and Quin appear as patients of the asylum/skull:

> The thin one chafed to run about, but the youth had thrown himself down in the shade of a rock, like Sordello, but less noble, for Sordello resembled a lion at rest, and clung to it with both hands. (262)
>
> Le maigre avait envie de courir dans toute l'île, mais le jeune s'était couché à l'ombre d'un rocher, et cela le faisait ressembler, en moins fier, à Sordello, qui lui avait l'air d'un lion au repos, et il s'y accrochait. (214)

In *Malone meurt/Malone Dies* Murphy, rather than the 'I', is superimposed upon the Sordello/Belacqua figure. The 'gallery of moribunds', namely the list of Beckettian characters from Murphy onwards, is frequently mentioned in the *Three Novels*, in which 'each successive character in the series [is] conceived of as a repetition and a reimagination at the same time'.[42] The names of Sordello and Belacqua have a function similar to that of the other names coming from the 'Beckett canon'; they are part of the open-ended series of reduplications and mirrorings which structure the narrative.[43]

The function of Dante in the *Three Novels* is that of a fading memory, which 'comes and goes'. The relationship between inventing and remembering is increasingly destabilised, and the recognition of a difference between the two is questioned. As the 'I' in *Molloy* puts it:

> Perhaps I had invented him [Molloy or Mollose], I mean found him ready-made in my head. There is no doubt one sometimes meets with strangers who are not entire strangers, through their having played a part in certain cerebral reels. This had never happened to me, I considered myself immune from such experiences, and even the simple *déjà vu* seemed infinitely beyond my reach. But it was happening to me then, or I was greatly mistaken. (103)
>
> Peut-être l'avais-je inventée, je veux dire trouvé toute faite dans ma tête. Il est certain qu'on rencontre parfois des inconnus qui ne le sont pas tout à fait, pour avoir joué un rôle dans certaines sequences cérébrales. Cela ne m'était jamais arrivé, je ne me croyais pas fait pour des experiences pareilles, et même le simple déjà vu me paraissait infiniment hors de ma portée. Mais cela avait tout l'air de m'arriver alors. (172)

The confusion between Sordello and Belacqua, stated in *Molloy*, is implicitly re-elaborated in *Malone meurt/Malone Dies*. The position of Sordello, like a lion at rest on a rock, is merged with that of Belacqua crouching in the shade of a rock. The memory that keeps surfacing is always a non-coinciding re-imagination. The text of the *Comedy*, 'just' remembered in *The Calmative*, has lost its reassuring power.

Dante is part of the movement of repetition, observed by Connor at work in *Molloy*, which 'itself produces the play of sameness and difference which is the text'.[44] The numerous references in *L'innomable/The Unnamable* to spiralling movement, to islands, sea, and to hell and paradise can be read in the light of Connor's argument:

> To tell the truth – no, first the story. The island, I'm on the island, I've never left the island, God help me. I was under the impression I spent my life in spirals round the earth. Wrong, it's on the island I wind my endless ways. The island, that's all the earth I know. I don't know it either, never having had the stomach to look at it. When I come to the coast I turn back inland. And my course is not helicoidal, I got that wrong too, but a succession of irregular loops (300)

> A vrai dire – non, l'histoire d'abord. Pour porter à son comble mon mal de cœur. L'île, je suis dans l'île, je n'ai jamais quitté l'île, pauvre de moi. J'avais cru comprendre que je passais ma vie à faire le tour du monde, en colimaçon. Erreur, c'est dans l'île que je ne cesse de tourner. Je ne connais rien d'autre, seulement l'île. Elle non plus je ne la connais pas, n'ayant jamais eu la force de la regarder. Quand j'arrive au rivage, je m'en retourne, vers l'intérieur. Ce n'est pas une spirale, mon chemin, là aussi je me suis gouré, mais des boucles irrégulières (81)

> He hears, that's all about it, he who is alone, and mute, lost in the smoke, it is not real smoke, there is no fire, no matter, strange hell that has no heating, no denizens, perhaps it's paradise, perhaps it's the light of paradise, and the solitude, and this voice the voice of the blest interceding invisible, for the living, for the dead, all is possible. (330)

> Il entend, un point c'est tout, lui qui est seul, et muet, perdu dans la fumée, c'est ne pas de feu, ça ne fait rien, drôle d'enfer, non chauffée, non peuplée, c'est peut-être le paradis, c'est peut-être la lumière du paradis, et la solitude, et cette voix celle des bienheureux qui intercèdent, invisibles, pour les vivants, pour les morts, tout est possible. (147–148)

The references to Dante also work in connection with authority. As observed by Moorjani, the time and place of the Easter excursion in *Malone Dies* 'evoke Beckett's birth during Easter week and Dante's Easter ascent in the *Divine Comedy*'.[45] And yet, every date is like the mythical reference to 1900 in *Mercier et/and Camier*. As we read in *The Unnamable*:

> For I am obliged to assign a beginning to my residence here, if only for the sake of clarity. Hell itself, although eternal, dates from the revolt of Lucifer. It is therefore permissible, in the light of this distant analogy, to think of myself as being here forever. This will greatly help me in my relation. Memory, notably, which I did not think myself entitled to draw upon, will have its word to say, if necessary. (271)

These scattered allusions do not allow us to speak of the *Three Novels* as a 'reworking of Dante's *Inferno* and *Purgatorio*'; rather, they constitute Dante's *Comedy* as a flickering, non-coinciding, intratextual memory which underlines the secondariness of language.[46] Dante is not present in the *Three Novels* as a model masterpiece against which Beckett's fictional masterpiece moulds itself; instead, Dante inscribes the mark of literature in a series of texts which explore the modalities according to which literature works.

One last example of how the Beckett canon shapes itself as a series of 'self-contextualizing texts' is provided by the way in which a few terms intratextually related to the *Comedy* are employed, like the following:[47]

> I sometimes see shining afar and how is it the moon where *Cain toils bowed beneath his burden* never sheds its light on my face? (203; emphasis mine)

> Mais comment se fait-il alors que mon petit espace ne bénéficie pas des astres qu'il m'arrive de voir briller au loin et que cette lune ou Caïn peine sous son fardeau ne m'éclaire jamais le visage? (86)

> But for the moment let him *toss and turn* at least, roll on the ground, damn it all, since there's no other remedy, anything at all, to relieve the monotony, damn it all, look at the burnt alive, they don't have to be told, when not lashed to the stake, to rush about in every direction, without method, crackling, in search of a little cool (338; emphasis mine)

> Pour l'heure qu'au moins il s'agite, qu'il se roule par terre, que diable, puisqu'il n'y a pas d'autre remède, n'importe quoi, pour rompre la monotonie (164–165)

The first example, both from the English and from the French texts, once again connects the term 'toil' with the image of Cain from the *Comedy*, first adopted in *Dream*. The second one alludes, but only in the English text, to the 'tossing and turning' of the 'Sedendo and Quiesciendo' [sic] section of *Dream* which uses the simile between Florence and the sick patient in *Purgatorio* VI.

These inter- and intratextual scattered fragments, do not, however, reconstitute the 'ventriloquist' that the 'I' in *The Unnamable* claims was visible in *Murphy* (320). They are part of the textual memory made of voices at once internal and external, new and already seen, through which 'the very drive to fix or position the self as an entity ... brings about the splitting of the self into simulacra'.[48] The 'I' oscillates from the position of a 'ventriloquist' to that of 'a mere ventriloquist's dummy'.[49] As said in *The Unnamable*: 'it's entirely a matter of voices, no other metaphor is appropriate' (298).

The allusions to Dante are in the *Three Novels* part of the process which transforms any text into a voice and any voice into a text. We can read Dante as part of the oscillation between the 'I' as ever-shifting memory and unoriginal invention. Angela Moorjani observes that in Beckett's *Three Novels* writing entails 'a process of fraying a path into the embedded archives of the mind consisting of the records of previous frayings and the inscriptions of the past.' These 'embedded records' can never be transcribed accurately, but they are 'full of flaws and gaps through which are noticeable the traces of another text ... and so on to infinity'.[50] Dante is part of the 'Beckett archive'.

Bits and scraps flickering on and off

In the *Textes pour rien/Texts for Nothing* 'it's too late now, too late to deny it, the knowledge is there, the bits and scraps, flickering on and off, turn about, winking on the storm, in league to fool me' (86), 'mais il est trop tard, trop tard pour le nier, les connaissances sont là, elles luisent tour à tour, proches et lointaines, clignent sur l'abîme, complices' (146). The stars promising guidance in *Malone Dies* are still a textual memory.[51] However, these texts point out what was said in *Molloy*, namely that 'if it happens that I speak of the stars it is by mistake' (16). Dante is part of what Carla Locatelli calls 're-membering', that is to say the way in which 'the strong intertextuality of the Beckettian texts is itself a condition for calling to our attention semiosis as a process in which the creation of meaning is the product of the dynamics of reference as interpretive performance.'[52]

Similarly to *Le calmant/The Calmative*, the thirteen texts allude to Dante in different ways. In the English version there are a number of words intratextually associated with a Dantean context, such as 'toiling' (78), 'arsy-varsy' (128), and expressions such as 'quick quick all die' (134) and 'a pity hope is dead' (84). These refer to the English part of Beckett's *oeuvre*, since 'arsy-versy' – encountered in 'Text', *More Pricks Than Kicks*, *Mercier and Camier*, and *All That Fall* – is in the French 'tout de travers' (206) (rather than 'cul-à-cul', as in *Mercier et Camier*). Similarly, the pun on 'quick' and 'dying', which intratextually resurfaces in 'Text' and 'Dante and the Lobster' is not present in 'vite vite tous meurent' (213). 'Dommage que l'espoir soit mort' (142) is, however, very close to 'pity all hope is dead', both intratextually referring to a Dantean context.

In one instance, the correspondence between French and English is very close; 'toiling up the slope, or in the bracken by the wood' (78) is in the French: 'peinant à mi-versante, ou dans les fougeraies qui bordent le bois' (132). The whole passage reads:

> and yet it's not, not certain, what is not certain, absolutely certain, that night prevents what day permits, for those who know how to go about it ... the wind

> freshen and the whole night sky open over the mountain, with its lights, including the Bears, to guide me once again on my way, let's wait for night. All mingles, times and tenses, at first I only had been here, now I'm here still, soon I won't be here yet, toiling up the slope, or in the bracken of the wood ... for the moment I'm here, always have been, always shall be, I won't be afraid of the big words any more, they are not big. (78)
>
> qu'est-ce qui n'est pas sûr, absolument sûr, que la nuit empêche ce que le jour permet, à ceux qui savent s'y prendre ... le vent fraîchira, la nuit venue, et sur la montagne ce sera tout le ciel nocturne, avec ses luminaires, dont les chariots, pour me servir de guide, encore une fois, de guide à mes pas, attendons la nuit. Tout s'emmêle, les temps s'emmêlent, d'abord j'y avais seulement été, maintenant j'y suis toujours, tout à l'heure je n'y serai pas encore, peinant à mi-versant, ou dans les fougeraies qui bordent le bois ... pour l'instant je suis là, depuis toujours, pour toujours, je n'aurai plus peur des grands mots, ils ne sont pas grands. (132–133)

The Purgatorial rule expressed by Sordello, that 'night prevents what day permits' (*Purg.* VII, 48–60), which entails the vertical progression up the Purgatorial mount, is no longer certain. Yet the *Texts*, like the *Nouvelles* before them, can still look at a sky in which help and guidance from the stars can be sought. The passage recalls *The Expelled*: 'But first I raised my eyes to the sky, whence cometh our help' (13) and *The End*: 'There were stars in the sky, quite a few' (71). The repetitive quality of the image, underlined by 'once again', is then 'mingled' by the succession of past continuous, present and future. 'Here', at first constructed as 'toiling up the slope', is gradually emptied of its reference. The 'imagined' future appearance of the guiding stars is built through a memory which, however, can never be identical to itself, which cannot guarantee either the past or the future.

The claustrophobic space of the *Texts* is limited by the hypothesis of an 'above' (*Text 2*, 81) and of a 'way out' (*Text 9*, 117), which anticipate the structure of *Comment c'est/How It Is* and *Le dépeupleur/The Lost Ones*. 'Above' can be interpreted, as Moorjani points out, as a 'textual direction', the "see above (earlier)" correspond[s] to the "past-above" conceptualization' (63). The stars acquire in *Text 9* a specific Dantean connotation; their being 'above' creates Dante as 'past', as memory:

> And I have no doubts, I'd get there somehow, to the way out, sooner or later, if I could say, There's a way out there, there's a way out somewhere, the rest would come, the other words, sooner or later, and the power to get there, and the way to get there, and pass out, and see the beauties of the skies, and see the stars again. (121)

> Et je suis tranquille, j'y irais, à l'issue, tôt ou tard, si je la disais là, quelque part, les autres mots me viendraient, tôt ou tard, et de quoi pouvoir y aller, et y aller, et passer à travers, et voir les belles choses que porte le ciel, et revoir les étoiles. (196)

In the French text the allusion is very close to *Inferno* XXXIV, 135–139:

> e sanza cura aver d'alcun riposo,
> salimmo sú, el primo e io secondo,
> tanto ch'i' vidi de le cose belle
> che porta 'l ciel, per un pertugio tondo.
> E quindi uscimmo a riveder le stelle.

> and caring not for any rest, we climbed up, he first and I second, so far that through a round opening I saw some of the beautiful things that Heaven bears; and thence we issued forth to see again the stars.

In *Text 9* the wish that memory 'could be wiped from knowledge' (82) is phrased as a wish 'to have done, with worlds, with creatures, with words, with misery, misery' (118). The impossibility of cessation is articulated through the hypothesis that opens the text: 'If I said, there is a way out there, there is a way out somewhere, the rest would come' (117). The impossibility of a way out which would entail 'the rest' (but 'what does that mean, the rest?' 117) coexists with the impossibility of having 'done' with it. By hypothesising an impossible utterance, the text at once tenders it and retracts it: 'it must be said, since I just said it' and 'What am I waiting for then, to say it?' Simultaneously, the wish for cessation is still a wish for a way out for the non-coinciding subject:

> wordshit, bury me, avalanche, and let there be no more talk of any creature, nor of a world to leave ... Which no sooner said, Ah, says I, punctually, if only I could say, There's a way out there, there's a way out somewhere, then all would be said, it would be the first step on the long travelable road, destination tomb, to be trod without a word, tramp tramp (118)

> Fatras, mets-toi autour de moi, avalanche, qu'il ne soit plus question de personne, ni d'un monde à quitter ... Et pas plus tôt dit, Ah, que je me dis, il faillait s'y attendre, si seulement je pouvais dire, Là il y a une issue, tout serait dit, ce serait le premier pas, du long voyage faisable, destination tombe, à faire dans le silence (191)

The 'long travelable road', the promise of 'the rest', the 'way out' is, at the end of the text, the passage out of the *Inferno*. The stars are, once again, the theo/teleological promise of the Dantean system, and the way out is the 'round opening' through which they can be seen. The way out into an 'above' is also a way out into the text of the *Comedy*, into the promise of the guiding lights for the pilgrim and the scribe. The 'impossible' ending effectively becomes the ending of the text. And yet in Dante this is both a threshold and an ending; it is the beginning of the *Purgatorio* and not only the end of the first canticle.

Thus, the impossible 'rest' is also the impossible end of the text. 'Rest' means 'the rest to come', the impossible future continuation of the text, but it also means 'repose', 'tranquillity', 'death', and 'residuum'. The allusion to *Inferno* XXXIV is all this at once. It is the soothing promise of a future of tranquillity, represented by the story that can calm. It is also the image of the literary text, which represents the very possibility of literature. It is a residuum, too, a rest from a textual past, a memory which cannot be cancelled, the promise of a future which can only exist in the past.

The apparently soothing quality of the past is to be found again in connection to Dante in *Text 6*:

> I was, I was, they say in Purgatory, in Hell too, admirable singulars, admirable assurance. Plunged in ice up to the nostrils, the eyelids caked with frozen tears, to fight all your battles o'er again, what tranquillity, and know there are no more emotions in store, no, I can't have heard aright. (104)

> Je fus, je fus, disent ceux du Purgatoire, ceux des Enfers aussi, admirable pluriel, merveilleuse assurance. Plongé dans la glace, jusqu'aux narines, les paupières collées de larmes gelées, revivre ses campagnes, quelle tranquillité, et se savoir au bout de ses surprises, non, j'ai dû mal entendre. (172)

The precise allusion is to a canto already mentioned in relation to *Watt* in which the punishment consists, 'in being entombed up to the neck in ice. Dante sees two so buried, and so close together that their very hair is interwoven', as an early 'Dante' notebook puts it or, as 'dread nay' does, 'in hellice eyes / stream till / frozen to / jaws rails / gnaw gnash / teeth with stork / clack chatter':[53]

> li occhi lor, ch'eran pria pur dentro molli,
> gocciar su per le labbra, e 'l gelo strinse
> le lagrime tra essi rinserrolli. (*Inf.* XXXII, 46–48)

their eyes, which before were moist only within, walled up with tears, which ran down over the lips, and the frost bound each to each and locked them even tighter.

The subject tells a story to himself in his icy bed; as in *Le calmant/The Calmative* it is connected to the reassuring character attributed to such a possibility. The possibility of saying 'I was' and of fighting 'your battles o'er again' is at first described as the 'tranquillity' guaranteed by a self-identical future which will not entail new 'emotions'. The tears, marks of this emotionality, are frozen, as in *Mal vu mal dit/Ill Seen Ill Said*: 'L'œil reviendra sur les lieux de ses trahison. En congé séculaire de là où gèlent les larmes', 'The eye will return to the scene of its betrayals. On centennial leave from where tears freeze.'[54]

The admirable assurance of the 'I was' is what, according to the (admirably self-assured) Animator in *Rough for Radio II*, characterises the *Purgatorio*: 'A: Not read the Purgatory? ... There all sighs, I was, I was. It's like a knell. Strange, is it not?' In the radio drama the repeated 'I was' is not reassuring, since its 'strangeness' derives from its impossibility either to retrieve accurate memories or to live in hope, as the Animator explains: 'Why, one would rather have expected, I shall be. No?'[55] In *Text 6* this 'admirable assurance' is only initially attributed to the *Comedy*, the text alluded to, in which the absolute past is still possible. However, the final sentence 'I can't have heard aright' destabilises both the *Comedy* as text and the possibility of reproducing it as memory.

The passage also blurs the textual spaces; we can hypothesise that the 'I' places himself in the position of Dante the pilgrim listening to the 'people'/'characters' inhabiting the *Inferno* and the *Purgatorio*, and questions his powers as witness. At the same time, however, the use of acoustic rather than visual terminology ('hear' rather than, say, 'read') mobilises the text alluded to and makes it unstable. The 'I', external to the *Comedy*, has misheard the voices coming from there, has misinterpreted the text.

Thus, the intertext is initially given the meaning of the soothing ever-identical past tense, capable of freezing the unpredictable emotionality of the future. This meaning, however, is later questioned through the volatile notion of 'hearing'. The *Comedy* itself becomes a 'voice' that the 'I' can 'mishear'; it is not an immobile, given 'text' to which only one meaning can be attached, but it is the scene of interpretation. The use of acoustic terminology in this passage calls into question the possibility of the 'I' as reliable witness and the authenticity of his 'experience'. It also inscribes an oscillating, unstable quality in the alluded text itself, which can no longer be regarded as the 'source text' to which only one meaning can be attached. Furthermore, 'I can't have heard aright' critiques the possibility of repeating the 'source text', now transformed into a 'voice', and marks the loss of the reassuring quality of allusion and quotation.

In the *Textes pour rien/Texts for Nothing* the metaphor of the voice at underlines the instability of the text and evokes the impossible guarantee of authenticity.[56] The following paragraph, which deals explicitly with the 'mythic images of earth and sky', plays with the ambiguities raised by the metaphor of the voice and that of the scribe:[57]

> the sky and the earth, I've heard great accounts of them, now that's pure word for word, I invent nothing. I've noted, I must have noted many a story with

them as setting, they create the atmosphere ... The sea too, I am conversant with the sea too, it belongs to the same family, I have even gone to the bottom more than once, under various assumed names, don't make me laugh, if only I could laugh, all would vanish, all what, who knows, all, me, it's noted. (*Text 5*, 97)

le ciel et la terre, j'en ai beaucoup entendu parler, ça alors c'est du vrai mot à mot, je n'invente rien. J'ai noté, j'ai dû noter beaucoup d'histoires les ayant pour décor, ils créent l'ambiance ... la mer aussi, je suis au courant de la mer aussi, elle fait partie de la meme série, je m'y suis même noyé à plusieurs reprises, sous diverses fausses appellations, laisse-moi rire, si seulement je pouvais rire, tout disparaîtrait, quoi, qui sait, tout, moi, embarqué. (162–163)

The 'sky and the earth', and 'the sea too' are always inevitably unoriginal, part of the same 'family' or 'série'. The 'I' claims to have heard 'great accounts' of them and to reproduce them 'pure[ly]', 'word for word'. The 'mythic images' initially appear to be transcriptions, the result of a 'simple' noting down of the accounts heard. But just as such a 'recording' is posited as faithful and identical repetition, the 'I' explicitly invents 'fictive' descents to the bottom of the sea under 'various assumed' personae ('fausses appellations'). This questions the very possibility of self-identical repetition and makes the hypothesis of transcription laughable. Furthermore, the play with different personae is enacted by the statement 'don't make me laugh', which constructs a 'you' as the source of ridiculous writing. This means that to this 'you' can be attributed the descent to the bottom of the sea 'under various assumed names'. The 'you' then becomes what the narrative has been presenting as the 'I' so far; this creates both positions as part of an enclosed textual circle, whose infinity makes the wish for an end crumble, together with the conceptualisations of a unitary subject and object. The redeeming possibility of laughter is denied by 'it's noted', which suggests another unreliable 'scribe', caught in the same circular movement of impossible repetition and identity.

The 'earth', the 'sea', and the 'sky', are secondary elements which 'create the atmosphere', endlessly reproduced but never self-identical. The 'guiding stars' have a similar function in the texts from the *Novellas* to the *Texts for Nothing*; they construct fiction as the unaccountable 'rest' of repetition.

Notes

1. Samuel Beckett, *Stories and Texts for Nothing* (New York: Grove Weidenfeld, 1967) and *Nouvelles et textes pour rien* (Paris: Les Éditions de Minuit, 1958).
2. Steven Connor, *Samuel Beckett: Repetition, Theory and Text* (Oxford: Blackwell, 1988), p. 76.

3 John Pilling, *Beckett Before Godot* (Cambridge: Cambridge University Press, 1997), p. 221.
4 Pilling, *Beckett Before Godot*, p. 218.
5 *Premier amour* was published separately from the rest of the *Nouvelles et textes pour rien*. Samuel Beckett, *Premier amour* (Les Éditions de Minuit, 1970); Samuel Beckett, *First Love*, in S. E. Gontarski (ed.), *Samuel Beckett: The Complete Short Prose 1929–1989* (New York: Grove Press, 1995), pp. 25–45.
6 In *La fin/The End* one allusion to *Inferno* V is maintained both in the French and in the English text. *La fin* reads: 'au-delà du stupide espoir de repos ou de moindre peine' (103); *The End* reads: 'beyond the stupid hope of rest or less pain' (62). *Inferno* V, 44–45 reads: 'nulla speranza li conforta mai, / non che di possa, ma di minor pena' (No hope of less pain, not to say of rest, ever comforts them). Francesca Del Moro has drawn attention to this allusion in her '"The Divine Florentine": Dante nell'opera di Samuel Beckett', dissertation, University of Pisa, 1996, p. 90.
7 Samuel Beckett, *Happy Days* (New York: Grove Weidenfeld, 1961), p. 57.
8 Samuel Beckett, *The Beckett Trilogy: Molloy, Malone Dies, The Unnamable* (London: Picador, 1979), p. 364.
9 The *Paradiso* is, however, based on this failure, and the textual examples can be many. See, for example, *Par.* XIV, 103–108; XVIII, 8–12; XXIII, 61–63. For a discussion of how the canticle uses impotence see Teodolinda Barolini, *The Undivine Comedy: Detheologizing Dante* (Princeton: Princeton University Press, 1992).
10 For a liberal humanist interpretation of the passage see Jean-Pierre Ferrini, 'À partir du desert: Dante et l'aphonie de Virgile dans "Le calmant" de Samuel Beckett', *Samuel Beckett Today/Aujourd'hui*, 13 (2003), 201–212; Ferrini's reading is indebted to Kelly Anspaugh's view of *The Calmative* as a subversion of the *Comedy* in his 'The partially purged: Samuel Beckett's "The Calmative" as anti-*Comedy*', *Canadian Journal of Irish Studies*, 22:1 (1996), 30–41.
11 A number of English translations of the *Comedy* render 'fioco' by 'hoarse'. However, this is not the case with Cary's translation, owned by Beckett, which reads: 'I fell, my ken discern'd the form of one / Whose voice seem'd faint through long disuse of speech.' *The Vision of Dante Alighieri, or Hell, Purgatory and Paradise*, translated by the Rev. H. F. Cary (London: Bell and Daldy, 1869), p. 16. The phrase 'per lungo silenzio parea fioco' follows Virgil's allegorical description in TCD MS 10963, fol. 2.
12 Vittorio Sermonti, *L'Inferno di Dante* (Milan: Rizzoli, 1988), p. 9; Giovanni Getto, 'Inferno I', in *Lectura Dantis Scaligera. Inferno* (Florence: Le Monnier, 1967), p. 12. Most critics follow Getto's interpretation. See for example Pompeo Giannantonio, '*Inferno* I', in Pompeo Giannantonio (ed.), *Lectura Dantis Neapolitana* (Naples: Loffredo, 1986). The passage has also been allegorically interpreted as the dim surfacing of reason after its long silence from the sinner's conscience. See Emilio Pasquini and Antonio Quaglio (eds), *Commedia* (Milan: Garzanti, 1987).
13 Gérard Genette, *Narrative Discourse* (Oxford: Blackwell, 1980), p. 236; the author's italics.
14 'I took it eagerly and put it in my mouth, the old gesture came back to me' (33). In the French the word 'bouche' is not repeated: 'les enfers' 's'ouvrent', the 'bonbon' is put 'dans [ma] bouche', the 'phrase' is 'prononcée', and the boy is 'à l'orée de la vie' (53–54). For a discussion of the use of 'mouth' in Beckett, with some references to Dante's Bocca degli Abati in *Inferno* XXXII, see Keir Elam, 'World's End: West Brompton, Turdy and

other godforsaken holes', *Beckett Today/Aujourd'hui. Crossroads and Borderlines, L'œuvre carrefour/l'œuvre limite*, 6 (1997),165–179.

15 The 'murmuring' and 'buzzing' are relevant in *Molloy* too: 'And the words I uttered myself, and which must nearly always have gone with an effort of the intelligence, were often to me as the buzzing of an insect' (47).

16 I am arguing against Michael Riffaterre's claim that 'the text does not signify unless as a function of a complementary or contradictory intertextual homologue'. Riffaterre claims that the intertextual reading is 'an operation of the reader's mind, but it is an obligatory one, necessary to any textual decoding'. Michel Riffaterre, 'Intertextual representation: on mimesis as interpretive discourse', *Critical Inquiry*, 11:1 (September 1984), 142–162, 142–143.

17 Angela Moorjani, *Abysmal Games in the Novels of Samuel Beckett* (Chapel Hill: North Carolina Studies in the Romance Languages and Literatures, 1982), p. 62.

18 My reading differs from Theoharis Constantine Theoharis's, who claims: 'The conviction Dante felt, the heroic sense of guilt and purposeful atonement, has faded to irritation and unavailing complaint for Beckett.' Theoharis Constantine Theoharis, '"Che la diritta via era smarrita": Dante's *Commedia* in Beckett's *Texts for Nothing*', *Journal of the Short Story in English*, 41 (2003), 25–39, 38.

19 Samuel Beckett, *Mercier and Camier* (London: Picador, 1988), p. 123. In the French: 'la vie de la survie'. Samuel Beckett, *Mercier et Camier* (Paris: Les Éditions de Minuit, 1970), p. 211.

20 For a discussion of the role of the 'outrageously inauthentic' devices at work in the *Comedy* see Barolini, *The Undivine Comedy*, pp. 13 and 48–73.

21 For a discussion of literary overdetermination in Beckett see Aldo Tagliaferri, *Beckett e l'iperdeterminazione letteraria* (Milan: Feltrinelli, 1976).

22 One of the working titles of *Mercier et Camier* was *Le Voyage de Mercier et Camier autour du Pot dans le Bosquet de Bondy*.

23 For a reading of *The Calmative* as a subversion of the *Comedy* see Anspaugh, 'The partially purged'.

24 'E come quei che con lena affannata, / uscito fuor di pelago a la riva, / si volge verso a l'acqua perigliosa e guata, / così l'animo mio, ch'ancor fuggiva, / si volse a retro a rimirar lo passo / che non lasciò già mai persona viva' (And as he who with laboring breath has escaped from the deep to the shore turns to look back on the dangerous waters, so my mind which was still fleeing turned back to gaze upon the pass that never left anyone alive) (*Inf* I, 22–26).

25 See Carla Locatelli, *La disdetta della parola: l'ermeneutica del silenzio nella prosa inglese di Samuel Beckett* (Bologna: Patron, 1984); Angela Moorjani, *Abysmal Games*, p. 49; Dina Sherzer, *Structure de la Trilogie de Beckett* (The Hague: Mouton, 1976), p. 86.

26 Beckett writes: '"sì che 'l piè fermo sempre era 'l più basso" ... true for one walking on the flat. But Dante is already on the *piaggia*, gentle slope that preceeds the steep (erba). Meant probably to suggest hesitancy of forward reaching foot', TCD MS 10966, fol. 1. The line translates as 'so that the firm foot was always the lower'. Allegorical readings of different kinds have been proposed as possible explanation of this 'impossible' limp. 'Impossible' because, even if limping on the slope of a hill, one would have to put one's weight alternatively on one and the other foot in order to proceed.

27 The 'I' also says that he enters the town through the 'Shepherds' Gate'. St Peter, the guardian of the Gate of Purgatory, is called 'archimandrita' (archimandrite) in *Paradiso*

XI, 99 and 'Archimandrita nostro' (our archimandrite) in *Monarchia*, III, IX, 17. The allusion to the 'Shepherds' Gate' reappears in *Molloy*, as pointed out by Connor, *Samuel Beckett*, p. 83.

28 The first entry of the first of the 'three postcards' reads: 'Pur. I, 22 / I' mi volsi a man destra / (in Hell turn always to the left / ' Purg ' ' ' ' right)', RUL MS 4123.
29 In the French: 'Mais bientôt m'apercevant de la pente je fis demi-tour et repartis dans l'autre sens, car je craignais en descendant de retourner à la mer, où j'avais dit que je ne retournerais plus' (60).
30 'Or have I been dreaming, am I dreaming?' (43). But see also 'The End': 'I had a vague vision, not a real vision' (53). The term 'dream' is also reminiscent of the posthumously published *Dream of Fair to Middling Women*, thus building in a further intratextual layer. 'Vision' is a crucial term in the *Comedy*; one of Beckett's own copies of the text was entitled *The Vision of Dante Alighieri: or Hell, Purgatory, and Paradise* translated by the Rev. Henry Francis Cary (London: Bell & Daldy, 1869).
31 *Purg.* XII, 1–12; see also *Purg* V, 1–2; VI, 25–27; XVII, 1–12; XXX, 1–6; XXV, 109–111.
32 *Purg.* III, 15–18 and XXVI, 1–12.
33 RUL MS 4123.
34 A list of other elements, which are vaguely reminiscent of the *Comedy*, follows. The character goes to a jetty, whose deserted aspect 'might change from one moment to the next and be transformed like magic before my eyes'. He also hypothesises that he might 'slip unnoticed aboard' and that he would 'achieve a little encounter' or 'exchange a few words with a navigator', to 'add to his collection'. All these elements are reminiscent of *Inferno* III, the encounter with Charon, the crossing of the Acheron, and the dialogue with Ulysses. Furthermore, the character gazes at a vessel reminiscent of the 'vasello leggero e snelletto' (vessel ... swift and light) of *Purgatorio* II, 41, and sees lights flashing on the water (*Inf.* II, 134). The 'atrocious brightness' is reminiscent of the *Paradiso*, while the mass of bright flowers fading in an exquisite cascade of paling colours recalls *Purgatorio* XXX, 28. The swoon might be related to *Inferno* III, 136. The reference to the 'verdigrised copper', followed by the remark 'phew, if that's not clear' (36) can be read as an intratextual reference to the copper beech of *Mercier et/and Camier*, interpreted by Levy as the tree of the earthly paradise. In *The Calmative* it caps the 'little dome' whose spiral staircase the 'I' climbs and which sports a 'projecting gallery'.
35 Beckett, 'Dante...Bruno.Vico..Joyce', in Ruby Cohn (ed.), *Disjecta: Miscellaneous Writings and a Dramatic Fragment* (New York, Grove Press, 1984), p. 32; Beckett, *Mercier and Camier*, p. 13.
36 Samuel Beckett, *From An Abandoned Work*, in S. E. Gontarski (ed.), *Samuel Beckett: The Complete Short Prose 1929–1989* (New York: Grove Press, 1995), pp. 155–168, p. 162.
37 Moorjani, *Abysmal Games*, p. 41.
38 Moorjani discusses how the images of island, sea, plain, and town are used in the *Three Novels*.
39 The stone is described on line 9 as 'livid'.
40 Samuel Beckett, 'Le Concentrisme', in Ruby Cohn (ed.), *Disjecta*, pp. 35–42, p. 37.
41 In the '*Dream*' notebook we also read: 'leccare lo specchio di Narcisso', from *Inferno* XXX, 128.
42 Connor, *Samuel Beckett*, p. 50.
43 Parallel to the migration of the man carrying the board folded in two from *Mercier et/and Camier* to *The End* and vice versa, in the *Three Novels* there are a number of allusions and

reinscriptions of figures encountered in *Mercier et/and Camier*. Steven Connor has pointed out some of them; Connor, *Samuel Beckett*, pp. 82–83. In *Molloy*, 'a fine rain begins to fall, as from a rose, highly important' (28), 'une pluie fine se met à tomber, comme d'une pomme d'arrosoir. Voilà qui est important' (41), as in *Mercier et/and Camier* (52, 34). In *Malone Dies/Malone meurt* a 'mixed choir' is heard (191, 62), as in *Mercier et/and Camier* (25, 37).
44 Connor, *Samuel Beckett*, p. 58. He refers to *Molloy*, but his argument can be applied also to the *Three Novels*.
45 Moorjani, *Abysmal Game*, p. 123.
46 Katherine Travers Gross, 'In other words: Samuel Beckett's art of poetry', Ph.D. thesis, Columbia University, 1972, p. 91. Kevin O'Neill argues that the movement from 'taire' to 'terre' in the *Three Novels* can be related to Dante's ascent, while observing a correspondence between the use of what Benveniste calls 'histoire' in *Molloy* and the *Inferno*, the use of 'discourse' in *L'innomable* and the *Paradiso*, and the shift between the two modes in *Malone meurt* and the *Purgatorio*. Kevin O'Neill, 'Two trilogies: notes on Beckett and Dante', *Romance Notes*, 32:3 (Spring 1992), 235–240.
47 Carla Locatelli, '"My life natural order more or less in the present more or less": textual immanence as the textual impossible in Beckett's works', in Lois Oppenheim and Marius Buning (eds), *Beckett On and On ...* (Madison: Fairleigh Dickinson University Press, 1996), pp. 127–147, p. 142. See also her *Unwording the World: Samuel Beckett's Prose Works After the Nobel Prize* (Philadelphia: Pennsylvania University Press, 1990).
48 Connor, *Samuel Beckett*, p. 50.
49 Beckett, *Text 8*, p. 113.
50 Moorjani, *Abysmal Games*, p. 149.
51 'the promise it [the rain] contained of stars a little later, to light his way and enable him to get his bearings, should he wish to do so,' Beckett, *Malone Dies*, p. 220.
52 Carla Locatelli, 'My life natural order', p. 142.
53 TCD MS 10963, fol. 79. Samuel Beckett, 'dread nay', in *Collected Poems 1930–1978* (London: Calder, 1984), p. 33.
54 Samuel Beckett, *Mal vu mal dit* (Paris: Les Éditions de Minuit, 1981), p. 32 ; Samuel Beckett, *Ill Seen Ill Said* (New York: Grove Press, 1981), p. 27.
55 Samuel Beckett, *Rough for Radio II*, in *Collected Shorter Plays of Samuel Beckett* (London: Faber and Faber, 1984), pp. 113–124, p. 118.
56 For a discussion of how voice and speech have been constructed as the site of original plenitude in Western culture see Jacques Derrida, *Of Grammatology*, transl. Gayatri Chakravorty Spivak (Baltimore: Johns Hopkins, 1976), and *La voix et le phénomène* (Paris: Presses Universitaires de France, 1967).
57 Moorjani, *Abysmal Games*, p. 95.

7 Staging the *Inferno* in *How It Is*

> E fango è il mondo (Giacomo Leopardi, 'A se stesso')

In *How It Is/Comment c'est* a creature panting in the mud murmurs 'his "life" as he hears it obscurely uttered by a voice inside him' while he journeys from left to right.[1] Scholars have often seen Dante lurking behind the 'I''s dreams of places 'above' and 'below' the mud, and they have argued that the *Comedy* mediates this spatially oriented tripartite narrative.[2] The text appears in print as a series of versets of various lengths, which have been visually compared to Dante's terza rima, a poetic form that uses repetition according to the spiral movement of 'unceasing forward motion and recurrent backward glances'.[3] The predominant role of mud, the name of Belacqua, and a number of allusions to the *Inferno* have secured that the name of Dante is often evoked in relation to *How It Is/Comment c'est*.

Things, however, are more complicated than this: the creature crawling and panting in the mud is far from being a character, and although geometry and spatial arrangements play an important role, *How It Is/Comment c'est* is remarkable for its intractability rather than for its geometrical clarity. Transparency is not what this muddy text is about. The main fiction of *How It Is/Comment c'est* is that of constructing itself as voice (communication in progress) while being a written text.[4] The text plays with its structure of presence and its literary status of communication in absence.

Reading Dante as an *auctoritas* in *How It Is/Comment c'est* does not mean to foist upon the text a deeper or additional layer of meaning in order to reduce its opacity, but rather to view Dante as part of the text's critique of depth and originality. The voice is paradoxically both an utterance and a quotation, and Dante is the intractable source which oscillates between being located 'within' and 'without'.[5]

Dante is also part of the textual cycle of absorption and expulsion: in *How It Is/Comment c'est* writing ('from left to right') becomes 'ruins' and 'dejections' through a process of digestion ('from top to bottom'). Discarding is also part of the interpretative process elicited by *How It Is/Comment c'est*; the absence of punctuation and the syntax maximise the process of choosing between alternative meanings and following different associative patterns. The chosen version is constantly haunted by the abandoned combinations, leading us to establish hierarchies and to acknowledge the instability of the text, which can be thought of as the impossible sum of the various patterns. This is further complicated by the coexistence of the English and the French versions. *How It Is/Comment c'est* therefore offers itself as the impossible sum of all the possible syntactical combinations which the text allows in both languages.

The 'scraps' of voice and 'script' which make up this text are signs to which different meanings can be assigned, and yet they also resist the production of meaning, playing with the opposition between language and matter, between voice and mud. Dante stands for the 'light above' while also being the stuff of which this muddy text is made.

A voice comes to one in the dark

> how it was I quote before Pim with Pim after Pim how it is three parts I say it as I hear it
>
> comment c'était je cite avant Pim avec Pim après Pim comment c'est trois parties je le dis comme je l'entends[6]

For Bersani and Dutoit this first paragraph announces 'the entire work as an act of quotation'. 'I say it as I hear it', they argue, 'initiates an infinite regression of sources. A speech act that posits itself as a dictation immediately attributes this reference to the dictating source itself, thus reversing the direction of language's referentiality from the world (where the response might stop) to the chimerical origins of a speech that is never begun but always heard, never initiated but always repeated.'[7] By presenting itself as orality, *How It Is/Comment c'est* lends itself to a reading of the 'I quote' and 'I hear it as I say it' as both marks of the non-originality of what is being said (everything is being repeated) and as pointing towards an infinitely regressive chain of (pseudo-)sources, unable to indicate the division between what is being reproduced and what (if anything) added. From the very first paragraph the text questions notions of origin, beginning, and presence, as the French title also does by punning on the homophony between 'comment c'est' and 'commencer'. The voice is neither original, since it is quoting, and might even be quoting 'I say it as I hear it', nor is it originary, since its origin is infinitely regressive. Its presence is the result of repetition; it is an 'invocation' of a presence and a present which can be called such only when it no longer is: *How It Is*/'how it *is*' can only be about 'how it was', can only occur *after* 'how it was' and '*after* Pim'. From its very beginning, *How It Is/Comment c'est* also problematises the unity of the voice, which in the text cannot be taken as a sign of the existence of an individual. The 'saying' and 'hearing' are articulated around a grammatical 'I', which, although a 'subject', is also 'a kind of stopping point for voices, an intersection of extortionary speech acts, a collecting depot for all the words whose source of transmission remains uncertain'.[8] The voice is multiple ('quaqua on all sides') and does not belong to a unitary self ('in me not mine').

The disunity of the self and the notions of source, origin, and beginning can be scrutinised further through the familiar figure of Belacqua, who appears in the text as:

> knees drawn up back bent in a hoop I clasp the sack to my belly I see me now on my side I clutch it the sack we're talking of the sack with one hand behind my back I slip it under my head without letting it go I never let it go (10)

> genoux remontés dos en cerceau je serre le sac contre mon ventre là alors je me vois sur le flanc je le tiens le sac on parle du sac d'une main derrière le dos je le glisse sous ma tête sans le lâcher je ne le lâche jamais (14)

Belacqua appears again a few pages later, and his name is mentioned:

> asleep I see me asleep on my side or on my face it's one or the other on my side it's preferable which side the right it's preferable the sack under my head or clasped to my belly clasped to my belly the knees drawn up the back bent in a hoop the tiny head near the knees curled round the sack Belacqua fallen over on his side tired of waiting forgotten of the hearts where grace abides asleep (24)

> endormi je me vois endormi sur le flanc ou sur le ventre c'est l'un ou l'autre sur le flanc lequel le droit c'est mieux le sac sous la tête ou serré contre le ventre serré contre le ventre les genoux remontés le dos en cerceau la tête minuscule près des genoux enroulé autour du sac Belacqua basculé sur le côté las d'attendre oublié des cœurs où vit la grâce endormi (36–37)

In both passages we encounter the 'Belacqua posture' occurring in many other Beckett texts; however, the knee-and-elbow position is in this text 'fallen over on his side' and is one of the ways in which the 'speaking I' chooses to 'see' himself ('on my side or on my face it's one or the other').[9] Belacqua thus negotiates an idea of the self as being capable of 'seeing' itself only by splitting itself.

Belacqua is also the 'I''s fantasy of sleep, and it works as both his memory and as intertextual memory. However, the truth value attached to the notion of memory in part one (which oscillates between a memory of 'how it was', a memory of the 'journey', and a dream) is questioned and disrupted by terms such as 'figure', 'fancy', or 'fantasy' used in relation to the 'images' (probably three) occurring to the 'I'. Belacqua, the figure who informs Dante through few mocking and lapidary statements that he is waiting in order to be saved, has fallen on his side; he has also forgotten about the people (those who abide in grace) praying for him in order to shorten his waiting time, and is dreamt, or imagined, to be asleep. This modification of the 'Belacqua episode' is reproduced in Beckett's letter to Kay Boyle on 29 August 1960: 'Belacqua for me is no more than a kind of fetish. In the work I have finished he appears "basculé sur le côté las d'attendre oublié des cœurs où vit la grâce endormi" (cor che in grazia vive), and I hope that's the end of him.'[10] This is not the end of Belacqua, however: he is also referred to in part two of *How It Is/Comment c'est*, and 'the old lutist' is still able to wrench a 'wan smile' from Dante in *The Lost Ones/Le dépeupleur* and *Company/Compagnie*.[11] Belacqua first is evoked in relation to the 'fable' of the 'eastern sage' who, 'having clenched his fists from the tenderest age ... was enabled to see them emerging at last on the other side':

> the curtains parted part one I saw his friends come to visit him where squatting in the deep shade of a tomb or a bo his fist clenched on his knees he lived thus
>
> ... I saw him dreaming the mud parted the light went on I saw him dreaming (53)
>
> les rideaux s'écartaient première partie je voyais les amis venus le voir où accroupi à l'ombre profonde d'une tombe ou d'un bo les poings serrés sur les genoux il vivait ainsi
>
> ... je le voyais rêvant la boue s'écartait ça s'allumait je le voyais rêvant (83)

These images can be read as variations on the Belacqua theme, especially from an intratextual perspective; 'squatting' is the verb describing in *Dream* and *Murphy* the 'old lutist', but in *How It Is* it also applies to the scribe 'squatting on the little stool old style' (81). This 'character' is squatting in the shade of a 'tomb' and can be read as a variation of Belacqua lying in the 'lee' of a 'rock' in *Murphy*.[12] The image of the friends coming to visit him can also be read in intertextual perspective, painting a homely picture of Dante and Virgil visiting Belacqua.[13] This Belacqua is a dream of a figure dreaming, thus creating a similarity both with the previous images of Belacqua asleep and with the Belacqua fantasised by Murphy, who covets the possibility to 'have a long time lying there dreaming, watching the dayspring run through its zodiac, before the toil up hill to Paradise'.[14]

The numerous theatrical metaphors – 'nails' which 'play a part', 'curtains' and 'mud' which 'part', alternating darkness and light – make of the Belacqua episode a 'light intermission'.[15] Lights go on and the 'little scene' acts as a diversion, providing a degree of familiar comic relief. The mud with its darkness is the space of representation, and the anecdote, which merges the figure of the 'extreme eastern sage' with that of Belacqua, is an intermission.

Belacqua is characterised by not only his posture ('in the deep shade of a tomb') but also his lapidary statements: he again appears in the second part of *How It Is/Comment c'est* in relation to the issue of voice:

> a human voice there within an inch or two my dream perhaps even a human mind if I have to learn Italian obviously it will be less amusing (56)

> une voix humaine là à quelques centimètres mon rêve voire peut-être une pensée humaine si je dois apprendre l'italien évidemment ce sera moins drôle (88)

In the second part of *How It Is/Comment c'est*, which is devoted to the time 'I' spends with Pim, Belacqua is 'company', as a 'voice [which] comes to one in the dark'. This can be read as a variation of the role that Belacqua's voice plays in *Dream*, in which he is a humorous figure of unlocatable source. Since this 'little scene' is framed as 'my dream perhaps', it can be read as yet another 'invocation' of the 'Murphy fantasy': this 'human voice' speaking Italian can be read as 'scraps of an ancient voice in me not mine'. The voice is 'in me' but 'not mine', it is 'with/out', thus articulating that the notion of within and togetherness can be observed only from outside. Belacqua, the voice speaking Italian, mediates the idea of the self; in order to hear his voice, it splits into self and non-self. To be heard as 'in him' the voice has to be no longer 'his'.

The inference of a human being attached to the voice implies a concept of the 'human' as owning a voice, but the voice cannot signal the 'originary presence' of 'the being which is human' because voice and humanity are demonstrated as being mutually dependent. Inferring is here a process of following pre-established patterns, which, however necessary, do not prove ontological existence. Origin and presence are thus notions deriving from the movement of repetition, as Bersani and Dutoit point out when writing: '*How It Is* diagrams a type of being (the being which is human) structured as the unending repetition of its own origination. As if the deepest structure of being could be anything but that: the beginning again of its own beginnings' (59). Although Bersani and Dutoit convincingly argue against a humanist view of this 'being which is human', they then define it as the 'deepest structure of being', thus contradicting their own argument about origins. 'Deepest' suggests that Beckett has finally shown the truth about being, and therefore attributes ontological validity to a text that deconstructs the notion of ontology as the basis of truth. Rather, the text plays with Western and Christian notions of being, questioning the presuppositions on which their validity rests.

A third Belacqua passage also criticises the traditional rationalist equivalence between human person and human mind, by ironically stating 'human voice there within an inch or two my dreams perhaps even a human mind' (56).

By claiming 'if I have to learn Italian obviously it will be less amusing' (56), the text humorously draws attention to the materiality of the voice, to the fact that, in order to be recognised, the voice has to speak a language, and this might create problems. In order to be recognised as a voice, the sounds have first to be recognised as language, and then the language has to be understood, otherwise 'it would be less amusing'. The Belacqua episode, which in *Dream* complicates the idea that the voice has an origin, in this text questions the cognitive relationship between presupposition and perception.[16]

Another voice from the *Comedy*, which has been already analysed in relation to *Le calmant/The Calmative*, is used in this text:

> question if what he has said or rather I heard of that voice ruined from such long silence a third two fifths or every word question if there when it stops if somewhere there food for thought prayer without words against a stable-door long icy toil towards the too late all-forgiving what else night at dead water on the deep on the little sea poor in isles or else some other voyage (91)

> question ce qu'il vient de dire plutôt moi d'entendre de cette voix ruinée de s'être si longtemps tue le tiers les deux cinquièmes ou alors tout chaque mot question si là quand elle s'arrête si là-dedans quelque part matière à réflexion prière sans paroles contre la porte d'une étable longue montée glacée vers la toute pardonnante trop tard quoi encore la nuit au large à la morte-eau sur la petite mer pauvre en îles ou alors quelque autre voyage (143)

The 'voice ruined from such long silence', 'cette voix ruinée de s'être si longtemps tue' is a reference to *Inferno* I, 63, which describes Virgil, appearing for the first time to a frightened Dante, as 'chi per lungo silenzio parea fioco' ('one who seemed faint through long silence'). As I have already discussed in the previous chapter, the passage is also reproduced in the 'Whoroscope' notebook as 'hoarse from long silence: Virgil to Dante / (chi per lungo silenzio parea fioco: Inf I)'.[17]

In *The Calmative* the image has a soothing, if faintly disturbing, quality, since the 'rattle, unintelligible even to me who knew what was intended ... was nothing, mere speechlessness due to long silence.'[18] However, in *How It Is* the voice is 'ruined', thus joining the economy of the text, and the 'rattle' could be due either to the broken sound of the mouth clogged with mud or to the impaired hearing of the 'I'. The paragraph is also sprinkled with words that have Dantean relevance in the Beckett canon, such as 'icy' and 'toil', a word used for the purgatorial ascent from *Dream* to *The Calmative*. In the French, the verb used in the sentence 'quand elle s'arrête', lead us, via *Premier amour*, 'là où le verbe s'arrête, on dirait du Dante' (44). Furthermore, the 'dead water', 'morte-eau', is the Dantean 'morta gora', which describes the Stygian bog, a central setting for this Beckett text.

'E fango è il mondo': the *Inferno* performed

Mud is the main Danteian element in *How It Is/Comment c'est*.[19] Michael Robinson states that the narrator 'exists in a landscape which is composed of a number of details from different circles of the *Inferno*. The mud through which he crawls is reminiscent of the fifth Circle, where the Wrathful are confined.'[20] William Hutchings, Francesca Del Moro, John Fletcher, Neal Oxenhandler, Gabriele Frasca, and Philip Terry have also noticed the importance of canto VII.[21] In *Inferno* VII Dante 'sees many fighting and wrangling above the mud, and his guide assures him that there are as many sighing beneath it – and hence the many bubbles on the surface. All gurgle a piteous lament', as Beckett put it in an early notebook which reproduces lines 121–124. Lines 121–123 appear also in the 'Whoroscope' notebook, which reads:

> tristi fummo
> nell'aere dolce che dal sol s'allegra,
> portanto [*sic*] dentro accidioso fummo.
> (Inf VII. 123)

we were sullen in the sweet air that is gladdened by the sun, bearing within us the sluggish fumes; now we are sullen in the black mire [22]

The sentence, omitted in the English, refers to the following lines in the *Comedy*:

> L'acqua era buia assai più che persa;
> e noi, in compagnia de l'onde bige,
> intrammo giù per una via diversa.
> In la palude va ch'ha nome Stige
> questo tristo ruscel, quand'è disceso
> al piè de le maligne piagge grige.
> E io, che di mirare stava inteso,
> vidi genti fangose in quel pantano,
> ignude tutte, con sembiante offeso.
> Queste si percotean non pur con mano,
> ma con la testa e col petto e coi piedi,
> troncandosi co'denti brano a brano.
> Lo buon maestro disse: 'Figlio, or vedi
> l'anime di color cui vinse l'ira;
> e anche vo' che tu per certo credi
> che sotto l'acqua è gente che sospira,
> e fanno pullular quest'acqua al summo,
> come l'occhio ti dice, u' che s'aggira.
> Fitti nel limo dicon: "Tristi fummo

> ne l'aere dolce che dal sol s'allegra,
> portando dietro accidïoso fummo:
> or ci attristiam ne la belletta negra".
> Quest'inno si gorgoglian ne la strozza,
> ché dir nol posson con parola integra'.
> Così girammo de la lorda pozza
> grand'arco, tra la ripa secca e 'l mezzo,
> con li occhi vòlti a chi del fango ingozza.
> Venimmo al piè d'una torre al di sezzo.

> The water was far darker than perse; and we, in company with the murky waves, entered down through a strange way. This dismal little stream, when it has descended to the foot of the malign grey slopes, flows into the marsh that is named Styx; and I, who standing intent to gaze, saw a muddy people in that bog, all naked and with looks of rage. They were smiting each other not with hand only, but with head and chest and feet, and tearing each other piecemeal with their teeth.
>
> The good master said, 'Son, you see now the souls of those whose anger overcame; and I would also have you know for certain that down under the water are people who sigh and make it bubble at the surface, as your eye tells you wherever it turns. Fixed in the slime they say, "We were sullen in the sweet air that is gladdened by the sun, bearing within us the sluggish fumes; now we are sullen in the black mire." This hymn they gurgle in their throats, for they cannot speak it in full words.'
>
> Thus we compassed a great arc of that foul pond between the dry bank and the slough, with eyes turned on those that swallow the mire; and we came at length to the foot of a tower. (*Inf.* VII, 103–130)

In the passage from Dante the reality of the people immersed in the mud and the truthfulness of what they say are produced by the pilgrim's faith in Virgil's words. Not all the damned of this circle are visible, but the active wrathful souls can be seen by Virgil and Dante while 'si percotean non pur con mano, / ma con la testa e col petto e coi piedi, / troncandosi tra loro a brano a brano' (They were smiting each other not with hand only, but with head and chest and feet, and tearing each other piecemeal with their teeth). However, the slothful souls, structurally parallel to the slothful Belacqua in the *Purgatorio*, have a different torment inflicted on them. They are immersed under the 'dead' muddy water of the Stygian bog and create 'bubbles' on the surface of the water by 'bubbling' or 'gurgling' their hymn in their throats. These bubbles are all Dante's moving eye can 'tell' him ('come l'occhio ti dice, che s'aggira') and are interpreted and translated by Virgil, who repeats the words of their hymn. This 'hymn', produced by their throats and mouths clogged with mud, cannot be 'whole'.

We encounter the mud on the first page of the text, in which 'past moments old dreams back again or fresh like those that pass or things things always and memories I say them as I hear them murmur them in the mud' (7). The mud is thus the setting of the exchange between the voice and the hearer who repeats it. The 'I''s 'thirst for labials' (108), his 'murmuring in the mud', is the figure of this broken (as opposed to 'parola integra' or whole word) and intermittent (as visually produced by the typographical blanks) 'gurgling in the throat' (gorgogli[arsi] nella strozza). The 'I' repeats what he hears in the mud, both in the sense of repeating it while being in the mud and hearing it in the mud. The mud is at once what permits the passing on of the murmuring and what hinders it, thus reproducing the situation of the slothful damned of the fifth circle, doomed to sing their 'hymn' of damnation.

The passage from the *Comedy* is therefore important both for the materiality of the text and for the issues of reproduction and repetition as constitutive of reality. *Inferno* VII is reconstructed in *How It Is/Comment c'est*'s painfully detailed exploration of the materiality of speech and in its investigation of how repetition and reproduction confer the status of reality upon invisibility. However, *How It Is/Comment c'est* not only thematises materiality but also constructs itself *as* the mud, as 'bubbles' in opposition to 'meaning': 'such a bubble at such a time it bursts the day can't do much more to me' (41). The text creates a tension between non-meaning as residual materiality and the impossibility of avoiding meaning; the 'scraps' and 'bubbles', which constitute it, at once resist and enable meaning, while they also prevent the formation of a coherent self.

The *Comedy* generates a repetition of inaudibility, in order to testify to the presence of the damned; the bubbles' visible materiality and the damned souls' invisibility are transformed into presence by Virgil's language. By presenting itself as repetition, Virgil's words construct the originality and the presence of the hymn and of the damned themselves. In *How It Is/Comment c'est*, the 'scraps of an ancient voice in me not mine' (7), 'bribes d'une voix ancienne en moi pas la mienne' (9), cannot reproduce the presence of a unitary self. The voice is 'in me' but 'not mine', oscillating between self and non-self. Similarly, the hearing, which is necessary for the voice to exist – to be recognised as voice rather than noise – cannot constitute a unitary point of reception, nor can it guarantee a unified and coherent text.

The text thus fashions a reader/hearer who can be thought of neither as a unitary self nor as a final receiver. Forced to perform the endlessly repetitive task of extorting meaning from a language which constitutes itself as materiality, the reader/ear is plunged into the Hell of fragmentation of self and non-self.[23] This movement is not devoid of humour: the text is Hell, reading it means to be able to force neither a unity upon the text, nor a non-unity, 'damned' and 'demon' at once (36). The text can neither be reconstructed as a 'hymn' (as 'parola integra', whole word), nor apprehended as materiality (mud), since it oozes 'broken' meaning. In the words of *Waiting for Godot*: 'V: "This is becoming really insignificant." E: "Not enough."'[24]

Inferno VII is therefore not a source in the traditional sense of the word; rather, it participates in the intractable economy of the text by being an 'unthinkable beginning', an already said/written which constitutes itself as the transcription of an already said. The voice can exist as voice only if it is heard and if it has been heard before, and therefore can be recognised as voice rather than indistinct sound or noise. Similarly, Dante is inscribed in Beckett's text as what we can hear/read only if we have heard/seen it before. However, the existence of the voice does not coincide with the self; it cannot guarantee a unitary self-presence. Similarly, Dante cannot be thought of as a presence in the text. Rather than being located in hell, *How It Is/Comment c'est* enacts an inferno with Dante. The intertextual strategies of the text mirror its overall structure.

Mud and speech are further correlated in *How It Is/Comment c'est* by the ways in which the text explores in painful detail the deterioration of speech caused by the mud clogging the mouth. The mud is both what impairs speech and what abates the 'I''s thirst, although at first it remains in question if it would nourish when swallowed: 'the tongue gets clogged with mud that can happen too only one remedy then pull it in and suck it and swallow the mud or spit it out ... and question is it nourishing' (28), 'la langue se charge de boue ça arrive aussi un seul remède alors la rentrer et la tourner dans la bouche la boue l'avaler ou la rejeter question si elle est nourissante' (42). The mud is also a source of 'oral' pleasure: when 'the mouth opens the tongue comes out lolls in the mud that lasts a good moment they are good moments ... the mouth open the mud in the mouth thirst abating humanity regained' (27), 'la bouche s'ouvre enfin la langue sort va dans la boue ça dure un bon moment ce sont des bons moments ... la bouche ouverte la boue dans la bouche la soif qui se perd l'humanité reconquise' (41).

The materiality of the production of speech is the pleasure of the mouth exploring the materiality of the mud, thus constituting an interminable movement between language as matter and matter as language: the clogged tongue and the mouth filled with mud are an attempt of the self to merge into the materiality of the mud. Parallel to this movement is the way in which the 'I' becomes part of a 'vast imbrication of flesh'; the bodies are 'glued together' and negotiate the movement between self and non-self, between the impossibility of the individual's self-presence in the text and the aspiration towards a materiality 'without breach or fissure'. The dynamic between tormentor and tormented visible in the figure of those 'glued together like a single body in the dark the mud' (122), 'collés ensemble à ne faire qu'un seul corps dans le noir le boue' (141) is part of this eroticised final judgement which makes use of *Inferno* XXXII, a canto which *Watt* adopted as one of its figures of inversion:

> heads together necessarily my right shoulder overriding his left I've the upper everywhere but how together like two old jades harnessed together no but mine my head its face in the mud and his its right cheek in the mud his mouth against my ear *our hairs tangled together* impression that to separate us one would have to sever them good so much for the bodies the arms the hands the heads (91; emphasis mine)

> tête contre tête fatalement mon épaule droite ayant grimpé sur sa gauche à lui j'ai le dessus partout mais contre comment comme deux vieux canassons attelés ensemble non mais la mienne ma tête la face dans la boue la sienne sur la joue droite sa bouche contre mon oreille *nos poils emmêlés* impression que pour nous séparer il aurait fallu les trancher bon voilà pour les corps les bras les mains les têtes (143; emphasis mine)

The Dantean 'due sì stretti, / che 'l pel del capo avieno insieme misto' (two who were pressed so close together that they had the hair of their head intermixed) (*Inf.* XXXII, 41–42), becomes in *Comment c'est* 'nos poils emmêlés', the obsessively repeated figure of the endless infernal genealogy: 'in reality we are one and all from the unthinkable first to the no less unthinkable last glued together in a vast imbrication of flesh without breach or fissure' (140), 'mais qu'en réalité nous sommes tous depuis l'impensable premier jusqu'au non moins impensable dernier collés les uns aux autres dans une imbrication des chairs sans hiatus' (217). Both the disintegration of speech caused by the mud clogging the mouth and the merging of the self in an inseparable continuum of flesh exist as the oscillation between self and non-self, between language and matter, and both are given an erotic and violent quality at once: 'a hundred thousand prone glued two by two together' (112), 'cent mille gisant collés deux par deux' (174).

The mud is a 'resource'; it is nourishment, able to abate thirst, even a mark of 'humanity', and it can open up 'vistas'. It is interesting to notice the function of the verb 'to open'. It is used throughout the text as the action of the (can)-opener which gives the 'I' access to food ('tunny', 'sardines') and as the action of 'opening' Pim, which is 'the can opened by this instrument [the can-opener], and his words are the sustenance that is disgorged'.[25] The 'warmth of primeval mud impenetrable dark' is therefore 'vomit' and 'shit', the non-self of an already fragmented self:

> suddenly like all that was not then is I go not because of the shit and vomit something else not known not said whence preparatives sudden series subject object subject object quick succession and away (11)

> soudain comme tout ce qui n'était pas puis est je m'en vais pas à cause des saletés autre chose on ne sait pas on ne dit pas d'où préparatifs brusque série sujet objet sujet objet coup sur coup et en avant (16)

The text *is* mud; it is discarded and digested materiality, which, however, is also 'nourishment' giving sustenance to these 'perpetual revictuallings narrations and auditions' (139). The mud is both an oral and an aural pleasure; the pleasure of the tongue lolling in it, sucking and swallowing is equated with the pleasure of hearing words – in their turn equivalent to food – and of disgorging, gurgling them in the mouth. The mud is also the pleasure of the text itself aspiring to become the materiality of the eroticised body without fissures, and the pleasure of the self looking at its 'quaqua'/faeces, as its 'voice in me not mine', as both self and non-self.[26]

Occasionally, relief is provided from this amorphousness in the form of the mud opening to 'vistas', acting as a window, or, indeed, as a stage on which the text performs what part two nostalgically recalls as 'little scenes' when 'the curtains parted the mud parted the light went on' (73):

> the scene is empty in the mud ... find something else to last a little more questions who were they what beings what point of the earth that family whence this dumb show better nothing eat something (32)

> la scène est vide sous la boue ... trouver autre chose pour durer encore des questions de qui il s'agissait quels êtres quel point de la terre cette famille d'où me vient ce cinéma ce genre plutôt rien manger un morceau (49–50)

The mud is the stage, where the curtains part; as observed above in relation to Belacqua, the light goes on, rather than off, suggesting that the little scenes are 'intermissions' within the ongoing representation in/of the darkness of the mud. The 'little scenes' are more narrative than the rest, even when the scene is empty. Other theatrical metaphors are sprinkled throughout the text. In part two, part one is twice described as 'the script'; the French equivalent 'graphie' stresses the meaning of 'script' as 'inscription' and 'writing' while sustaining its theatrical denotation by the use of a number of other words related to performance. The hellishly funny 'table of basic stimuli', in which a torment corresponds to a number and a mechanical action – 'one sing nails in armpit two speak blade in arse three stop thump on skull four louder pestle on kidney five softer index in anus six' (69), 'un chante ongles dans l'aisselle deux parle fer de l'ouvre-boîte dans le cul trois stop coup de poing sur le crâne quatre plus fort manche de l'ouvre-boîte dans le rein cinq moins fort index dans l'anus' six (108–109) – is interrupted by a series of mock joyful exclamations ('bravo clap', 'bravo claque', and 'encore') from an imaginary public.

This cruel puppet theatre, recalling the importance that puppets have in *Murphy*, puns, as often in Beckett's English *oeuvre*, on the double meaning of 'quick': 'Pim never be but for me anything but a dumb limp lump flat for ever in the mud but I'll quicken him you wait and see and how I can efface myself behind my creature when the fit takes me' (52).[27]

William Colerick has read one of these 'little scenes' as a reference to the episode of Ulysses's voyage as represented in the *Comedy*:

> astern receding land of brothers dimming lights mountains if I turn water roughening he falls I fall on my knees crawl forward clink of chains perhaps it's not me perhaps it's another perhaps it's another voyage confusion with another what isle what moon you say the thing you see the thoughts sometimes that go with it it disappears the voice goes on a few words it can stop it can go on depending on what it's not known it's not said (86)

If, with Colerick, we accept that the details of the ship, the mountain, the dimming light, and the roughening water refer to Ulysses' tale in the *Comedy*,[28] we can nevertheless read the passage differently. Rather than symbolising the ultimate salvation of the *Purgatorio* that neither Ulysses nor the narrator of *How It Is* will ever be able to reach, the excerpt is another example of the staging of an infernal 'obligation to express', to say 'something ... that's what was needed seen something called it above said it was so said it was me' (86). Since the 'above' is also the 'above mentioned', it can be read in an intertextual perspective, in which the 'above mentioned' is not only textual but also intertextual. This example shows how a number of scenes are not precise allusions, but rather a 'familiar' murmur, as what has already been said.[29]

Other references to the *Inferno* are to be found in part one, in which, within a context scattered with 'souls in torment' and 'demons', we encounter a reference to Paolo and Francesca and to the 'banner' reminiscent of *Inferno* III. Although Neal Oxenhandler has suggested that the 'banner' refers to *Inferno* XXXIV, where the Easter hymn 'the royal banners forward go' is modified as 'the banners of hell go forth', Katherine Travers Gross argues that it refers to *Inferno* III.[30] Reading the poem 'Enueg I', she points out a number of Dantean references, among which are 'the bright stiff banner of the hoarding', 'the banner of meat bleeding', and the 'secret things', claiming that this image from *Inferno* III 'is an obsessive image in Beckett's canon', as demonstrated by the narrator of *How It Is* who 'envisions himself as a flagpole bearing the banner of *Inferno* III' and by the 1935 'Enueg I' in which the narrator tells again of 'these secret things ... the heart's outpourings day by day'.[31] However, 'banner' is a word that in the Beckett canon suggests Rimbaud. Lawrence Harvey has pointed out that 'Enueg I' directly translates from 'Barbare' the line 'Le pavillon en viande saignante sur la soie des mers et des fleurs arctiques; (elle n'existent pas)' as 'Ah the banner / the banner of meat bleeding / on the silk of the seas and the arctic flowers / that do not exist'.[32] The 'banner' can also be found in Beckett's translation of Arthur Rimbaud's 'Le bateau ivre', in which 'Ni traverser l'orgueil des drapeaux des flammes' is translated as 'Nor breast the arrogant oriflammes and banners'.[33] Both in 'Enueg I' and in the passage from *How It Is/Comment c'est*, 'banner' is to be found in a context with Dantean elements, thus not excluding a possible coexistence of the references both to the *Inferno* and to Rimbaud.

This passage is 'an old view', which 'has faded' and which cannot be 'believed' (36); lights go on again and the 'I' 'sees' himself 'arse bare on the summit of a muckheap':

> holding in my mouth the horizontal staff of a vast banner on which I read
>
> in thy clemency now and then let the great damned sleep here something illegible in the folds then dream perhaps of the good time their naughtiness procured them what time the demons may rest ten seconds fifteen seconds ... dream come of a sky an earth an under-earth where I am inconceivable aah no sound in the rectum a redhot spike that day we prayed no further (36–37)
>
> entre les dents la hampe horizontale d'une vaste vexille où je lis
>
> en ta clémence de temps à autre qu'ils dorment les grands damnés ici des mots illisibles dans les plis puis rêver peut-être du bon temps que leur valurent leurs errements pendant ce temps les démons se reposeront dix secondes quinze secondes ... rêve viens d'un ciel d'une terre d'un sous-sol où je sois inconcevable aïe aucun son dans le cul un pal ardent ce jour-là nous ne priâmes pas plus avant (56–57)

This scene anticipates one of the torments which the 'I' inflicts on Pim and which in its turn he will later fall victim to: 'take the opener in my right hand move it down along the spine and drive it into the arse' (67), 'prends l'oeuvre-boîte dans ma droite le descends le long de l'échine et le lui enforce dans le cul' (105). The context of violent sodomy, involving the redhot spike from Marlowe's *Edward II* and the position in which the 'I' sees himself, are later modified as: 'drive it into the arse not the hole not such fool the cheek a cheek he cries I withdraw' (67) and: 'five softer index in anus' (69).

Inferno III is also intratextually relevant through the term 'naughtiness' in the English version, a word which is quite conspicuous in this context. The passage 'all this tenement of naught from top to bottom' (36) leads me to read 'naughtiness', which of course carries with it both a child-related and a sexual sense, primarily as a derivative of 'naught'. We can thus read it as referring, to what the poem 'Text' calls the victims 'of an ingenious damnation' in canto III. 'Coloro / che visser senza 'nfamia e senza lodo' (those who lived without infamy and without praise) (*Inf.* III, 35–36) are not even accepted, owing to their 'naughtiness', within *Inferno*. This hypothesis is sustained by the phrase 'great damned', which refers back to 'colui che fece per viltade il gran rifiuto' (the shade of him who from cowardice made the great refusal) (*Inf.* III, 59–60) via 'What a Misfortune' and *Eleuthéria*.[34] In 'What a Misfortune' Mrs bboggs (who 'would probably have [been] disliked' by Dante 'on this account') is 'almost as non-partisan as Pope Celestine the fifth' (126). The historical character whom the critical tradition has identified as the maker of the 'gran rifiuto', Celestino V, is linked to the 'grand refus' in *Eleuthéria*.[35] The paradoxical juxtaposition of 'greatness' and 'naughtiness' can therefore be read against 'Text' and the pride of an 'ingenious damnation'. The presence of 'something illegible in the folds', which in the French is specified as 'des mots illisibles dans les plis', can also be read in the context of canto III via the 'ingenious damnation'. This canto withholds the identity of the neutrals, and does not name the soul who made 'the great refusal', who, however, is recognised (but not named) by Dante the character. *How It Is*/*Comment c'est* reproduces the reticence of *Inferno* III. Furthermore, the 'dream perhaps of the good time their naughtiness procured them' alludes to Belacqua dreaming, and to the 'blissful' state, which his sloth secured him.

As seen in other Beckett works analysed in this study, each text shapes its own idea of intertextuality, which coheres with its narrative strategies. This 'trituration' of Dante is a strategy coherent with that of the whole text, which at once appropriates and denies ('in me not mine') 'scraps of an ancient voice'. The 'Paolo-Francesca episode', described in 'Papini's Dante' as 'the imperishable reference ... to the incompatibility of the two operations [i.e. reading and loving]' has fallen into the 'muckheap' too: 'quel giorno più non vi leggemmo avante' (that day we read no further) (*Inf.* V, 138) becomes 'that day we prayed no further' (36), 'ce jour-là nous ne priâmes pas plus avant' (57).[36] The 'imperishable reference' participates in the 'interminable procession' of 'scraps' of voices being heard and reproduced, an interpretive process of extorting meaning that is both violent and pleasurable.[37]

Geometries of passion

The opaque, dense, amorphous, impairing materiality of the mud is also the place of divisions. The mud is the only 'surface' in the text and constructs the text's spatiality. In part one, the 'warmth of primeval mud impenetrable dark' (11) is open to 'vistas' of the 'light above', 'above if I were above the stars already' (43), where one could 'raise the eyes look for faces in the sky animals in the sky' (45). The dark surface of the mud makes possible the hypothesis of a Dantean above, marked by the presence of the stars, which, as in *The Calmative*, are the 'Bears', thus 'animals'.[38]

The mud is also 'infernal' by virtue of being 'darkness below', spatially opposed to an 'above', which is, similarly to *Text 5*, the place both of the visibility of the stars – 'above if I were above the stars already' (43) – and of the presence of light: 'your life above YOUR LIFE pause my life ABOVE long pause above IN THE in the LIGHT pause light his life above in the light almost an octosyllable come to think of it a coincidence' (72). The geometric division between above and below is also a temporal division between before and after. The passage from *Inferno* VII which appears in the 'Whoroscope' notebook, and which I have analysed earlier, is also functional to this division:

> the people above whining about not living strange at such a time such a bubble in the head all dead now others for whom it is not a life and what follows very strange namely that I understand them (41)

> les gents là-haut qui se lamentaient de ne pas vivre étrange à un tel moment une telle bulle dans la tête tous morts à présent d'autres à présent pour qui ce n'est pas une vie et la suite très étrange à savoir je les comprends (64)

The syntax suggests that people 'whining about not living' are 'above'. This inverts the situation of canto VII, in which the people below, both in the sense of down in Hell and below the surface of the mud of the Styx, lament the 'accidioso fummo' (sluggish fumes). This has ruined their life above on earth, where the sun shines, and has condemned them to the mud ('we were sullen in the sweet air that is gladdened by the sun, bearing within us the sluggish fumes; now we are sullen in the black mire'). What in canto VII was the effect of their speaking and the only visible sign of their existence, namely the bubbles produced by their voices, becomes in Beckett 'such a bubble in the head'. The Dantean 'scraps' turn into 'a bubble in the head' of a light-headed 'I'. The passage carries the parallel with canto VII further; the people above are all dead and others have taken their place, following an infernal economy of substitution and repetition. The final remark 'very strange namely that I understand them' goes against Dante's need for Virgil's interpretation as the place of unusual communicability.

The mud is not only the place of the division between above and below but also what has always been there, the 'primeval' warmth and the mass of human 'de-jections', at once 'originelle' and the place of 'saletés':

> vite une supposition si cette boue soi-disant n'était que notre merde à tous parfaitement tous si on n'est pas des billions en ce moment et pourquoi pas puisq'on voilà deux on le fut des billions à ramper et à chier dans leur merde en serrant comme un trésor dans leur bras de quoi ramper et chier encore maintenant mes ongles (82)

> quick a supposition if this so-called mud were nothing more than all our shit yes all if there are not billions of us at the moment and why not the moment there are two there were yes billions of us crawling and shitting in their shit hugging like a treasure in their arms the wherewithal to crawl and shit a little more now my nails (52)

William Hutchings has analysed the text's prominent scatology in relation to Dante; he describes *How It Is/Comment c'est* as the 'scatological eschatological', comparing Dante's journey and 'passage through the literal bowels of the earth' to the 'intestinal odyssey of Beckett's narrator'.[39] Since, in another critic's words, 'Dante ... makes his final hair-borne descent through the crevice near "the point where the thigh / Begins its swelling curve to meet the haunch" (*Inf* XXXIV, 72-73), and ... emerges "seeking once more to return / Up to the world of light"', Dante's progress can be compared to the scatological being 'shat into grace' of *How It Is/Comment c'est*.[40]

The passage also goes back to the second *bolgia* of the eighth circle, namely *Inferno* XVIII, one of the most scatological passages of Dante's poem, which is quoted in the following order in an undated Beckett card held at Trinity College Dublin:

> Le ripe eran grommate d'una muffa,
> Per l'alito di giù che vi s'appasta,
> Che con gli occhi e col naso facea zuffa (106–108)

The banks were crusted over with a mold from the vapor below that sticks on them and that did battle with the eyes and with the nose

> Vidi gente attuffata in uno sterco
> Che dagli uman privadi parea mosso.
> E mentre ch'io là giù con l'occhio cerco,
> Vidi un col capo sí di merda lordo
> Che non parea s'era laico o cherco. (113–117)

I saw down in the ditch a people plunged in filth that seemed to have come from human privies.

And while I was searching down there with my eyes, I beheld one whose head was so befouled with ordure that it did not appear whether he was layman or cleric.

> Quaggiù m'hanno sommerso le lusinghe
> Ond'io non ebbi mai la lingua stucca. (125–126)

Down to this the flatteries wherewith my tongue was never cloyed have sunk me

> Di quella sozza e scapigliata fante
> Che là si graffia con le unghie merdose (130–131)

that fouled and disheveled wench who is scratching herself there with her filthy nails

In *How It Is/Comment c'est* scatology makes this text a 'throwing away' and 'throwing down' of words, which fall in the 'muckheap' made of previous (s)crap(s), residua, fragments, debris. Ingurgitating and disgorging, the text is the 'abject' 'infinite loss without profit' (112); time is described through a digestive metaphor ('tracts of time') and its scatological materiality constitutes the 'primeval' as the 'already there' and the 'unthinkable beginning'.[41]

At once hindering and permitting speech and progress, a surface which makes possible a dream of 'above', the mud can retain 'a few traces that's all' (103). The mud is a figure of the primeval as residual and of the impossibility of absolute amorphousness; there is no simple 'nostalgie de la boue' in this text, since mud is a figure of the impossibility both of a full and original self and of an absolute non-self. The 'I' in the text can be neither transparent meaning nor opaque materiality; it takes shape in the movement between the two.

The mud is subjected to internal unstable divisions. The infernal repetitiveness and the darkness of the mud can occasionally possess a reassuring quality: 'safe places one after another infernal homes' (95). However, this uniformity can also be subdivided: 'B to C C to D from hell to home hell to home to hell always at night Z to A divine forgetting enough' (79). Within the mud itself, which is infernal, the movement from the position of tormented to that of tormentor is rephrased as that from Hell to home. The text constitutes itself as the infernal fragmentariness of self and non-self, as the always already divided materiality of body parts, as the impossible complete amorphousness of the mud.

The text keeps positing divisions that are then eroded, crossed, and shifted. Its overall tripartite division follows this dynamic as well. The voice keeps subdividing the story into three phases and crossing those same limits, at once declaring the impossibility of doing without discriminations, and the impossibility for these divisions to be stable. Thus, the text recurrently 'dreams' that it might organise itself into the three neatly divided parts 'of a sky an earth an under-earth where I am inconceivable' (37) and wants to 'divide into three a single eternity for the sake of clarity' (24).

Although one of the possible meanings of the number three in the Beckett canon might well have a Dantean connotation (as suggested by 'Dante... Bruno.Vico..Joyce'), I would prefer not to force correspondences between the two systems. Rather, I would suggest that the text's tripartite division is part of a larger 'critical' reading of the notion of 'critique' in its etymological sense of 'judging' and 'dividing'. That is to say, by positing these divisions, the text critically interrogates the presuppositions on which any division rests: divisions can neither be trusted nor avoided. The presence in the text of a number of institutional disciplines presiding over these critical practices can be read in this light. For example, the movements by which the 'I' advances are chopped up and schematised, in a mechanical parody reminiscent of *Watt*:

> my arm bends therefore my right it's preferable which reduces from very obtuse to very acute the angle between the humerus and the other the *anatomy* the *geometry* and my right hand seeks his lips let us try and see this pretty movement more clearly (55–56)

> mon bras se plie donc le droit c'est mieux ce qui ramène de très obtus en très aigu l'angle entre l'humérus et l'autre l'anatomie la géométrie et ma main droite cherche ses lèvres tâchons de voir ce joli mouvement de plus près (87)

In order to 'see' this ironically 'pretty' movement we are offered geometry and 'anatomy' (54–56), 'algebra' (51), 'arithmetic' (37), 'mathematics', 'astronomy', 'physics', 'history', and 'geography' (41). Meaning needs to be produced through discriminations; and yet, the power that these discriminations have to create the real as given and a-temporal is suffocated and engulfed by the muddy materiality of meaning itself.

The text's passion for geometry is part of the infernal torment of infinite fragmentation and repetition through which the spatiality of *How It Is/Comment c'est* is produced. At the same time, the text's geometry is a figure of passion: the endless chain of tormented bodies 'glued together' is also a source of violent pleasure. 'Passion' thus refers to the relationship between tormentor and tormented, structured according to an alternating dynamic of activity and passivity. The victim is passive (Latin *patire*) but active in his speaking, while the tormentor acts but is confined to silence. 'Passion', for Jacques Derrida, connotes 'toujours en mémoire de la signification christiano-romaine, le martyre, c'est-à-dire, comme son nom l'indique, le témoignage'.[42] Both martyrdom and witnessing are important elements in the text; the 'moderate' 'martyring and being martyred' (127) is the specific figure of the closed structure of extorting and passing on 'the story' along the chain through the infliction of bodily pain, of torture. At the same time, both hearing and producing speech are pleasurable activities, identified with the opening of the can of food and the 'good moments' experienced by the tongue lolling in mud and feeding itself with it. Furthermore, the fragmented body parts scattered through the text and constituting the fragmented self of the text are eroticised in the image of the 'imbrication of flesh without fissures': 'sadism pure and simple no since I may not cry' (63).

'Passion' also connotes 'la passibilité, c'est-à-dire aussi l'imputabilité, la culpabilité, la responsabilité, un certain *Schuldigsein*, une dette originaire de l'être-devant-la-loi'.[43] This is the situation of the beings in the text, tormentors and tormented; this is their condition of 'being in justice' (124) and their belonging to the infinite procession organised according to a geometric system. The term 'passion' is also suggestive of the text's Christian imagery, since the organisation of the narrative flow of information is related to 'God that old favourite' (70), the ear who listens to the murmuring, the Love, the source of provisions. Therefore, to speak of 'geometries of passion' in relation to Dante means understanding how the text's spatiality is mediated not only by explicitly Christian but also by specifically Dantean connotations.

As clarified by Bersani and Dutoit, the structure of the journey is organised as a geometric model, which allows a triadic series of relationships thanks to four elements. The movement from A to B is the 'journey', identified in the narration with part one, the tormenting of B by A is the 'with Pim', namely part two, and the abandonment of B by A, which waits for a tormentor to arrive, is part three. Bersani and Dutoit point out that A will only know B and D, never C, while 'B will never have any other tormentor than A, no other victim but C'.[44] This geometric structure explains why the text thus requires four elements in order to have three parts. This is why the text asserts that 'in trying to present in three parts or episodes an affair which all things considered involves four one is in danger of being incomplete', calls for a supplementary structure, 'to this third part now ending at last a fourth should normally be appended', and declares 'our total life it states only three quarters' (130).

In *How It Is/Comment c'est*, this structure is closely related not only to the idea of authority (as discussed in relation to *Mercier and Camier* and *Watt*), but also of time and autobiographical writing. The division 'before Pim with Pim after Pim' is continuously stated and continuously collapsed, outfaced by the impossibility of grasping the present, which can only be reformulated as present afterwards. In order to speak about his life – 'it's my life we're speaking of, my life, what else' – the 'I' always has to leave off the 'last quarter', in the 'present formulation'. The division of time into 'history prophesy and latest news' (129) describes this impossibility, which is also the impossibility of the 'I' as self-presence.[45] This structure is imagined according to two different 'figures', to adopt a term frequently occurring in the text: the ellipse around the earth, which makes possible a finite number of 'players', and the straight line, for which an infinite number of players must be devised (116–117).

The reference to the elliptical movement, which embraces the girdle of the earth, brings us back to the etymological root of geo-metry, from the Greek 'earth' and 'measurer'. The 'equivalent' of the girdle of the earth is the measure of the movement of the 'being which is human': 'and so in the mud the dark on the belly in a straight line as near as no matter four hundred miles in other words in eight thousand years if I had not stopped the girdle of the earth meaning the equivalent' (41). The hypothesis of the ellipses is at one point suggested as possible only 'above in the light where their space is measured', since 'here the straight line the straight line eastward strange and death in the west as a rule' (123). Thus, an above where space can be measured is hypothesised from a below in which the straight line is privileged since it entails either solitude or an infinite number of members ('either I am alone ... or else we are innumerable and no further problem either'), and cannot be measured: 'a procession in a straight line with neither head nor tail in the dark the mud with all the various infinitudes that such a conception involves' (124).

The distinctions between above and below and between the ellipsis and the straight line, are, however, not so 'neat'. The procession both 'advances from left to right', 'wends as we have seen from left to right or if you prefer from west to east' (123)', and 'turns deasil' (118). The 'confused reckonings to the effect I can't have deviated more than a second or so from the direction imparted to me' obsessively reiterate how this direction, imparted 'at the inconceivable outset' (40), is 'from left to right ... from west to east ... from left to right in the dark the mud' (125).

'Death' is always assumed to be 'in the west as a rule', a 'rule' strongly connoted by centuries of Christian thought, and, possibly, by Dante too. The relevance of Dante in matters of directionality has been discussed in relation to other works, such as *Le calmant/The Calmative*, and it is explicitly stated in the first 'Dante postcard' and in *Compagnie*, in which the direction is the opposite of that of *Comment c'est*. While in the latter we read: 'supposition qu'on tourne destrorsum' (183), *Compagnie* states: 'Senestrorsum ... Comme aux enfers' (68).[46] In *How It Is* the 'rumour [is] transmissible ad infinitum in either direction ... from left to right ... from right to left' (120), but the direction is that described in the 'first postcard' as 'in Purg. always to the right'.[47] Thus, the Purgatorial direction of salvation, framed into the larger Christian 'rule' which prescribes that 'death lies in the west', can be read as one of the overdetermined meanings with which the text plays. This directionality conspicuously refers to another movement, that of writing; Leslie Hill has observed that 'the theme of the journey, ... which sustains the novel's overall structure, is quite closely exploited as a metaphor for the act of writing'.[48] The movement of the pen from left to right is also the movement of the torturer inscribing painful words on the body of his victim, 'from left to right and top to bottom as in our civilisation I carve my Roman capitals' (70).[49]

If the Purgatorial winding movement from left to right, away from death, is framed by a logic which connotes the 'above' as the place of salvation, this is short-circuited by the more technical sense of 'above' as 'above mentioned.' The above becomes the already said, 'my voice is going it will come back my first voice no voice above none there either' (79), creating the textual loop: 'so eternally I quote on' (115). This endless repetition/repetitiveness is, as we have seen, the 'infernal' passion of the 'beginning again of its own beginnings'. Furthermore, the above and below are also part of the 'top to bottom' digestive circularity of the text, in which shit and vomit are food and nourishment.

The witness and the scribe

How It Is/Comment c'est stages *Inferno* VII by enacting its hellish repetitiveness and playing with its muddy materiality. We have seen how in canto VII invisibility and inaudibility are transformed by Virgil's persuasive rhetoric into testimonies of truth. Dante the witness reports the words of Virgil (whose 'ornate word' has been strongly questioned in the same canto), who, in his turn, is translating and assembling a hymn that cannot be sung in 'full words'. In *Watt*, Virgil's refusal to 'add fair words' ('parole non ci appulcro') questions the function of the 'Addenda'. In *How It Is/Comment c'est*, the passage from invisibility and inaudibility to testimony operated by Virgil's words questions the reality of the voice.

In other sections of this volume I have argued, with Teodolinda Barolini, that the *Comedy*'s 'outrageously inauthentic devices' construct the narrative as 'truth', and, using Singleton's well-known definition, that 'the fiction of the *Comedy* is that there is no fiction'.[50] The episode of the sullen souls in canto VII is a good example of how a complex narrative strategy of passing on the 'murmuring in the mud' can become an act of witnessing the truth. *How It Is/Comment c'est* plays on this process: the 'reality' of the scene is based on what in the English text is the sequence 'say what you hear see what you say say you see it' (105), which elaborates on the succinct French 'dire ce qu'on entend le voir' (163). The 'heard' is made by the 'saying', the 'saying' by the 'seeing' and the 'seeing' by the 'saying', thus creating reality through the repetitiveness of the said.

The issue of testimony becomes a central one through the figures of the witness and of the scribe. Witness and scribe in *How It Is/Comment c'est* strongly question vision and written recording in their traditional reifying roles.[51] At the same time, these two figures of authority demand an ear in order for the voice to exist as fragmentary movement between self and non-self. We encounter the figure of the witness quite early in the text:

> that's the speech I've been given part one before Pim question do I use it freely it's not said or I don't hear it's one or the other all I hear is that a witness I'd need a witness

> he lives bent over me that's the life he has been given all my visible surface bathing in the light of his lamps when I go he follows me bent in two (18)

> voilà la parole qu'on m'a donnée première partie avant Pim question si j'en use beaucoup on ne dit pas ou je n'entends pas c'est l'un ou l'autre on dit qu'un témoin qu'il me faudrait un témoin

> il vit penché sur moi voilà la vie qu'on lui a donnée toute ma surface visible plongée dans la lumière de ses lampes quand je m'en vais il me suit courbé en deux (26–27)

We can read the passage as the 'invocation' for the scribe coming from the 'I', in need of knowing if he either does not hear 'it', or if 'it' is not said. However, it can also be read as the 'I' hearing, and repeating, the voice from which he quotes declaring the need for a witness. The syntax reproduces the oscillation between undecidability and interpretation, and the invocation of a witness is an invocation for 'reality' and 'truth' within this framework. It is an 'invocation', a conjuring up of a voice, which would then be caught in the same need for a witness not only in order to be interpreted, but also to exist. In fact, the witness in the text is the figure of the 'ear'; the voice cannot be a voice if there is nobody to hear it.

The posture of the witness bent over the 'I', following him everywhere, illuminating him with the lamp, indicates that he is at once his double and a variation on the theme of closeness between tormentor and tormented, between self and non-self. The necessity for 'good eyes' and a 'good lamp' points to light and vision as *topoi* of knowledge and reason in Western culture.[52]

> he would need good eyes the witness if there were a witness good eyes a good lamp he would have them the witness the good eyes the good lamp

> to the scribe sitting aloof he'd announce midnight no two in the morning three in the morning Ballast Office brief movements of the lower face no sound it's my words cause them it's they cause my words it's one or the other I'll fall asleep within humanity again just barely (44–45)

> il lui faudrait de bonne yeux au témoin s'il y avait un témoin de bons yeux une bonne lampe il les aurait les bons yeux la bonne lampe

> au scribe assis à l'écart il annoncerait minuit non deux heures trois heures heure du Ballast Office brefs mouvements du bas du visage aucun son c'est mes mots qui font ça ça qui fait mes mots je m'endormirai encore dans l'humanité tout juste (69)[53]

The lamp is both what allows the witness to see, thus making him a witness, and an instrument for extorting confessions, similar to the function of the spot in *Play*. To see *is* to extort; the act of witnessing as martyr '*makes* reality' or, as Derrida points out, amounts to '*faire la vérité*, selon l'expression d'Augustin'. The link between witnessing and martyrdom, on which *How It Is/Comment c'est* elaborates, is also linked to the constant possibility that witnessing could turn into perjury: 'Si le témoignage est passion, c'est aussi parce qu'il souffrira toujours et d'avoir indécidablement partie liée avec la fiction, le parjure ou le mensonge et de ne jamais pouvoir ni devoir, faute de cesser de témoigner, devenir une preuve.'[54]

Judiciary figures, as in *Text 5*, the witness and the scribe are part of the system of justice based on the endless 'moderate' martyrdom, caught between the impossibility of repetition (the possibility of fiction) and the construction of truth through repetition:

> wrong for never twice the same unless time vast tracts aged out of recognition no for often fresher stronger after than before unless sickness sorrow they sometimes pass one feels better less wretched after than before
>
> unless recordings on ebonite or suchlike a whole life generations on ebonite one can imagine it nothing to prevent one mix it all up change the natural order play about with that (107)
>
> attention jamais deux fois la même ou alors le temps des temps énormes vieillie méconnaissable non car souvent plus fraîche plus forte après qu'avant à moins que la maladie les malheurs quelquefois ça passe on est mieux moins mal après qu'avant
>
> ou alors enregistrements sur ébonite ou similaire toute une vie des générations sur ébonite on peut l'imaginer rien ne vous en empêche mélanger changer l'ordre naturel jouer avec ça (166)

The ebonite recording does not bear witness to life's 'natural order', and repetition can never be absolutely self-coinciding, cannot guarantee the truthfulness of memories, which are eroded, modified, used as cathartic instruments, as *Krapp's Last Tape* illustrates too. On the other hand, repetition 'makes reality', reifies discourse into history. I would read in this light the families and dynasties in which witness and scribe, named Kram and Krim (a pun on 'the German *Krimskrams* or junk'), are inserted:[55]

> all alone and the witness bending over me name Kram bending over us father to son to grandson yes or no and the scribe name Krim generations of scribes keeping the record a little aloof sitting standing it's not said yes or no samples extracts (80)
>
> tout seul et le témoin penché sur moi nom Kram penché sur nous de père en fils en petit-fils oui ou non et le scribe nom Krim générations de scribes tenant le greffe un peu à l'écart assis debout on ne dit pas oui ou non échantillons extraits (125)
>
> what's the use of that Krim (81)
>
> à quoi ça sert Krim (127)
>
> Krim dead are you mad one doesn't die here (93)
>
> Krim morts tu est malade on ne meurt pas ici (146)
>
> Kram who listens Krim who notes or Kram alone one is enough Kram alone witness and scribe his lamps their light upon me Kram with me bending over me till the age-limit then his son his son's son so on (133)
>
> pour Kram qui écoute Krim qui note ou Kram seul un seul suffit Kram seul témoin et scribe ses feux qui m'éclairent Kram avec moi penché sur moi jusqu'à la limite d'âge puis son fils son petit-fils ainsi de suite (207)

Just as the witness duplicates the 'I', the scribe duplicates the witness. Inscribed in a written text that claims to be an oral/aural communication, the witness and the scribe are the two figures of authority that mirror this double aspect of narration. The scribe is a reduplication of the witness; the 'three books' are a 'rich testimony' (83):

> little private book these secret things little book all my own the heart's outpourings day by day it's forbidden one big book and everything there Krim imagines I am drawing what then places faces loved forgotten
>
> that's enough end of extracts yes or no yes or no no no no witness no scribe all alone and yet I hear it murmur it all alone in the dark the mud and yet (84)
>
> petit calepin à part ces notes intimes petit calepin à moi effusions de l'âme au jour le jour c'est défendu un seul grand livre et tout dedans Krim s'imagine que je dessine quoi paysages visages aimés oubliés
>
> assez fin des extraits oui ou non oui ou non non non pas de témoin pas de scribe tout seul et cependant je l'entends le murmure tout seul dans le noir la boue et cependant (131)

In the English text 'secret things' refer to the 'secrete cose', mentioned above in relation to 'Enueg I'; Dante calls 'secrete cose' the other world he will discover after he has gone through the gate announcing the end of hope:

> E poi che la sua mano a la mia puose
> con lieto volto, ond'io mi confortai,
> mi mise dentro a le secrete cose. (*Inf.* III, 19–21)

> And when he had placed his hand on mine, with a cheerful look from which I took comfort, he led me among the secret things.

The 'secret things' in this context are the 'I''s confessions in his 'little book'. The scribe watches and imagines what he is 'drawing' in the book/diary. But this sentimental outburst of expression is itself made by 'extracts' from other books. Following Travers Gross, we can read these 'heart's outpourings' against 'my darling's red sputum' of 'Enueg I'. The 'extracts' can be read as referring to the confessional early poem, once again metamorphosising passages from previous books into other texts belonging to the Beckett canon. In line with a practice already observed in *Watt* and the *Three Novels*, the text transforms the whole canon into what *How It Is* calls a 'perpetual revictuallings, narrations and auditions' (139).

The figure of the witness and the scribe are figures of authority not only because they are parallel to the originating movement of the text's claim to a simultaneous oral and written status but also because they question the possibility of infinitude, absolute non-hierarchical transmission of indistinct murmuring. In other words, the witness and the scribe point to the necessarily 'aloof' position of the one who writes the story. The attempt 'to present in three parts or episodes an affair which all things considered involves four one is in danger of being incomplete ... in the present formulation', 'qu'à vouloir présenter en trois parties ou épisodes un affaire qui à bien y regarder en comporte quatre on risque d'être incomplet ... dans la présente rédaction', is the need of a 'fourth part to be appended' (130), 's'ajouter une quatrième' (201–202). The 'affair' can be regarded as concluded only from an outside, aloof position; it can be reified only by an appendix, by a supplement, which its own external status makes into the 'impossible last'. In *Mercier et/and Camier* the narration of the couple can exist only insofar as it depends on a third observer, and Dante is a figure of this problem of authority. In *How It Is/Comment c'est*, the witness and the scribe have a similar function; they are the necessary hypothesis for the voice to be called voice, for the text to exist. Their collapsing first into one single figure, then into God, and later into the 'I', sketches how the text cannot possibly state the absolute absence of teleology, cannot deny its being a written piece of work, even when its genealogy coincides with the German word for junk.

In Dante, the figure of the scribe is one of the *loci classici* of the *Comedy*, in which his self-definition is both a declaration of humility and of supreme authority:

> Or ti riman, lettor, sovra 'l tuo banco,
> dietro pensando a ciò che si preliba,
> s'esser vuoi lieto assai prima che stanco.
> Messo t'ho innanzi: omai per te ti ciba;
> ché a sé torce tutta la mia cura
> quella materia ond'io son fatto scriba. (*Par.* X, 22–27)

> Now remain, reader, upon your desk, reflecting on this of which you have a foretaste, if you would be glad far sooner than weary. I have set before you; now feed yourself, because that matter of which I am made the scribe wrests to itself all my care.[56]

The self-definition as scribe is within an address to the reader, who is pictured as sitting at his desk, transformed into a student *of* Dante *by* Dante. However, thinking is also a movement; as in *Paradiso* II, 3, the reader has to follow behind Dante's ship 'that singing makes her way' ('seguiti / dietro al mio legno che cantando varca'), here he has to 'think behind' what he has been offered. The scribe can no longer help him to feed himself; he will have to do it on his own, because the 'matter of which [he is] made scribe' absorbs all his energies. Dante terms himself as scribe while his reader cannot demand any more help and has to realise the difficulty of *a tëodia* (divine song).[57]

The image can be related to a no less famous passage of the *Comedy*, in which Dante places himself at the receiving end of a dictation:

> E io a lui: 'I' mi son un che, quando
> Amor mi spira, noto, e a quel modo
> Ch'e' ditta dentro vo significando'. (*Purg.* XXIV, 52–54)

> And I to him: 'I am one who, when Love inspires me, takes note, and goes setting it forth after the fashion which he dictates within me.'[58]

The passage from canto XXIV illustrates the 'dolce stil novo' (mentioned in line 57), or, as Beckett puts it in 'Home Olga', 'the sweet noo style.' Love is the dictator, and Dante can 'take' his 'new rhymes' from being a perfect scribe, noting what Love dictates and reproducing it faithfully in the process of signifying. If in the *Purgatorio* Dante retrospectively creates a poetic school and a genre through the image of the 'dittator d'Amore', in the *Paradiso* the writer is still a scribe, but his dictator is no longer Love, but rather God himself. From being Love's scribe the poet has become the Divine Love's scribe, able to 'faithfully reproduce' the 'secret things' of life beyond life. Dante appropriates the scribe's

STAGING THE *INFERNO* IN *HOW IT IS*

power of 'reproducing' in order to create his own 'tëodia' and to speak as 'scriba Dei'. He thus invests himself with an authority 'at least equal to that of the author of the Apocalypse (John agrees with him on a visionary detail in *Purgatorio* XXIX – not the other way around!)'.[59]

Rather than seeing Beckett's work as a denial or a reversal of the Dantean teleology, I would argue that the witness and the scribe are figures of the necessary 'auditor' for the voice to exist. This 'ear' is gradually transformed into the 'love' which guarantees provisions, justice, and ultimately narration itself, thus impersonating the problem of authority. Witness and scribe are collapsed into one single figure:

> cumulation of offices most understandable if it will be kindly considered that to hear and note one of our murmurs is to hear and note them all (138)

> cumul d'emplois facile à admettre si l'on veut bien considérer que l'écoute d'un seul de nos murmures et sa rédaction sont l'écoute et la rédaction de tous (215)

The killing off of Kram results in the hypothesis of 'the ear, we're talking of an ear above in the light' (134–135):

> the panting stops I hear it my life I have it murmur it it's preferable more logical for Kram to note and if we are innumerable then Krams innumerable if you like or one alone my Kram mine alone he's enough here where justice reigns one life all life not two lives our justice one Kram not one of us there's reason in me yet his son begets his son leaves the light Kram goes back up into the light to end his days

> or no Kram that too when the panting stops an ear above somewhere above and unto it the murmur ascending (134)

> ça cesse de haleter je l'entends ma vie je l'ai la murmure c'est mieux plus logique pour Kram qui peut noter et si nous sommes sans nombre des Kram sans nombre si l'on veut ou un seul le mien mon Kram à moi il suffit ici où la justice regne une seule vie toute la vie pas deux vies notre justice Kram n'est pas des nôtres de la raison il m'en reste son fils fait son fils quitte la lumière Kram y remonte finir ses jours

> ou pas de Kram ça aussi quand ça cesse de haleter une oreille quelque part là-haut et jusqu'à elle le murmure qui s'éleve (208)

The ear is given transcendental characteristics, since it is the place to which the 'fallen words' – 'scraps of other scraps of other scraps of an antique rigmarole' (134), 'ces bribes d'autres bribes d'un antique cafouillis' (209) – can ascend. This transcendental ear, a fragment of the body, becomes not only the absolute hearer/writer, thus duplicating the witness/scribe couple, but also the source of provisions: 'the gift of understanding the care for us the means of noting what does it matter ... whose his charge of the sacks' (135), 'le don de comprendre le souci de nous les moyens de noter ... à qui au préposé aux sacs' (210). 'He' is even called 'a love' (138), 'un amour' (214), which guarantees justice. This witness/scribe, who hears and notes, is necessary for the narration to exist and thus becomes the author. This does not mean, however, that either 'narrations' or 'auditions' can be reconstructed as 'whole'; the hellish fragmentariness persists in the 'ill-inspired ill-told and so ancient so forgotten at each telling' stories, which are 'the ballast that chains the dog to his vomit'.[60]

Witness and the scribe first merge, then are transcendentally transformed, and they ultimately collapse into the figure of a God-author: 'there he is then at last that not one of us ... when he lends his ear to our murmur does no more than lend it to a story of his own devising ill-inspired ill-told and so ancient so forgotten at each telling that ours may seem faithful that we murmur to the mud to him' (139), 'le voilà donc ce pas des nôtres ... en prêtant l'oreille à notre murmure ne fait que la prêter à une histoire de son cru mal inspirée mal dite et chaque fois si ancienne si oubliée que peut lui paraître conforme celle qu'à la boue nous lui murmurons' (215). To him the procession of murmuring voices is 'indebted', not only because only through his ear they exist as voices and through his notes they can exist as text but also because he is the 'source' of food, the love which guarantees the 'victuals'. The source of both narration and food, which are equated, is the end point of these 'perpetual revictuallings narrations and auditions' (139). To him the power of ending is allocated: 'God knows who could blame him' for wanting to 'put an end' to this inferno. However, this God-ear, which can also be read as referring to the Old Testament tradition of God as voice, cannot be the ultimate closing point. The text is the process of digestion: it feeds, regurgitates, and expels language as matter and matter as language.[61]

God-ear, this figure of authority, presiding over the 'infinite loss without profit' (112), is disposed of through a move which is at once the beginning of the end and the assumption of authority on the 'I''s part:

has he not staring him in the face I quote on a solution more simple by far and by far more radical

a formulation that would eliminate him completely and so admit him to that peace at least while rendering me in the same breath sole responsible for this unqualifiable murmur of which consequently here the last scraps at last very last (144)

n'a-t-il pas sous la main je cite toujours une solution plus simple de beaucoup et plus radicale

> une formulation qui en même temps qu'elle le supprimerait tout à fait et lui ouvrirait le voie de ce repos-là au moins me rendrait moi seul responsable de cet inqualifiable murmure dont voici par conséquent enfin les dernières bribes tout à fait (223–224)

The 'I' takes up 'sole responsibility', legally admits his guilt, confesses, states that 'the whole story from beginning to end yes completely false yes ... yes all balls only one voice here yes mine yes' (144–145), 'toute l'histoire d'un bout à l'autre oui complètement faux oui ... oui de la foutaise oui qu'une voix ici oui la mienne oui' (224).

However, the text's critique of the notions of absolutely reliable reproduction or absolute betrayal, of matter as amorphousness or language as transparent, does not allow any stable conclusion, not even a negative one. Looking for 'proof' and meaning amounts to continuing the 'infinite' passion of ingestion and de-jection: 'stab him simply in the arse that is to say speak and he will say anything what he can whereas proof I need proof so stab him in a certain way signifying answer once and for all which I do therefore what an improvement how I've improved' (71), 'le piquer simplement au cul c'est-à-dire parle il dira n'importe quoi ce qu'il peut alors que la prevue il me faut la prevue donc le piquer de façon spéciale signifiant une fois pour toutes réponds c'est donc ce que je fais quel mieux comme j'ai gagné' (111–112).

Dante, we have seen, plays a number of different roles in *How It Is/Comment c'est*: Belacqua is a familiar memory and his mocking lapidary quality has 'fallen over on his side' ('basculé sur le côté'), providing, yet again, a brief comic relief. *Inferno* VII does not just question the reality of *How It Is/Comment c'est*'s incessantly repeated murmurings; it also performs the textual negotiation between language and materiality. The witness and the scribe are *How It Is/Comment c'est*'s translation of the *Comedy*'s take on authority, and the purgatorially oriented circular movement pralleled by the chain of imbricated bodies explores the necessary teleological structure of the narrative. This problem, first encountered in *Dream*, assumes global proportions in *How It Is/Comment c'est*, in which it is extended to an endless procession, 'from next mortal to the next leading nowhere', 'de mortel suivant en mortel suivant ne menant nulle part sans autre'. The material and the literary (and the violent and the pleasurable) are inextricably joined by the tormentor's injunction to 'cleave' to the tormented and to 'give him a name train him up bloody him all over with Roman capitals gorge on his fables unite for life in stoic love to the last shrimp and a little longer' (62), 'le nommer le dresser le couvrir jusq'au sang de majuscules romaines me gaver de ses fables nous unir pour la vie dans l'amour stoïque jusq'au dernier hareng gai et un peu plus' (97).

In *How It Is/Comment c'est* Dante is one of the murmured voices both 'within' and 'without' the text and one of its flickering 'figures'. 'Figure', as Erich Auerbach points out, shares its grammatical root with 'fingere', 'figulus', 'fictor', and 'effiges';[62] the word oscillates between the mathematical reassuring power of the 'dear figures when all fails a few figures' (47) and fiction.

The figures of Belacqua and of the witness and the scribe, and the algebraic figures trying to account for the constantly redrawn and collapsed divisions of mud and bodies indicate that *How It Is/Comment c'est* rewrites an inferno with Dante, enacting the problems of visibility and audibility present in *Inferno* VII and turning them into questions about the reality of fiction, performing the muddy materiality of the canto, and staging the problems of directionality and testimony which haunt the *Purgatorio* through a repetitiveness which is tormenting, unavoidable, and, at times, hellishly funny.

Notes

1 Letter to Donald McWhinnie, 6 April 1960 (RUL) quoted in James Knowlson, *Damned to Fame: The Life of Samuel Beckett* (London: Bloomsbury, 1996), pp. 461–462.
2 Ruby Cohn, *A Beckett Canon* (Ann Arbor: University of Michigan Press, 2001), pp. 256–257.
3 Teodolinda Barolini, *The Undivine Comedy. Detheologizing Dante* (Princeton: Princeton University Press, 1992), p. 25. Neal Oxenhandler, 'Seeing and believing in Dante and Beckett', in Mary Ann Caws (ed.), *Writing in a Modern Temper: Essays on French Literature and Thought in Honor of Henri Peyre* (Saratoga: Anma Libri, 1984), pp. 214–223, p. 218.
4 On the notion of literature as communication in the absence of speaker and listener see Carla Locatelli, '"My life natural order more or less in the present more or less": textual immanence as the textual impossible in Beckett's works', in Lois Oppenheim and Marius Buning (eds), *Beckett On and On ...* (Madison: Fairleigh Dickinson University Press, 1996), pp. 127–147, p. 128. See also Marcello Pagnini, *Pragmatica della letteratura* (Palermo: Sellerio, 1980).
5 Cohn, *A Beckett Canon*, p. 256.
6 Samuel Beckett, *How It Is* (New York: Grove Press, 1964), p. 7; Samuel Beckett, *Comment c'est* (Paris: Les Éditions de Minuit, 1961), p. 9. Subsequent references are given in the text.
7 Leo Bersani and Ulysse Dutoit, *Arts of Impoverishment: Beckett, Rothko, Resnais* (Cambridge, MA: Harvard University Press, 1993), pp. 59–60. On the infinitely regressive movement started by the 'I quote' see also Peter Boxall, 'Beckett's negative geography: fictional space in Beckett's prose', Ph.D. thesis, University of Sussex, 1996, p. 146.
8 Bersani and Dutoit, *Arts of Impoverishment*, p. 60.
9 See Beckett, *Dream of Fair to Middling Woman* (New York: Arcade, 1992), p. 66; *More Pricks Than Kicks* (New York: Grove Weidenfeld, 1972), pp. 38–39 and 47; *Murphy* (London: Picador, 1973), p. 48; *Molloy, The Beckett Trilogy* (London: Picador, 1979), p. 12; *Waiting for Godot* (London: Faber and Faber, 1988), p. 70; *All Strange Away, The Complete Short Prose 1929–1989* ed. S. E. Gontarski (New York: Grove Press, 1995),

p. 171; *The Lost Ones* (New York: Grove Weidenfeld, 1972), p. 56; *Company* (London: Calder, 1980), p. 85.
10 Letter to Kay Boyle, 29 August 1960, HRHRC, University of Texas, Austin.
11 Beckett, *The Lost Ones*, p. 14, *Le dépeupleur*, p. 13, *Company*, p. 85, *Compagnie* (Paris: Les Éditions de Minuit, 1985), p. 84.
12 Murphy 'renounced the lee of Belacqua's rock and his embryonal repose.' Beckett, *Murphy*, p. 48.
13 Francesca Del Moro interprets 'no callers' (12), 'ni de visiteurs' (17) as a reference to Dante and Virgil visiting the damned. Francesca Del Moro, '"The Divine Florentine": Dante nell'opera di Samuel Beckett', dissertation, University of Pisa, 1996, p. 194.
14 Beckett, *Murphy*, p. 48.
15 Ruby Cohn has pointed out that 'curtains open on a scene, as in the theatre, and images vanish through "brief void" or "brief black", like cinematic blackouts'. Cohn, *Back to Beckett* (Princeton: Princeton University Press, 1973), p. 232.
16 See Carla Locatelli, *Unwording the World: Samuel Beckett's Prose Works After the Nobel Prize* (Philadelphia: University of Pennsylvania Press, 1990), pp. 112–154 and 188–224.
17 RUL MS 3000.
18 Beckett, *The Calmative*, in *Stories and Texts for Nothing*, p. 33.
19 Ruby Cohn notices that the mud appears in the Leopardi epigraph to the 1931 edition of *Proust*: 'e fango è il mondo' (and mud is the world). Cohn, *Back to Beckett*, p. 232. William Hutchings, too, draws attention to Leopardi's *A se stesso* in *Proust* (79), '"Shat into grace" or, a tale of a turd: why it is how it is in Samuel Beckett's *How It Is*', *Papers on Language and Literature: A Journal for Scholars and Critics of Language and Literature*, 21:1 (Winter 1985), 64–87. Many others establish the connection between the mud of *How It Is/Comment c'est* and Dante's *Inferno*; see for instance Francesca Del Moro, 'The Divine Florentine', p. 194; Kateryna Arthur, 'T. S. Eliot, Samuel Beckett, and Dante', Ph.D. thesis, University of Sussex, 1982, p. 228; John Fletcher, *Samuel Beckett's Art* (London: Chatto & Windus, 1971), p. 118; Gabriele Frasca, *Cascando: Tre studi su Samuel Beckett* (Naples: Liguori, 1988), pp. 18–19; Oxenhandler, 'Seeing and believing in Dante and Beckett', pp. 214–223; Michael Robinson, 'From purgatory to inferno: Beckett and Dante revisited', *Journal of Beckett Studies*, 5 (Autumn 1979), 79; Jean-Pierre Ferrini, *Dante et Beckett* (Paris: Hermann, 2003).
20 Michael Robinson quotes from canto VII, 109–111, 112–125, and 125–126.
21 William Hutchings also quotes canto VII, 118–126. Hutchings's first parallel between the Dantean passage and *How It Is* is based on a close reading of a 1948 English translation (by Thomas G. Bergin) of the *Comedy*, and it is quite misleading. Philip Terry, 'Waiting for God to go: *How It Is* and *Inferno* VII–VIII', *Samuel Beckett Today/Aujourdhui: Beckett Versus Beckett*, 7 (1998), 349–360.
22 TCD 10963, fols 18–19. RUL MS 3000. *Foirade IV* also has a reference in Italian to the same passage from the *Comedy*: 'Je rentre à la nuit, ils s'envolent, ils lâchent mon petit chêne et s'en vont, gavés, dans les ombres. Tristi fummo ne l'aere dolce. Je rentre, lève le bras, saisis la branche, me met debout et rentre dans la maison.' Samuel Beckett, *Pour finir encore et autres foirades* (Paris: Les Éditions de Minuit, 1976), p. 45.
23 This is parallel to what *What Where* does through the last sentence 'make sense who may', thus explicitly placing the reader in the position of the next tormentor/tormented. See Samuel Beckett, *What Where*, in *Collected Shorter Plays of Samuel Beckett* (London: Faber & Faber, 1984), pp. 307–313, p. 313.

24 Samuel Beckett, *Waiting for Godot* (London: Faber and Faber, 1988), p. 68.
25 Cohn, *Back to Beckett*, p. 238.
26 'The *masochist body*: it is poorly understood in terms of pain; it is fundamentally a question of the BwO [Body without Organs]. It has its sadist or whore sew it up; the eyes, anus, urethra, breasts, and nose are sewn shut. It has itself strung up to stop the organs from working; flayed, as if the organs clung to the skin; sodomized, smothered, to make sure everything is sealed tight.' Gilles Deleuze and Félix Guattari, *A Thousand Plateaus: Capitalism and Schizophrenia* (London: Athlone, 1988), vol. 2, p. 150; the authors' emphasis.
27 In *Murphy* all the characters but Murphy are called 'puppets'. The French version reads instead: 'Pim à tout jamais qu'une carcasse inerte et muette à jamais alatie dans la boue sans moi mais comment que je vais l'animer vous allez voir et si je sais m'effacer derrière ma creature quand ça m'arrive' (82).
28 'e volta nostra poppa nel mattino, / de' remi facemmo ali al folle vole, / sempre acquistando dal lato mancino. / Tutte le stelle già dell'altro polo / vedea la notte, e 'l nostro tanto basso, / che non surgea fuor del marin suolo. / ... quando n'apparve una montagna, bruna / per la distanza, e parvemi alta tanto / quanto veduta non avëa alcuna. / Noi ci allegrammo, e tosto tornò in pianto; / ché de la nova terra un turbo nacque / e percosse del legno il primo canto. / Tre volte il fé girar con tutte l'acque; / a la quarta levar la poppa in suso / e la prora ire in giù, com'altrui piacque, / infin che 'l mar fu sovra noi richiuso' (And turning our stern to the morning, we made of our oars wings for the mad flight, always gaining on the left. The night now saw the other pole and all its stars, and ours so low that it did not rise from the ocean floor ... when there appeared to us a mountain dark in the distance, and to me it seemed the highest I had ever seen. We rejoiced, but soon our joy was turned to grief, for from the new land a whirlwind rose and struck the forepart of the ship. Three times it whirled her round with all the waters, and the fourth time it lifted the stern aloft and plunged the prow below, as pleased Another, till the sea closed over us) (*Inf.* XXVI, 124–129 and 133–142).
29 The term 'family' occurs in the text in the sense of 'category', which in the French appears as 'genre'. Beckett, *How It Is*, pp. 9 and 12, *Comment c'est*, pp. 13 and 17. It also occurs in relation to the 'dynasty' of Kram, *How It Is*, p. 83.
30 This hypothesis accounts for the correspondence between the French 'vexille' in *Comment c'est* and the Latin 'vexilla' in canto XXXIV; Neal Oxenhandler, 'Seeing and believing', p. 222.
31 Katherine Travers Gross, 'In other words: Samuel Beckett's art of poetry', Ph.D. thesis, Columbia University, 1972, p. 167. Christopher Ricks also writes of 'the Dantesque "abandon hope"' Christopher Ricks, *Beckett's Dying Words* (Oxford: Oxford University Press, 1995), p. 145.
32 Lawrence E. Harvey, *Samuel Beckett: Poet and Critic* (Princeton: Princeton University Press, 1970), p. 72.
33 Samuel Beckett, *Collected Poems 1930–1978* (London: John Calder, 1984), p. 137.
34 Francesca Del Moro, '"The Divine Florentine"', p. 86.
35 '*Dr. Piouk*: ... Allez! Le grand refus, pas le petit, le grand, ce que seul l'homme peut, ce qu'il peut de plus glorieux, le refus de l'être! *(s'essuie le front)*' and '*Mme Krap* – Ne faites pas attention. Il se croit au cercle. *M. Krap* – Je suis. Au neuvième.' Samuel Beckett, *Eleuthéria* (Paris: Les Éditions de Minuit, 1995), pp. 159 and 29–30.
36 Samuel Beckett, 'Papini's Dante', in Ruby Cohn (ed.), *Disjecta: Miscellaneous Writings and a Dramatic Fragment* (New York: Grove Press, 1984), pp. 80–81, p. 81.

37 The connection between the 'interminable processions' and digested materiality is made in *Watt*, in which pleasure can be derived by the bathetic outcome: 'And the poor old lousy old earth, my earth and my father's and my mother's and my father's father's and my mother's mother's and my father's mother's and my mother's father's and my father's mother's father's and my father's mother's mother's ... and mothers' mothers' mothers'. An excrement. The crocuses and the larch turning green every year a week before the others and the pastures red with uneaten sheep's placentas and the long summer days ... and then the whole bloody business starting all over again. A turd.' Samuel Beckett, *Watt*, (New York: Grove Weidenfeld, 1959), pp. 46–47.

38 'But in vain I raised without hope my eyes to the sky to look for the Bears.' Beckett, *The Calmative*, p. 46. The reference is to *Purgatorio* I, 28–30.

39 Hutchings, '"Shat into Grace"', 75. On scatology in Beckett and its 'hellish' connotation, see Keir Elam, 'World's End: West Brompton, Turdy and other godforsaken holes', *Samuel Beckett Today/Aujourd'hui*, 6 (1997), 165–180.

40 Elam, 'World's End', 170.

41 A similar connection between *Inferno* XVIII, 17 and 'mud' can be found in *Watt*: 'My friend call me Dum, said Mr Spiro, I am so bright and cheerful. D-U-M. Anagram of mud ... Our advertisements are extraordinary. We keep our tonsure above water.' *How it Is/Comment c'est* expands upon the suggestion of equivalence between mud and excrement, which in *Watt* is also made through the allusion to Dante's Alessio Interminelli da Lucca, 'so befouled with ordure that it did not appear whether he was layman or cleric'. Beckett, *Watt*, p. 27.

42 Jacques Derrida, 'Demeure: fiction et témoignage', in Michel Lisse (ed.), *Passions de la littérature: avec Jacques Derrida* (Paris: Galilée, 1996), pp. 13–73, pp. 21–22.

43 Derrida, 'Demeure', p. 21.

44 Bersani and Dutoit, *Arts of Impoverishment*, p. 56.

45 See Beckett, *How It Is*, p. 129.

46 *Company* reads: 'withershins'. The adverb comes 'from Middle Low German *weddersins*, from Middle High German *widersinnes*, from *wider* "against" + *sin* "direction"; the second element was associated with Scots "sun"' (*OED*). In the English text the explicit reference to Hell is lost, although implicitly suggested by the adverb. In the 'romantic picnic' scene of *How it Is/Comment c'est*, we read: 'we let go our hands and turn about I dextrogyre she sinistro' (29), 'nous nous lâchons la main et faisons demi-tour moi dextrorsum elle senestro' (45).

47 See the first of the three 'Dante postcards', RUL MS 4123.

48 Leslie Hill, *Beckett's Fiction in Different Words* (Cambridge: Cambridge University Press, 1990), p. 137.

49 The 'Roman capitals' are inscribed in the body of the text itself; the capitalisation, used in part two during the torture (*How It Is*, pp. 90 and 96), appears again at the very end of the text (pp. 144–147). I am indebted to Dr Steven Barfield for this observation made during a meeting of the London Beckett Seminar, held at Birkbeck College in 1999.

50 Charles S. Singleton, *Commedia: Elements of Structure* (Cambridge, MA: Harvard University Press, 1954), p. 90. See also Teodolinda Barolini, *Dante's Poets: Textuality and Truth in the* Comedy (Princeton: Princeton University Press, 1984), p. 90, and *The Undivine Comedy*, p. 18.

51 On witness and scribe as figures of repetition in *How It Is* see Ewa Plonowska Ziarek, *The Rhetoric of Failure: Deconstruction of Skepticism, Reinvention of Modernism* (Albany: State University of New York Press, 1996), pp. 157–199, p. 178.

52 In *How It Is*, the relationship between light and reason is made quite clear: 'this voice yes the sad truth is there are moments when I fancy I can hear it and my lamps that my lamps are going out Krim says I'm mad' (p. 83) and 'under the ideal observer's lamp' (p. 95) and 'no knowing our senses our lights what do they amount to' (p. 83). See also *Watt*: 'But what kind of witness was Watt, weak now of eye, hard of hearing, and with even more intimate senses greatly below par? A needy witness, an imperfect witness. The better to witness, the worse to witness. That with his need he might witness its absence. That imperfect he might witness it ill', p. 203.

53 'Time on the ballastoffice is down.' 'Mr Bloom smile O rocks at two window of the ballastoffice', and 'the flags of the Ballast office and Custom House were dipped in salute as were also those of the electrical power station at the Pigeonhouse and the Poolbeg Light.' James Joyce, *Ulysses*, eds Hans Walter Gabler, Wolfhard Steppe and Claus Melchior (Harmondsworth: Penguin, 1986), pp. 126 and 280.

54 Jacques Derrida, 'Demeure', pp. 21–22.

55 Cohn, *A Beckett Canon*, p. 258.

56 I substitute 'desk' for Singleton's 'bench'; the Italian 'banco' ('desk', but also 'school-desk') creates the reader as student.

57 Teodolinda Barolini, discussing the use of 'tëodia' in the *Comedy*, states that *Paradiso* XXV is 'the canto in which Dante implicitly aligns his poetry with David's by calling his poem a *poema sacro*; here, as part of his examination on hope, Dante translates word from word from David's ninth (now tenth) Psalm: "Sperino in te", ne la sua tëodia / dice, "color che sanno il nome tuo" ("Let them hope in thee," he says in his *tëodia*, "who know Thy name", 73–74). The term *tëodia*, "divine song" coined to describe the Psalms, is easily tranferred to Dante's own *poema sacro*: needing a new descriptive term for his new genre, Dante invents it with the rest of the *Comedy*'s basic poetic baggage ... True to his fundamental procedural principles of appropriation and revision, he first appropriates a standard rhetorical term, *comedìa*, and then – having redefined it from within as a *poema sacro* – replaces the original term with a new one: *tëodia*.' Barolini, *Dante's Poets*, p. 277.

58 Philip Terry, also, establishes the parallel between Purgatorio XXIV and the dictation taking place in *How It Is*. Terry, 'Waiting for God', 350.

59 Barolini, *The Undivine Comedy*, p. 8. See also the entry 'dittare' in *Enciclopedia dantesca*, by Bruno Basile, who points out some *auctoritates* in which a similar use of 'dittare' can be found, most notably in Richard of Saint Victor and Guido Cavalcanti. Philip Terry points out (via David H. Higgins) that 'Alcuin of York saw God as the "dictator" under whom holy men write'. Terry, 'Waiting for God', 350.

60 Samuel Beckett, *Proust* (New York: Grove Press, 1957), p. 8.

61 This does not mean that the text configures itself as 'body', as the container of the digestive process. Rather, as I have observed above, the text is made of body fragments, severed from a thus-already-fragmented self.

62 Erich Auerbach, *Studi su Dante* (Milan: Feltrinelli, 1989 [1963]), pp. 176–226.

8 'In the words of the poet': *The Lost Ones*

The Lost Ones/Le dépepleur has been described as a 'Dantean hellscape,' for more than one reason: the English title evokes the 'perduta gente' ('the lost people' or 'the lost ones') mentioned on the gate of the *Inferno* in canto III; the text refers to the final line of the *Paradiso*, it groups the beings inhabiting the concentrically divided 'closed place' into categories according to their postures and orientation, and it is concerned with 'a way out' of this faintly lit rotunda.[1]

If in *How It Is* Dante participates in the game between saying and quoting (within and without), here Dante's visibility is part of the tension between blindness and insight. *The Lost Ones* has been said to be 'filled with a wealth of subtle allusions', while also exhibiting an irritating rhetorical 'flatness'.[2] In the critical literature, the surprise at the relative transparency of the writing of this late text goes hand in hand with the invocation of a – more or less – dysfunctional 'allegory'.[3] In other words, Beckett criticism has interpreted this text at once as flat and convoluted, dully transparent and opaquely allegorical.[4]

I argue that the text plays with notions of transparency and opacity, inside and outside, and perception and construction, in order to critique them as oppositions. By presenting itself as a 'long observation', the text attempts to be a sensory experience, 'witnessing', or non-language.[5] Of course, it can only do so *through* and *as* language, narration, and text. Being language, the text can be neither completely transparent, nor absolutely opaque, although these are the two poles around which an unresolved tension is created. *The Lost Ones* uses romantic notions of perception, experience, landscape, and unspeakability, playing them against ideas of language and textuality.[6]

The text's intertextuality is displayed in this strategic adoption and critique of the oppositions between perception and language, spatial organisation, and inside and outside. Rather than being one of the 'subtle allusions' which add to the text's value, Dante's visibility in *The Lost Ones/Le dépepleur* is produced by what the *Comedy* calls 'ravening eyes', by the concentric division of space, and by the presence of the vanquished subjected to iron rules. Significantly, Dante's presence within the text is also questioned by positing the last lines of the *Comedy* as the impossible 'way out' of this infernal system.

Ravening eyes

Both *The Lost Ones* and *Le dépeupleur* claim their original unoriginality in their very titles; the French title *Le dépeupleur* refers to the poem 'L'isolement' by Lamartine, a poet also quoted later in the text.[7] Moreover, as pointed out by Edward Colerick, the English title alludes to Dante's *Inferno* III, in which the inscription on the gate of hell reads:[8]

> Per me si va ne la città dolente,
> per me si va ne l'etterno dolore,
> per me si va tra la *perduta gente*. (*Inf.* III, 1–3)
>
> THROUGH ME YOU ENTER THE WOEFUL CITY,
> THROUGH ME YOU ENTER ETERNAL GRIEF,
> THROUGH ME YOU ENTER AMONG *THE LOST*.[9]

Dante and Lamartine are the two *auctoritates* who give a name to the texts, marking their individuality, and characterise them as already written. The titles inaugurate a dynamic between originality and unoriginality, and between outside and inside. This dialectic parallels both the untenable opposition between sensory experience and textuality, and the oscillation, already observed in *Mercier and/et Camier*, between narration as the reportage of an external reality and as the invention of a microcosm 'teeming' with 'little people'.

The beginning of the text sets up this contrast between the notion of a reality 'out there', retrievable through observation, and that of reality made of language: 'Abode where lost bodies roam each searching for its lost one. Vast enough for search to be in vain. Narrow enough for flight to be in vain' (7), 'Séjour où des corps vont cherchant chacun son dépepleur. Assez vaste pour permettre de chercher en vain. Assez restreint pour que toute fruite soit vaine' (7). The 'abode' can 'subsist' only according to certain parameters, which draw attention to the narrative as fabrication.[10] This is enhanced later in the text, which establishes the dimensions of the cylinder 'for the sake of harmony' (7). The compositional problem of 'harmony', a term that frequently occurs in the text, is juxtaposed against the description of a number of natural factors: light, temperature ('climate'), sound, and customs of the inhabitants of the cylinder.[11] The tension between textuality and experience is echoed by the tension between composition and nature and narration and vision.

Dante's visibility in *The Lost Ones* can be understood only if we explore further this tension. For instance, although presenting itself as observation, the text deconstructs all the elements on which visual perception is based, such as the perceiving subject and the perceived object, the position of the observer, and the material conditions of visibility.

The narrator claims that the 'aperçus' of the cylinder are 'from a certain angle', 'from above', or 'from below'; however, the position of the narrator/observer can be neither internal nor external: *Imagination Dead Imagine* phrases this problem as an injunction: 'No way in, go in, measure.'[12] Since *The Lost Ones* excludes a 'way out', and therefore a way in, the observer has no openings from which to peruse the closed cylinder. However, he cannot be within the cylinder either, since he states that 'it is doubtful' that 'such a one exists' with 'a perfect mental image of the entire system', which would allow him to 'relish' the 'harmony' of the 'irregular' quincunxial disposition of the niches (11–12).[13] This proposition further complicates matters; the knowledge deriving from experience can give shape to a 'perfect mental image', which should allow the subject to relish the harmony of the disposition of the niches. The 'harmony' (a term implying composition) is the result of an observation (its own) of the disposition of the niches; yet, there cannot be a subject capable of relishing this harmony precisely because he lacks the complete experience, which can produce the perfect mental image. The text, therefore, creates a loop: harmony, the result of experience (observation) can be experienced (relished) only by those who have sufficient experience, and therefore a perfect mental image; but it is doubtful that such a one exists. Sensory experience is created by a mental image, in its turn created by sensory experience, 'and so on infinitely' (50).

The observer can be neither external nor internal; the text asserts a harmonic disposition denying the existence of an internal subject within the cylinder able to experience it, while it also denies the existence of an external space from which the observation could have taken place.

This paradox is paralleled by the juxtaposition of the absolute visibility reigning in the cylinder against the invisibility of the niches 'from below'. The narrator/observer asserts that everything is 'agleam', even the inside of the tunnels and niches. Shadows are limited to 'those cast by the bodies pressing on one another wilfully or from necessity as when for example on a breast to prevent its being lit or on some private part the hand descends with vanished palm' (40). However, 'seen from below the wall presents an unbroken surface all the way round and up to the ceiling' (55). Hence, 'the dim omnipresent light' has a 'levelling effect', causing the invisibility of the niches; however, the text declares them as invisible, thus creating a visible invisibility. At the same time, the cylinder is dominated by the absolute visibility of 'even some of its [the tunnel's] folds and recesses in so far as the air enters in'; so much so that 'light is not the word' (40).

The text creates not only a visible invisibility but also an invisible visibility, a 'darkness visible', to borrow a Miltonian expression from *Company*; it does so by telling us what can be seen during the 'momentary lull[s]' (36), when the light goes off and the temperature down. We are told of how the 'stillness heightened tenfold of the sedentary and vanquished makes that which is normally theirs seem risible in comparison' (37), and how 'the fists on their way to smite in anger or discouragement freeze in their arcs' (37): 'The effect of those brief and rare respites is unspeakably dramatic to put it mildly' (36). Invisible visibility goes hand in hand with visible blindness; the deterioration of sight proceeds 'by such slow and insensible degrees to be sure as to pass unperceived even by those most concerned' (39). Death is 'so gradual and to put it plainly so fluctuant a death as to escape the notice even of a visitor' (18), the vanquished 'stray unseeing through the throng indistinguishable to the eye of flesh from the still unrelenting' (31).

The material conditions of visibility are further explored through the 'observation' of the 'repercussions on the organ' (38) of the paradoxical 'fiery flickering murk' (38). The text often refers to the visual 'organ', the 'eye', in the singular, punning on the divide between observing subject and observed object: 'Consequences of this light for the searching eye' (8).

The 'searching eye' increasingly 'reddens' and its pupil deteriorates, dilating until it 'devours' the whole 'orb'. The searchers in the arena are 'devouring with their eyes' the occupants of the climbers' territory; their 'eyes ... fixed as they burn to enter the first [zone]' (46) create a 'second even narrower belt' between the arena and the climbers' zone (29). The 'last of all if a man' devours the face of the vanquished woman (62), and 'the spent eyes may have fits of the old craving' (31). The painful and hopeless sexual encounters at once imply and deny vision: the 'spectacle' of 'man and wife' 'in camera' can be seen 'without their knowledge', thus 'verging ... on the obscene'.[14] 'Stranger still at such times all the questing eyes ... suddenly go still and fix their stare on the void or on some old abomination as for instance other eyes and then the long looks exchanged by those fain to look away' (54). Those 'fain' (both pleased and compelled) to look away do exchange long looks; fixing other eyes is defined as an abomination, a thing causing hatred and disgust, implying the act of turning away.[15] This is an 'obscene scene' of unseeing people at once staring and turning away their looks.[16]

The 'eyes' of the little people ravenously scrutinise the 'fiery flickering murk' while searching for their lost ones. These eyes are voracious, devouring, famished: 'The spent eyes may have fits of the old craving ... Then the eyes suddenly start to search afresh as famished as the unthinkable first day' (31–32). The 'unceasing eyes' (33) not only devour but also are devoured by the 'fiery flickering murk'; they are victims of 'ocular fever', subjects *of* and *to* their passion, within a predator/prey dynamic, to which not even the vanquished are exempt, since 'even they may experience a return of "ocular fever", replete with "ravenous eyes"'.[17]

Dante's visibility emerges via these predatory, ravening eyes, which are encountered in a passage from *Inferno* IV quoted twice in the 'Whoroscope' notebook.

> Cesare armato con gli occhi *grifagni*.
> (20.123) [sic]
> Cesare armato con gli *occhi grifagni*
> (Inf IV 123)
> falcon-eyed Cesar armed

The 'ravenous' or 'ravening' eyes are the 'yeux grifanes' (the adjective 'grifagno' can be translated as 'predatory' and 'ravenous') also found in *Vieille terre/Old Earth*, in which the 'I' which calls himself 'me' sees with his 'other's ravening eyes': the split self is the split I/eye: 'Vieille terre, assez menti, je l'ai vue, c'était moi, de mes yeux grifanes d'autrui, c'est trop tard' (45), 'Old earth, no more lies, I've seen you, it was me, with my other's ravening eyes, too late' (238).[18]

The link between perception, vision, relationality, and desire has been present in Beckett's works since *Proust*, in which perception is described as the process in which 'the observer infects the observed with his own mobility'.[19] The theorised mobility of both subject and object leads to the conclusion that 'whatever the object, our thirst for possession is, by definition, insatiable'.[20] In *Murphy* too, the act of looking and devouring is connected to 'the type-tragedy of the human relationship whose failure is preordained'.[21] Ruby Cohn has pointed out the parallel between Murphy's scrutiny of Mr Endon's eyes and the last paragraph of *The Lost Ones*, in which the last searcher inspects the vanquished woman's unseeing eyes.[22] Susan Brienza has further discussed the similarity between the deterioration of Mr Endon's 'prodigiously dilated' pupils and those of the inhabitants of the cylinder.[23] Perception and visibility are crucial also for *Film*, in which Berkeley's 'esse est percipi' is reformulated as an act of self-perception.[24] In *The Lost Ones*, as in the *Foirade* mentioned above, there is no reconstitution of a final unitary subject; the eye's search for its lost ones (even when articulated as the search for the self) can only be vain.

In *The Lost Ones* the well-worn puns between 'eye' and the 'I', and 'seen' and 'scene', are connected to the paradoxical position of the subject of the observation/narration, which is neither internal nor external. The frequent use of the singular – 'eye', 'searching eye', 'the eye of flesh' – produces an ambiguity about whose eye the text is speaking of: the little people's, the observer/narrator's, or the reader's. The 'eye of flesh' cannot perceive what in the text is being described as perceived, since the vanquished 'may stray unseeing through the throng indistinguishable to the eye of flesh from the still unrelenting' (31) and 'the bed of the cylinder comprises three distinct zones separated by clear-cut mental or imaginary frontiers invisible to the eye of flesh' (43). The text claims 'to see' something indistinguishable or invisible to the 'eye of flesh'; the narrator becomes – *ex negativo* – the 'mind's eye'. Able to see through darkness and through a light which is not a light, at once internal and external, invisible in so far as it is also the subject of the scrutiny, the 'eye' becomes the 'I', the split subject of a process of self-perception within the 'skullscape'. The subject of the scrutiny cannot see himself while seeing; the self is the non-coinciding process of its creation, it cannot be grasped as a unity through sight: 'none looks within himself where none can be' (30).

The use of the term 'aperçu' not only in the French but also in the English text draws attention to introspection, since, as pointed out by Susan Brienza, it does not only mean 'glimpse', 'glance', and 'outline', but also 'insight'. *The Lost Ones* is as a 'skullscape', a closed scene/seen of an I/eye created by its own process of perception and construction, an imprisoned landscape constituted by a mind, which is both perceiver and perceived: 'By nature I mean here, like the naivest realist, a composite of perceiver and perceived, not a datum, an experience.'[25] Berkeley's 'esse est percipi' is confined within the closed space of the mind perceiving itself. The representation of mind exploring itself is closely related to Descartes' *Meditations*; *The Lost Ones* even refers to 'the thinking being' and to 'data' and 'evidences': 'And the thinking being coldly intent on all these data and evidences could scarcely escape at the close of his analysis the mistaken conclusion' (39). Descartes' second meditation, 'Of the nature of the human mind, and that it is more easily known than the body', supposes the fallacy of perception in order to arrive at the 'cogito ergo sum' and at the definition of the self as 'une chose qui pense', a 'res cogitans'.[26]

The text is the mind, and therefore the mind is the text. Through a process similar to that observed above in relation to experiences and mental images, what the text reports to 'see' is always already in the mind and vice versa; experience must have been already constructed as such in order to be. In this text, the saying says to be the seeing and the seeing cannot be outside the saying. Textuality presents itself as perception, experience, non-linguistic transparency and/or opacity; however, perception as non-language can only 'subsist' in language as text, thus feeding back into the loop. In *The Lost Ones*, as in any text, the seeing cannot 'go without saying' (57).

Closed places

This dynamics between perception and language, inside and outside, and visibility and invisibility is mediated by the *Comedy*'s 'ravening eyes' and it is linked to another role played by Dante in *The Lost Ones*.

Ruby Cohn has noticed that in *Se voir/Closed Place* 'the concentric circles of ditch and track also mirror the human eye, which thus "se voit"', establishing a clear link between the split perceiving self and the spatial organisation of this *Foirade*.[27] Such a link can be extended to *The Lost Ones/Le dépeupleur* too, as its closed space consists in 'a belt' running 'all along the wall ... about one metre wide [is] reserved for the carriers' (27); 'when weary of searching among the throng' the searchers 'turn towards this zone [the climbers' territory] ... Their slow round counter-carrierwise creates a second even narrower belt respected in its turn by the main body of the searchers ... Which suitably lit from above would give the impression at times of two narrow rings turning in opposite directions about the teeming precinct' (29). We therefore have 'Three distinct zones separated by a clear-cut mental or imaginary frontiers invisible to the eye of flesh. First an outer belt ... Next a slightly narrower inner belt where those weary of searching in mid-cylinder slowly revolve in Indian file intent on the periphery. Finally the arena proper' (43).

This division of space has a Dantean dimension, since *Inferno* XIV (the third *girone* of the seventh *cerchio* occupied by the violents against God, nature and art) is a 'spazzo' (ground) made of 'una rena arida e spessa' (a dry deep sand). In it Dante has seen:

> D'anime nude [vidi] molte gregge
> che piangean tutte assai miseramente,
> e parea posta lor diversa legge.
> Supin giacea in terra alcuna gente,
> alcuna si sedea tutta raccolta,
> e altra andava continüamente. (*Inf.* XIV, 19–24)

> many herds of naked souls, who were all lamenting very miserably; and different laws seemed to be imposed upon them. Some were lying supine upon the ground, some sitting all crouched up, and others were going about incessantly

The word 'rena' echoes the English 'arena' and even more closely the French 'arène', which shares with the Italian the meaning of 'sand'. Both the English and the French terms appear in *Closed Place/Se voir* too, in which the 'closed place' is also divided into three zones: an 'arena', 'aréne', 'ditch', 'fosse' and 'track', 'piste', concentrically arranged: the 'arena' is surrounded by the 'ditch', and 'between the two skirting the latter a track', which is just wide enough to allow for 'the average sized body' (236).[28] Within the black vast arena there is 'room for millions' (236), which appear 'six time smaller than life' and never see, hear, or touch one another. The track is made of 'dead leaves', which 'are dry': 'dead but not rotting. Crumbling into dust rather' (237).

Francesca Del Moro has pointed out the similarity between this division and that of the seventh circle of *Inferno* (cantos XII–XVI), which is divided into a 'fosso' (ditch), a 'selva' (wood, thicket), and a 'spazzo' (ground, yard, arena) made of 'rena arida e spessa' (dry and deep sand): 'La dolorosa selva l'è ghirlanda / Intorno, come 'l fosso tristo ad essa; / ... Lo spazzo era una rena arida e spessa' (The woeful wood is garland round about it, as round the wood the dismal ditch ... The ground was a dry deep sand) (*Inf.* XIV, 10–11; 13).[29]

In the sandy ground the damned souls are divided into three categories, according to different laws, precisely as in *The Lost Ones*. They can 'lie down' ('supin giacea'), 'crouch' or 'squat' ('sedea tutta raccolta'), or 'feverishly teem the precinct' ('altra andava continüamente'). Lying down is at once denied and inscribed in *The Lost Ones*: 'Lying down is unheard of in the cylinder and this pose solace of the vanquished is forever denied them here' (60).

The crouching or squatting posture is the by now familiar Belacqua posture, which is alluded once in the text through a mention of Dante:

> Fourthly those who do not search or non-searchers sitting for the most part against the wall in the attitude which wrung from Dante one of his rare wan smiles. (14)

> Quatrièmement ceux qui ne cherchent pas ou non-chercheurs assis pour la plupart contre le mur dans l'attitude qui arracha à Dante un de ses rares pâles sourires. (13)

Dante smiling is to be found also in the first of the three Beckett postcards, where Casella and Manfredi are recorded as respectively the first and the second 'shade to smile' at Dante, while under the title '4', standing for *Purgatorio* IV, the card reads:

> 122 Dante smiles (at Belacqua)
> D's 1st smile?[30]

At first the text assimilates Belacqua's posture to that of the fourth group of inhabitants of the cylinder, the 'non-searchers' or 'vanquished'. The fifth vanquished, the woman who 'is the north', 'squats against the wall with her head between her knees and her legs in her arms' (56–57). The verb 'to squat' also refers intratextually to the Belacqua posture, encountered from *Dream* to *How It Is*. The vanquished, however, are not all in this position: 'Cleave ... to the wall both sitting and standing four vanquished out of five' (29). They not only sit against the wall but also stand. Furthermore, the vanquished are not the only ones to crouch; people described as 'sitting or standing against the wall' are, later in the text, said to belong to the third category of 'sedentary searchers'. These are a 'sort of semi-sages among whom all ages are to be admired from old age to infancy' and 'inspire in those still fitfully fevering if not a cult at least a certain deference' (28).[31]

The climbers, too, share the Belacqua posture; once they have reached their niches, they 'crouch down after a fashion' (11). The climbers crouching in their niches recall another image from the *Purgatorio*, this time from canto XIII, in which Dante compares the narrow stair he had to climb to that of San Miniato, with this difference, that this one 'quinci e quindi l'alta pietra rade' (the high rock presses close on this side and on that) (*Purg.* XII, 108). When they have reached the top of this stair, in canto XIII, Virgil says to Dante: 'Ma ficca li occhi per l'aere ben fiso, / e vedrai gente innanzi a noi sedersi, / e ciascun è lungo la grotta assiso' (But fix your eyes full steadily through the air and you will see people sitting there in front of us, and each is seated against the rock). 'Grotta' also means 'cave' or 'grotto', thus reinforcing the parallel. The mount of *Purgatory* 'teems' with steep stairs, which the pilgrims have to climb.[32] In Italian, as in French, no difference is made between 'stairs' and 'ladder'; the word 'scala' (échelle) is used for both. Faced by the steep ladder in canto III, Virgil asks himself 'Or chi sa da qual man la costa cala ... sì che possa salir chi va senz'ala?' (Now who knows on which hand the hillside slopes ... so that he can ascend who goes without wings?) (*Purg.* III, 52–54): in the *Purgatorio*, as in the cylinder, some ladders 'call for acrobatics' (10). The ladder in canto XXV is described as 'la scala / che per artezza i salitor dispaia' (the stairway which by its straitness unpairs the climbers) (*Purg.* XXV, 8–9); in *The Lost Ones* 'it is the custom not to climb two or more at a time' (11).

The crouching Belacqua posture characterises more than one category of little people, but pervades the microcosm of the cylinder. Belacqua's attitude participates in the 'oscillation' between perception and imagination. Although the crouching attitude is posited as the result of a 'natural' observation, from which the four categories are deduced, its referring to Belacqua disrupts the idea that subdivisions, categories, and language are the result of visual perception and indicate that the 'natural' is the result of language. Vision, perception, experience, and body are the result of a linguistic visibility obtained through repetition.

In the *Inferno* the division of the damned is regulated, as in the cylinder, by 'different laws', reflecting the 'harmony between order and licence' (44) 'the repeated violation of which would soon transform the abode into a pandemonium' (26). The term 'pandemonium' inscribes the infernal qualities of the text while denying them through the institution of 'laws', which are themselves similar to those of Dante's *Inferno*. A similar strategy is adopted in the following sentence: 'the sensation of yellow [the gloom] imparts not to say of sulphur in view of the associations' (36). Once again, the 'sensation' can only derive from a 'word' carrying 'associations'.

A few pages later we are told about the 'motion'; 'For one entering this zone head-on the nearest queue is on the right and if it does not please it is only by going right that a more pleasing can be found' (48). The direction towards the right which the climbers have to follow is the one followed by the protagonist of *Le calmant/The Calmative*, in *How It Is/Comment c'est*, and in the first of the three Beckett postcards referring to Dante. The direction towards the right is that followed by the pilgrims in the *Purgatorio*. In the first 'Dante postcard' line 22 of *Purgatorio* I appears – 'I' mi volsi alla man destra' – followed by: '(In Hell turn always to the left / in Purg turn always to the right).[33] In *The Lost Ones* the queuing searchers move on the right, while the slow movement 'counter-carrierwise creates a second even narrower belt'.

The two narrow rings and the Indian file are to be encountered in *Purgatorio* XXVI, where the lustful penitents appear to Dante;

> ché per lo mezzo del cammino acceso
> venne gente col viso incontro a questa,
> la qual mi fece a rimirar sospeso.
> Lì veggio d'ogne parte farsi presta
> ciascun' ombra e basciarsi una con una
> senza restar, contente a brieve festa (*Purg.* XXVI, 28–33)

for through the middle of the burning road people were coming with their faces opposite to these, and made me gaze in suspense. There on every side I see all the shades making haste and kissing one another, without stopping, content with brief greeting

Malebolge presents a similar image; the damned walk in two opposite 'rings'; those walking in the larger ring come towards the poet, those in the narrower one walk in his direction: 'dal mezzo in qua ci venien verso 'l volto / di là con noi, ma con passi maggiori' (on our side of the middle they came facing us, and, on the other side, along with us, but with greater strides) (*Inf.* XVIII, 26–27). An image 'which suitably lit from above would give the impression at times of two narrow rings turning in opposite directions' (29).

Section seven of *The Lost Ones* is devoted to the 'transport' of the ladders. A rule requires the carrier of the ladders 'to hug the wall at all times eddywise' (27). Together with 'the prohibition to climb more than one at a time' (27), this rule is part of the 'conventions' which 'regulate' the use of the ladders; 'in their precision and the submission they exact from the climbers [they] resemble laws' (21). Yet, it is declared that there is 'Nothing more natural' (27) than 'rule[s]' and 'prohibition[s]'. The text ironises 'naturalness'; without the rules which organise the text 'life in the cylinder would soon become untenable', that is to say the text (even the text *as* life) could not exist. Naming implies 'the order of the law'.[34]

Other passages of *The Lost Ones* which refer both to physical and spatial divisions are reminiscent of the *Comedy*. The 'consequences of this climate for the skin' are that the skin 'shrivels' and 'the bodies brush together with a rustle of dry leaves' (8), 'this desiccation ... transforms into a rustling of nettles the natural succulence of flesh against flesh' (53). In *Inferno* III, 112, the damned on the banks of the Acheron are queuing to be transported by Charon to hell; at Charon's words they 'huddle together ... a mere jumble of intermingled flesh';[35] later, they appear to Dante the observer as:

> Come d'autunno si levano le foglie
> l'una appresso de l'altra, fin che 'l ramo
> vede a la terra tutte le sue spoglie,
> similemente il mal seme d'Adamo
> gittansi di quel lito ad una ad una (*Inf.* III, 112)

> As the leaves fall away in autumn, one after another, till the bough sees all its spoils upon the ground, so there the evil seed of Adam: one by one they cast themselves from that shore

In *Se voir/Closed Place* the dry, dead leaves, 'dead but not rotting. Crumbling into dust rather' (237) echo Dante's presence in *The Lost Ones/Le dépeupleur*. In the words of *Waiting for Godot* we could say that 'all the dead voices ... make a noise like ...leaves. Like sand. ... They rustle. They murmur. They rustle.'[36] The skin 'shrivels' also in *Purgatorio* XXIII, in which the gluttons expiate their sin; they are incredibly thin and their skin is called 'squama' [scurf], because, as Forese Donati tells the pilgrim, 'l'asciutta scabbia / [che] mi scolora ... la pelle' (the dry scab [that] discolors my skin).

As in the case of *How It Is*, the violence in *The Lost Ones* can also be related to some passages from the *Inferno*. The 'little people' (as Dr Johnson called Swift's characters) 'dash against them [floor and wall of solid rubber] foot or fist or head' (8), during the 'momentary lull', 'the fists on their way to smite in anger or discouragement freeze in their arcs until the scare is past and the blow can be completed or volley of blows' (37).[37] There are many passages describing violence in the *Inferno*; in canto VII, the souls of the damned in the mud of the Styx 'si percotean non pur con mano, / ma con la testa e col petto e coi piedi' (They were smiting each other not with hand only, but with head and chest and feet) (*Inf.* VII, 112–114). In canto IX, the Erinyes 'battiensi a palme' (beating themselves with their palms) (*Inf.* IX, 50); in canto XVIII, part of which is reproduced in an undated card held at Trinity College Dublin, we read 'Quindi sentimmo gente che ... sé medesma con le palme picchia' (From there we heard people ... smiting themselves with their palms) (*Inf.* XVIII, 103–105).[38] In *Purgatorio* X, a canto which focuses on vision and representation and which was quoted in *Proust*, Dante 'disentangles' with his sight the figures of the proud souls, who are bent under the weight of the stones, from the background of the terrace, while Virgil invites him to 'scorger ... come ciascun si picchia' (discern how each beats his breast).[39] *Purgatorio* X can be read as a reflection on the notion of mimesis of the *Comedy*, which creates its reliability through the figures of the witness and the scribe.[40] Dante the witness sees on the wall of the terrace of pride engravings representing examples of humility. These are seen as God's work, and they achieve their supreme realism by surpassing nature herself: 'non pur Policleto, / ma la natura lí avrebbe scorno' (not only Polycletus but Nature herself would there be put to shame) (*Purg.* X, 32–33). The engraved characters are endowed in Dante's narrative with speech; they can speak, and therefore they are 'alive'. The canto is based on the notion of 'visibile parlare' (visible speech). Dante, by putting himself 'in the position of having to re-present God's realism with his own', blurs the boundaries between art and life.[41] He does so by describing art as real and reality in terms of art, the latter through the image of the caryatids: 'The real people seem like sculptures, and the sculpted reliefs seem like real people: which is imitation and which is being imitated?'[42] This confuses the division between God's representation and the representation that represents it; Dante, the *scriba Dei*, has crafted his own authoritative 'visibile parlare' by playing with the notions of reality and representation.[43] The violence in the closed place of *The Lost Ones/Le dépeupleur* begins to display the 'monumental simplicity of the final fiction.'[44]

The sun and other stars would still be shining

Although the 'impersonal declarative sentences' and the painstaking division of space optimistically state 'certitudes', 'in the cylinder certitudes are not to be found'.[45] Dante is teasingly presented as the hypothetical possibility of a way out of this claustrophobic rotunda only to be reintegrated into the closed place. The fourth paragraph of the text, which in a manuscript of the French version is entitled 'Issue', reads:

> Regarding the nature of this way out and its location two opinions divide without opposing all those still loyal to that old belief. One school swears by a secret passage branching from one of the tunnels and leading in the words of the poet to nature's sanctuaries. The other dreams of a trapdoor hidden in the hub of the ceiling giving access to a flue at the end of which the sun and other stars would still be shining. (18)

> Sur la nature de l'issue et sur son emplacement deux avis principaux divisent sans les opposer tous ceux restés fidèles à cette vieille croyance. Pour les uns il

ne peut s'agir que d'un passage dérobé prenant naissance dans un des tunnels et menant comme dit le poète aus asiles de la nature. Les autres rêvent d'une trappe dissimulée au centre du plafond donnant accès à une cheminée au bout de laquelle brilleraient encore le soleil et les autres étoiles. (17)[46]

'Nature's sanctuaries', 'asiles de la nature', alludes to Lamartine's poem *Le Vallon*; 'the sun and other stars' is a literal translation of the last words of the *Comedy*, the end of the *Paradiso*: 'l'amor che move il sole e l'altre stelle' (*Par.* XXXIII, 145). The allusion also refers to the end of all three canticles of the *Comedy*. The 'trapdoor hidden in the hub of the ceiling giving access to a flue' is a reversal of the path followed by Dante and Virgil on their way out from the *Inferno*. They get out by climbing a 'natural burella' ('natural dungeon', but also 'tunnel') and, through their 'cammino ascoso' (hidden road), finally reach a 'pertugio tondo' (a 'round opening', a term which can be related to the word 'hub' via the Franch 'trappe'), from which they get out 'to see the stars again'.[47] Furthermore, the 'ascent' up the ladders in order to get to the 'stars' also recalls the end of the *Purgatorio*, in which Dante, after having climbed the stairs of mount Purgatory, is 'ready to ascend to the stars' (puro e disposto a salire a le stelle) (*Purg.* XXXIII, 145).

The *Comedy*'s last words refer to the stars' function of promise and ending; here they are a 'myth' of a 'way out'. Both Lamartine's and Dante's words are related to an idea of nature in *The Lost Ones*, to 'earth and sky' (21) as a space outside both cylinder and text. 'Earth and sky', together with the stars '*still shining*', are the 'myth' of solidity, atemporality, escape from language.[48] But the text can create its 'outside' only through the 'words of the poet', that is to say, *in* and *as* language. As argued earlier in this chapter, the text's spatiality adopts and collapses the divisions between internal and external. In *The Lost Ones*, the division between outside and inside, which according to Bachelard 'has the sharpness of the dialectics of *yes* and *no*', is similar to that of *Murphy*: 'yes and no' are 'the eternal tautology'.[49]

Furthermore, *The Lost Ones*' intertextuality problematises the text as an 'inside' opposed not only to an 'outside reality' but also to 'outside texts'. This problem is not explored, like in *How It Is*, through the notion of quotation, but brings us back to Dante's role in *Premier amour*. The 'words of the poet' are the words of this particular 'poet' (Beckett) repeating the words of other poets and constructing their own 'external' position precisely by writing them, that is to say by internalising them. The allusion is produced by the repetition of the words of some 'poets', but language is repetition of others' words. This Beckett text fashions Dante as a principle of authority on which writing as repetition is based. It does so within the specific concern of spatiality and visibility, inside and outside, perception and composition.

This passage from *The Lost Ones* does not so much 'mock the escapist notions of Romantic poets perhaps', as investigate Romantic notions of visibility and invisibility, experience outside of language, description and composition of landscape/skullscape, and self-perception.[50] In *The Lost Ones*, as in *Ill Seen Ill Said*, 'what is seen has always already been said'.[51] 'The words of the poet' are simultaneously Dante's and Beckett's words; they are the repeatability that makes language, the authority that constitutes the text, the outside which is also the inside.

In *The Lost Ones*, the 'words of the poet' take part in the construction of visibility as repetition and reality as the result of language. The 'subtle allusions' do not work as 'wealth', as added literary value to the text, but they contribute to the dismantling of the opposition between the seen as outside language and the said. *The Lost Ones* uses discourses marked by the sign of the author ('stelle' in Dante) in order to make visible the principle of repetition according to which visibility itself is created. Dante is one of the authorities according to which the intertextuality in this text works to 'show' the seen as the (already) said.

It is therefore irrelevant to try to locate *The Lost Ones*, characterising it as either Purgatorial or Infernal. Elements from both are adopted and refashioned in order to disrupt the opposition between experience and language, inside and outside. *The Lost Ones* constructs itself as the observation of an 'abode'/'séjour', which, however, is 'text', 'the words of the poet'. The terms 'abode' and 'séjour', respectively in their sense of 'the action of waiting, delay' and 'résidence plus ou moins longue dans un lieu dans un pays', 'intervalle de repos que l'on prend en voyage', constitute the text as a 'purgatorial villeggiatura'.[52] The little people, squatting like Belacqua, intratextually mirror the action of a Berkeleyan and Cartesian self-perception with which the figure of Belacqua has been associated throughout the Beckett canon. In their turn, these acts of introspection doomed to failure mirror the construction of the text as skullscape. However, as stated in *Proust*, *Dream*, and *Murphy*, there can be no coincidence of perceiver and perceived. The Belacqua bliss is unattainable and self-perception also becomes the infernal process of the ravening, devouring eye being devoured, the non-coincidence of seer and seen; 'séjour', also denotes 'séjour infernal', 'l'enfer'.[53]

The 'aperçu' of this 'abode' is a Belacqua-like act of introspection doomed never to attain the constitution of a unitary 'I'. The 'eye' of the mind constructs the categories according to which it can see: the text produces itself as mind while necessarily producing the mind as text. Experience can exist only as text: the 'observed' attitudes are those already 'in the words of the poet', Dante's just as much as Beckett's.

Notes

1 Linda Ben-Zvi, *Samuel Beckett* (Boston: Twayne Publishers, 1980), p. 117. Samuel Beckett, *The Lost Ones* (New York: Grove Weidenfeld, 1972); *Le dépeupleur* (Paris: Les Éditions de Minuit, 1970). Subsequent references are given in the text.
2 While the back cover of the Grove Weidenfeld American edition of *The Lost Ones* praises such 'wealth of allusions', John Pilling comments on the text's rhetorical flatness. John Pilling, *Samuel Beckett* (London, Henley and Boston: Routledge and Kegan Paul, 1976), p. 33.
3 For a well-documented allegorical reading of *The Lost Ones* and Dante see Sebastian Neumeister, 'Das allegorische Erbe: zur Wiederkehr Dantes bei Becketts (*Le dépeupleur*, 1970)', in Manuel Lichtwitz (ed.), *Materialen zu Samuel Becketts* Der Verwaiser (Frankfurt: Suhrkamp,1990), pp. 107–128.
4 For an example of this oscillation see the conclusion of Susan Brienza's article '*The Lost Ones*: the reader as searcher', *Journal of Modern Literature*, 6:1 (1977), 148–168.
5 *The Lost Ones* presents many similarities with 'Long Observation of the Ray', an unpublished work held at the Beckett International Foundation, RUL. For a reading of this text see Steven Connor, 'Between theatre and theory: "Long Observation of the Ray"', in John Pilling and Mary Bryden (eds), *The Ideal Core of the Onion: Reading Beckett Archives* (Reading: Beckett International Foundation, 1992), pp. 79–98. Connor also points out a number of similarities and contrasts between 'Long Observation of the Ray', *The Lost Ones*, *Ping*, *All Strange Away*, and *Closed Space*. See also the undated RUL MS 1536/1, which reads: 'Through very different formally these 2 MSS [*Le dépeupleur* and *Bing*] belong together. *Bing* may be regarded as the result or miniaturization of *Le dépeupleur* abandoned because of its intractable complexities.'
6 For a discussion of Beckett and English Romanticism see Elizabeth Barry, '"Take into the air my quiet breath": Samuel Beckett and English Romanticism', *Journal of Beckett Studies*, 10:1–2 (Fall 2000/Spring 2001), 207–221.
7 Ruby Cohn, *Back to Beckett* (Princeton: Princeton University Press, 1973), p. 257. Neumeister also clarifies how the passage reading 'comme dit le poète aux asiles de la nature' (17), 'in the words of the poet to nature's sanctuaries' (18) refers to Lamartine's 'Le vallon' (1819): 'Prêtez-moi seulement, vallons de mon enfance, / Un asile d'un jour pour attendre la mort. (Strophe I) Repose-toi, mon âme, en ce dernier asile, (Strophe X)'. Neumeister, 'Das allegorische Erbe', 126, note 11. See also Lamartine, *Méditations* (Paris: Éditions Garnier Frères, 1968), pp. 4 and 22–23, respectively.
8 Edward Colerick, 'The syntax of life: strategies of representation in Samuel Beckett's middle to late longer prose 1947–1983', Ph.D. thesis, University of Kent, 1997, p. 98, note 20.
9 Emphasis mine. Singleton's capitalisation.
10 'But enough will always subsist to spell for this little people the extinction soon or late of its last remaining fires', p. 15. The verb 'to subsist' suggests the presence of a law according to which certain rules remain in force or in effect; at the same time, however, the verb also entails the idea of maintaining or supporting one's existence at the minimal level. That is to say, the verb takes part in the oscillation which problematises the opposition between a reality fabricated according to rules and laws and an 'existence' outside language.

11 In one passage 'harmony' is related to composition, sound and hearing, thus foregrounding the musical meaning of the word: 'They [the ladders] are propped against the wall without regard to *harmony* ... Its *composition* is no less familiar therefore than that of floor and wall. Dash a rung against it and the *sound* is scarcely *heard*' (9). Emphasis mine.
12 Samuel Beckett, *Imagination Dead Imagine*, in *The Complete Short Prose 1929–1989*, ed. S. E. Gontarski (New York: Grove Press, 1995), pp. 182–185, p. 182. Samuel Beckett, *Imagination morte imaginez* (Paris: Les Éditions de Minuit, 1965).
13 The last paragraph, added in 1970, narrates the death of the last one among the lost ones, thus implying the notion of an external perspective.
14 The whole passage plays hide and seek using theatrical and legal terms such as 'spectacle', 'in camera', and 'ob-scene'. Steven Connor argues that the 'abstruse "in camera" for "en chambre" ... suggests that the difference between public and private love-making is merely the difference between an open and a closed trial – witnessed or unwitnessed it is still an ordeal. The incongruity is the more delicious for the fact that "in camera" seems like the most literal translation of "en chambre", but is, in fact, at the opposite pole from it.' Steve Connor, *Samuel Beckett: Repetition, Theory and Text* (Oxford: Blackwell, 1988), p. 109.
15 The word comes from the Latin verb *abominari*, from *ab* 'away, from' + *omen, omin* 'omen'. However, the *New Oxford English Dictionary* states that 'It was once widely believed to be from *ab* "away from" + Lat. *homine* (from *homo* "human being"), thus "inhuman, beastly", and frequently spelled *abhominable* until the 17th century'.
16 See also *Ill Seen Ill Said*: 'The eye will return to the scene of its betrayals' (New York: Grove Press, 1981), p. 27.
17 Cohn, *Back to Beckett*, p. 260.
18 Francesca Del Moro, '"The Divine Florentine": Dante nell'opera di Samuel Beckett', dissertation, University of Pisa, 1996, p. 91. *Foirade IV*, published in English as *Fizzle VI*, has a further reference in Italian to the *Comedy*: 'Je rentre à la nuit, ils s'envolent, ils lâchent mon petit chêne et s'en vont, gavés, dans les ombres. Tristi fummo ne l'aere dolce. Je rentre, lève le bras, saisis la branche, me met debout et rentre dans la maison' (45). The sentence is omitted in the English. The same passage from *Inferno* VII, 121–123 from the 'Whoroscope' notebook has been discussed it in relation to *How It Is*.
19 Samuel Beckett, *Proust* (New York: Grove Press, 1957), p. 6.
20 Beckett, *Proust*, p. 7.
21 Beckett, *Proust*, p. 7.
22 Cohn, *Back to Beckett*, p. 260.
23 Samuel Beckett, *Murphy* (London: Picador, 1973), pp. 139–140. Susan Brienza misquotes from *Murphy*, substituting 'as though by permanent excess of light' for the Beckettian 'as though by permanent lack of light'. Brienza, 'The Lost Ones', 153.
24 See Sylvie Debevec Henning, 'Samuel Beckett's *Film* and *La dernière bande*: intratextual and intertextual doubles', *Symposium*, 35:2 (Summer 1981), 131–153.
25 Samuel Beckett, 'Three Dialogues', in Ruby Cohn (ed.), *Disjecta* (New York: Grove Press, 1984), pp. 138–145, p. 138. Similarly, in *Film*, the mind is 'both the knower and the known, the subject and the object of the act of knowing'. Debevec Henning, 'Samuel Beckett's *Film*' 139.
26 René Descartes, 'Of the nature of the human mind, and that it is more easily known than the body', *Discourse on Method and Meditations*, ed. and transl. Laurence J. Lafleur

(Indianapolis: The Library of Liberal Arts, 1960), pp. 81–90, p. 85. *Le dépeupleur* uses 'être pensant' (35). For a brilliant reading of the Cartesian *cogito* in relation to Beckett see Daniel Katz, *Saying I No More: Subjectivity and Consciousness in the Prose of Samuel Beckett* (Evanston, IL : Northwestern University Press, 1999).
27 Cohn, *A Beckett Canon*, p. 304.
28 Samuel Beckett, *Closed Place*, in S. E. Gontarski (ed.), *The Complete Short Prose 1929–1989*, pp. 236–238, p. 236; *Se voir, Pour finir encore et autres foirades* (Paris: Les Éditions de Minuit, 1976), pp. 51–53, p. 51.
29 Del Moro, '"The Divine Florentine"', pp. 191–192.
30 RUL MS 4123. Beckett, *Compagnie*, p. 84, and *Company*, p. 85.
31 The reference to the semi-sages intratextually refers to *Proust*, in which 'the wisdom of all sages, from Brahma to Leopardi' is 'the wisdom that consists not in the satisfaction but in the ablation of desire' (7). Nevertheless, in *The Lost Ones*, not the 'ablation of desire' shown by the vanquished, but rather the susceptibility of the semi-sages 'inspire[s] in those still fitfully fevering if not a cult at least a certain deference' (28); the vanquished, who 'may be walked on without their reacting' (29), cannot be called 'sages'. The 'certain deference' to the semi-sages, still now and again victims of their need to climb, is a consequence of their being 'morbidly susceptible to the least want of consideration' (28).
32 It should be noted that the contemporary meaning of 'bolgia' in Italian is a Dantean derivation which means 'a place teeming with noisy and turbulent people.'
33 RUL MS 4123. The 'deasil'/'dextrorsum' movement is to be encountered also in *Still/Immobile*, in which it denotes the movement of the hand and the arm. *Still*, in Gontarski (ed.), *The Complete Short Prose*, p. 241; *Immobile*, in Beckett, *Pour finir encore*, p. 22.
34 Carla Locatelli, *Unwording the World: Samuel Beckett's Prose Works After the Nobel Prize* (Philadelphia: University of Pennsylvania Press, 1990), p. 192.
35 The souls 'si ritrasser tutte quante insieme, / forte piangendo, a la riva malvagia' (Then, weeping loudly, all drew to the evil shore) (*Inf*. III, 106). Dorothy L. Sayers translates as 'Then, huddling hugger-mugger, down the scud, / Dismally wailing, to the accursed strand'; Dorothy L. Sayers, *The Divine Comedy* (Harmonsdsworth: Penguin, 1949).
36 Samuel Beckett, *Waiting for Godot* (London: Faber and Faber, 1988), pp. 62–63.
37 John Fletcher, *Samuel Beckett's Art* (London, Chatto & Windus, 1971), p. 72.
38 In *Inferno* IX, 50, I have substituted 'palms' for Singleton's 'hands'.
39 'E chi più pazienza avea ne gli atti / parea dicer: – Più non posso' (and he who showed the most suffering in his looks, seemed to say, weeping, 'I can no more'). Beckett, *Proust*, p. 58. 'scorger ... come ciascun si picchia' has also been read as 'discern how they are pressed by the weight of the stones they are carrying'. Another episode of violence in *The Lost Ones* is analogous to a 'verbal image' of the *Comedy*. The reaction of the queuing climbers against the 'rash searcher' who 'carried away by his passion dare lay a finger on the least among them' (59–60) is phrased as follows: 'Like a single body the whole queue falls on the offender'. In *Inferno* VIII, Dante sees the damned 'attuffa[ti] in quella broda' 'quello strazio / far di costui a le fangose genti, / che Dio ancor ne lode e ne ringrazio. / Tutti gridavano: "A Filippo Argenti!"' (such rending of him by the muddy folk that I still praise and thank God for it. All cried: 'At Filippo Argenti!') (*Inf*. VIII, 58–61): indeed, 'Of all the scenes of violence the cylinder has to offer none approaches this'.

40 Teodolinda Barolini, *The Undivine Comedy: Detheologizing Dante* (Princeton: Princeton University Press, 1992), p. 122.
41 Barolini, *The Undivine Comedy*, p. 123.
42 Barolini, *The Undivine Comedy*, p. 125.
43 In the terrace of pride Dante carves out his place in the history of literature; in the words of Omberto Aldobrandesco: 'Credette Cimabue ne la pittura / tener lo campo, e ora ha Giotto il grido, / sí che la fama di colui è scura. / Cosí ha tolto l'uno a l'altro Guido / la gloria de la lingua; e forse è nato / chi l'uno e l'altro caccerà dal nido' (Cimabue thought to hold the field in painting, and now Giotto has the cry, so that the other's fame is dim; so has the one Guido taken from the other the glory of our tongue – and he perchance is born that shall chase the one and the other from the nest) (*Purg.* XI, 94–99). The names of the precursors are there only to be 'chased' away; the scribe claims as his only precursor God, the author of the book of nature.
44 Cohn, *A Beckett Canon*, p. 368.
45 Cohn, *A Beckett Canon*, p. 309.
46 MS 1536/9, dated 'Ussy, mai 66', presents a list of the sections up to number 8, each bearing a title: 1 is called 'Séjour'; 2 'Population et notion'; 3 'Séjour 2'; 4 'Issue'; 5 'Zénith'; 6 'Échelle code'; 7 'Échelle transport'; 8 'Sédentaire'.
47 *Inf.* XXXIV, 98; 133; 138. Neumeister, 'Das allegorische Erbe', p. 111.
48 The outside/'without' is also defined as 'nothing but mystery': 'For in the cylinder alone are certitudes to be found and without nothing but mystery' (42). The mystery is opposed to the 'harmony' reigning in the cylinder; such a distinction, however, is constantly set up and collapsed by the text's contradictory claims to 'truth' ('The truth is ...', 14) and insufficiency: 'All has not been told and never shall be' (51).
49 Gaston Bachelard, *The Poetics of Space* (Boston: Beacon Press, 1969), p. 211. Beckett, *Murphy*, p. 27. Another example of deconstruction of a dichotomy can be found in the passage of *Ill Seen Ill Said*, which reads: 'Such the confusion now between real and – how says its contrary? ... Real and – how ill say its contrary? The counter-poison.' Samuel Beckett, *Ill Seen Ill Said* (New York: Grove Press, 1981), p. 40.
50 Brienza, '*The Lost Ones*', 163.
51 Carla Locatelli, *Unwording the World*, p. 189.
52 *Littré*. *OED*. Samuel Beckett, *Dream of Fair to Middling Women* (New York: Arcade, 1993), p. 184. The Italian 'villeggiatura' is close to the French 'séjour'.
53 *Littré*. The first word of the French text, 'Séjour', replaces 'Espace' in RUL MS 1536/9, dated 'Ussy, mai 66'.

Conclusion Farewell to the old lutist

Dante in Beckett is a figure of the 'belatedness, secondary, and debt' which characterise the Beckett canon.[1] Dante is 'the impossible first' and the 'impossible last': it is company throughout, 'on the way from A to Z'.[2]

Scholars who have analysed the work of Joyce, Eliot, or Pound in relation to Dante have suggested various forms of teleological development: Lucia Boldrini interestingly indicates that Mary Reynolds's thematic approach to Dante is acceptable up to *Ulysses* but fails with regard to *Finnegans Wake*, a text in which 'Joyce's use of Dante becomes most pervasive and far-reaching'; Dominic Manganiello juxtaposes the early Eliot of 'the Boston doubt' against the late Eliot who 'understands Dante's total vision as relevant for the present time'; Stephen Sicari rejects Steve Ellis's portrayal of a Pound who uses Dante in piecemeal and random ways in order to claim that Dante gradually becomes central to Pound's epic ambitions.[3]

Unlike them, I have read the Beckett *corpus* as resisting an idea of progression which presupposes a growing consciousness behind the work and as exploring instead the production of such a figure of authority. Different Beckett texts construct different 'Dantes', in line with their main representational concerns, and the Dante of *Dream of Fair to Middling Women* is as different from that of *How It Is* as are the notions of source and progression in the two texts. However, to argue that one kind of complexity is more 'successful' than the other because it reflects a maturation in the writing would not do justice to the different kinds of complexity in the two novels. Beckett texts read like 'something out of Beckett' because the Beckett canon opposes the idea of an authentic voice in a paradoxically coherent manner. In the Beckett *oeuvre*, understood as odds and ends, disjecta, and detritus, Dante contributes to the stubborn questioning of 'textual theology and directionality', as Belacqua's refusal to observe 'the rule of the road' demonstrates.[4] This 'indolent' critique entails however some residual form of progression, since troubling teleology cannot simply result in an absolute lack of direction: as seen in *Dream*, the 'going up' always leads somewhere, brings something. There is no neutral or free position from where to speak in or about Beckett.

'Like the presence of a third party', Dante comes and goes in Beckett. The chronological arrangement of the chapters in this book is thus a structure akin to the 'way from A to Z' in *Company*: a conventional arrangement, which cannot avoid suggesting progress, even when it questions it.

The idea of a stable, anterior text, or set of texts marked by Dante's signature to which predetermined meanings can be attributed, is challenged by the ways in which Dante keeps changing in the Beckett *oeuvre*, while also being an element of continuity that produces this *oeuvre* and 'Mr Beckett' as the author responsible for it. Different Dantes work as sources, quotations, allusions, models to be parodied, at once configuring the conventional presuppositions on which these notions rest and questioning them. Beckett's texts do not develop what Pound calls, referring to Eliot, 'the true Dantescan voice': when we hear a 'true' Dantescan voice in Beckett, like *Dream*'s 'l'andar su che porta?', we soon learn that 'Mr Beckett' is ventriloquising Dante in order to get 'the bay about his brow'.[5]

Eliot's essay on Dante uses the 'most *universal* of poets' as 'the gauge by which to measure the achievements of other writers', juxtaposing the imitators of Dante (who run the risk of being pedestrian and flat) against the imitators of Shakespeare (who run the risk of making utter fools of themselves).[6] Beckett's works upset such ideas of value and imitation by producing a series of 'marginal', 'minor', or 'disfunctional' Dantes which paradoxically play a major role within the *oeuvre*. This strategy cannot be 'carefully folded' into a neat quantitative model able to defend Mr Beckett from accusations of having a limited knowledge of Dante. The complexly 'incompetent' ways in which each Beckett text constructs the 'competent' poet as source, allusion, and model to parody do not suggest that there is one Dante, or one *Comedy*, whose meaning Beckett more or less accurately and faithfully understands, reproduces, or rejects. Instead, the different Dantes in Beckett are elements outside the text which question the very idea of an outside-text, thus being intratextual unifying elements which constitute the Beckett *oeuvre* as remarkably interconnected and consistent.

Such a destabilising view of Dante does not entail the simplistic belief that any meaning could be attached to the sign 'Dante', but encourages us to explore instead, after Foucault, the ways in which author-functions circulate, are valorised, appropriated, and attributed. Thus, Dante's presence (even Dante's paradoxically invisible, residual, or marginal presence) confers on 'Mr Beckett' the 'bay about his brow'. Dante is one of the ways in which Beckett's texts configure themselves into a *corpus* dominated by the idea of an author responsible for their consistency and interconnectedness; at the same time, they incessantly question the issues of teleology and authority which such a *corpus* implies. The case study of Beckett and Dante might thus contribute to new research interested in considering the power structures of intertextuality within other contexts, and it might indicate a way forward for studies of intertextuality interested in developing the valuable work done by Boldrini, Katz,

Uhlmann, and Van Hulle on the relationship between Dante, Joyce, and Beckett, or in exploring further the uses of Dante in modernism.[7]

This understanding of the Dante intertexts as part of a larger economy of gain and loss, and of origin and finality, is reflected in the many Beckett characters who embark on faltering and digressive journeys or sit and see themselves raise and go, tentatively suggesting a farewell that fails to materialise, in *Ohio Impromptu* as in *Waiting for Godot*: 'Yes, let's go. *They don't move.*'[8]

In *Company/Compagnie* such an attempt to say farewell is directed at Belacqua:

> So sat waiting to be purged the old lutist cause of Dante's first quarter-smile and now perhaps singing praises with some section of the blest at last. To whom here in any case farewell. (85)

> Ainsi se tenait en attendant de pouvoir se purger le vieux luthier qui arracha à Dante son premier quart de sourire et peut-être déjà enfin dans quelque coin perdu du paradis. A qui ici dans tous le cas adieu. (84)

Company plays with the confessional mode and with the deceptive directness of childhood memories in order to question, in line with the rest of the Beckett *oeuvre*, autobiographical self-expression and the assumption of a stable self. In this text the 'I' 'is as much a figure of finality as of origin, or, more precisely, is the figuring of origin *as* finality, and vice versa'.[9] Belacqua reflects this: the 'old lutist' is, in the words of the Anonimo Fiorentino, 'dimestico', intimate with both Dante and Beckett. Such familiarity is produced by the recurrent presence of Belacqua throughout the Beckett canon, which shapes itself as a continuum haunted by tedium: 'now perhaps singing praises with some section of the blest at last'. And yet, the linear temporality suggested in the passage by the 'now' and the 'here' fails to extricate finality from origin. Belacqua is both the originary character of the early novels and the unavoidable legacy of Dante, which can neither be forgotten nor abandoned. Belacqua Shuah's origins are multiple (merging Florence with the purgatorial island of Ireland, inverting the authorial initials S.B., incorporating commentaries to the *Comedy*) and so are his farewells, which happen 'in any case'. 'In any case' does not just add a flippant note to this relatively sentimental adieu; it also indicates that Belacqua, and Dante with him, critique the notions of source and presence. They are part of what Molloy's calls the '*déjà vu* ... infinitely beyond my reach', which pervades the *oeuvre*: Murphy will never be able to attain the Belacqua bliss; Mercier and Camier cannot understand the 'vague shadowy shapes' of authority that menacingly accompany them; Dantesque analogies have to be kept out of sight in the 'Whoroscope' notebook; a Virgilian hoarseness prevents the 'I''s mouth from articulating meaningful words in *The Calmative*, while the slothful damned of the fifth circle of Hell cannot do much better in *How It Is*; even when, as in *The Lost Ones*, the text presents itself as a simple record of an observation, the last words of the poet still echo in the rotunda, failing to guarantee a way out and yet waving a tentative goodbye ('the sun and other stars').

The impossibility of such an adieu can be gauged from a diachronic point of view too. In 'Dante and the Lobster' Belacqua Shuah ruminates over the translation of Dante's 'great phrase', which has already been translated in the published poem 'Text'. Similarly, even though *Company* says farewell to Belacqua (who had already 'fallen over to his side' in *How It Is*), this is not the end of Dante in Beckett: in *Ill Seen Ill Said/Mal vu mal dit* the eye (omnipresent in *The Lost Ones*) 'will return to the scene of its betrayal. On centennial leave from where tears freeze', 'reviendra sur les lieux de ses trahisons. En conge séculaire de là où gèlent les larmes'.[10] The frozen tears of the intertwined treacherous brothers immersed in the ice of Cocytus in *Inferno* XXXII (encountered in an early 'Dante' notebook, *How It Is*, and 'dread nay') lead us back to the negotiation between saying and betraying ('ill saying') and self and other (the I looking at itself).[11]

The passage also troubles chronology, since the betraying eye is predicted to return in an undetermined future from a place in which time can be suspended through 'centennial leave'. Moreover, such a leave will make the eye 'Free again an instant to shed them scalding. On the blest tears once shed' (27), 'Libre encore un instant de les verser chaudes. Sur les bienheureuses larmes qui furent' (32). The tears are now 'blest' (rather than damned) and they are situated in a momentary present ('an instant') which links them to past tears. The association to the *Paradiso* created by the adjective 'blest' (which appears in *Company* too) is complicated by the purgatorial and infernal associations of the French 'furent', a simple past tense linked to both French and English versions of *Rough for Radio II/Pochade radiophonique* and *Text for Nothing 6/Texte pour rien 6*: 'Je fus, je fus, disent ceux du Purgatoire, ceux des Enfers aussi, admirable pluriel, merveilleuse assurance. Plongé dans la glace, jusqu'aux narines, les paupières collées de larmes gelées, revivre ses campagnes, quelle tranquillité, et se savoir au bout de ses surprises, non, j'ai dû mal entendre' (172).[12]

Canto XXXII in *Ill Seen Ill Said/Mal vu mal dit* cannot function as simply 'the past', either the literary past or the past within the chronology of Beckett's work; it is projected into a future ('the eye will return'), into the hypothetical freedom of a momentary present ('free again an instant'), and into the past of the narrative ('the blest tears once shed'). The last farewell to Dante is a 'return to the scene of its betrayals'.

Notes

1. Daniel Katz, *Saying I No More: Subjectivity and Consciousness in the Prose of Samuel Beckett* (Evanston, IL: Northwestern University Press, 1999), p. 14.
2. Samuel Beckett, *Company* (London: Calder, 1980), p. 30; 'sur le chemin de A à Z'. Samuel Beckett, *Compagnie* (Paris, Les Éditions de Minuit, 1985), p. 30.
3. Lucia Boldrini, *Joyce, Dante and the Poetics of Literary Relations* (Cambridge: Cambridge University Press, 2001), p. 6; Dominic Manganiello, *T. S. Eliot and Dante* (Basingstoke: Macmillan, 1989), p. 165; Steve Ellis, *Dante and English Poetry* (Cambridge: Cambridge University Press, 1983); Stephen Sicari, *Pound's Epic Ambition* (Albany, NY: SUNY Press, 1991), p. 11.
4. Katz, *Saying I No More*, p. 165.
5. 'His was the true Dantescan voice – not honoured enough, and deserving more than I ever gave him.' Ezra Pound, 'For T.S.E.', in Allen Tate (ed.), *T. S. Eliot: The Man and His Work* (New York: Dell, 1966), p. 89.
6. Manganiello, *T. S. Eliot and Dante*, p. 164. T. S. Eliot, 'Dante' (1929), in Frank Kermode (ed.), *Selected Prose of T. S. Eliot* (London: Faber and Faber, 1975), pp. 205–230, p. 217.
7. Interesting examples in relation to art history and cultural studies are Mieke Bal, *Quoting Caravaggio* (Chicago and London: The University of Chicago Press, 1999) and Jonathan Bignell, 'Question of Authorship: Samuel Beckett and *Film*', in Jonathan Bignell (ed.), *Writing and Cinema* (New York and London: Longman, 1999), pp. 29–42. On Dante in relation to Beckett and Joyce, see Boldrini, *Joyce, Dante, and the Poetics*; Katz, *Saying I No More*; Anthony Uhlmann, *Beckett and Poststructuralism* (Cambridge: Cambridge University Press, 1999); Dirk Van Hulle, *Joyce and Beckett, Discovering Dante* (Dublin: National Library of Ireland, 2004). On Dante in the twentieth century, see Stuart Y. McDougal (ed.), *Dante Among the Moderns* (Chapel Hill: The University of North Carolina Press, 1985); Ellis, *Dante and English Poetry*; Manganiello, *T. S. Eliot and Dante*; Sicari, *Pound's Epic Ambition*; Peter Kuon, *'Lo mio maestro e 'l mio autore': die productive Rezeption der Divina Commedia in der Erzählliteratur der Moderne* (Frankfurt am Main: Klostermann, 1993); N. R. Havely (ed.), *Dante's Modern Afterlife: Reception and Response from Blake to Heaney* (Basingstoke: Macmillan, 1998); Eric Griffiths and Matthew Reynolds, *Dante in English* (Harmondsworth: Penguin, 2005).
8. Samuel Beckett, *Waiting for Godot* (London: Faber and Faber, 1988), pp. 54 and 94.
9. Katz, *Saying I No More*, p. 168.
10. Samuel Beckett, *Ill Seen Ill Said* (New York: Grove Press, 1981), p. 27. Samuel Beckett, *Mal vu mal dit* (Paris: Les Éditions de Minuit, 1981), p. 32.
11. TCD MS 10963, fol. 79. Samuel Beckett, 'dread nay', in *Collected Poems 1930–1978* (London: Calder, 1984), p. 33.
12. Samuel Beckett, *Nouvelles et textes pour rien* (Paris: Les Éditions de Minuit, 1958). 'I was, I was, they say in Purgatory, in Hell too, admirable singulars, admirable assurance. Plunged in ice up to the nostrils, the eyelids caked with frozen tears, to fight all your battles o'er again, what tranquillity, and know there are no more emotions in store, no, I can't have heard aright.' Samuel Beckett, *Stories and Texts for Nothing* (New York: Grove Weidenfeld, 1967), p. 104.

Bibliography

Works by Beckett

Texts in English

As the Story Was Told. Uncollected and Late Prose (New York: Riverrun Press, 1990).
The Beckett Trilogy: Molloy, Malone Dies, The Unnamable (London: Picador, 1979).
Beckett's Dream *Notebook*, ed. John Pilling (Reading: Beckett International Foundation, 1999).
Collected Poems 1930–1978 (London: John Calder, 1984).
Collected Shorter Plays of Samuel Beckett (London: Faber & Faber, 1984).
Company (London: Calder, 1980).
The Complete Short Prose 1929–1989, ed. S. E. Gontarski (New York: Grove Press, 1995).
Disjecta: Miscellaneous Writings and a Dramatic Fragment, ed. Ruby Cohn (New York: Grove Press, 1984).
Dream of Fair to Middling Women (New York: Arcade, 1993).
Endgame (London: Faber & Faber, 1958).
Happy Days (New York: Grove Weidenfeld, 1961).
How It Is (New York: Grove Press, 1964).
Ill Seen Ill Said (New York: Grove Press, 1981).
The Lost Ones (New York: Grove Weidenfeld, 1972).
Mercier and Camier (London: Picador, 1988).
More Pricks Than Kicks (New York: Grove Wiedenfeld, 1972).
Murphy (London: Picador, 1973).
Proust (New York: Grove Press, 1957 [1931])
Stories and Texts for Nothing (New York: Grove Weidenfeld, 1967).
Waiting for Godot (London: Faber & Faber, 1988).
Watt (New York: Grove Weidenfeld, 1959).
Worstward Ho (London: John Calder, 1980).

Uncollected texts in English

'Che Sciagura', *T.C.D.: A College Miscellany*, 36:622 (Thursday 14 November 1929).
'Dante and the Lobster', *This Quarter* (December 1932), 222–236.
'From the Only Poet to a Shining Whore', in Henry Crowder, *Henry-Music* (Paris: The Hours Press, 1930), pp. 12–14.
'Hell Crane to Starling', 'Casket of Pralinen for a Daughter of a Dissipated Mandarin', 'Yoke of Liberty', *The European Caravan: An Anthology of the New Spirit in European Literature* (New York: Brewer, Warren, and Putnam, 1931), pp. 475–476, 476–478, 480. Reprinted in Lawrence Harvey, *Samuel Beckett Poet and Critic* (Princeton: Princeton University Press, 1970).
'Sedendo et Quiesciendo' [sic], *transition*, 21 (March 1932), 13–20.
'Text', *The European Caravan: An Anthology of the New Spirit in European Literature* (New York: Brewer, Warren, and Putnam, 1931), 478–480; reprinted in *The New Review*, 1:4 (Winter 1931–32), 338–339.

Texts in French

Comment c'est (Paris: Les Éditions de Minuit, 1961).
Compagnie (Paris: Les Éditions de Minuit, 1985).
Le dépeupleur (Paris: Les Éditions de Minuit, 1970).
Eleuthéria (Paris : Les Éditions de Minuit, 1995).
Imagination morte imaginez (Paris : Les Éditions de Minuit, 1965).
L'innomable (Paris: Les Éditions de Minuit, 1952).
Malone meurt (Paris: Les Éditions de Minuit, 1951).
Mal vu mal dit (Paris: Les Éditions de Minuit, 1981).
Mercier et Camier (Paris: Les Éditions de Minuit, 1970).
Molloy (Paris: Les Éditions de Minuit, 1950).
Murphy (Paris: Les Éditions de Minuit, 1965).
Nouvelles et textes pour rien (Paris: Les Éditions de Minuit, 1958).
Pour finir encore et autres foirades (Paris: Les Éditions de Minuit, 1976).
Premier amour (Paris: Les Éditions de Minuit, 1970).
Watt (Paris: Les Éditions de Minuit, 1968).

Unpublished works consulted

RUL = Reading University Library
TCD = Trinity College, Dublin

'Whoroscope' notebook, RUL MS 3000.
'Sottisier' notebook, RUL MS 2901.

'*Dream*' notebook, RUL 5000.
'Dante' notebooks, TCD 10962, 10963, 10963a, 10965, 10965a, 10966, 10971/1–11.
RUL MS 4123.
RUL MS 3059.
RUL MSS 1536/1–10.
'Echos' Bones' Typescript. Dartmouth College Library.

Works by Dante

La Commedia secondo l'antica vulgata, ed. Giorgio Petrocchi (Milan: Mondadori, 1966–67).
Convivio, Opere minori, I, ii, eds Cesare Vasoli and Domenico De Robertis (Milan and Naples: Ricciardi, 1988).
De vulgari eloquentia, Opere minori, V, ii, ed. Pier Vincenzo Mengaldo (Milan and Naples: Ricciardi, 1979).
Vita Nuova, ed. Domenico De Robertis (Milan and Naples: Ricciardi, 1980).
Rime, ed. Gianfranco Contini (Turin: Einaudi, 1946).
Concordanza della Commedia di Dante Alighieri eds Luciano Lovera, Rosanna Bettarini, and Anna Mazzarello, preface by Giovanni Contini (Turin: Einaudi, 1975).
Dartmouth Dante Project, www.princeton.edu/~dante/dante2.html.
La Divina Commedia, ed. Enrico Bianchi (Florence: Salani, 1921 and 1922).
La Divina Commedia, ed. G. A. Scartazzini, eighth edition, largely revised by G. Vandelli with an improved rhyming dictionary by L. Polacco. Third run, revised and corrected (Milan: Hoepli, 1922).
La Divina Commedia *di Dante Alighieri*, col commento di Pompeo Venturi (Florence: Ciardetti, 1821 reprint).
La Divina Commedia *di Dante Alighieri*, illustrata di note da Luigi Portirelli (Milan: Tipografia dei classici italiani, 1804–5).

Translations

Dante in Hell: The De Vulgari Eloquentia, ed. Warman Welliver (Ravenna: Longo, 1981).
Dantis Alagherii Epistolae: The Letters of Dante, ed. Paget Toynbee (Oxford: The Clarendon Press, 1920).
The Divine Comedy, translated with a commentary by Charles S. Singleton (Princeton: Princeton University Press, Bollingen Series LXXX, 3 vols, 1973).

The Divine Comedy. Hell, trans. Dorothy L. Sayers (Harmondsworth: Penguin, 1949).
The Divine Comedy, trans. Henry Cary, introduction by Edmund Gardner (London: Everyman's Library, 1967).
The Vision of Dante Alighieri: or, Hell, Purgatory, and Paradise, trans. Rev. Henry Francis Cary (London: Bell and Daldy, 1869).

Secondary texts and other works cited

Critical studies on Beckett and Dante

Anspaugh, Kelly, 'Faith, hope, and – what was it? Beckett reading Joyce reading Dante', *Journal of Beckett Studies*, 5:1–2 (Autumn 1995 and Spring 1996), 19–38.
—— 'The partially purged: Samuel Beckett's "The Calmative" as anti-Comedy', *Canadian Journal of Irish Studies*, 22:1 (1996), 30–41.
Arthur, Kateryna, 'Murphy, Gerontion and Dante', *AUMLA, Australian University Language and Literature Association*, 55 (May 1981), 54–67.
—— 'T. S. Eliot, Samuel Beckett, and Dante', Ph.D. thesis, University of Sussex, 1982.
Bryden, Mary, 'Beckett and the three Dantean smiles', *Journal of Beckett Studies*, n.s. 4:2 (September 1995), 29–33.
—— 'No stars without stripes: Beckett and Dante', *The Romanic Review*, 87:4 (1996), 541–556.
Carey, Phyllis, 'Stephen Dedalus, Belacqua Shuah, and Dante's *Pietà*', in Phyllis Carey and Ed Jewinski (eds), *RE: Joyce 'n Beckett* (New York: Fordham University Press, 1992), pp. 104–116.
Caselli, Daniela, '"Looking it up in my big Dante": a note on "Sedendo et Quiesciendo" [sic]', *Journal of Beckett Studies*, 6:2 (Spring 1997), 85–93.
—— '"L'andar su che porta?": Dante nel primo Beckett', *The Italianist*, 18 (1998), 130–154.
—— '"The Florentia edition in the ignoble Salani collection": a textual comparison', *Journal of Beckett Studies*, 9:2 (2001), 1–20.
—— 'Shadows of Belacqua in *Dream of Fair to Middling Women* and *How It Is*', *Samuel Beckett Today/Aujourd'hui*, 11 (2001), 463–470.
—— 'God that old favourite: issues of authority in Beckett's *How It Is*', *Samuel Beckett Today/Aujourd'hui*, 9 (2001), 150–172.
—— 'The promise of Dante in Beckett's manuscripts', *Samuel Beckett Today/Aujourd'hui*, forthcoming.
Cohn, Ruby, 'A note on Beckett, Dante, and Geulincx', *Comparative Literature*, 12 (1960), 93–94.

Colerick, Edward, 'The syntax of life: strategies of representation in Samuel Beckett's middle to late longer prose 1947–1983', Ph.D thesis, University of Kent, 1997.

Cuddy, Lois A., 'Beckett's "dead voices" in *Waiting for Godot*: new inhabitants of Dante's *Inferno*', *Modern Language Studies*, 12:2 (Spring 1982), 48–61.

De Logu, Pietro, 'The unifying power of tradition: the presence of Dante in W. B. Yeats's and Samuel Beckett's works', in Wolfgang Zach (ed.), *Literature(s) in English: New Perspectives* (Frankfurt: Peter Lang, 1990), pp. 61–67.

Del Moro, Francesca, '"The Divine Florentine": Dante nell'opera di Samuel Beckett', dissertation (tesi di laurea), University of Pisa (Italy), 1996.

Doran, Eva, 'Au seuil de Beckett: quelques notes sur "Dante...Bruno.Vico.. Joyce"', *Stanford French Review*, 5:1 (Spring 1981), 121–127.

Federman, Raymond, *Journey to Chaos: Samuel Beckett's Early Fiction* (Berkeley: University of California Press, 1965).

Ferrini, Jean–Pierre, *Dante et Beckett* (Paris: Hermann, 2003).

——'À partir du desert: Dante et l'aphonie de Virgile dans "Le calmant" de Samuel Beckett', *Samuel Beckett Today/Aujourd'hui*, 13 (2003), 201–212.

Fletcher, John, *Samuel Beckett's Art* (London: Chatto & Windus, 1971).

—— 'Beckett's verses: influences and parallels', *French Review*, 37:1 (October 1963), 320–331.

—— 'Beckett's debt to Dante', *Nottingham French Studies*, 4 (May 1965), 41–52.

Fowlie, Wallace, 'Dante and Beckett', in Stuart Y. McDougal (ed.), *Dante Among the Moderns* (Chapel Hill: University of North Carolina Press, 1985), pp. 129–152.

Frasca, Gabriele, *Cascando: Tre studi su Samuel Beckett* (Naples: Liguori, 1988).

Gleason, Paul, 'Dante, Joyce, Beckett and the use of memory in the process of literary creation', *Joyce Studies Annual*, 10 (Summer 1999), 104–142.

Green, David D., 'Beckett's *Dream*: more niente than Bel', *Journal of Beckett Studies*, 5:1 and 2 (1995–96), 67–80.

Gross, Katherine Travers, 'In other words: Samuel Beckett's art of poetry', Ph.D. thesis, Columbia University, 1972.

Gussow, Mel, 'Interview with Samuel Beckett', *The New York Times* (31 December 1989), Arts and Leisure section.

Harvey, Lawrence, *Samuel Beckett: Poet and Critic* (Princeton: Princeton University Press, 1970).

Hayman, David, 'Quest for meaninglessness: the boundless poverty of *Molloy*', in W. O. S. Sutherland Jr (ed.), *Six Contemporary Novels* (Austin: University of Texas Press, 1962), pp. 90–112.

Hutchings, William, '"Shat into grace" or, a tale of a turd: why it is how it is in Samuel Beckett's *How It Is*', *Papers on Language and Literature: A Journal for Scholars and Critics of Language and Literature*, 21:1 (Winter 1985), 64–87.

Kennedy, Sighle, 'Beckett's schoolboy copy of Dante: a handbook for liberty', *Dalhousie French Studies*, 19 (Fall–Winter 1990), 11–19.

Leventhal, A. J., 'The Beckett hero', in Martin Esslin (ed.), *Samuel Beckett: A Collection of Critical Essays* (Englewood Cliffs: Prentice Hall Inc., 1965), pp. 37–51.

Levy, Eric P., *Beckett and the Voice of Species: A Study of the Prose Fiction* (Totowa: Barnes & Noble, 1980).

McQueeny, Terence, 'Samuel Beckett as critic of Proust and Joyce', Ph.D. thesis, University of North Carolina, 1977.

Neumeister, Sebastian, 'Das allegorische Erbe: zur Wiederkehr Dantes bei Becketts (*Le dépeupleur*, 1970)', in Manuel Lichtwitz (ed.), *Materialen zu Samuel Becketts* Der Verwaiser (Frankfurt: Suhrkamp, 1990), pp. 107–128.

Nykrog, Per, 'In the ruins of the past: reading Beckett intertextually', *Comparative Literature*, 36:4 (Fall 1984), 289–311.

O'Brian, William, 'To Hell with Samuel Beckett', in John V. Apczynski (ed.), *Foundations of Religious Literacy* (Chico: Scolar Press, 1983), pp. 165–174.

Oliva, Renato, 'Appunti per una lettura dell'ultimo Beckett', in Samuel Beckett, *Senza e Lo spopolatore*, ed. Renato Oliva (Turin: Einaudi, 1972).

O'Neill, Kevin C., 'Two trilogies: notes on Beckett and Dante', *Romance Notes*, 32:3 (Spring 1992), 235–240.

—— 'The voyage from Dante to Beckett', Ph.D. thesis, University of California, 1985.

Oxenhandler, Neal, 'Seeing and believing in Dante and Beckett', in Mary Ann Caws (ed.), *Writing in a Modern Temper: Essays on French Literature and Thought in Honor of Henri Peyre* (Saratoga: Anma Libri, 1984), pp. 214–223.

Pilling, John, 'From a (W)horoscope to *Murphy*', in John Pilling and Mary Bryden (eds), *The Ideal Core of the Onion: Reading Beckett Archives* (Reading: Beckett International Foundation, 1992), pp. 1–20.

Robinson, Michael, 'From purgatory to inferno: Beckett and Dante revisited', *Journal of Beckett Studies*, 5 (Autumn 1979), 69–82.

Roig, Michel, '*Malone meurt*: jeux de miroirs', *Littératures*, 19 (automne 1988), 147–154.

Schödel, Kathrin, 'Intertextuelle Dialog: Dantes "Belaqua" in Samuel Becketts Roman *Dream of Fair to Middling Women*', *Deutsches Dante Jahrbuch*, 77 (2002), 149–173.

Smith, Fredrik N., 'Dating the "Whoroscope" Notebook', *Journal of Beckett Studies*, n.s. 3:1 (1993), 65–70.

Strauss, Walter A., 'Dante's Belacqua and Beckett's tramps', *Comparative Literature*, 11 (Summer 1959), 250–261.

Terry, Philip, 'Waiting for God to go: *How It Is* and *Inferno* VII–VIII', *Samuel Beckett Today/Aujourd'hui: Beckett Versus Beckett*, 7 (1998), 349–360.

Theoharis, Constantine Theoharis, '"Che la diritta via era smarrita": Dante's *Commedia* in Beckett's *Texts for Nothing*', *Journal of the Short Story in English*, 41 (2003), 25–39.

Van Hulle, Dirk, *Joyce and Beckett, Discovering Dante* (Dublin: National Library of Ireland, 2004).

Visconti, Laura, 'Il purgatorio sferico: la poetica di Samuel Beckett', in Giorgio Melchiori (ed.), *Joyce Studies in Italy* (Rome: Bulzoni, 1984), pp. 55–74.

Critical studies on Beckett

Abbott, H. Porter, *Beckett Writing Beckett: The Author in the Autograph* (Ithaca: Cornell University Press, 1996).

Ackerley, C. J., 'Fatigue and disgust: the Addenda to Watt', *Samuel Beckett Today/Aujourd'hui: Beckett in the 1990s*, 2 (1993), 175–188.

—— 'Beckett's "Malacoda": or, Dante's devil plays Beethoven', *Journal of Beckett Studies*, 3:1 (Autumn 1993), 59–64.

—— 'Demented particulars: the annotated *Murphy*', *Journal of Beckett Studies*, 7:1–2 (Autumn 1997–Spring 1998).

Ackerley, C. J., and S. E. Gontarski, *The Grove Companion to Samuel Beckett* (New York: Grove Press, 2004).

Admussen, Richard, *The Samuel Beckett Manuscripts: A Study* (Boston: G. K. Hall & Co., 1979).

Anzieu, Didier, 'Le théâtre d'Echo dans les récits de Beckett', *Revue d'Esthétique*, numéro hors-série (1986), 39–43.

Bair, Deidre, *Samuel Beckett: A Biography* (New York and London: Harcourt Brace Jovanovich, 1978).

Barry, Elizabeth, '"Take into the air my quiet breath": Beckett and English Romanticism', *Journal of Beckett Studies*, 10:1–2 (Fall–Spring 2001), 207–221.

Begam, Richard, *Samuel Beckett and the End of Modernity* (Stanford: Stanford University Press, 1996).

Ben-Zvi, Linda, *Samuel Beckett* (Boston: Twayne Publishers, 1980).

—— 'Fritz Mauthner for Company', *Journal of Beckett Studies*, 9 (1984), 65–69.
Bernold, André, *L'Amitié de Beckett : 1979–1989* (Paris: Herman, 1992).
Bersani, Leo and Ulysse Dutoit, *Arts of Impoverishments: Beckett, Rothko, Resnais* (Cambridge, MA: Harvard University Press, 1993).
Bignell, Jonathan, 'Question of authorship: Samuel Beckett and *Film*', in Jonathan Bignell (ed.), *Writing and Cinema* (New York and London: Longman, 1999), pp. 29–42.
Bloom, Harold (ed.) *Samuel Beckett: Modern Critical Views* (New York: Chelsea House Publishers, 1985).
Boxall, Peter, 'Beckett's negative geography: fictional space in Beckett's prose', Ph.D. thesis, University of Sussex, 1996.
Brater Enoch (ed.), *The Drama in the Text: Samuel Beckett's Late Fiction* (New York: Oxford University Press, 1994).
—— 'Intertextuality', in Lois Oppenheim (ed.), *Palgrave Advances in Samuel Beckett Studies* (Basingstoke: Palgrave, 2004).
Brienza, Susan, '*The Lost Ones*: the reader as searcher', *Journal of Modern Literature*, 6:1 (1977), 148–168.
Bryden, Mary, *Women in Samuel Beckett's Prose and Drama: Her Own Other* (Basingstoke: Macmillan, 1993).
—— *Beckett and the Idea of God* (New York: St Martin's Press, 1998).
Butler, Harry L., 'Balzac and Godeau, Beckett and Godot: a curious parallel', *Romance Notes*, 3:2 (Spring 1962), 13–17.
Carlton, Lake (ed.), *No Symbols Where None Intended: A Catalogue of Books, Manuscripts, etc. to Samuel Beckett in the Collection of the Humanities Research Center* (University of Texas at Austin: The Library Chronicle, 1984).
Carey, Phyllis and Ed Jewinski (eds), *RE: Joyce 'n Beckett* (New York: Fordham University Press, 1992).
Casanova, Pascale, *Beckett l'abstracteur: anatomie d'une révolution litteraire* (Paris: Éditions du Seuil, 1997).
Caselli, Daniela, 'Beckett's intertextual modalities of appropriation: the case of Leopardi', *Journal of Beckett Studies*, 6:1 (Autumn 1996), 1–24.
Clément, Bruno, *L'Oeuvre sans qualités: rhétorique de Samuel Beckett* (Paris: Éditions du Seuil, 1994).
Coetzee, J. M., 'The English fiction of Samuel Beckett: an essay in stylistic analysis', Ph.D. thesis, University of Texas at Austin, 1969.
Cohn, Ruby, '*Watt* in the light of *The Castle*', *Comparative Literature*, 13 (1961), 154–166.
—— *Samuel Beckett: The Comic Gamut* (New Brunswick: Rutgers University Press, 1962).

—— *Back to Beckett* (Princeton: Princeton University Press, 1973).
—— *A Beckett Canon* (Ann Arbor: University of Michigan Press, 2001).
—— 'Joyce and Beckett, Irish cosmopolitans', in Francois Jost (ed.), *Proceedings of the Fourth Congress of International Comparative Literature Association* (The Hague and Paris: Mouton & Co., 1966), pp. 109–113.
—— (ed.), *Disjecta: Miscellaneous Writings and a Dramatic Fragment* (New York: Grove Press, 1984).
Connor, Steven, *Samuel Beckett: Repetition, Theory and Text* (Oxford: Blackwell, 1988).
—— 'Negativity and the question of value: Beckett's *Worstward Ho*', *Paragraph*, 15:2 (1992), 121–135.
—— 'Authorship, authority, and self-reference in Joyce and Beckett', in Phyllis Carey and Ed Jewinski (eds), *RE: Joyce 'n Beckett* (New York: Fordham University Press, 1992), pp. 147–159.
—— 'Between theatre and theory: "Long Observation of the Ray"', in John Pilling and Mary Bryden (eds), *The Ideal Core of the Onion: Reading Beckett Archives* (Reading: Beckett International Foundation, 1992), pp. 79–98.
Cronin, Anthony, *Samuel Beckett: The Last Modernist* (London: HarperCollins Publishers, 1996).
Dearlove, J. E., *Accomodating the Chaos: Samuel Beckett's Non-relational Art* (Durham, NC: Duke University Press, 1982).
Debevec Henning, Sylvie, *Beckett's Critical Complicity: Carnival, Contestation and Tradition* (Lexington: The University Press of Kentucky, 1988).
—— 'Samuel Beckett's *Film* and *La Dernière Bande*: intertextual and intratextual doubles', *Symposium*, 35:2 (Summer 1981), 131–153.
De Clerque, Martine, 'Different forms of intertextuality in Beckett's bilingual work', in *Fiction, texte, narratologie, genre: actes du symposium international de littérature comparée* (Frankfurt: Peter Lang, 1989), pp. 131–137.
Drew, Anne Marie, *Past Crimson Past Woe: The Shakespeare-Beckett Connection* (New York: Garland Publishing Inc., 1993).
Elam, Keir, '*Not I*: Beckett's mouth and the ars(e) rhetorica', in Enoch Brater (ed.), *Beckett at 80/Beckett in Context* (New York: Oxford University Press, 1986), pp. 124–148.
—— 'World's End: West Brompton, Turdy and other godforsaken holes', *Samuel Beckett Today/Aujourd'hui: Crossroads and Borderlines/L'œuvre carrefour/L'œuvre limite*, 6 (1997), 165–180.
Esslin, Martin (ed.), *Samuel Beckett: A Collection of Critical Essays* (Englewood Cliffs: Prentice Hall Inc., 1965).

Farrow, Anthony, *Early Beckett: Art and Allusion in* More Pricks Than Kicks *and* Murphy (Troy, NJ: The Whitston Publishing Company, 1991).
Federman, Raymond, and John Fletcher, *Samuel Beckett: His Works and His Critics: An Essay in Bibliography* (Berkeley: University of California Press, 1970).
Federman, Raymond, and Lawrence Graver (eds), *Samuel Beckett: The Critical Heritage* (London: Routledge and Kegan Paul, 1979).
Fitch, Brian T., *Beckett and Babel: An Investigation into the Status of the Bilingual Work* (Toronto: University of Toronto Press, 1988).
—— 'Beckett's literary cathedrals: speculations on Beckett's achievement as a writer of prose fiction', *Samuel Beckett Today/Aujourd'hui: Beckett in the Nineties*, 2 (1993), 124–131.
Fletcher, John, *The Novels of Samuel Beckett* (London: Chatto and Windus, 1964).
—— 'Samuel Beckett and the philosophers', *Comparative Literature*, 17 (1965), 42–56.
Friedman, Alan Warren, Charles Rossman, and Dina Scherzer (eds), *Beckett Translating/Translating Beckett* (University Park: The Pennsylvania State University Press, 1987).
Friedman, Malvin J., 'The novels of Samuel Beckett: an amalgam of Joyce and Proust', *Comparative Literature*, 12 (1960), 47–58.
—— 'A note on Leibniz and Samuel Beckett', *Romance Notes*, 4:2 (Spring 1963), 93–96.
—— (ed.), *Samuel Beckett Now* (Chicago: The University of Chicago Press, 1970).
Gessner, Niklaus, *Die Unzulänglichkeit der Sprache: eine Untersuchung über Formzerfall und Beziehungslosigkeit bei Samuel Beckett* (Zurich: Juris Verlag, 1957).
Gibson, Andrew, *Reading Narrative Discourse: Studies in the Novel from Cervantes to Beckett* (Basingstoke: Macmillan, 1990).
—— 'One kind of ambiguity in Joyce, Beckett, and Robbe-Grillet', *Canadian Review of Comparative Literature*, 12 (September 1985), 409–421.
Gontarski, S. E. (ed.), *On Beckett: Essays and Criticism* (New York: Grove Press, 1986).
Harvey, Lawrence E., *Samuel Beckett: Poet and Critic* (Princeton: Princeton University Press, 1970).
Hill, Leslie, *Beckett's Fiction in Different Words* (Cambridge: Cambridge University Press, 1990).
Juliet, Charles, *Rencontre avec Samuel Beckett* (Paris: Éditions Fata Morgana, 1986), trans. Janey Tucker, *Conversations with Samuel Beckett and Bram van Velde* (Leiden: Academic Press, 1995).

Katz, Daniel, *Saying I No More: Subjectivity and Consciousness in the Prose of Samuel Beckett* (Evanston, IL: Northwestern University Press, 1999).

Kenner, Hugh, *Samuel Beckett: A Critical Study* (New York: Grove Press, Inc., 1961).

Knowlson, James, *Damned to Fame: The Life of Samuel Beckett* (London: Bloomsbury, 1996).

Knowlson, James and John Pilling, *Frescoes of the Skull: The Later Prose and Drama of Samuel Beckett* (London: John Calder, 1979).

Lernout, Geert, 'James Joyce and Fritz Mauthner and Samuel Beckett', in Friedhelm Rathjen (ed.), *In Principle, Beckett Is Joyce* (Edinburgh: Split Pea Press, 1994).

Leventhal, A. J., 'Samuel Beckett: poet and pessimist', *The Listener*, 57 (May 1957), 746–747.

Locatelli, Carla, *La disdetta della parola: L'ermeneutica del silenzio nella prosa inglese di Samuel Beckett* (Bologna: Patron, 1984).

—— *Unwording the World: Samuel Beckett's Prose Works After the Nobel Prize* (Philadelphia: University of Pennsylvania Press, 1990).

—— '"My life natural order more or less in the present more or less": textual immanence and the textual impossible in Samuel Beckett's works', in Lois Oppenheim and Marius Buning (eds), *Beckett On and On ...* (Madison, NJ, and London: Associated University Press, 1996), pp. 127–147.

Moorjani, Angela B., *Abysmal Games in the Novels of Samuel Beckett* (Chapel Hill: North Carolina Studies in the Romance Languages and Literatures, 1982).

Murphy, P. J., *Reconstructing Beckett: Language for Being in Samuel Beckett's Fiction* (Toronto: University of Toronto Press, 1990).

—— 'Language and being in the prose works of Samuel Beckett', Ph.D. thesis, University of Reading, 1979.

O'Hara, J. D., *Samuel Beckett's Hidden Drives: Structural Uses of Depth Psychology* (Gainsville: University Press of Florida, 1997).

Pilling, John, *Samuel Beckett* (London, Henley and Boston: Routledge, 1976).

—— *Beckett Before Godot: The Formative Years (1929–1946)* (Cambridge: Cambridge University Press, 1997).

—— *Beckett's Dream Notebook* (Reading: Beckett International Foundation, 1999).

—— *Companion to* Dream of Fair to Middling Women (Tallahassee, FL: Journal of Beckett Studies Books, 2004).

—— (ed.), *The Cambridge Companion to Beckett* (Cambridge: Cambridge University Press, 1994).

—— 'Beckett's Proust', *Journal of Beckett Studies*, 1:1 (Winter 1976), 8–29.
—— 'Beckett's Stendhal: "Nimrod of novelists"', *French Studies*, 6 (1980), 56–62.
—— 'Review article: *Company* by Samuel Beckett', *Journal of Beckett Studies*, 7 (Spring 1982), 127–131.
—— 'Losing one's classics: Beckett's small Latin, and less Greek', *Journal of Beckett Studies*, 4: 2 (Spring 1995), 5–14.
—— 'Guesses and recesses: notes on, in, and towards *Dream of Fair To Middling Women*', *Samuel Beckett Today/Aujourd'hui: Beckett Versus Beckett*, 7 (1998), 13–23.
Rabinovitz, Rubin, *The Development of Samuel Beckett Fiction* (Urbana: University of Illinois Press, 1984).
—— 'Molloy and the archetypal traveller', *Journal of Beckett Studies*, 5 (Autumn 1979), 25–44.
Renton, Andrew, '"He all but said ...": evasion and referral in the later prose and drama of Samuel Beckett', Ph.D. thesis, University of Reading, 1989.
Ricks, Christopher, *Beckett's Dying Words* (Oxford: Oxford University Press, 1995).
Sherzer, Dina, *Structure de la Trilogie de Beckett* (The Hague: Mouton, 1976).
Smith, Russell, 'Someone (the other Beckett)', *Journal of Beckett Studies*, 10:1–2 (Fall 2000–Spring 2001), 1–16.
Stevenson, Kay Gilliland, 'Belacqua in the moon: Beckett's revision of "Dante and the Lobster"', in Patrick A. McCarthy (ed.), *Critical Essays on Samuel Beckett* (Boston: G. K. Hall, 1986).
Tagliaferri, Aldo, *Beckett e l'iperdeterminazione letteraria* (Milan: Feltrinelli, 1976).
Uhlmann, Anthony, *Beckett and Poststructuralism* (Cambridge: Cambridge University Press, 1999).
Verdicchio, Massimo, 'Examination round the fictification of Vico and Joyce', *James Joyce Quarterly*, 26:4 (Summer 1989), 531–539.
Wood, Rupert, 'Murphy, Beckett, Geulincx, God', *Journal of Beckett Studies*, 2:2 (1993), 27–51.
Wright, Ian, 'What matter who's speaking?: Beckett, the authorial subject and contemporary critical theory', *Comparative Criticism*, 5 (1983), 59–86.
Ziarek, Ewa Plonowska, *The Rhetoric of Failure: Deconstruction of Scepticism, Reinvention of Modernism* (Albany: State University of New York Press, 1996).

Zurbrugg, Nicholas, *Beckett and Proust* (Totowa: Barnes and Noble, 1988).
—— 'Beckett, Proust, and *Dream of Fair to Middling Women*', *Journal of Beckett Studies*, 9 (1984), 43–64.

Critical studies on Dante

Albertini, Stefano, 'Questione linguistica e questione politica nelle opere minori di Dante', *Canadian Journal of Italian Studies*, 18:51 (1995), 111–135.

Auerbach, Erich, *Mimesis: The Representation of Reality in Western Literature*, trans. William R. Trask (Princeton: Princeton University Press, 1953).
—— *Dante: Poet of the Secular World*, trans. Ralph Manheim (Chicago: The University of Chicago Press, 1961).
—— *Studi su Dante* (Milan: Feltrinelli, 1963)

Avalle, D'Arco Silvio, *Modelli semiologici nella* Commedia *di Dante* (Milan: Bompiani, 1975).

Baranski, Zygmunt G., 'The power of influence: aspects of Dante's presence in twentieth-century Italian culture', *Strumenti Critici*, n.s. 1:3 (September 1986), 343–376.
—— 'Benvenuto da Imola e la tradizione dantesca della "Comedía": appunti per una descrizione del *Comentum*', in P. Palmieri and C. Paolazzi (eds), *Benvenuto da Imola: Lettore degli antichi e dei moderni* (Ravenna: Longo, 1991).
—— 'A note on the Trecento: Boccaccio, Benvenuto, and the dream of Dante's pregnant mother', in *Miscellanea di Studi Danteschi in memoria di Silvio Pasquazi* (Naples: Federico & Ardia, 1993), pp. 69–82.
—— '*Sole nuovo, luce nuova*': *saggi sul rinnovamento culturale in Dante* (Turin: Scriptorium, 1996).

Barbi, Michele, *Dante: Vita, opere e fortuna* (Florence: Sansoni, 1933).

Barolini, Teodolinda, *Dante's Poets: Textuality and Truth in the* Comedy (Princeton: Princeton University Press, 1984).
—— *The Undivine Comedy: Detheologizing Dante* (Princeton: Princeton University Press, 1992).

Battaglia Ricci, Lucia, *Dante e la tradizione medievale* (Pisa: Giardini, 1983).

Boccaccio, Giovanni, *Trattatello in laude di Dante*, ed. Pier Giorgio Ricci (Milan: Mondadori, 1974).

Carugati, Giuliana, *Dalla menzogna al silenzio: la scrittura mistica della* Commedia *di Dante* (Bologna: Il Mulino, 1991).

Contini, Gianfranco, *Varianti e altra linguistica* (Turin: Einaudi, 1970).
—— *Un'idea di Dante* (Turin: Einaudi, 1970).

Corti, Maria, *Dante a un nuovo crocevia* (Florence: Sansoni, 1981).

—— *La felicità mentale: nuove prospettive per Cavalcanti e Dante* (Turin: Einaudi, 1983).
De Benedetti, Santorre, 'Comunicazione su Belacqua', *Bullettino della Società Dantesca Italiana*, 13 (1906), 222–233.
Del Lungo, Isidoro, *Dal secolo e dal poema di Dante: altri ritratti e studi* (Bologna: Zanichelli, 1898).
De Sanctis, Francesco, *Lezioni e saggi su Dante*, ed. Sergio Romagnoli (Turin: Einaudi, 1955).
—— *Storia della letteratura italiana* (Turin: Einaudi-Gallimard, 1996).
Dolfi, Anna, 'Dante e i poeti del Novecento', *Studi danteschi*, 58 (1986), 307–342.
Dragonetti, Roger, *Aux frontières du langage poétique: études sur Dante, Mallarmé, Valéry* (Gent: Romanica Gardensia, 1961).
—— 'The double play of Arnaut Daniel's *Sestina* and Dante's *Divina Commedia*', in Shoshana Felman (ed.), *Literature and Psychoanalysis: The Question of Reading: Otherwise* (Baltimore: Johns Hopkins University Press, 1982), pp. 227–252.
Eliot, T. S., 'Dante' (1929), in Frank Kermode (ed.), *Selected Prose of T. S. Eliot* (London: Faber and Faber, 1975).
Ellis, Steve, *Dante and English Poetry* (Cambridge: Cambridge University Press, 1983).
Enciclopedia Dantesca, eds, Umberto Bosco and Giorgio Petrocchi, 6 vols (Rome: Istituto dell'Enciclopedia Italiana, 1970–78).
Freccero, John, *Dante: The Poetics of Conversion* (Cambridge, MA: Harvard University Press, 1986).
Getto, Giovanni, 'Inferno I', in *Lectura Dantis Scaligera: Inferno* (Florence: Le Monnier, 1967).
Giannantonio, Pompeo, '*Inferno* I', in Pompeo Giannantonio (ed.), *Lectura Dantis Neapolitana* (Naples: Loffredo, 1986).
Hollander, Robert, *Allegory in Dante's Divine Comedy* (Princeton: Princeton University Press, 1969).
—— *Il Virgilio dantesco: tragedia nella* Commedia (Florence: Olschki, 1983).
—— 'Dante and his commentators', in Rachel Jacoff (ed.), *A Cambridge Companion to Dante* (Cambridge: Cambridge University Press, 1993).
Iannucci, Amilcare (ed.), *Dante e la 'bella scola' della poesia: autorità e sfida poetica* (Ravenna: Longo, 1993).
Luzi, Mario, 'Dante, scienza e innocenza', *Vicissitudini e forma* (Milan: Rizzoli, 1974).
Mazzotta, Giuseppe, *Dante Poet of the Desert: History and Allegory in the* Divine Comedy (Princeton: Princeton University Press, 1979).

—— *Dante's Vision and the Circle of Knowledge* (Princeton: Princeton University Press, 1993).
McDougal, Stuart Y. (ed.), *Dante Among the Moderns* (Chapel Hill: The University of North Carolina Press, 1985).
Mengaldo, Pier Vincenzo, *Linguistica e retorica di Dante* (Pisa: Nistri-Lischi, 1978).
—— (ed.), *De vulgari eloquentia* (Padua: Antenore, 1968).
Muscetta, Carlo and Giuseppe Savoca (eds), *Sovra il monumento di Dante che si preparava in Firenze, Canti, Poesie varie, Traduzioni poetiche e Versi puerili, Parnaso Italiano*, vol. IX (Turin: Einaudi, 1968).
Nardi, Bruno, *Dante e la cultura medievale: nuovi saggi di filosofia dantesca* (Bari: Laterza, 1942).
Noferi, Adelia, *Il gioco delle tracce. Studi su Dante, Petrarca, Bruno, il Neo-classicismo, Leopardi, l'Informale* (Florence: La Nuova Italia, 1979).
—— 'Dante e il Novecento', *Studi Danteschi*, 48 (1971), 185–209.
Palmieri, Pantaleo, and Carlo Paolazzi (eds), *Benvenuto da Imola lettore degli antichi e dei moderni* (Ravenna: Longo, 1991).
Papini, Giovanni, *Dante vivo* (Florence: Libreria Editrice Fiorentina, 1933).
Pasolini, Pier Paolo, 'La volontà di Dante a essere poeta', *Empirismo eretico* (Milan: Garzanti, 1972).
Pasquini, Emilio (ed.), *Intertestualità dantesca: letture classensi*, vol. 25 (Ravenna: Longo, 1996).
Pasquini, Emilio, and Antonio Quaglio (eds), *Commedia* (Milan: Garzanti, 1987).
Petrocchi, Giorgio, and Giannantonio, Pompeo (eds), *Questioni di critica dantesca* (Naples: Loffredo, 1969).
Quartieri, Franco (ed.), *Benvenuto da Imola: un moderno antico commentatore di Dante* (Ravenna: Longo, 2001).
Ricci, Corrado, *L'ultimo rifugio di Dante* (Ravenna: Longo, 1965 [1891]).
Sanguineti, Edoardo, *Interpretazione di Malebolge* (Florence: Olschki, 1961).
Sermonti, Vittorio, *L'Inferno di Dante*, supervised by Gianfranco Contini (Milan: Rizzoli, 1988).
—— *Il Purgatorio di Dante*, supervised by Gianfranco Contini (Milan: Rizzoli, 1990).
—— *Il Paradiso di Dante*, supervised by Cesare Segre (Milan: Rizzoli, 1993).
Singleton, Charles S., Commedia: *Elements of Structure* (Cambridge, MA: Harvard University Press, 1954).
—— *Journey to Beatrice* (Cambridge, MA: Harvard University Press, 1958).
Symonds, J. A., *An Introduction to the Study of Dante* (London: Adam and Charles Black, 1893).
Toynbee, Paget, *A Dictionary of Proper Names and Notable Matters in the Works of Dante* (Oxford: The Clarendon Press, 1898).

—— *Dante Studies and Researches* (London: Methuen, 1902).
—— *Dante in English Literature from Chaucer to Cary (c. 1380–1844)* (London: Methuen, 1909).
Vallone, Aldo, *La critica dantesca nel Novecento* (Florence: Olschki, 1976).
—— *Antidantismo politico e dantismo letterario* (Rome: Bonacci, 1988).

Critical studies on intertextuality

Allen, Graham, *Intertextuality* (New York and London: Routledge, 2000).
Bal, Mieke, *Quoting Caravaggio* (Chicago and London: The University of Chicago Press, 1999).
Bakhtin, Mikhail, *The Dialogic Imagination: Four Essays by M. M. Bakhtin*, Michael Holquist (ed.), trans. Caryl Emerson and Michael Holquist (Austin: University of Texas Press, 1981).
Barthes, Roland, *The Rustle of Language*, trans. Richard Howard (Oxford: Blackwell, 1986).
Bassnett–McGuire, Susan, *Comparative Literature: A Critical Introduction* (Oxford: Blackwell, 1993).
Ben-Porat, Ziva, 'The poetics of literary allusion', *PTL: A Journal for Descriptive Poetics and Theory of Literature*, 1 (1976), 105–128.
Bloom, Harold, *The Anxiety of Influence* (New York: Oxford University Press, 1973).
—— *The Western Canon* (Basingstoke: Macmillan, 1995).
Boening, John, 'Some recent theories of reception and influence: their implication for the study of international literary relations', *Proceedings of the Eighth Congress of International Comparative Literature Association* (Stuttgart: Bieber, 1980), 543–550.
Boitani, Piero, *L'ombra di Ulisse: figure di un mito* (Bologna: Il Mulino, 1992).
Boldrini, Lucia, *Joyce, Dante, and the Poetics of Literary Relations: Language and Meaning in* Finnegans Wake (Cambridge: Cambridge University Press, 2001).
Borges, Jorge Luis, 'Kafka and his precursors', in *Labyrinths: Selected Stories and Other Writings*, ed. Donald A. Yates and James E. Irby, preface by André Maurois (New York: New Directions, 1964), pp. 199–202.
Caselli, Daniela, 'Rifunzionalizzare la nozione di intertestualità: alcune proposte italiane', *Strumenti Critici*, n.s. 80:11 (January 1996), 75–92.
Clayton, Jay, and Rothstein, Eric (eds), *Influence and Intertextuality in Literary History* (Madison: The University of Wisconsin Press, 1991).
Compagnon, Antoine, *La seconde main ou le travail de la citation* (Paris: Seuil, 1979).

Conte, Gian Biagio, *Memoria dei poeti e sistema letterario: Catullo, Virgilio, Ovidio, Lucano* (Turin: Einaudi, [1974] 1985).
Coombs, James H., 'Allusion defined and explained', *Poetics*, 13:6 (December 1984), 475–488.
Culler, Jonathan, *On Deconstruction* (London: Fontana, 1983).
Dällenbach, Lucien, *Le récit spéculaire: essai sur la mise en abyme* (Paris: Éditions du Seuil, 1977).
—— 'Intertexte et autotexte', *Poétique*, 27 (1976), 282–296.
Dasenbrock, Reedway, *Imitating the Italians: Wyatt, Spenser, Synge, Pound, Joyce* (Baltimore: Johns Hopkins University Press, 1991).
Derrida, Jacques, 'Qual quelle: Valéry's sources', *Margins of Philosophy*, trans. Alan Bass (Brighton: The Harvester Press, 1982), pp. 273–306.
Eliot, T. S., *What Is a Classic?* (1944) (London: Faber and Faber, 1945).
—— 'Tradition and the individual talent' (1917), *Selected Prose of T. S. Eliot*, ed. Frank Kermode (London: Faber and Faber, 1975), pp. 37–44.
Genette, Gérard, *Introduction à l'architexte* (Paris: Seuil, 1979).
—— *Narrative Discourse* (Oxford: Blackwell, 1980).
—— *Palimpsestes: la littérature au second degré* (Paris: Seuil, 1982).
—— *Paratexts: Thresholds of Interpretation* (Cambridge: Cambridge University Press, 1997).
—— 'Transtextualité', *Magazine Littéraire*, 192 (février 1983), 40–41.
Griffiths, Eric, and Matthew Reynolds, *Dante in English* (Harmondsworth: Penguin, 2005).
Guillén, Claudio, *L'uno e il molteplice: introduzione alla letteratura comparata* (Bologna: Il Mulino, 1992).
Havely, N. R. (ed.), *Dante's Modern Afterlife: Reception and Response from Blake to Heaney* (Basingstoke: Macmillan, 1998).
Hebel, Udo J., *Intertextuality, Allusion, and Quotation: An International Bibliography of Critical Studies*, Bibliography and Indexes in World Literature, vol. 18 (New York: Greenwood Press, 1989).
Helbig, Jörg, *Intertextualität und Markierung* (Heidelberg: Universitätsverlag C. Winter, 1996).
Hillman, Richard, 'The anxiety of intertextuality', *Semiotica*, 107 (1995), 98–126.
Jenny, Laurent, 'La strategie de la forme', *Poétique*, 27 (1976), 257–281.
Johnson, Barbara, *A World of Difference* (Baltimore: Johns Hopkins University Press, 1987).
Kermode, Frank, 'Institutional control of interpretation', *Salmagundi*, 43 (1979), 72–86.

Kirkpatrick, Robin, *English and Italian Literature from Dante to Shakespeare: A Study of Sources, Analogy, and Divergence* (London: Longman, 1995).
Kristeva, Julia, 'Problèmes de la structuration du texte', *Théorie d'ensemble* (Paris: Éditions du Seuil, 1968).
—— 'The Ruin of a Poetics', *Twentieth Century Studies*, 7–8 (1972), 102–119.
—— *Desire in Language: A Semiotic Approach to Literature and Art*, trans. Thomas Gora, Alice Jardine, and Léon S. Roudiez (New York: Columbia University Press, 1980).
—— *Revolution of Poetic Language* (New York; Columbia University Press, 1984).
Kuon, Peter,*'Lo mio maestro e 'l mio autore': die productive Rezeption der* Divina Commedia *in der Erzählliterature der Moderne* (Frankfurt am Main: Klostermann, 1993).
Manganiello, Dominic, *T. S. Eliot and Dante* (Basingstoke: Macmillan, 1989).
Pagnini, Marcello, *Pragmatica della letteratura* (Palermo: Sellerio, 1980).
—— *Semiosi: Teoria ed ermeneutica del testo letterario* (Bologna: Il Mulino, 1988).
Perri, Carmela, 'On alluding', *Poetics*, 7:3 (September 1978), 289–307.
Plett, Heinrich F. (ed.), *Intertextuality* (Berlin: Walter de Gruyter, 1991).
Reynolds, Mary T., *Joyce and Dante: The Shaping Imagination* (Princeton: Princeton University Press, 1981).
Riffaterre, Michael, 'The self-sufficient text', *Diacritics*, 3 (1973), 39–45.
—— 'Intertextual scrambling', *Romanic Review*, 67 (1977), 197–206.
—— 'La syllepse intertextuelle', *Poétique*, 40 (1979), 496–501.
—— 'Syllepsis', *Critical Inquiry*, 6 (1980), 625–38.
—— 'La trace de l'intertexte', *La Pensée*, 215 (1980), 4–18.
—— 'Interpretation and undecidability', *New Literary History*, 12 (1981), 227–242.
—— 'Semanalyse de l'intertexte', *Texte*, 2 (1983), 171–175.
—— 'Intertextual representation: on mimesis as interpretive discourse', *Critical Inquiry*, 11:1 (September 1984), 141–162.
—— 'The intertextual unconscious', *Critical Inquiry*, 13 (Winter 1987), 371–385.
San Juan, E. Jr, 'From Bakhtin to Gramsci: intertextuality, praxis, hegemony', *The New Orleans Review*, 18:4 (Winter 1991), 75–85.
Segre, Cesare, *I segni e la critica* (Turin: Einaudi, 1969).
—— 'Intertestuale, interdiscorsivo: appunti per una fenomenologia delle fonti', in C. Di Girolamo and I. Paccagnella (eds), *La parola ritrovata: Fonti e analisi letteraria* (Palermo: Sellerio, 1982), pp. 15–28.

Sicari, Stephen, *Pound's Epic Ambition: Dante and the Modern World* (Albany: State University of New York Press, 1991).
Spivak, Gayatri Chakravorty, *In Other Worlds: Essays in Cultural Politics* (New York: Methuen, 1987).
Steiner, George, *What Is Comparative Literature?* (Oxford: The Clarendon Press, 1995).
Worton, Michael, and Judith Still, *Intertextuality: Theory and Practices* (Manchester: Manchester University Press, 1990).

Other critical works

Bachelard, Gaston, *The Poetics of Space*, trans. Maria Jolas (Boston: Beacon Press, 1969).
Bickersteth, Geoffrey L. (ed.), *Poems of Leopardi* (New York: Russell and Russell, 1973).
Butler, Judith, *Bodies That Matter* (London and New York: Routledge, 1993).
Currie, Mark (ed.), *Metafiction* (London: Longman, 1995).
Deleuze, Gilles, *Difference and Repetion*, trans. Paul Patton (London: Athlone Press, 1994).
Deleuze, Gilles, and Félix Guattari, *A Thousand Plateaus: Capitalism and Schizophrenia* (London: Athlone, 1988).
Derrida, Jacques, *La voix et le phénomène* (Paris: Presses Universitaires de France, 1967).
—— *Of Grammatology* (Baltimore: Johns Hopkins University Press, 1976).
—— *Writing and Difference* (London: Routledge, 1978).
—— *Acts of Literature*, ed. Derek Attridge (London: Routledge, 1992).
—— 'Demeure : Fiction et témoignage', *Passions de la littérature: avec Jacques Derrida*, ed. Michel Lisse (Paris: Galilée, 1996), pp. 13–73.
Descartes, René, *Discourse on Method and Meditations*, trans. Laurence J. Lafleur (Indianapolis: The Library of Liberal Arts, 1960).
Foucault, Michel, *Madness and Civilization: A History of Insanity in the Age of Reason*, trans. Richard Howard (London: Routledge, 1995).
—— 'What is an Author?' (1969), in Paul Rabinow (ed.), *The Foucault Reader* (Harmondsworth: Penguin, 1984), pp. 101–120.
Greenblatt, Stephen, *Hamlet in Purgatory* (Princeton: Princeton University Press, 2001).
Joyce, James, *Ulysses*, eds Hans Walter Gabler, Wolfhard Steppe, and Claus Melchior, with a new preface by Richard Ellmann (Harmondsworth: Penguin, 1986).
Grésillon, Almouth, *Élements de critique génétique: lire le manuscrits modernes* (Paris: PUF, 1994).

—— *Literarische Handschriften: Einführung in die 'critique génétique'* (Bern: Peter Lang, 1999).

Grésillon, Almouth and Jean-Louis Labrave, *Écrire aux XVIIe et XVIII3 siècles. Genèses de textes littéraires et philosophiques* (Paris: CNRS Éditions, 2000).

Hunt, P. W., *The History of Grammar in the Middle Ages* (Amsterdam: G. L. Bursill-Hall, 1980).

Le Goff, Jacques, *The Birth of Purgatory*, trans. Arthur Godhammer (London: Scolar Press, 1984).

Lesnik-Oberstein, Karín, '*Oliver Twist*: the narrator's tale', *Textual Practice*, 15:1 (2001), 87–100.

Locatelli, Carla, 'Considerazioni sulle varianti del testo letterario: tra "genesi" e "ricezione"', in L. Innocenti, F. Marucci and P. Pugliatti (eds), *Semeia. Itinerari per Marcello Pagnini* (Bologna: Il Mulino, 1994), pp. 29–38.

McGann, Jerome, 'Literary Pragmatics and the Editorial Horizon', in Philip Cohen (ed.), *Devils and Angels: Textual Editing and Literary Theory* (Charlottesville VA: University of Virginia Press, 1991), pp. 1–21.

Minnis, A. J., *Medieval Theory of Authorship: Scholastic Literary Attitudes in the Later Middle Ages* (London: Scolar Press, 1984).

Minnis, A. J., and A. B. Scott, with the assistance of David Wallace, *Medieval Literary Theory and Criticism* (Oxford: Clarendon Press, 1988).

Prince, Gerald, *Dictionary of Narratology* (Aldershot: Scolar Press, 1988).

Index

Abbott, H. P. 58, 77
Ackerley, C. J. 7, 87, 90–91, 93, 99, 100
Addenda 6, 88–91, 93–94, 97, 99, 113, 169
Alba 46, 62, 65, 67, 80
Alberigo (de' Manfredi) 70
Alessio (Interminelli da Lucca) 81
allegory 26–30
Allen, G. 9
anagogy 28–29
Anonimo Fiorentino 38, 39, 41, 43–45, 54, 59, 203
　see also Belacqua; Benvenuto da Imola
Anspaugh, K. 7, 8, 65, 78, 79, 144, 145
Antepurgatory 20, 36, 50–52, 87
Argenti, Filippo 116
Aristotle 39, 41, 45
arsy-versy (arsy-varsy) 80, 94, 96, 117, 138
Arthur, K. 8, 21, 33, 179
auctor 29, 39–41, 48, 49, 56, 57, 87
　see also auctoritas
auctoritas 17, 19, 21–22, 30, 39, 41, 81, 109, 111, 113–115, 121, 126, 182, 184
auctoritates *see* auctoritas
Auerbach, E. 178, 182
authorial intentionality
　critique of 3–5, 58, 81–85, 201–204
　see also authority; Foucault, M.
authority
　cultural value 4, 49, 107, 116–117
　　God 175–177
　　mimesis 91–93
　　witness and scribe 142–143, 170–175, 194
　　see also authorial intentionality; Connor, S.; Foucault, M.; intertextuality; intratextuality

Bachelard, G. 200
Bal, M. 205
Baranski, Z. 31, 54, 55, 56
Barbi, M. 32
Barolini, T. 33, 52, 55, 56, 70, 80, 92, 99, 118, 144, 145, 169, 178, 181, 182, 200
Barry, E. 55, 197
Barthes, R. 55
Baudelaire, 28, 30, 121–123
Beatrice 65–66, 76
　'Blissful Beatrice' 58–59, 62, 73, 77
　in the brothel 35, 67
　and the spots on the moon 58–62
Beckett, S.
　'Mr Beckett' 3, 6, 45–49, 57, 104, 107, 108, 114, 202
　'Alba' 60
　All Strange Away 79, 178, 197
　All That Fall 80, 95, 117, 138
　Beckett Trilogy, The: Molloy, Malone Dies, The Unnamable (*Three Novels*) 144, 173
　calmant, Le, 120, 123–132, 138, 141, 153, 168
　Calmative, The, 7, 120, 121, 123–132, 138, 141, 146, 153, 168, 181, 203
　'Casket of Pralinen for a Daughter of a Dissipated Mandarin' 78
　Closed Place 189, 193, 197, 199
　Collected Poems 1930–1978 180
　Come and Go 65
　Comment c'est 6, 148–178
　Compagnie 151, 168, 179, 199, 205
　Company 9, 55, 108, 151, 178, 181, 199, 201, 203–204, 205
　'concentrisme, Le' 54, 146

INDEX

'Dante and the Lobster' 36, 58–62, 64, 68, 70, 73, 76, 95, 107, 138, 204
'Dante...Bruno.Vico..Joyce' 3, 5, 8, 9, 10–22, 23, 24, 30, 62, 66, 83, 108, 131, 146, 166
'Dante' notebooks TCD 10962, 32, 55; TCD 10963 53, 54, 118, 141, 147, 179, 204, 205; TCD 10963a 33, 54, 80; TCD10965 78;10965a 78; TCD 10966 53, 80, 145; 'Dante' postcards (MS4123) 56, 100, 101, 118, 146, 168, 181, 190, 192
dépeupleur, Le 6, 139, 151, 183–196, 197
'Ding-Dong' 57, 58, 62, 63–67, 68, 70, 76, 112
'Draff' 62, 73–77 *passim*, 94
'dread nay' 96, 101, 141, 147, 201, 202, 205
'Dream' notebook (RUL MS 5000) 54, 78, 133, 134
Dream of Fair to Middling Women 2, 3, 22, 35–53, 57, 59, 62, 63, 65, 67, 72, 73, 75, 76, 77, 80, 81, 88, 98, 104, 107, 117, 118, 131, 133, 137, 153, 178, 190, 196, 200
'Echo's Bones' (story) 57, 67, 75–77
Echo's Bones and Other Precipitates 57, 95
Eleuthéria 80, 162, 180
End, The 106, 121, 139, 144, 146, 162
Enough 22
'Enueg I' 79, 95, 160, 161, 173
Expelled, The 139
Film 187, 198
fin, La 106, 144
'Fingal' 57, 58, 62
First Love 121–123, 144
Foirade IV 179
Happy Days 95, 122, 144
'Hell Crane to Starling' 79
'Home Olga' 65, 67, 174

How It Is 5, 6, 8, 21, 95, 96, 104, 148–178, 183, 190, 193, 195, 201, 204
Ill Seen Ill Said 96, 141–142, 147, 198, 200, 204, 205
Imagination Dead Imagine 185, 198
L'innomable 136–138
'Intercessions by Denis Devlin' 77
Krapp's Last Tape 171
'Letter to Axel Kaun' 63, 79
Letter to Kaye Boyle 151, 178
Letter to Mary Hutchinson 7
Letter to MacGreevy 80
Letter to McWhinnie 178
Lost Ones, The 5–6, 139, 151, 178, 183–196, 197, 199, 204
'Love and Lethe' 68
'Malacoda' 73, 76, 95
Malone Dies 21, 117, 134–136, 138, 147
Malone meurt 134–136, 147
Mal vu mal dit 141–142, 147, 204, 205
Mercier and Camier 6, 9, 80, 102–117, 119, 120, 121, 124, 126, 127, 129, 131, 136, 138, 145, 146, 173
Mercier et Camier 6, 102–117, 118, 119, 120, 121, 124, 125, 126, 127, 128, 129, 131, 136, 145, 146, 173
Molloy 21, 36, 118, 132, 133–135, 138, 145, 147, 178
Molloy (French) 132, 133–135, 147
More Pricks Than Kicks 3, 36, 57–77, 80, 81, 88, 92, 138, 178
Murphy 6, 36, 55, 81–88, 99, 100, 103, 108, 117, 118, 137, 151, 160, 178, 179, 180, 187, 195, 196, 198
Nouvelles et textes pour rien 6, 120–132, 138–143, 205
Ohio Impromptu 203
Old Earth 187
'Papini's Dante' 162, 180
Pochade radiophonique 204

Premier amour 121–123, 144, 153, 195
Proust 3, 22–30, 33, 42, 55, 75, 80, 179, 182, 187, 194, 196, 198
Rough for Radio II 10, 142, 147, 204
'Sanies I' 78
'Sedendo et Quiesciendo' [sic] 38, 42, 43, 54, 137
'Serena III' 95
Se voir 189, 193, 199
'Smeraldina Billet-Doux, The' 57
Stories and Texts for Nothing 6, 8, 117, 120–132, 138–143, 205
TCD 10402 54, 120
'Text' (poem) 61, 66, 70–71, 73, 78, 80, 95, 138, 162, 204
Text 2 125–126, 139
Text 5 163, 171
Text 6 101, 134, 141, 142, 204
Texte 6 134, 141, 204
Text 8 147
Text 9 139, 140
Texte 9 140
'Three Dialogues' 198
Unnamable, The 52, 80, 122, 128–129, 136–138
Vielle terre 187
Waiting for Godot 8, 22, 95, 157, 178, 179, 193, 199, 203, 205
'Walking Out' 58, 68, 80
Watt 6, 46, 55, 80, 81, 88–97, 99, 100, 108, 117, 131, 132, 141, 158, 166, 169, 173, 180, 181
'*Watt*' notebook 118
'Wet Night, A' 57, 62, 65–68, 76
'What a Misfortune' 57, 58, 68–73, 76, 162
What Where 179
'Whoroscope' notebook (RUL MS 3000) 9, 54, 81–88, 98, 118, 124, 128, 179, 187, 198, 203
'Yoke of Liberty' 79
Begam, R. 100
Belacqua 2, 35–53, 134–135, 190, 201, 203
'l'andar su che porta?' ('andare in sù che porta?') 35, 37, 46–49, 54

Belacqua bliss 88, 162, 203
bogged 43, 58–60, 63, 70, 76, 79
posture 36, 38, 43, 64, 132, 150–151, 177, 178, 191, 204
'qui vive la pietà' 35, 61, 69, 70, 96, 116, 138, 204
'sedendo et quiescendo' 38–42, 80
third being 43–46
see also Anonimo Fiorentino; Beckett, S., 'Mr Beckett', *Dream of Fair to Middling Women*; Benvenuto da Imola; Dante, (Dante Alighieri) works, *Purgatorio*, IV
'bella menzogna' *see Convivio*
Benvenuto da Imola 32, 38–41, 59
'aliquando etiam pulsabat' 38, 40, 43, 44
see also Anonimo Fiorentino, Belacqua
Ben-Zvi, L. 197
Berkeley, 187–188
Bersani, L. and U. Dutoit 149, 152, 167, 178, 181
Bianchi, E. 54, 98
Bignell, J. 205
Bloom, H. 4, 9
Boccaccio, G. 16–19, 32, 66, 79
Boldrini, L. 14, 15, 31, 32, 34, 79, 201, 202, 205
Boniface VIII 18, 71
Borges, J. L. 9
Boxall, P. 36, 54, 77
Brienza, S. 187, 188, 197, 200
Browning, R. 56
Bryden, M. 7, 56, 79
Butler, J. 4, 9
Byron, G. 53

Cain 60–61
Carey, P. 8, 9
Cary, H. F. 144, 146
Casanova, P. 33
Casella 41
Caselli, D. 54, 55, 77, 79, 98
Castiglione, B. 18
Catalano (dei Malvolti) 10
Cavalcanti, G. 13, 28
Celestine V 71, 80

INDEX

cellineggiare *see* Cellini
Cellini, B. 44, 45
Cino da Pistoia 13
Clément, B. 80
Cocytus 70, 204
Coetzee, J. M. 99
Cohn, R. 96, 100, 101, 178, 179, 181, 187, 189, 197, 198, 199, 200
Colerick, E. 8, 160, 184, 197
Connor, S. 55, 99, 112, 117, 118, 135, 136, 143, 146, 147, 197, 198
Constance (Costanza) 35, 54
Conte, G. B. 56
Contini, G. 31, 84
Corti, M. 19, 33
Cottignoli, A. 55
Cronin, A. 7
Cuddy, L. A. 8
Currie, M. 104, 117

Dällenbach, L. 94, 99
Dante (Dante Alighieri) works
   Comedy 1, 2, 3, 5, 6, 11
   Convivio 11, 16, 21, 24, 28–29, 32–34, 58, 74–76, 92
   De Monarchia 19, 79
   De vulgari eloquentia 11–19, 21, 31–32, 58, 66
   Epistle to Cangrande 32
   Inferno 1, 5, 24, 52, 56, 88, 95, 126, 137, 142, 148, 191; I 100, 107, 113, 114, 124, 127, 145; II 111, 129, 130, 146; III 35 71, 72, 74, 80, 95, 118, 146, 160, 161, 162, 173, 184, 193, 199; IV 187; V 35, 54, 67, 68, 79, 144, 162; VII 5, 8, 59, 77, 89, 91, 114, 154–158, 163, 169, 177, 179, 193; VIII 116, 130, 131, 199; IX 23, 193, 199; XII–XV 190; XVI 118, 190; XVII 119; XVIII 99, 100, 164, 165, 181, 192, 193; XX 35, 60, 61, 69, 78, 80, 95–97, 101, 116–118; XXI 73, 101; XXIII 10; XXV 108; XXVI 180; XXIX 54, 78; XXX 54, 146; XXXI 54, 79; XXXII 95, 96, 101, 141, 158; XXXIII 70; XXXIV 140–141, 160, 200
   Paradiso 88, 183, 204; II 59, 77, 128, 174; III 54, 59–60, 128, 133–134; IV 65; X 174; XI 145–146; XIV 144; XVIII 144; XXIII 144; XXX 35, 54, 65, 114, 123; XXXIII 195
   Postille cassinesi 54
   Purgatorio 20, 21, 23, 30, 38, 41, 47, 62, 65, 68, 80, 82, 83, 88, 95, 107, 126, 127; I 77, 87, 128–132, 142, 155, 160, 192; II 41, 116, 146; III 109, 118, 129, 146, 191; IV 2, 35–38, 40–41, 44, 46–48, 54, 59–60, 79, 87, 118, 132, 190; V 129, 146; VI 18, 35, 50, 137, 146; VII 50, 80, 139; VIII 50; IX 50, 52, 200; X 25, 26, 107, 193–194; XII 146, 191; XIII 133, 191; XIV 56; XVII 146; XIX 65; XXIII 193; XXIV 174; XXV 111, 146, 191; XXVI 100, 146, 192; XXVII 100, 118; XXIX 175; XXX 146; XXXI 68, 74; XXXII 131; XXXIII 67; XXXIII 195
   Vita Nuova 65, 79
De Benedetti, S. 55
déjà vu 3, 116, 120, 126, 129, 134, 203
Deleuze, G. and F. Guattari, 179, 180
Del Moro, F. 7, 32, 78, 79, 80, 144, 154, 179 180, 190, 198, 199
De Logu, P. 7, 33
Derrida, J. 9, 93, 99, 118, 147, 166–167, 171, 181, 182
De Sanctis, F. 23, 26–30, 33, 34, 51, 52, 56
Descartes, R. 188, 198
dolce stil novo (sweet noo style) 67, 174
   see also Beckett, S., 'Mr Beckett', 'Home Olga'
Dolfi, A. 31, 34
Doran, E. 8
Dragonetti, R. 19, 33
Duppa, R. 53

Elam, K. 144, 145, 181
Eliot, T. S. 31, 32, 56, 102, 117, 201–202
Ellis, Steve, 201, 205
Ellmann, R. 84–86, 98
Esposito, B. 1

Farrow, A. 62, 65, 68, 77, 78, 79, 80
Federman, R. and J. Fletcher 77, 79
Ferrini J-P. 7, 54, 118, 144, 179
Fitch, B. T. 86, 98, 112
Fletcher, J. 7, 154, 179, 199
Florence 35, 40, 44, 72–73, 137, 203
 see also Dante (Dante Alighieri) works,
  Purgatorio, VI
Foucault, M. 9, 55, 81, 97, 202
Fournier, E. 24, 33
Fowlie, W. 8
Frasca, G. 8, 154, 179
Freccero, J. 8

Gabler, H. W., 85, 86, 98
Galilei, G. 53
Genette, G. 9, 89, 99, 144
Getto, G. 144
Giannantonio, P. 144
Giudecca 56
Gleason, P. 8, 79
gongorzola 61, 78
Gontarski, S. E. 7, 144, 178, 188, 199
Gréssilon, A. 98
Gréssilon, A. and J–L. Lebrave 84, 98
Griffiths, E. and M. Reynolds 205
Guittone (d'Arezzo) 12
Gussow, M. 7

Harvey, L. 7, 73, 77, 78, 79, 161, 180
Havely, N. R. 205
Hayman, D. 7
Hill, L. 168, 169, 181
Hutchings, W. 8, 154, 164, 179, 181

Joyce, J. 10–11, 16, 18, 20–23, 62, 201,
 203
 'Dead, The' 65
  Finnegans Wake 15, 80, 201
  Ulysses 33, 78, 84–86, 98, 182,
   201

  Work in Progress 10, 15, 30
Joyce, L. 53
Juliet, C. 55

Katz, D. 9, 80, 199, 202, 205
Kaun, A. 63
Kennedy, S. 7
Knowlson, J. 7, 53, 54, 178
Kristeva, J. 8, 9
Kuon, P. 205

intertextuality 1–6, 201–204
 authority 1–3, 23–26, 35–36, 46–49,
  97, 102, 105–108, 201
 manuscripts 81–87
 narration 103, 105–108
 paratexts 89–91
 translation 112–116, 127, 138
 visibility 10, 83–84, 109–112, 121,
  183–188
 see also auctoritas; authority,
  Bal, M.; Bloom, H.; Genette, G.;
  Kristeva, J.; Riffaterre, M.;
  Segre, C.; textual stability
intratextuality 57–58, 64, 76, 77, 120
 authority 3, 58, 121, 202
 see also intertextuality

Lamartine, A. d. 184, 195
Latin
 English 11–12
  'forma locutionis' 19–20
  vernacular 14, 17–18, 41
 see also vulgare illustre (vernacular),
  vulgare latium
Leopardi, G. 10–11, 22, 30, 148, 179
Lernout, G. 98
Lesnik-Oberstein, K. 56
Leventhal, A. J. 8
Levy, E. P., 33, 107, 108, 109, 110, 112,
 117, 118, 119
Limbese 43, 51, 53
 see also Limbo
Limbo 10, 44, 52
Locatelli, C. 55, 56, 99, 117, 118, 138,
 145, 147, 178, 199, 200
Loderingo (degli Andalò) 10

McDougal, S. Y. 205
McGann, J. 85, 98
MacGreevy, T. 54
McQueeny, T. 8, 26, 28, 32, 33, 34
Malebolge 56, 70
Manganiello, D. 201, 205
Manto 63, 78, 116, 119
Marlowe, C. 119, 161
Medwin, T. 53
Mengaldo, P. V. 13, 31–33
Mercuri, R. 32, 39, 55
Minnis, A. J. and A. B. Scott, 34, 55, 56
mise en abyme 2, 11, 90–91, 93–94, 96–97
Miss Florence *see* Florence
Moorjani, A. 94, 99, 100, 118, 126, 132–133, 138–139, 145, 146, 147
Murphy, P. J. 102, 105, 117

Nabokov, V. 81, 86
Narcissus 56, 134, 146
Nardi, B. 33
Neumeister, S. 7, 197
Noferi, A. 31
Nykrog, P. 8

O'Hara, J. D. 86, 98, 99
Oliva, R. 8
Omberto (Aldobrandesco) 200
O'Neill, K. 8, 147
Ottolenghi (Signorina) 61–62
Oxenhandler, N. 154, 160, 178, 179, 180

Pagnini, M. 178
palimpsest 108–111, 126
    see also intertextuality; intratextuality
Pasquini, E. and A. Quaglio 144
Petrocchi, G. 31, 54
Piccarda Donati 35, 54, 59–60
Pilling, J. 7, 33, 52, 54, 55, 56, 77, 78, 79, 80, 98, 100, 118, 119, 121, 144, 197
Pilling, J. and M. Bryden 98, 197
Poliziano 18
Pound, E. 56, 201–202, 205

Proust, M. 22–25
Ptolemy *see* Tolomea (Ptolemy)

Quartieri, F. 54

Rabinovitz, R. 93, 99, 100, 118
Racine, J. 121–123
Ravenna 35, 53, 67
Renton, A. 77
Ricci, P. G. 32
Ricks, C. 180
Riffaterre, M. 2, 9, 145
Rimbaud, A. 161
Robinson, M. 8, 9, 21, 33, 154, 179
Ruby (Ruby Tough) 65

St Lucy 53
Salsano, F. 47, 55
Schödel, K. 54
Schopenhauer, A. 22, 25
Segre, C. 9
Semiramis 35, 54
Sermonti, V. 77, 144
shadow (ombra) 43, 100, 107, 128–129, 185
Shelley, P. B. 53
Sicari, S. 201, 205
Singleton, C. 31, 99, 169, 181, 182
sloth 43, 45, 48, 155, 162
    see also Belacqua
Smeraldina Rima 36–37, 42
Smith, F. N. 98
Smith, R. 9
Sordello 50, 51, 52, 53, 68, 72, 128, 132, 134–135, 138–139
Strauss, W. A. 21, 33
Stygian *see* Styx
Styx 5, 56, 153
'sweet noo style' *see* 'dolce stil novo'
Symonds, J. A. 32
Syra-Cusa 35

Tagliaferri, A. 145
teleology
    critique of 5, 20–21, 37, 42–43, 51–53, 62, 81, 84, 139–141, 167–169, 173, 201–204

see also Belacqua; Beckett, S., Mr Beckett,
    Dream of Fair to Middling Woman
Terry, P. 21, 33, 154, 179, 182
textual stability
  critique of 1–4, 23, 44–45, 89–91, 202
Theoharis, T. C. 8, 145
Tolomea (Ptolemy) 23, 67, 79
Toynbee, P. 38–40, 53, 54
Travers Gross, K. 7, 78, 94–95, 101, 147,
    160, 173, 180

Uhlmann, A. 9, 202, 205

Van Hulle, D. 203, 205
Vanni (Fucci) 108
vernacular
  see Boccaccio, G.; Latin; *vulgare illustre*
    (vernacular), *vulgare latium*
Virgil 44, 50, 51, 68, 69, 70, 82, 83, 87,
    91–94, 96, 113–115, 116, 144,
    154–158, 203
'Voi ch'intendendo' *see Convivio*
Voltaire 57
vulgare illustre (vernacular) 12–16, 67
vulgare latium 13
see also Boccaccio, G.; *vulgare illustre*

Ziarek, E. P. 181

EU authorised representative for GPSR:
Easy Access System Europe, Mustamäe tee 50,
10621 Tallinn, Estonia
gpsr.requests@easproject.com

www.ingramcontent.com/pod-product-compliance
Lightning Source LLC
Chambersburg PA
CBHW070941230426
43666CB00011B/2514